Lombroso in the Americas

History of Crime, Deviance and Punishment

Academic interest in the history of crime and punishment has never been greater and the *History of Crime, Deviance and Punishment* series provides a home for the wealth of new research being produced. Individual volumes within the series cover topics related to the history of crime and punishment, from the later medieval to modern period and in both Europe and North America, and seek to demonstrate the importance of this subject in furthering understanding of the way in which various societies and cultures operate. When taken together, the works in the series will show the evolution of the nature of illegality and attitudes towards its perpetration over time and will offer their readers a rounded and coherent history of crime and punishment through the centuries. The series' broad chronological and geographical coverage encourages comparative historical analysis of crime history between countries and cultures.

Published:

Policing the Factory, Barry Godfrey

Crime and Poverty in 19th-Century England, Adrian Ager

Print Culture, Crime and Justice in Eighteenth-Century London, Richard Ward

Rehabilitation and Probation in England and Wales, 1900-1950, Raymond Gard

The Policing of Belfast 1870-1914, Mark Radford

Crime, Regulation and Control during the Blitz, Peter Adey, David J. Cox and Barry Godfrey

The Italian Prison in the Age of Positivism, 1861-1914, Mary Gibson

Life Courses of Young Convicts Transported to Van Diemen's Land, Emma D. Watkins

Fair and Unfair Trials in the British Isles, 1800-1940, eds. David Nash and Anne-Marie Kilday

Photographing Crime Scenes in Twentieth-Century London, Alexa Neale
Combating London's Criminal Class, Matthew Bach
Sex and Violence in 1920s Scotland, Louise Heren

Forthcoming:

Feminist Campaigns against Child Sexual Abuse: Britain and India, 1860–1947, Daniel Grey

Deviance, Disorder and Music in Modern Britain and America, Cliff Williamson

Prison and Workhouse Reform in 19th-Century England: Shaping Incarceration, Lewis Darwen and David Orr

Crime and Criminal Justice in Early Modern Ireland: Developing a Colonial Institution, Coleman A. Dennehy

Motor Bandits in Interwar England: Criminal Mobility in the Modern Age, Alyson Brown

Prosecuting London's Fraudsters 1760–1820: Swindlers, Tricksters and the Law, Cerian Griffiths

Lombroso in the Americas

A Transatlantic History of a Controversial Criminologist

Edited by
Silvano Montaldo and Franco Orlandi

BLOOMSBURY ACADEMIC
LONDON • NEW YORK • OXFORD • NEW DELHI • SYDNEY

BLOOMSBURY ACADEMIC
Bloomsbury Publishing Plc, 50 Bedford Square, London, WC1B 3DP, UK
Bloomsbury Publishing Inc, 1385 Broadway, New York, NY 10018, USA
Bloomsbury Publishing Ireland, 29 Earlsfort Terrace, Dublin 2, D02 AY28, Ireland

First published in Great Britain 2026

Cover image: Unidentified photographer, *Instituto de Identificação Laboratorio de Policia Técnica*, police booking card of a man (detail) arrested and identified on homosexuality charges by the police in São Paulo (Brazil), two silver gelatin prints on card, *c.* 1930. Archive of the Cesare Lombroso Museum of criminal Anthropology, University of Turin

A catalogue record for this book is available from the British Library.

A catalog record for this book is available from the Library of Congress.

ISBN: HB: 978-1-3505-7121-1
ePDF: 978-1-3505-7122-8
eBook: 978-1-3505-7124-2

Series: History of Crime, Deviance and Punishment

Typeset by Newgen KnowledgeWorks Pvt. Ltd., Chennai, India

For product safety related questions contact productsafety@bloomsbury.com.

To find out more about our authors and books visit www.bloomsbury.com and sign up for our newsletters.

Contents

Illustrations

Acknowledgments

This volume collects together the papers presented at the conference *Lombroso in the Americas*, which took place from September 26 to 28, 2023, at the University of Turin's Palazzo degli Istituti Anatomici. The conference and the production of this volume were made possible by the support of the Department of Historical Studies and the University Museum System of the University of Turin; the *Scicomove* project (Scientific Collections on the Move: Provincial Museums, Archives, and Collecting Practices, 1800–1950, funded by the Horizon 2020 research and innovation program of the European Union under the Marie Skłodowska-Curie grant agreement No. 101007579); and the History Department of KU Leuven. Furthermore, study trips and exchanges facilitated by *Scicomove* between Europe and South America helped the establishment of connections between many of the contributors whose papers are collected here.

The editors of this volume would like to express their heartfelt thanks to Prof. Gianluca Cuniberti, then director of the Department of Historical Studies at the University of Turin; Prof. Kaat Wils, head of the History Department at KU Leuven; Prof. Nathalie Richard, scientific coordinator of *Scicomove*; Dr. Cristina Cilli, curator of the Cesare Lombroso Museum of Criminal Anthropology collections; and all the contributors for participating with such enthusiasm in this project.

The editors would also like to express their gratitude to the two anonymous reviewers for their encouragement and insightful comments, as well as to our publishers at Bloomsbury, Maddie Smith and Niamh Coffey, for their editorial assistance and patience throughout the submission process. Finally, for having assisted us with insight and professionalism, we would like to express our heartfelt thanks to Dr. Matthew Armistead, who translated or reviewed nearly all the texts in this volume.

Abbreviations

Archives

ACLM	Archive of the Cesare Lombroso Museum of Criminal Anthropology, University of Turin
AGEP	Archivo General del Estado de Puebla
AGN	Archivo General de la Nación de México
AHCDMX	Archivo Histórico de la Ciudad de México
AHMNA	Archivo Histórico del Museo Nacional de Antropología
CURB	Columbia University, Rare Book & Manuscript Library, New York, Guglielmo Ferrero Papers
ETSGP	Harvard Law School Library, Historical & Special Collections, Cambridge MA, Eleanor T. and Sheldon Glueck Papers, HOLLIS 601652
IDCH	Instituto de Documentação e Investigação em Ciências Humanas, Universidade do Estado de Santa Catarina
LP	Lombroso Project (online archive): https://lombrosoproject.unito.it/

Journals

AAC	*Archivio di antropologia criminale, psichiatria e medicina legale*
APC	*Archivos de Psiquiatría y Criminología*
APS	*Archivio di psichiatria, antropologia criminale e scienze penali*

Introduction

Silvano Montaldo and Franco Orlandi

Despite several invitations, Cesare Lombroso never visited the American continent. However, his ideas circulated widely and at length: by the late nineteenth century, Lombroso was the most frequently cited Italian author in US newspapers. The diffusion of criminal anthropology in that country was also extraordinarily quick. On January 6, 1875, the *Daily Clarion* of Jackson, Mississippi, informed its readers about certain somatic traits that, according to the Italian scholar, were characteristic of criminals (Results of Observation of Criminals 1875). On March 14, 1878, the *Freie Press für Texas* of San Antonio summarized certain chapters from *L'uomo delinquente* (Verbrechen 1878).

In Latin America, the first public presentation of criminal anthropology was a lecture by the physician José Rafael Montalvo at the Ateneo of Havana, Cuba, which was still a Spanish colony (E. B. E. 1879). The earliest known references in Portuguese were by Antônio Herculano de Sousa Bandeira Filho in an article on the question of prisons in Brazil, published in *O Direito* (De Sousa 1881: 6, 10, 192). Long before Lombroso's books were translated and published in the Americas, newspapers, journals, and lectures helped disseminate the principles of criminal anthropology. This contributed to shaping the image of the recidivist and incorrigible criminal, which, in the United States—studied by Silvano Montaldo—aligned with the judicial system's "punitive turn" and the adoption of the indeterminate sentence, first experimented at the Elmira Reformatory.

Later, in the late 1880s and early 1890s, while individual chapters of *L'uomo delinquente* were being translated, studies on criminal anthropology written by American scholars began to circulate. Following two essays published in 1888 by the Argentine authors Francisco Ramos Mejía and Luis Drago—the same year the Society of Legal Anthropology was founded in Buenos Aires—the first work dedicated to Lombrosian theory in the English-speaking Americas was *The Criminal* by the British author Havelock Ellis. It was published in a dual edition on both sides of the Atlantic in 1890. Translations of Lombroso's books arrived later: in 1893, *Escritos de polémica* was published in Spanish, along with *Aplicaciones judiciales y médicas de la antropología criminal*, which collected Lombroso's articles previously published in *España moderna. Revista Ibero-americana*. The following year, *Los anarquistas* was published in Madrid.

The Female Offender, in 1895, was the first book on criminology published by Lombroso in the United States.

Alongside Lombroso's theories, the works of his disciples quickly spread throughout the Americas, particularly those of Enrico Ferri and Raffaele Garofalo, who adapted and transferred the principles of criminal anthropology into penal theory. However, the reaction of classical legal thought was just as swift: echoes of the same debates that Lombroso's ideas had provoked in Italy, France, and the rest of Western Europe were also heard in the Americas. The *Revista forense chilena* translated an open letter, previously published in a French journal, addressed from the Italian jurist Luigi Lucchini to Charles Lucas, the patriarch of prison reform in Europe. In it, Lucchini announced that the Lombrosians had been defeated politically and scientifically in the debate over the Kingdom of Italy's new penal code (Lucchini 1888a). The significance of this letter, which reappeared the following year in the Mexican journal *El Foro* (Lucchini 1889), is worth underlining, as it united two generations of legal experts against Lombroso and his disciples in favor of the legacy of legal ideas from the Enlightenment.

In essence, the arrival of Lombroso's ideas in the Americas radically renewed the debate launched by Catholic and liberal thinkers in the early nineteenth century. At the time, this was described as a kind of theoretical revolution in thinking about criminality. The simultaneity and breadth of this debate are well documented in several national contexts. Máximo Sozzo identifies three distinct yet coexisting attitudes that defined the Argentine reception of Lombroso's doctrine: adoption, transaction, and rejection. The first, exemplified by Ramos Mejía, was characterized by an apologetic embrace and a rather superficial use of Lombroso's ideas. The second, represented by Drago—whose book was translated and published in Italy in 1890—involved a partial acceptance of Lombroso's doctrine while rejecting some of its core principles, such as atavism as a causal factor of crime and the significance of physical anomalies as indicators of criminality. In the introduction to the Italian edition, the father of criminal anthropology extolled the "extraordinary" spread of his new doctrine in South America, which was all the more remarkable given the strong opposition his ideas faced both in Italy and in much of Europe (Lombroso 1890a: XXXI). Lombroso could not help but seek a theoretical explanation for this phenomenon, which he found in the inverted relationship between racial degeneration, genius, and success: the older a "race," the more susceptible it was to the degenerative phenomena that also fostered genius, which nevertheless found great difficulty in asserting itself due to the strong conservative tendencies of the environment in which it arose. Conversely, in "younger races," the resistance to new ideas was much weaker. Thus, his theory, which had been mocked in Europe (the Second International Congress of Criminal Anthropology had concluded in Paris just a few months earlier), found refuge and understanding in the New World (ibid.: XXXV–XXXIX).

However, this reassuring thought would soon be disproved, as the third attitude identified by Sozzo emerged. This was evident in the work of Antonio Dellepiane, published in 1892, which was characterized by a complete rejection of Lombroso's theories and the attribution of crime to social and psychological causes. What set Dellepiane's book apart from those of Ramos Mejía and Drago was precisely the influence of the Second Congress, which was a severe setback for the credibility of the anthropological interpretation of crime among scholars of law, anthropology, and sociology. This credibility was relegated to the realms of forensic medicine, forensic policing, and prison management. A similar development took place in Argentina, which had initially been highly receptive to Lombroso's theories. In the following years, Lombroso's presence in that country remained multifaceted, and positivist criminology in Argentina emerged both because of and in spite of him.

In Chile, in the years between 1890 and 1954, the ideas of the Lombrosian school shaped societal perceptions, reinforcing prejudices against marginalized groups. As Marco Antonio León León demonstrates in his chapter, despite international criticism of biological determinism, Lombroso's doctrine remained embedded in Chilean law enforcement and public discourse. Authorities targeted groups deemed incompatible with the sociopolitical order, including vagrants, alcoholics, and anarchists. These ideas also fueled misogynistic narratives, depicting women as both primitive and deceptively cunning criminals. The case of Bolivia, studied by Françoise Martinez and Pablo Quisbert, first highlights the strong resistance that criminal anthropology encountered upon its arrival in the Americas. At the same time, it also reveals the reasons why young professionals with liberal ideas became deeply interested in it. Under Baptista's conservative government, strong anti-Lombrosian sentiment prevailed in academic institutions such as the University of La Paz, where Lombroso's rejection of free will was deemed unacceptable from a Catholic perspective. In 1893 Rodolfo Soria Galvarro was expelled from the Law School for having used Lombroso's studies. During the subsequent twenty-year period of liberal government, the Lombrosian doctrine gained prominence, as evidenced by contemporary press coverage and several criminal trials. In particular, criminal anthropology was believed to provide scientific validation for the widespread belief that the Indigenous population was inherently savage and criminal, and represented the primary obstacle to Bolivia's modernization. From the 1920s onward, Bolivia entered a new phase marked by fluctuating attitudes toward Lombroso's ideas, alternating between rejection and reinterpretation.

In Peru at the turn of the century, as examined by Gabriella Chiaramonti, crime was widely perceived as a persistent threat to the country's development, creating—at least in theory—a receptive environment for the ideas of the Lombrosian school. However, an analysis of doctoral theses discussing Lombroso at the University of San Marcos in Lima between 1899 and 1910 reveals that most authors expressed strong doubts about the reliability of his data, the theory of the born criminal, and his stance on the death penalty. Furthermore, Lombroso's influence on debates regarding the alleged criminality of the Indigenous "race" was minimal, as these discussions were shaped more by enduring colonial discourses than by his criminological theories. The most significant and lasting legacy of the Lombrosian school in Peru lay in the legal and penal systems, as demonstrated by the Criminal Code of 1924, which fully embraced the principles of social defense and the individualization of punishment.

Criminal anthropology was developed in Italy during a time when the patriotic enthusiasm of the Risorgimento was beginning to wane due to a growing perception of crisis within the political system that had emerged from national unification. Beneath the sense of national solidarity and idealistic fraternity that had fueled that process—rooted in the late-eighteenth-century revolutionary ideals and the democratic nationalism of Giuseppe Mazzini—a belief took hold, further reinforced by the spread of debates on scientific racism, that Italy was divided into two irreconcilable parts: the North and the South. Lombroso was among the scholars most committed to defining this perceived difference, which he attributed in part to distinct ethnic origins. He viewed the nascent Southern Question—the South's relative underdevelopment—primarily as a criminal issue. When transported to the American context, criminal anthropology immediately became intertwined with debates on the ethnic composition of certain states undergoing a process of nation-building, as seen in the case of Bolivia and, to some extent, Peru.

Maria Teresa Milicia reconstructs the key stages of the scientific debate that followed Lombroso's supposed "discovery" of the median occipital fossa in the skull of Giuseppe Villella in 1870, which became the foundation of his doctrine of criminal atavism. From the moment Lombroso announced his finding, the scientific community questioned the atavistic nature of this anatomical feature. The Italian criminologist believed he had definitively proven his theory of atavism when he identified the fossa in four Aymara skulls in 1883, leading him to rename it the "Aymara fossa." With the spread of Lombroso's theories to South America, the concept of the *fosita aymará* reached Peru, where it was critically reassessed by Carlos Morales Macedo in 1911. Although he agreed with Lombroso on the fossa's atavistic significance, he rejected any association with criminality, instead concluding that the Aymara were an ancient race, not a criminal one.

The spread of criminal anthropology in Mexico was significant, to the point that Lombroso had the study on Mexican criminals by Francisco Martínez Baca and Manuel Vergara (1894) translated and published in Italian. Laura Cházaro García and Gerardo García Rojas demonstrate that, although Lombroso's ideas were never fully embraced in Mexico, they nonetheless found their way into spaces such as prisons, laboratories, and museums in the late nineteenth century. At the State Penitentiary of Puebla, physicians conducted anthropometric studies to identify the defining traits of Mexican criminals and the distinctive features of the so-called Indigenous race. In the laboratories of the National Institute of Medicine, teams of doctors carried out research on the anthropometric and physiological characteristics of school-age children with behavioral problems, influenced by Lombroso's belief that deviant children could be treated and reformed. Meanwhile, at the National Museum of Mexico, crania and skeletal remains were collected and studied in an effort to establish a racial classification of the Indigenous population. The data and statistics produced within these spaces contributed to the categorization of different typologies of Mexicans—an epistemic construction that was, at least in part, informed by Lombroso's theories.

Prejudices against Southern Italians were absorbed into the American debate regarding mass immigration from Mediterranean countries. Alessandra Lorini's chapter examines how social scientists in the United States repurposed the theories of the Lombrosian school to reinforce preexisting racial prejudices against new foreign immigrants and to shape public debate against mass immigration between the 1890s and the 1920s. Despite Lombroso's favorable opinion of Sicilians, the notion that Southern Italians were born criminals circulated widely in the national press, fueling a climate of hatred that culminated in violent episodes such as a lynching in New

Orleans in 1891. The reports of the Dillingham Commission, along with the writings of leading eugenicist Madison Grant, selectively cited Giuseppe Sergi and Alfredo Niceforo as scientific authorities to justify restrictive immigration measures and to draw a racial distinction between Northern and Southern Italians. However, they carefully omitted any reference to Sergi's argument that the Mediterranean race had once been superior to the Aryan race and that the civilization of classical Greece and Rome had an African-Mediterranean origin.

Complicating the connection between racism and criminal anthropology was Lombroso's own background in the world of secular, assimilated Judaism. The criminologist positioned himself as a defender of this community in response to growing concerns about the dangers of modern anti-Semitism, even before the eruption of the Dreyfus Affair. Emanuele D'Antonio explores the limited yet significant reception of Lombroso's critique of anti-Semitism in the United States during the Progressive Era. The racial anthropologist and leading figure of the nativist anti-immigration movement, William Z. Ripley, made instrumental use of Lombroso's work, adopting his thesis that Jews were a racially mixed Aryan-Semitic group while rejecting the conclusion that this made them more assimilable into European (and American) civilization. In contrast, the Jewish physician and anthropologist Maurice Fishberg, who defended the idea that Jews were capable of assimilating into American society, used Lombroso's *L'antisemitismo* as a source on the biosocial characteristics of contemporary Jews but questioned his methodology and interpretation. Lombroso's scientific authority was also mobilized by the American Jewish press to counter unfounded accusations that Jews contributed disproportionately to crime in the United States.

Lombroso's conception of the criminal individual's distinctiveness was not limited to the biological sphere but also encompassed cultural aspects, even though he was convinced that physical traits primarily determined behavior and thought expression. To demonstrate this rigidly determinist core idea, he also explored the cultural dimensions of the criminal world, gathering extensive documentation. Diego Galeano investigates the South American reception of Lombroso's ideas on prison literature and the vanity of criminals, as well as their impact on criminological interpretations of mass culture consumption from the 1880s to the mid-1910s. Criminological knowledge about the literary production of inmates and concerns over the risks of its circulation traveled across both sides of the Atlantic. Lombroso translated and incorporated prison poetry sent to him from Brazil into *L'uomo delinquente*, while his work—known even to prisoners themselves—inspired South American criminologists such as Elisio de Carvalho and José Ingenieros to conduct their own research into prison literature and the alleged vanity of delinquents. Similarly, the debate on the perils of contagion and imitation associated with the consumption of such literature, initiated in Italy by Enrico Ferri and Scipio Sighele, found particularly fertile ground in South America, where it fueled preexisting anxieties about the detrimental role of mass media.

In turn, the father of criminal anthropology also drew inspiration from American authors. One significant influence on his criminological ideas was the New Yorker Richard Louis Dugdale, who in 1877 published *The Jukes*, a study on the spread of criminality, prostitution, pauperism, and mental illness across generations of families (Dugdale 1877). Lombroso reported on it in the second edition of *Uomo delinquente* the following year, but he interpreted it in a deterministic manner, using it as evidence of the biological inheritance of antisocial behaviors, while excluding the American author's reflection on the degraded environmental context and the impact of educational and emotional deficiencies on the lives of those families (Lombroso 1878: 269–74). Another influence on Lombroso from the New World was George Miller Beard, whose theory of *American Nervousness* (1881), a syndrome caused by his countrymen's highly competitive way of life, was referenced in the 1888 edition of *L'uomo di genio*, his first book to be translated into English (1891).

However, the American who had the greatest impact on Lombroso's development was José Maria Ramos Mejía, brother of the aforementioned Francisco, and author of *Las neurosis de los hombres célebres en la historia argentina* (1878–82). This study, which proposed a "biopathography" of Juan Manuel Rosas and other South American dictators and leaders, demonstrated how mental illness had shaped the lives of those populations. There were many points in common with Lombroso's research on the influence of madness and climatic factors in human history, starting from a theoretical framework rooted in early-nineteenth-century French physiology and alienism, Henry Maudsley's organic psychiatry, and German scientific materialism. Lombroso, who referred to Ramos Mejía as "one of the greatest alienists of the two worlds" (Lombroso 1890a: XXXI), saw in his work further confirmation of the link between genius and madness (Lombroso 1888b: 3–4, 93–5).

Lombroso incorporated Mejía's ideas into the development of what he termed the zoo-psychiatric theory of political action, beginning with a lecture he gave alongside Rodolfo Laschi in Rome in 1885 at the first international congress of criminal anthropology (Actes 1886–7: 380, 382) and later when writing *Il delitto politico e le rivoluzioni* (Lombroso and Laschi 1890: 57, 92, 133, 277–8, 299, 370). This line of thought gave birth to the 1894 book *Gli anarchici*, which, as already mentioned, was immediately translated into Spanish.

The chapter by Martín Albornoz reveals that the relationship between Lombroso and the anarchist movement in South America was far more complex and dynamic than previously thought, challenging the historiographical notion that it was purely antagonistic. It was an anarchist publisher who brought the first Spanish translation of *Gli anarchici* to America in 1895, and the anarchist press paid unanimous tribute to Lombroso after his death in 1909. He was often invoked by anarchists either as a scientific authority who confirmed certain aspects of their doctrine or else was mocked for his ludicrous criminological theories and classifications. Regardless, the Italian criminologist remained an omnipresent figure, both in criminological discourses on anarchism and within anarchist circles themselves.

Lombroso's interest in the anarchist movement was also responsible for a series of photographs preserved at the Cesare Lombroso Museum of Criminal Anthropology in Turin, related to the trial following the Haymarket affair in Chicago in 1886. The scientific exchange between the Lombrosian school in Italy and the Americas also took the form of material objects traveling across both sides of the Atlantic, as Nadia Pugliese shows in her chapter on the photographic collection from the United States at the Lombroso Museum. The history of what remains of this partially lost collection reveals the widespread popularity Lombroso enjoyed in late-nineteenth-century North

America, where he established connections with prominent figures such as the governor of Colorado and the director of *The Monist*. Photographs from the United States continued to be donated to Lombroso's family after his death. Pugliese hypothesizes that Lewis Hine's 1909 set of photographs of immigrant camps along the State of New York's New Barge Canal and the New York Aqueduct, which has been missing from the museum's collection since the late 1970s, was likely donated by the women's rights activist Mary Dreier to Gina Lombroso after her trip to the United States.

As a keen observer of American society, Lombroso dedicated a significant portion of a book, *Delitti vecchi e delitti nuovi*, published in 1902, to this topic. The book was a collection of essays and articles published in previous years, including one on the rise of homicides in the United States, which had been published in two installments in *North American Review* in 1897 and 1898. To the young Lombroso, a scholar of anthropology, the country seemed to represent the pinnacle of human civilization, thanks to the racial selection experienced by the Anglo-Saxon race. Later, Lombroso viewed the United States with great interest for the experimentation with penal innovations that aligned with the principles of criminal anthropology, such as the indeterminate sentence and early eugenic laws. However, by the end of the nineteenth century, he believed that American society was in a severe crisis, as evidenced by the increase in homicide rates. It was a commonly held belief among statisticians and criminologists that progress led to a reduction in violent crimes and an increase in crimes of deception, but this was not happening in the United States, where in the previous ten years the murder rate had increased well out of proportion with the rise in the population. Lombroso explained this anomaly by depicting the United States as a country torn between barbarism and civilization, where the white population retained a persistent spirit of domination inherited from the times of slavery and wars against the Native Americans, where mass immigration from semi-civilized or uncivilized nations was high, and, especially, where a primitive instinct remained within the Black population. In "Why Homicide Has Increased in the United States," an essay partly inspired by American segregationist literature, Lombroso's evolutionary racism could not be clearer (Lombroso 1897d; 1898b). However, even in this case, the theoretical framework was more complex. In *Delitti vecchi e delitti nuovi*, Lombroso included considerations about the progress made by the Black population, despite the ongoing discrimination they faced, which had been published by William Hooper Councill in *The Forum* in 1899. This further demonstrates how the Italian scholar constantly revised his ideas, without worrying about the contradictions that accumulated within them.

Two chapters in this volume explore the influence that criminal anthropology had on the early scholars of African culture in America. Livio Sansone sheds light on what he terms the "truncated influence" of Lombroso's ideas on Africa and Africans in the development of a new ethnographic sensibility toward Black cultural and religious forms in Brazil. The pioneers of research into the religiosity and fetishism of Black Brazilians in Bahia—namely Raimundo Nina Rodrigues, Oscar Freire, and Aurelino Leal—reflected both an adherence to and divergence from the Italian scientist's vision of Africans and racial mixing. Unlike Lombroso, Nina and Leal considered *métissage* as a cause of degeneration and weakness for the "Brazilian race." In contrast, Freire aligned more closely with Lombroso, viewing racial mixing as a source of vitality for Brazil and believing in the perfectibility of "African races."

Mario Valero's chapter shows that Lombroso also left his mark on the scientific work of Fernando Ortiz, widely regarded as the father of Afro-Cuban studies, even after his apparent shift from criminal anthropology to cultural anthropology. Although Ortiz increasingly interpreted crime as a culturally conditioned behavior, some of his studies continued to echo Lombroso's notion of atavism. Furthermore, his proposal for Cuba's new criminal code (1926) was clearly guided by positivist principles. Lombroso and Ortiz shared many similarities throughout their careers: both hoped their anthropological research would contribute to the nation-building process, believed in the importance of state-led preventive and reformatory measures, held a positive view of racial mixing, and developed an interest in spiritualism.

Finally, this volume contributes to one of the most debated issues in Lombroso scholarship: the fate of criminal anthropology in the decades following his death. The resilience of classical criminal law in the face of the challenge posed by the new conception of the criminal and criminality is well known, and was a phenomenon not only in Europe but also in the United States and Brazil. Equally clear is the central role that this conflict played in the development of twentieth-century legislation, which, while not abandoning the concepts of individual responsibility and retributivism of punishment, also incorporated measures of social defense based on the assessment of the subject's dangerousness and the prevention of recidivism (Pifferi 2022). In the Americas, attempts to punish dangerousness even in the absence of an actual crime, which emerged in plans for the Argentine penal code of 1924 and the Brazilian code of 1927, were unsuccessful, but the Peruvian penal code of 1924, the penal code for the Federal District and Mexican Territories of 1929, the Brazilian code of 1940, and the Chilean *ley de estados antisociales* of 1954 incorporated various elements of positivist proposals.

As a result, historians are divided between those who argue that Lombroso's death in 1909 marked the end of his criminological school and those who suggest that his legacy survived much longer (Orlandi 2024). Several chapters in this book support the second hypothesis. Franco Orlandi sheds light on the transatlantic legacy of Lombroso by focusing on the career and scientific production of Cuban criminal anthropologist Israel Castellanos, one of the most prominent and influential scientists of the country's Machado era and the recipient of the Lombroso Prize for the best work in criminal anthropology in 1929. The analysis of Castellanos's work reveals the extraordinary longevity of Lombrosian theories in Cuba, as they continued to be used to explain criminal behavior into the late 1930s. It also demonstrates that Lombrosian criminal anthropology contributed to the criminalization of the Black population and served as a tool for legitimizing Machado's political project, confirming the ease with which the Italian's ideas could be transferred from a liberal context to authoritarian regimes.

Similarly, Viviane Borges and Fernando Salla underscore the lasting influence of Lombroso's theories on prison practices in early-twentieth-century Brazil. Although the ideas of the Lombrosian school were not incorporated into the Brazilian penal code of 1890, they had a significant impact on institutions outside of the judiciary, such as prisons, long after Lombroso's death. An analysis of inmate records from the São Paulo and Florianópolis penitentiaries reveals that prison directors, doctors, and guards continued to place considerable importance on the physical traits of criminals and explicitly referred to Lombroso's classification of female offenders as late as the 1940s.

That Lombroso's conception of female criminality continued to be highly influential in the United States is demonstrated in Mary Gibson's chapter on the criminology of women. From the 1920s until the emergence of feminist criminology in the 1970s, theories of female crime repeated Lombroso's biological and psychological theories long after male crime had been explained in sociological terms. While US criminologists rejected Lombroso's theory of atavism and criticized his flawed methodology, they continued to echo his claim for fifty years that prostitution was the typical form of female criminality and that criminal women were "weak-willed, mentally deficient, overly emotional, and even hysterical."

The ambivalent attitude of US criminologists toward Lombroso is further highlighted by John Shepherd in his chapter on William Sheldon's and Sheldon and Eleanor Glueck's investigation of criminal somatotypes in the 1940s. The Gluecks strongly distanced themselves from Lombroso's theories, yet Lombrosian atavistic tropes seemed to resurface in their description of the mesomorphic delinquent. Sheldon, on the other hand, critiqued Lombroso but also acknowledged his importance as a precursor to modern biocriminology, establishing a direct connection between his study of criminal somatotypes and criminal anthropology. Lombroso thus remained a complex and contested reference point for mid-century US criminologists, even after his doctrine had been definitively eclipsed by competing criminological traditions in psychiatry and sociology.

Lombroso was regarded with similar ambiguity in Argentina, as Alejandra Mahile shows in her analysis of José Ingenieros's critical reception of criminal anthropology. A proponent of a psychopathological approach to the study of delinquency, Ingenieros vehemently attacked Lombroso for his emphasis on the criminal body and his interest in spiritualism, downplaying his role in the birth of criminology. However, as Mahile points out, Ingenieros's violent opposition to the Italian criminologist served to bolster his own career and establish his scientific authority in Argentina.

In conclusion, the presence of Lombroso's criminological theories in the Americas was precocious, pervasive, and enduring, extending from the late 1870s until—in countries such as Mexico, the United States, Cuba, Brazil, and Chile—the 1940s and 1950s. The relationship between Lombroso and the Americas was clearly extremely fertile, but it was never one of subordination. The father of criminal anthropology drew upon publications, human remains, and photographic portraits from the Americas to validate his theories and legitimize the prestige of his school, but in the Americas his ideas were almost never accepted uncritically. They were often challenged due to their rigid biological determinism and weak methodology. However, the continued ambivalence toward Lombroso in the Americas does not negate the fact that the work of the Italian criminologist remained, for better or worse, an indispensable reference for anyone studying crime and genius in the New World.

The case studies analyzed in this volume further reveal the considerable complexity of the image of Lombroso, whose intellectual legacy resists at hasty and reductive classifications. On the one hand, Lombroso was undoubtedly an evolutionary racist, and his criminological theories contributed to reinforcing preexisting racial prejudices against marginalized groups such as Indigenous people, Black people, and immigrants. His influence was an obstacle to the emancipation of women, contributed to the criminalization of prostitution, and was used by advocates of eugenics. On the other hand, he became an authoritative voice against American anti-Semitism, and his work had a significant influence on pioneering studies of Afro-American culture. His ideas, because of their ambiguity, found space in both authoritarian regimes and liberal governments, as well as in anarchist circles. The strength of these ideas was bolstered by an institutional environment interested in reforming systems of punishment, the social alarm over the spread of crime, and the tensions sparked by diverse ethnic compositions, all of which found convenient points of contact in Lombroso's racism, which was interpreted in various, even contradictory, ways.

Another factor facilitating the circulation of criminal anthropology was the use of Lombroso's ideas by mass-market newspapers, which were attracted by the sensationalism of his theories. This phenomenon was aided by the less hierarchical conception of culture in the Americas compared to Western Europe, where academic environments played a more prominent role in the cultural debate. Lombroso's ideas on crime and criminals were at the heart of this popular interest, but the strength of his proposals also stemmed from the fact that they were presented within a seemingly well-organized system of thought, bolstered by the trappings of cutting-edge scientific research. Lombroso was, in other words, a writer who managed to present himself as a "universal" intellectual, capable of expressing himself on topics far beyond criminology. For a long time, he succeeded in capturing the imagination of American readers with his paradoxes and attracting public curiosity with unusual, contrarian views, often while fanning the flames of social tensions and concerns from a position that was distant yet well-informed. In this sense, the success he achieved in the Americas and the long-lasting approval of his ideas, and the fact that they were considered credible for so long, seem symptomatic of a broader phase in the cultural history of the whole of the Americas and their difficult relationship with modern scientific thought.

Part I

The Criminal Man in the Americas

1

"Like a Literary Whale": The First Journeys of Lombrosian Theories in the United States (1870–95)

Silvano Montaldo

The Criminal Man Goes to the Far West

On Saturday, March 19, 1870, readers of *Appletons' Journal*, one of the most distinguished weekly publications of the post-Civil War era, discovered that a certain Professor Lombroso had presented a study on the physical structure of Italians at the International Medical Congress in Florence. His research revealed the significant influence of race and environment: a few drops of Greek or Norman blood made many Sicilians blonde, while Calabrians had disproportionately long arms resembling those of apes, and Sardinians had the smallest cranial capacity of all the subjects of the Kingdom of Italy (Physical Structure 1870). This was not the first time that Lombroso's name appeared in an American publication, but this brief article—imbued with Lamarckism, Darwinism, and a pronounced prejudice against Southern Italians—was probably the first published account in America of one of the Veronese scientist's areas of research: the construction of an anthropology of the Italians, a project pursued by some intellectuals of the Risorgimento (Barsotti 2021).

The second article to present Lombroso's theories in the United States, as far as the current research shows, appeared on Wednesday, August 21, 1872, in the *Deutsche Correspondent*. Readers from Baltimore's large German community learned that Italian doctors had recently begun studying an endemic disease called pellagra. One of these doctors, Lombroso, attributed this dreadful illness—of which there had been a few mild cases in Maryland—to the poor quality of corn provided to impoverished workers. Lombroso argued that neither the excessive consumption of corn, the staple food of Venetian peasants, nor a particular fungus that grew on it was to blame (Pellagra 1872).

Three years later, the residents of Jackson, Mississippi—a small community just beginning to recover from a terrible fire that had nearly destroyed it during the Civil War—read that Professor Lombroso had concluded that criminals were generally taller and heavier than honest men. Not only that, but they also had broader chests, darker hair and eyes, mostly brachycephalic skull shapes (especially the murderers), and frequent asymmetries. They were also weaker than average (though stronger than most lunatics), had sparse facial hair, slanted eyes, and large earlobes—traits that Lombroso claimed linked European criminals to the Australian and Mongolian races (Results of Observation of Criminals, 1875).

While the brief *Appletons' Journal* piece was written by its correspondent in Italy, and the article on pellagra appeared in the July 1, 1872, issue of the renowned *Rivista europea* (D'Antonio 2024: 41), the source of the third piece—published in the *Daily Clarion* on January 6, 1875, and reprinted in the *Weekly Clarion* the following day—is somewhat more surprising. Even Italian readers would have struggled to trace its origins, which can be found in the *Rendiconti del Reale Istituto Lombardo* (Proceedings of the Royal Lombard Institute), where Lombroso's study, presented at the institute's January 8, 1874, meeting, was published in two parts (Lombroso 1874a, b). These were among the earliest published materials of those which were compiled into *L'uomo delinquente* (The Criminal Man) two years later. It is astonishing how quickly news of the birth of criminal anthropology reached a small town in the Deep South, and it remains unclear how this could have happened. Notably, the *American Journal of Insanity*, the *American Journal of Science*, and the *New York Medical Journal*—three of the most prominent scientific journals in the United States—made no mention of this new area of study. Nor did the French *Annales d'hygiène publique et de médecine légale* and *Annales médico-psychologiques*, or Britain's *Journal of Mental Science*. All of these internationally recognized periodicals were widely read in the United States and were otherwise familiar with Cesare Lombroso and his studies.

Rather than the specialist press, the primary channel of transmission for criminal anthropology across the Atlantic appears to have been the newspapers, which had been devoting considerable space to crime reports for decades, fueling public interest (Wood 2016: 301–2). Unfortunately, surviving correspondence from Lombroso documents his connections with American journalists only from the early twentieth century (Rafter 2009: 287), making it challenging to identify the link—or links—between Milan's *Rendiconti* and Mississippi's *Daily Clarion*. One possibility is that a major European newspaper picked up the news, transmitting it to the United States; another is that the *Daily Clarion* had reprinted an article from a more prominent American newspaper with a correspondent in Italy or France.

The second mechanism may also have been at work on March 14, 1878, when the *Freie Press für Texas* of San Antonio printed a summary of the first six chapters of *L'uomo delinquente* (Verbrechen 1878), the second edition of which was published that year. The similarities between Jackson and San Antonio are notable: both were Reconstruction states with high crime rates, and in fact Texas had the highest levels of violence in the Western world at the time (Mac Mahon 2016: 117–19). These conditions may have made both newspapers particularly receptive to new discussions on criminality, fostering an environment favorable to criminal anthropology.

These were the years of a harshly repressive reform of American justice—the so-called "punitive turn" (Simon 2001)—and the entire American public was highly sensitive to the issue of crime. On August 8 of the following year, Vermont's *Burlington*

Weekly Free Press reviewed *Sull'incremento del delitto in Italia e sui mezzi per arrestarlo* (On the Increase of Crime in Italy and the Means of Stopping It), which Lombroso had published a few months earlier (Crime and Criminals 1879). The next day, the review was reprinted by the *Daily Cairo Bulletin* in Illinois (Paris Letter 1879a), and the following week by the *Lafayette Advertiser* of Vermilionville, Louisiana (Paris Letter 1879b). In the latter case, we have a firmer indication about the flow of information, as it was specified that the piece was written on July 23 by a correspondent in France. The editorial decision would have been motivated by the book's focus on the topic of crime rather than its emphasis on Italy, a distant country whose migration to the United States had not yet reached the mass scale it would soon achieve (Rauty 2010).

The first scientific articles on criminal anthropology appear to have come later. In 1880, E. P. Fowler presented in the *Medico-Chirurgical Quarterly* the research of the Austrian Moritz Benedikt on the brains of criminals, which in part supported Lombroso's ideas (Fink 1938: 99). In 1881, *Popular Science Monthly* published "New Phrenology" (De Varigny 1881), a piece on cerebral localization by a French scientist and popularizer originally written for the *Revue des Deux Mondes*. Two years later came "Tattooing among Civilized People," the text of a lecture by Robert Fletcher, an English physician who had moved to America and was one of the founders of the Anthropological Society of Washington (Fletcher 1883); and a study by Edward Charles Spitzka, a psychiatrist and anatomist, on Charles Guiteau, the assassin of President James A. Garfield. Lombroso had also examined Guiteau's case, using it to develop his concept of the "graphomaniac mattoid" type (Lombroso and Kornfeld 1881; Lombroso 1882: 216, 220, 331–9; Spitzka 1883: 212). The second half of the decade saw the publication of two texts considered among the first to spread Lombrosian criminology in the United States (Horton and Rich 2004: 386; Rafter 2009: 281): Jastrow's "A Theory of Criminality" (1886) and Noyes's "The Criminal Type" (1887). By this time, the name of Lombroso and the ideas of criminal anthropology had been known in the United States for a decade, although the theory of the born criminal seemed confined to small niches until the late 1870s. The first time that Lombroso was mentioned in an American scientific publication may have come in 1869, when the *American Journal of Insanity* referred to a project to collect international statistics on mental illnesses, launched at the first International Congress of Alienists held in Paris two years earlier. Lombroso was named as the project's point of contact in Italy (A Project of a System of Statistics 1869–70: 49, 52). A decade would pass before a second mention, which in fact came in the same journal, with the translation of an article by Clodomiro Bonfigli on moral insanity that referred to Lombroso's views on the matter (Bonfigli on Moral Insanity 1879–80: 490). Thus, Fletcher's lecture, which took place on December 19, 1882, at the Anthropological Society, was probably the first formal academic discussion of an aspect of the theory of criminal atavism—specifically, the idea that tattooing was an instinct connecting criminals and contemporary "savages" to primitive man. However, it is important to emphasize that this came after the reports published by small provincial newspapers, a fact that raises complicated questions about the connections that enabled this "knowledge in transit" (Secord 2004).

Lombroso and North American Popular Culture

Popular science played a crucial role in shaping the culture of an expanding population from the nineteenth to the early twentieth centuries. Building on Enlightenment ideals of scientific dissemination as a means to combat superstition and ignorance, journals, manuals, children's books, novels, and associations proliferated in countries like France, Germany, England, and the United States. Italy, too, had its own "science for all," and Lombroso participated actively by contributing to *Igea*, the first Italian journal on hygiene and preventive medicine (Govoni 2002), and by giving lectures and public talks for nonacademic audiences. Of course, the United States in the Gilded Age offered Lombroso a far larger and constantly evolving audience (Mott 1950: 404, 478).

Chronicling America, a service provided by the Library of Congress, allows searches of more than twenty-one million pages of North American newspapers from 1756 to 1963. A search for Lombroso's name returns 4,630 results, putting him in first position among Italian writers of his time, surpassing Giosuè Carducci (2,803), Giovanni Pascoli (1,867), and Edmondo De Amicis (1,531). If we narrow this to the nineteenth century—to avoid skewing the results with references to publications by his daughters Paola and Gina, to Gina's 1908 US visit with her famous husband, Guglielmo Ferrero, and to his grandson Cesare T. Lombroso, a professor at Harvard Medical School—Cesare Lombroso still ranks first among significant Italian authors, with 1,298 results. The anthropologist and ethnographer Paolo Mantegazza, a major popularizer of science somewhat comparable to Lombroso in terms of the popularity of his themes, was mentioned only 290 times. The relationship between Lombroso and the United States—the first mass society—thus highlights a significant overlap between public and scientific discourse which, while noted by historians (Horton and Rich 2004; Rafter 2009; Rafter and Ystehede 2009; Forno 2010; Pedersson 2018), nevertheless warrants deeper analysis.

It is worth noting from the beginning that Lombroso's critics were well aware of his inclination to seek "ascendancy over the masses" (Lucchini 1886: 115) through sensationalism, paradox, and polemic (Antropologia contro antropologia 1886, Lucchini 1888b). His search for support from the general public was no doubt influenced by his awareness that his audacious theories were often met with skepticism or outright hostility in scientific circles. He thus organized temporary criminal anthropology exhibitions and established a "psychiatric-criminological museum" in Turin specifically to encourage public engagement. In a letter to Ferrero, who was overseeing the English translation of *La donna delinquente*, Lombroso expressed frustration with the English editor's decision to cut out all references to the sexuality of prostitutes and criminals: "Regarding women, to tell the truth, I fear that starting with such drastic cuts will lead me to lose popularity."[1] It is therefore difficult to credit Lombroso with a sincere commitment to scientific dissemination or the "popularization" of a "science," however one understands that word. Rather, his eyes were on self-promotion and a propagandistic use of ideas that, while encountering growing opposition in academic circles in the Old Continent, found fertile ground in the United States, where a thriving publishing industry, an enthusiasm for science, and a culture less hierarchical than Western Europe (Pandora 2009: 351–5) offered great opportunities.

All twenty-six articles referencing Lombroso in *Chronicling America* from the 1880s were confined to local or non-English papers, although this may reflect a bias in the site's focus on local and multilingual publications. This is the impression that emerges when tracing the overseas success of "Délit politique au point de vue de l'anthropologie criminelle," an article Lombroso published in the May–June 1886 issue of the progressive Parisian journal *Nouvelle Revue* (Lombroso 1886). In this instance, we have sufficient information to map the transatlantic transfer and diffusion of Lombroso's ideas, as well as to hypothesize the motivations for their reception.

The original text was the first exposition of Lombroso's thoughts on politics to be published in French, ideas that would later be developed fully in *Il delitto politico e le rivoluzioni*, which he published with Rodolfo Laschi in 1890. Lombroso had explored these topics for years, seeking to uncover the great natural laws governing the development of mankind. The debut on the international stage of his biopsychological theory of political behavior coincided with a particularly tumultuous time in American society, which had just been shaken by the Haymarket affair—a massacre committed in Chicago during a labor dispute, followed by a show trial of eight, predominantly German, immigrant anarchists. The first US newspaper to report the originality of Lombroso's theories on revolts and revolutions was *Der Deutsche Correspondent*, which had also published his article on pellagra in 1872. In a lengthy article printed on June 5, the paper explained Lombroso's idea that natural factors like seasons, latitude, and madness influenced political violence (Eine neue Verbrecher-Theorie 1886). The German-language newspaper may have been trying to suggest a defense strategy for the compatriots arrested a month earlier. In subsequent years, some of Lombroso's insights on crowd psychology were occasionally employed, with some success, by Italian jurists sympathetic to socialism in trials of activists charged with striking and sedition.

A second, and far more impactful, channel also opened up as a result of the *Nouvelle Revue* article, when Joseph Jastrow, then an assistant in psychology at Johns Hopkins University, published a summary of it on July 2 in *Science*, the journal of the American Association for the Advancement of Science. Jastrow's piece was subsequently reprinted anonymously in *Public Opinion*, the weekly publication of the Washington DC news agency of the same name, and further circulated in local newspapers over the ensuing months, with mentions continuing as late as February 1889 in Wisconsin, North Carolina, Nebraska, Vermont, Minnesota, Dakota, and Maryland (A Theory of Criminality 1886; Physicians and Scientists 1886; Insanity and Crime 1886a, b, c, d; A Study of Criminal Types 1886a, b; Insanity and Crime 1889). The nine articles cataloged in *Chronicling America* probably represent only a portion of this sequence, considering the thousands of newspapers in circulation and the public interest in these topics during the trial and execution of the Chicago anarchists. A third and fourth wave was initiated by the *Chicago Tribune* and the *Baltimore Daily News*. In the case of the former, the source was the *Nouvelle Revue*, as evidenced by an article reprinted by *The Fairfield News and Herald* in South Carolina (The Revolutionists 1886). Meanwhile, the Maryland paper took Lombroso's theory in an extremely reactionary direction, branding all revolutionaries as insane. This was likely the first significant distortion of Lombroso's ideas in America and found an audience at least in Illinois, Kansas, and Tennessee (Socialism and Insanity 1886a, b, c).

The year 1886 thus saw the first widespread circulation of Lombroso's criminology in the United States, fueled by the clamor for information about the Haymarket affair. This was followed by a new wave of articles the following year, sparked by William Noyes, a physician at New York's Bloomingdale Insane Asylum, who gave a talk on the fundamentals of criminal anthropology at a conference. A summary of his talk, published in the *New York Tribune*, was reprinted in Kansas, Minnesota, Delaware, Nebraska, and Montana (The Criminal Type 1887a, b, c, d, e). Additionally, the *Illinois Staats-zeitung* of Chicago featured an extensive article on how science could assist the police by studying criminal jargon, tattoos, the use of the plethysmograph in interrogations, and photographic identification (Die Wissenschaft 1886).

We do not know the extent of Lombroso's awareness of his initial phase of popularity in the United States. However, the journalist Helen Zimmern reported that he received "daily an immense quantity of newspapers from all parts of the world in which Lombroso is spoken of" (One of the Great Men 1893). In any case, in 1891 Lombroso wrote about the Chicago anarchists in an article published in *The Monist*, igniting a debate with Michael Schwab, one of the three Haymarket defendants who had escaped the gallows (Lombroso 1891a: 338–42). This exchange was echoed in several local newspapers ("Curious Condensations" 1891; Professor Lombroso 1891a, b).

The "Lombroso moment"

The early 1890s marked the beginning of what could be called the "Lombroso moment" in North American culture. Figure 1.1 demonstrates the widespread presence of his name, both as an author and as a point of reference, in the generalist newspapers and weeklies included in *Chronicling America*, as well as in ten selected specialist journals related to his fields of work.[2]

One of the main reasons behind Lombroso's rapid rise to fame was the publication of *The Criminal* by British author Havelock Ellis. This was the first comprehensive summary of criminal anthropology available in English, copublished by Scribner & Welford in New York and Walter Scott in London (Ellis 1890). The book was positively reviewed by *Science* (Book Reviews 1890) and various generalist periodicals (Some New Books 1890; Science and Crime 1890; Our Boston Literary Letter 1890), and not only familiarized the American public with the details of Lombroso's theories but also established a connection between his ideas and North American punitive practices. Ellis highlighted the New York State Reformatory at Elmira as the institution that applied the treatments most closely aligned with the tenets of the new criminological science, noting its implementation of practices like separation, sentence gradation, incentives, and probation. These measures granted its director the discretion necessary to tailor punishment to the individual personality of young inmates (Ellis 1890: 59–273).

In Italy, the experiment in individualized sentencing undertaken by Zebulon Brockway at Elmira, which was in full development, had already caught the attention of the government. Martino Beltrani Scalia, the director general of Italian Prisons and an advocate of criminal anthropology, highlighted this experiment in the journal he directed, suggesting it as a model for the political class when drafting new prison

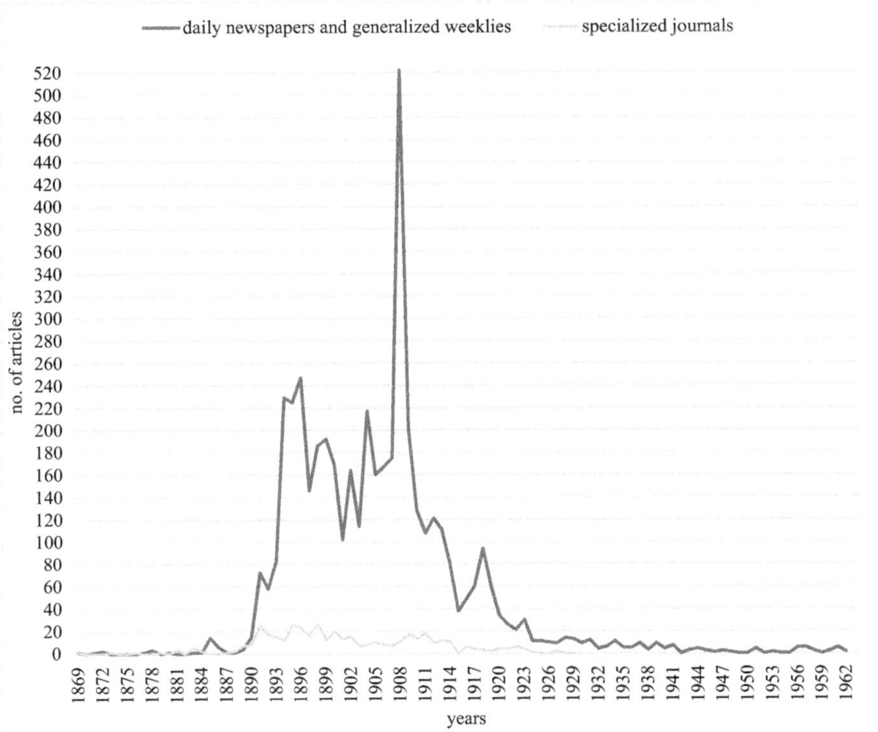

Figure 1.1 References to Cesare Lombroso in the American press, 1869–1962.

regulations (M. B. S. 1887: 311). This is how Lombroso's followers first became aware of Elmira. Notably, the first article in Lombroso's journal dedicated to the prison was a summary of Beltrani Scalia's text. Lombroso viewed Elmira not as an application of the ideas of the positive school but as embodying "the recommendations of the greatest American scholars in prison studies" (Lombroso 1887b: 547).

In a later commentary, Ellis further reinforced this connection, designating 1876—the year *L'uomo delinquente* was published and the Elmira reformatory was founded—as the beginning of a scientific reform of the penitentiary system, theorized by Lombroso and realized by Brockway (Ellis 1891: III–IV). Lombroso already admired Americans, whom he saw as the highest evolutionary expression of the white race, and their way of life (Lombroso 1871c: 103–6), believing that their "nervousness" signaled the advent of a more civilized form of humanity (Lombroso 1888b: 481). He thus became an avid observer of the country, partly because of his desire for information about penal experiments that the hostility of Italian "classical" jurists prevented at home. For Lombroso's followers, Elmira exemplified the influence that their ideas exerted in the world's most advanced nation, although Lombroso doubted that even the best rehabilitation programs could reform born criminals (Lombroso 1893e: 325–30; Carrara 1895).

In 1892, Arthur MacDonald—a Bureau of Education official who had visited several European universities and taught criminal anthropology at Clark University in Massachusetts—published *Criminology*, which received positive attention in the press (Criminology 1893; Blumenthal 2022: 217–19). Lombroso wrote the introduction, adopting his familiar tone of victimhood and expressing satisfaction that his theories, so contested in Europe, had taken "such deep root" in the United States and "found practical applications, as at Elmira." He hoped that, having been adopted in the New World, his ideas could return to the Old Continent, refined by experimentation (Lombroso 1892a: X).

The success of *The Criminal* and *Criminology* fueled interest in criminal anthropology but discouraged the English translation of *L'uomo delinquente* until after Lombroso's death. Consequently, his first book for English-speaking readers was *The Man of Genius* (Lombroso 1891b), released by the same publishers as *The Criminal* and part of a series directed by Ellis. In this book, Lombroso boldly combined the theory of reversion—the possibility of ancestral instincts and forms reappearing in the present—with the concept of degeneration. According to this theory, geniuses were degenerates, bound by a physiological law that deprived them of something in their general mental health and common values in return for their special intellectual gifts (ibid.: V–VI). Degeneration gave rise to genius, and also to the "mattoids," individuals who only appeared to possess genius but lacked its substance, but who could nevertheless perform an evolutionary function by being less inhibited than average people when faced with the new and thus able to direct the masses toward progress.

While academia received it with varying degrees of skepticism—*The American Journal of Insanity* explicitly labeled it a "pseudo-science" (J. B. 1891–2: 529)—the theory that genius was a form of neurosis and that madness had a key role in history gained traction in the major newspapers (Genius and Insanity 1891; Genius and Insanity 1892a; Insanity and Genius 1892 a, b, c; Not Consoling 1892). Lombroso's ideas thus became frequent reference points in commentaries on research into familial heredity and in biographies of prominent individuals (New Books, 1892a, b). *The Boston Globe* referred to him as "perhaps the most celebrated expert on insanity in Europe," a judgment echoed by other newspapers (Genius and Insanity 1892b).

Another factor in Lombroso's rise to prominence in the United States in the early 1890s was the founding of *The Monist*, a philosophical journal launched in October 1890 by entrepreneur Edward Carl Hegeler, who was interested in the dialogue between scientific thought and religion. In its early years, *The Monist* focused heavily on scientific materialism. Lombroso, who was in contact with the journal's first editor, Paul Carus, a German philosopher who had emigrated to the United States, made a major contribution, publishing five articles in its first year: three on criminal anthropology, one on psychology, and one on recent Italian literature.

By this time, then, Lombroso was no longer unknown to the American public, partly because, apart from the arguments already mentioned, he continually introduced new ones, sustaining a steady flow of interest and curiosity. Commenting on Lombroso's extraordinary pervasiveness, Warren Webster, a retired medical officer who contributed to various American and German scientific journals, wrote:

> He flits and floats with his productions through magazines and newspapers published all the way from the Mediterranean to the North Sea … At one time he dives into type through the columns of an English or German review, and speedily comes to surface again, like a literary whale, to blow through his favorite organ, the Paris *Revue des Revues*. (Webster 1895, 86)

The "female question"

Among the new topics tackled by Lombroso in the 1890s, his views on the anthropology of Western women stand out. The emergence of this theme in references to him in the worldwide press coincided with the preparation for the publication of *La donna delinquente* in 1893. Through public lectures and articles in major French and British periodicals, Lombroso and his student Ferrero presented strongly misogynistic arguments that reflected not only their views on female inferiority but also generated anticipation for their forthcoming book.

The reaction from the American public was much stronger than in Italy, where the so-called "female question" was less commonly debated. New York's *The Sun*, one of the most important newspapers of the time, reported that at a Milan conference Lombroso presented research claiming that women had a lower pain threshold than men, as their senses were less developed, making it easier for them to overcome moral suffering. He argued that the common belief that women were more sensitive than men was a misconception, stemming from their greater irritability and tendency to cry. Initially, the newspaper ridiculed these claims, referring to Lombroso as "the old porcupine" who, "inspired of course by the devil," had declared "that woman was an animal of an inferior grade" (Various Manifestations, 1891). The following year, however, when *The Sun* reported on a text containing similar theories that Lombroso submitted to the International Congress of Experimental Psychology in London, it noted that these ideas would make him "extremely unpopular in feminine circles," but also acknowledged him as one of the few "bold men in these effeminate days" (Latest News 1892). The *Salt Lake Herald* even called him "one of the great lights of modern scientific research" (How We Endure Pain, 1892). Lombroso, in other words, had begun to divide American public opinion, eliciting contrasting views that only increased his visibility.

Another example of this comes from a Minnesota newspaper, which devoted four articles to discussing Lombroso's theory—featured in the *Revue des revues*—that women had a natural, instinctive tendency toward lying and cruelty, unlike men (Are Women Liars? 1892; Women as Prevaricators 1892; Retaliation 1892; Are All Men Liars? 1892). The provocation was certainly successful, as newspapers from across the country, including Mississippi, Pennsylvania, Montana, Utah, New Jersey, Illinois, Kentucky, Louisiana, California, and Washington, all published texts by Lombroso, alongside reflections on differences between men and women, opinions of American doctors and dentists on their reactions to pain, views of physiologists on relative female insensitivity, discussions on the differences between European and American women, and even speculations on the Italian professor's personality and the state of his domestic life (Woman's Power 1892; A Woman's Heart 1892; Women Endure Pain 1892; Men, Women and Pain 1892; How We Endure Pain, 1892; Woman's Sensibility 1892a, b; Dissecting Female Theories 1892; The Sensibility of Women 1892).

The "female question," viewed through the lens of Lombrosian anthropology, continued to inspire American reporting for several more years (Geniusz 1893; Das Weib als Verbrecher, 1893; Nowe idee 1895; Love and Suicide 1895; Women's Criminal Instincts 1895; Das Weib als Verbrecher 1895), ensuring that American newspapers were primed for the release of *The Female Offender* (New Books 1895; Female Offender 1895; Female Criminals 1895). Despite being significantly abridged and modified by the Anglican priest who translated it—a fact Lombroso himself lamented in an interview (Lombroso's "Woman" 1895)—this was the first book on criminal anthropology to be translated into English. It enjoyed considerable and lasting success in the United States.

Adding to the resonance of Lombroso's research in fin-de-siècle culture was his conversion to Spiritualism, which in those years had become a social phenomenon in the United States, bolstered by the growing entertainment industry, the crisis of traditional beliefs, and the spread of alternative views of science (Natale 2016; Karpenko and Claggett 2017). This was particularly clear in 1909, at the time of his death, when many newspapers reported that he had promised his relatives that he would contact them from the afterlife. While North American academics were quick to criticize Lombroso's shift from initial skepticism to embracing the "silly humbug of old-time spiritualism" (The Spiritualists 1892), the major newspapers did not. For them, the interest of renowned thinkers in supernatural phenomena was a sign of courage and intellectual honesty (Science and the Spirits 1893; A Roman Seance 1894). Research on hypnosis and suggestion-induced crimes also tapped into widespread popular anxieties, amplified by the press on both sides of the Atlantic (Hughes 2015). This reinforced Lombroso's image as a bold explorer at the frontier of knowledge, transcending the routine of official science (A Psychic Suggestion 1894a, b).

The Helen Zimmern Interview

By this point, the time was ripe for American newspapers to feature an extensive interview with Lombroso. It was in fact a woman—Helen Zimmern—who took up the task in an article published by *The Sun* in 1893. A German-born Jewish journalist and writer with British nationality, Zimmern was well respected for her work as a translator and essayist. She was known for introducing English-speaking audiences to German and Italian artists, philosophers, and writers. After years of collaborating with Italian newspapers, she had settled in Florence (Del Vivo 2014), where she met Lombroso and Enrico Ferri during their visit to the city in April–May 1892 for a legal case.[3] The three spent time together discussing a variety of issues, and after a few days, an American friend of Zimmern's suggested the idea of an interview.

The friend hoped that Lombroso, whose name had been widely mentioned in the British press in debates on the English prison system (Serafini 2025), would defend the Elmira penitentiary from a scathing attack launched by William Tallack in a letter published in *The Times* of London. Tallack, secretary of the Howard Association and a convinced abolitionist, was considered an authority on prison issues. He viewed the parole system and the engagement of long-term inmates in work and managerial activities—practices pioneered by the Massachusetts prison—as serious lapses in disciplinary standards. American prisons, he argued, risked becoming schools of crime, unlike in England, where rules on separation and fixed-term punishment were properly respected. Tallack's article, which linked the methods adopted by Brockway to the precepts of criminal anthropology and the influence of Italian reformers, echoed throughout the American press (American Prison System 1892; Crime in Two Countries 1892; As to That English Screed 1892), leading to the suggestion for an interview with Lombroso on the subject of prison reform, which Zimmern took up with enthusiasm.

Time passed, however, and the interview was not published until June 11, 1893, by which time another storm had broken out over Elmira. Accusations of brutality and corporal punishment had emerged, implicating even Brockway himself. Titled "One of the Great Men," Zimmern's article reflected on Lombroso's visit, which was preceded by a correspondence that has since been lost. She played on the contrast between his fame and appearance, describing him as "a little roly-poly, good-humored looking, elderly gentleman," particularly in comparison to Ferri, "a tall, Apollo-like younger man." Aside for his gaze, Zimmern found nothing remarkable about Lombroso, noting he looked like "some peaceable notary." Even his speech was neither "easy" nor elegant"; his strong Venetian accent, use of Piedmontese terms, and rhapsodic discussions driven by fervent imagination made his delivery, like his writing, somewhat labored.

Zimmern did not shy away from Lombroso's reputation as "the bugbear of the superstitious, the laughing stock of the small-witted," yet she redirected the accusation of pseudoscience toward his critics, whom she held responsible for superficial interpretations. Only those able to follow his reasoning and grasp the novelty of his methods truly appreciated him. Loyal and devoted to his theories and followers, Lombroso despised those who opposed him, "seeing an enemy in every adversary." His restless mind had made him "impatient of all criticism," and the relentless and violent attacks he endured fostered "a kind of persecution mania," to the point that he believed his life was at risk.

Zimmern pointed out that Lombroso certainly did not lack enemies, especially among the clergy. Prominent Catholic newspapers in Turin had called for him to be stripped of his professorship for teaching "immoral doctrines." Women, too, largely disliked him—not so much Italian women, who at the time showed limited interest in emancipation, but the many mothers in Turin who were genuinely distressed that their sons attended the professor's lectures or read his books. To them, he was a "heretic, sacrilegious, cynic … an overthrower of all faith and illusions." Then there were the pranksters who amused themselves by visiting his office or attending his lectures while pretending to be mad, idiotic, or criminal, or else sent him fake documents. Some even presented themselves with fake tattoos that could be rubbed away with a damp finger.

Zimmern also offered a glimpse into Lombroso's personal life, which had become the subject of avid speculation in American newspapers. She described his special relationship with his two daughters, "high-minded, characteristic types of Hebrew women," who, while not neglecting their household duties, "helped him with his work, translating and writing for him." She explained that errors in his books arose because he used other people's publications without reading them in full, skimming the pages in search of what interested him. Nevertheless, Zimmern assured, his intellectual honesty and passion for research were beyond suspicion (Zimmern 1893b).

The portion of the interview concerning prison reform did not appear in *The Sun* but was published separately in the September 1893 issue of *Popular Science Monthly* (Zimmern 1893c). Here, Zimmern went as far as to portray Lombroso as the successor of Galileo, persecuted for the boldness of his ideas—a characterization that caused a stir in smaller American newspapers (Lombroso's Theory 1893a, b). A similar response followed in December, when the journalist enthusiastically reviewed *La donna delinquente*, offering its English-speaking audience a preview of its contents (Zimmern 1893a; Criminal Women 1893).

The Friendly Dispute with Max Nordau

In 1895, the English translation of *Degeneration* by Max Nordau—pseudonym of Simon Maximilian Südfeld, a Hungarian Jewish doctor, writer, and journalist of German culture based in Paris—was published. The book, which had already sparked significant controversy in Europe for its vehement condemnation of modern art and artists, was dedicated to Lombroso. In the introduction, Nordau addressed him as his "dear and honoured Master" (Nordau 1895, VII; Knepper 2010: 167–74). The two had developed a strong bond in the preceding years. Lombroso, who had admired Nordau's earlier work, *Les mensonges conventionnelles de notre civilisation*, was later being persuaded by him to join the Zionist movement, in which the Hungarian played a leading role. Yet despite this friendship, the Italian politely disagreed with the views expressed in *Degeneration*, arguing that eccentricity had always been a part of genius and that degeneration could have an evolutionary function (Lombroso 1895d). American newspapers seized upon their debate, as a dispute between two renowned scholars was the kind of melodrama that drove sales (Nordau and His Master 1895; Lombroso on Nordau 1895; Nordau's Errors 1895a, b).

Though the debate with Nordau was amicable, it further amplified Lombroso's fame in the United States. By this time, however, as we have seen, he was already a celebrity. Newspapers carried articles declaring that he was Jewish and that his father's name was Levi (Personal and Pertinent 1895), describing him as small in stature and modest in demeanor ("Lombroso" 1895), and reporting his thoughts about specific crimes (Is a Study in Crime 1895; Hayward a Degenerate 1895). His name even entered the popular vernacular in descriptions of unsettling people (Life in London 1895). When the case of Herman Webster Mudgett, alias Dr. Henry Howard Holmes—one of the deadliest serial killers in American history—came to light, the newspapers immediately made the association with Lombroso's notion of the "born criminal" (Holmes's Many Crimes 1895; The Holmes Horror 1895a, b; Der Champion Verbrecher, 1895). It is worth remembering that years later Lombroso would himself discuss Holmes, referring to him as the quintessential modern criminal (Lombroso 1902).

We have reached the end of 1895, and yet there remains much still to be said. The "Lombroso moment" in North American culture would persist for several more years, extending beyond even the peak reached when the newspapers carried the news of his death. One could, for instance, explore how the growing authority of experts in late-nineteenth-century American culture intersected with newspapers and magazines that continued to rely on sensationalism and pseudoscience to attract new readers (Mott 1950: 524–5, 539; Pandora 2009: 357). One thing is immediately clear. The remarkable popularity enjoyed by Lombroso in the United States—likely part of a broader international fame—was a genuine phenomenon that emerged almost entirely after 1889, the annus horribilis in which French, German, and Austrian criminologists, anthropologists, anatomists, and sociologists dismantled criminal anthropology point by point at the Paris congress. The fame that the Italian knew he had obtained in what he regarded as the most civilized country in the world must, in some way, have encouraged him to forge ahead, disregarding the criticisms of his academic opponents—or rather, his enemies.

Notes

1. CURB, Series I: correspondence, Box 32, folder nn., letter from Cesare Lombroso to Guglielmo Ferrero, February 19, 1894.
2. *The Alienist and Neurologist* (1880–1920); *The American Anthropologist* (1888–1938); *The American Journal of Insanity* (1869–1929); *The American Journal of Psychology* (1888–1929); *The American Journal of Sociology* (1895–1928); *The Medico-Legal Journal* (1883–1927); *The Monist* (1890–1922); *The New York Medical Journal* (1865–1922); *The North American Review* (1866–1914); *The Popular Science Monthly* (1872–1922). The final date of the research was defined by the limits of OCR-based research capabilities.
3. LP, Letter of H. Zimmern to C. Lombroso, May 12, 1892.

2

The Long Shadow of Lombroso: A Polyvalent Presence in the Birth of Positivist Criminology in Argentina

Máximo Sozzo

Introduction

From the mid-1880s, the medical and legal fields in Buenos Aires began importing from Europe, especially Italy, the discourse on the criminal question "in the name of science." This centered on the theoretical innovations of Cesare Lombroso and his colleagues and disciples.

In the medical domain, Argentina's leading journal, *Revista Médico-Quirúrgica* (established in 1864), promoted the First International Congress of Criminal Anthropology to be held in Rome in 1885 (Congreso y Exposición de Antropología Criminal 1885: 147). That same year, it published a short article on the "criminal anthropology" studies that Melendez and Coni—respectively the most important alienist and hygienist in Buenos Aires—were conducting in the city's insane asylum (Estudios de Antropologia Criminal 1885: 226).

In the legal field, the leading journal *Revista Jurídica* published two texts in 1886 that briefly referenced the ideas of the "Positive School" and presented the debates from the First International Congress of Criminal Anthropology (Piñero 1886; Brusa 1886; Congreso Penitenciario 1886). The following year, the chair of Criminal and Commercial Law (created in 1856) of the University of Buenos Aires's Faculty of Law and Social Sciences was split in two, thus creating dedicated space in the curriculum for criminal law. Norberto Piñero was appointed professor and immediately established a course based entirely on the teachings of the "Positive School" (Piñero 1887b; see Del Olmo 1992: 3–5; Creazzo 2007: 39–41; Sozzo 2015: 223–4). In the same year, *Revista Jurídica* published Piñero's inaugural lecture, in which he emphasized the importance of using the "positive method" as a starting point and referenced the "anomalous" character of the "delinquent man" and the need to determine the causes of crime (Piñero 1887a; see also Piñero 1888).

In February 1888, the Society of Legal Anthropology was founded in Buenos Aires with the participation of several prominent professionals in the fields of medicine and law. Its objective was to "study the person of the offender, to establish his degree of dangerousness and responsibility … in accordance with the principles of the new school." The society's president, Francisco Ramos Mejía, delivered its first lecture, *Antropología Jurídica. Principios fundamentales de la Escuela Positiva de Derecho Penal* (Legal Anthropology: Key Principles of the Positive School of Criminal Law), which was later published as a pamphlet (Ramos Mejía 1888; see Del Olmo 1981: 135; 1992: 5–6; Scarzanella 1999: 13; Creazzo 2007: 44–5). In the same year, another member of the society, Luis Drago, gave a lecture entitled *Los Hombres de Presa* (The Men of Prey), which was later expanded into the first book on "criminology" published in Argentina (Drago 1921 [1888]).

As demonstrated, the ideas of positivist criminology emerging from Europe were swiftly disseminated and debated in Argentina, marking one of the most rapid and decisive instances of cultural importation of these ways of thinking about the criminal question ever recorded globally. Positivist criminology quickly developed into a theoretical vocabulary that gained extraordinary cultural and political significance (Del Olmo 1981; 1992: 1–12; Marteau 2003: 103–9; Creazzo 2007: 29–57).

Although Lombroso never visited Argentina—unlike some of those close to him, including his daughter, Gina Lombroso, Guglielmo Ferrero, and Enrico Ferri (Sansone 2022: 105–63)—his influence was central to the rise of positivist criminology there. However, this influence was not always marked by uncritical acceptance, as a superficial view of this pivotal period might suggest. Such an oversimplification would not only overstate the impact of this intellectual figure but also reduce his presence to singular, monovalent force, producing an extraordinarily reductive picture of local intellectual production and debate.

In this chapter, I distinguish three attitudes among local intellectuals toward Lombroso's concepts and arguments in the literature produced during the early stages of this process of cultural importation. These attitudes carried relatively equal weight and articulated a gradation of the impact of his presence, while at the same time giving it different valences. First, I identify an attitude of *adoption*, characterized by an apologetic embrace of his ideas. Second, I observe an attitude of *transaction*, in which the adoption of Lombroso's theories is balanced with criticisms of important elements of his intellectual production. Finally, I discern an attitude of *rejection*, in which the figure of Lombroso is viewed negatively, even within the framework of a "scientific" approach to the criminal question. In this way, I show that Lombroso's presence during the early period of positivist criminology in Argentina was polyvalent. Indeed, one could argue that positivist criminology in Argentina emerged both because of and in spite of Lombroso.

Adoption

From the outset of Argentina's importation of positivist criminology, the participants in this process emphasized the rupture implied by its shift to a "scientific" perspective from the older "metaphysical" positions—both Catholic and liberal—that had shaped local knowledge on the criminal question since the early nineteenth century (Sozzo 2007; 2015: 59–194). Lombroso, as previously noted, was central to this transformation. His ideas were frequently adopted from an apologetic stance, focusing on four key axes: (a) the need for and justification of criminal anthropology as a new and distinct science founded on the positive method; (b) determinism as a framework for understanding the causes of crimes; (c) the image of the "delinquent man" or "born criminal"; and (d) the rejection of free will in favor of the imperative of social defense against criminals, which justified radical reforms of criminal law based on the dangerousness of offenders.[1]

However, this reception did not involve a deep engagement with Lombrosian concepts and arguments. His writings were often cited superficially. For the sake of brevity, I will highlight just one example out of many. Francisco Ramos Mejía,[2] president of the Society of Legal Anthropology, published a pamphlet entitled *Antropología Jurídica. Principios fundamentales de la Escuela Positiva de Derecho Penal,* one of the more developed efforts to translate Lombroso's ideas in this context. In it, Ramos Mejía defends this "special science" founded on the "positive method," which has shown that the "delinquent man" has "somatic and psychic anomalies of a determined character" and belongs to "a species, an abnormal variant," while crime itself is a "natural phenomenon," like birth or death (Ramos Mejía 1888: 114–16).

In Ramos Mejía's view, there exists "a human type dedicated to crime" characterized by "anatomical, physiological and physiognomic anomalies." Within this type, "the epileptic occupies the first degree, the moral madman the second, and the born criminal the third, all united by a degenerative element" (ibid.: 117–19). He emphasizes that the core question of this new science revolves around the causes that produced "this abnormal product," a "being inferior to the average type of humanity." Among these causes, he emphasizes "atavism": "The criminal is an inhabitant of the quaternary jungles lost in the civilization of the nineteenth century, and is at the same time a sick person or a degenerate" (ibid.: 119).

Ramos Mejía then elaborates, in great detail, on Lombroso's achievements, asserting that he deserves the "title of head of the school" for demonstrating the "atavism" of the "criminal man" and his kinship with the "savage" (ibid.: 120–2). However, he acknowledges that not all criminals are "born criminals" and, therefore, criminal anthropology is not limited only to them. It also includes "criminals due to causes external to the organism, such as the social and moral influences of the family and society … which produce the no less important branch of criminals of passion and occasion," even if they do not present "the anthropological characteristics of other criminals" (ibid.: 123).

In this way, the author acknowledges the work of classifying criminals undertaken by various proponents of the Positive School, such as Ferri, who were enabled and promoted by Lombroso himself. At the same time, he insists that a common element unites all types of criminals: *determinism*. According to Ramos Mejía, "crime is not the product of an autonomous will, but a necessary phenomenon governed by determined laws to which man is subjected" (ibid.: 123).

Recognizing that crime is the product of "multiple material causes to which man is subjected, under whose influence he acts unknowingly," Ramos Mejía argues that punishment cannot be based on the notion that "man, morally free and knowing his duties and rights, fails to fulfill some and infringes others consciously and deliberately." This stance effectively denies the idea of criminal responsibility rooted in the "metaphysical" principle of "free will," as upheld by legal tradition. However, Ramos Mejía clarifies that this does not imply denying "society" the right to defend itself as a "social function," as some critics of the "new school" claimed. On the contrary, he asserts that crime must be addressed on a "positive" basis, taking into account "the personal characteristics of the offender that make him either more or less dangerous to the society in which he lives." Crime is "repressed not because man is morally free" but to "defend society." In this way, "society eliminates him temporarily or perpetually, according to the more or less dangerous nature" of the individual and the causes that fatally led him to act (ibid.: 124).

Transaction

Perhaps the most significant text in the emergence of positivist criminology in Argentina was *Los hombres de presa*, published in 1888 by Luis M. Drago (Drago 1921 [1888]).[3] Stemming from a lecture given at the Society for Legal Anthropology, the book conveyed a notable reception of Lombroso's ideas concerning several of the fundamental axes outlined in the preceding section, along with numerous secondary topics. At the same time, Drago raised challenges regarding key elements of Lombroso's contributions, initiating a sort of transaction that did not entirely compromise the special connection with the Italian author and, more broadly, the Italian Positive School. This operation further contributed, in a more complex way, to acknowledging the centrality of Lombroso in this field of knowledge in Argentina.

Drago, like Ramos Mejía, begins by highlighting the "revolution" brought about by the adoption of the "positive method" in the "repressive sciences" (ibid.: 29). He underscores Cesare Lombroso's central role, referencing the third Italian edition of *L'uomo delinquente* from 1884 (ibid.: 31–2). Drago acknowledges that morphological, somatic, and physiognomic details can provide important clues for identifying the "delinquent man." However, as the "new school" cautions, these characteristics appear in only 40 percent of observed cases (ibid.: 38). Regarding craniometric data, he argues that they "rarely present themselves as a sure sign for the diagnosis of crime" (ibid.: 43).[4]

Nevertheless, Drago contends that this limitation reflects the "science in its infancy" and should not lead to the conclusion that "somatic characters are of little value" (ibid.: 44).[5] It is, however, undeniable in the eyes of the Argentine author that "psychic anomalies," at this juncture, "offer a greater guarantee of truth and thus constitute a more complete element of conviction to arrive at the inquiry of the criminal constitution." He emphasizes the "absence of moral sense," illustrating his point by citing cases of local criminals (ibid.: 46–8). This review of local cases is expanded in the appendix, which offers a detailed analysis of the cases of Castro Rodriguez and Castruccio (ibid.: 162–76; see Ruggiero 2004: 146–58).

Drago recognizes the kinship established by Lombroso between the born criminal, the morally insane, and the epileptic, describing them as "part of the same natural family." However, he also considers the criticisms made by other positivists regarding this relationship, noting the difficulty that persists within the new school on this point (Drago 1921 [1888]: 55–63). Ultimately, he concludes that no definitive conclusion can be reached on this point (ibid.: 63).

Drago also examines Lombroso's claims regarding the distinct traits of criminals, particularly their inclination to form associations for illicit activities, their use of slang and argot, their practice of tattooing, and their predisposition toward gambling, alcohol consumption, and orgies. To substantiate these points, he draws on various theoretical sources, notably the work of Tarde, as well as observations from the local context, particularly concerning the *lunfardos*. He recalls conversations he had with some of "the main and best known" individuals from this group (ibid.: 71–83).[6]

However, perhaps Drago's most significant departure from Lombroso lies in the "embryology of crime," where he challenges the notion of "atavism" as a causal factor (ibid.: 85–7). He argues that the somatic anomalies leading Lombroso to formulate "the hypothesis of a specific regression"—which Lombroso himself had previously acknowledged as having only a "relative value" in many cases—should not be attributed to the "influence of remote ancestors in the evolution of generations" but rather to "more direct causes." Specifically, Drago contends that these anomalies stem from an "acquired or congenital degeneration of the encephalic mass," which was not the result of "distant influences" (ibid.: 88). Thus "atavism would be excluded" and the supposed "psychic similarity with distant ancestors would be purely illusory" (ibid.: 89).[7]

Drago also challenges the fundamental assumption behind the theory of "atavism" thesis, namely the claim that all "primitive groups" are "antisocial and bloodthirsty" (ibid.: 90–1). He argues that this idea relies on travelers' accounts that, with "very rare exceptions," come from "men who have hastily traveled through the countries they describe and [are] ignorant of the language of the groups studied and have lacked sufficient preparation" (ibid.: 90–1). In particular, he remarks, "we Americans have special reasons for doubting some of the fantasies commonly accepted as truth. So many lies have been told about us, and false claims have been received unchecked by respectable authors!" (ibid.: 93). Drago cites laughable misrepresentations of Argentina found in books published in the United States and France, including works by the "well-known French anthropologist" Topinard (ibid.: 93–5). He therefore argues instead that "primitive groups" "in the same period of evolution" sometimes present "bloodthirsty and cruel tendencies" and at other times have a "gentle and humane" character. He supports this view with examples of "the native customs and tendencies of the aborigines" inhabiting Argentina and makes reference to "our own experience" and to "what we observed by our own eyes" and by visiting the Museum of Natural Sciences of La Plata where a dozen *fuegueños* were living, having "recently been brought from their wigwams" (ibid.: 95–7). From his perspective, this proves "that the various human aggregates cannot be classified by progressive series" and that "social groupings are far from following a homogeneously uniform march in their evolution, so from studying a contemporary savage tribe it cannot safely be concluded that it is in one of the earlier stages of the development of the present civilized nations" (ibid.: 97–8).

Moreover, Drago asserts that "civilization" is not exclusive to the "Indo-European family." As evidence, he cites the Incas, describing them as "a race with ethnic characters similar to those we are accustomed to consider peculiar to the savage type," yet one that inhabited South America and reached "such a degree of development that we, the descendants of the European conquerors, accustomed to looking elsewhere for the origins of all civilization, can hardly realize it by a powerful effort of the imagination" (ibid.: 99). Regarding "atavism," he concludes that "the theory, by proving too much would prove nothing" (ibid.: 108).

Rejecting the concept of "atavism," Drago argues instead that "degeneration" results from a combination of hereditary and environmental factors, though relative influence is difficult to determine given the "present state of knowledge." He suggests that perhaps "hereditary influences" are "nullified" by the "lack of appropriate conditions for their development," so that "the biological factor may exist but it is necessary to have the reactive one that produces the movement" (ibid.: 121–2). He clarifies: "The biological and sociological factors combine and interpenetrate so intimately in the production of crime that it is not possible to do without one or the other" (ibid.: 123). He considers this to be true for the different types of criminals, following Ferri in this argument without actually quoting him, and distinguishing between the "born or instinctive criminal," the "fortuitous or occasion criminal," the "criminal by profession or acquired habit," and the "criminal by impetus of passion" (ibid.: 122–3).

Los hombres de presa initiated a direct dialogue with Lombroso and his colleagues, leading to its translation and publication in Italian in 1890 under the title *I criminali nati*. This edition featured an introduction by Cesare Lombroso himself, spanning nearly forty pages on "the diffusion of criminal anthropology." This marked the first step in reversing the flow of discursive production within this field, shifting the circulation from the periphery back to the center (Drago 1890; Lombroso 1890a). A year earlier, in the *Archivio di psichiatria*, Enrico Ferri commented on the book, recognizing the "original ideas held by the author, with much sagacity and eloquence and with a perfect knowledge of all the publications not only of criminal anthropology, but also of scientific philosophy" (Ferri 1889: 102). He concluded: "We cannot but rejoice with the author for the brilliant essay he has given us, for his courage not only to disseminate the new critical theories but also to subject them to original and fruitful criticism and thus to correct and complete them" (ibid.: 103).

In his introduction to Drago's book, Lombroso reflects on the diffusion of criminal anthropology, remarking that "a phenomenon that perhaps in a few centuries will attract the attention of historians of human thought is the strange difference that is observed between countries in terms of the number and value of the disciples of the new penal school" (Lombroso 1890a: V). He notes that in the "Iberian race"—in Spain, Portugal, and particularly in Spanish and Portuguese America—these ideas "have acquired a great development" (ibid.: VII). Lombroso specifically praises the work of the Society for Legal Anthropology of Buenos Aires: "Credit is due to South America to have founded a criminal anthropological Society when in Europe there is a battle even to grant it a name" (ibid.: XXXIV). He then commends "Drago's truly masterful work, preceded by Ramos Mejía's brilliant preface, which shows that the acceptance of new ideas does not hinder the originality of research or the perfect independence of judgment, because if there are many confirmations of our theory, there are not few criticisms" (ibid.: XXXV). In a footnote, Lombroso addresses some of these criticisms:

> I would be disrespecting these illustrious writers if I did not respond with a few words. It is true what they say: slang is to some extent adopted by all classes, particularly the young. But apart from the fact that it differs in these by the intensity and absence of cynicism, cruelty, etc., the fact that it is widespread among the young confirms the embryonic, infantile tendency of crime. But the delinquent

> does not use slang only in his youth but does so even in extreme old age, and even uses it against himself. Tattoos may be explained as a consequence of leisure, but only to a certain extent, because it is never practiced in insane asylums and when it is found on normal men (sailors), it never has the cynical and obscene character nor the enormous diffusion that it has among criminals. (ibid.: XXXV)

It does not seem accidental that Lombroso's response overlooks Drago's rejection of "atavism" as an explanation for the "embryology of crime," his doubts about the significance of "somatic anomalies" as a symptom of the "delinquent man," and his questioning of the existence of a single process of "civilization" tied to the "Indo-European family." Instead, Lombroso chooses to highlight their common ground. He seeks to establish, maintain, and promote the intellectual connection between what he perceives as the center and the periphery, reinforcing the rather explicit hierarchy he describes in his text in the geographical distribution of "creators" and "disciples" of this new knowledge on the criminal question.

In Drago's book, this transaction can give rise to challenges—more or less contained—against concepts and arguments in Lombroso's vocabulary. These challenges often draw on empirical data from the local context to question the validity of general statements developed "there," in the central countries. In turn, this empirical evidence may come from first- or second-hand sources, sometimes referencing other authors who provided different kinds of observations. In this sense, the local context, with its distinct problems and questions, plays a crucial role (Salvatore and Aguirre 1996: 33; Sozzo 2006: 380–1, 383; Salvatore 2016: 1, 10–11).

Moreover, empirical information can also stem from observations made within central contexts, articulating the importation of other voices gestated in those settings. This process can, in more ambitious cases, lead to the more or less tentative development of an alternative general statement—one informed by other acts of translation and by other views generated within the central countries. In any case, such transaction creates a space for inventiveness and innovation among local intellectuals, complicating the process of importation beyond a simple act of adoption. While this does not erase the recognition of the link with the imported material—in this case the work of Lombroso—it does render that connection more intricate, and its contours more sinuous and flexible. Drago, in turn, might even boast that it is precisely because of this that the reversal of the flow of circulation becomes possible, in turn engendering a translation that allows his perspective to travel from the periphery to the center.

Rejection

As in other national contexts, the attempts to import positivist criminology, particularly Lombroso's concepts and arguments, into Argentina quickly encountered resistance from certain Catholic and liberal criminal law jurists, who rejected them outright (Lozano 1889; Prack 1892). In their writings, one can observe what might be described as a "struggle of schools" (Creazzo 2007: 50). However, during this early period, there were also intellectual efforts grounded in a positivist viewpoint that acknowledged the need for a "scientific" approach to the criminal question, while rejecting the core principles of Lombroso's perspective. Instead, these thinkers drew from other European authors who, in their own contexts, had expressed similar opposition to Lombroso. These efforts went beyond the compromise seen in Drago's book—which received praise from Lombroso and other key authors of the Italian Positive School, like Ferri—by advancing a more definitive confrontation. They even redefined what constituted the essence of a positivist perspective on crime and punishment. Among several examples, I have selected just one for brevity.

In 1892, Antonio Dellepiane[8] presented an important dissertation entitled *Las causas del delito* (The Causes of Crime) at the Faculty of Law of the University of Buenos Aires (ibid.: 117–23), in which he offered several radical criticisms of Lombroso's ideas. This work reflected the intellectual schism that occurred in Europe at the Second International Congress of Criminal Anthropology held in Paris in 1889 (Beirne 1993: 143–85; Renneville 1994; Digneffe 1998; Debuyst 1998; Gibson 2002: 55–62, 158–60; Frigessi 2003: 208–29).

Dellepiane begins by acknowledging the "revolution currently working in the very entrails of criminal law," driven by the growing trend to apply the "positive method" to the "study of social and human facts." He recognizes that "positivism … is in the air we breathe" (Dellepiane 1892: 7, 9) and expresses support for the method, stressing the importance of understanding the causes of crime (ibid.: 9, 12–15). However, he also recognizes the diversity of perspectives on the subject. He distinguishes between the "anthropological or pathological tendency," which deals "more with the delinquent than with crime," from the "sociological tendency," which deals "less with the delinquent than with crime" (ibid.: 15–17). From the outset, Dellepiane declares his opposition to the former approach (ibid.: 23), offering detailed criticisms of the perspective embodied in Lombroso's ideas.

On the one hand, Dellepiane firmly rejects the thesis of atavism outlined in *L'uomo delinquente*, which he read in its third Italian edition of 1884 (ibid.: 28). He states: "It is today a dead and buried theory … To fight atavism is almost like being angry with a corpse" (ibid.: 26). After summarizing Lombroso's argument and purported evidence (ibid.: 28–37), Dellepiane challenges several of Lombroso's claims, citing figures such as Aramburu, Joly, Tarde, and Colajanni.

First, Dellepiane questions Lombroso's assertion that there is no qualitative difference between humans and animals in relation to crime, emphasizing human freedom, rationality, and motives, as opposed to the needs and instincts of animals (ibid.: 38–9). Second, he refutes the claim that crime is a normal occurrence in "savage" peoples, pointing out that even within such groups, there exist distinctions between right and wrong, albeit different ones to those of more "civilized" people. He argues that actions considered crimes in these societies are still rooted in "fundamental ideas and feelings of the human nature" (ibid.: 39–42).

Third, Dellepiane criticizes Lombroso's assertion that children always display traits of the moral madman or born criminal, arguing that this is an exaggeration that generalizes traits only observed in exceptional cases (ibid.: 42). Fourth, he rejects Lombroso's notion of "a criminal type" defined by physical characteristics, contrasting numerous experimental observations demonstrating similarities between criminals and primitive men with observations and experiments yielding opposite conclusions (ibid.: 43–8). Finally, Dellepiane challenges Lombroso's view that slang and tattoos are symptoms of the criminal type, linked to the "savage" type. He refers to Tarde, who examines the differences between these practices among criminals and "savages" (ibid.: 48–50).

Dellepiane also takes aim at Lombroso's newer theories,[9] presented in the third edition of *L'uomo delinquente*, where criminality is linked to epilepsy. Lombroso suggests that "every epileptic would not be a criminal … but every criminal would be an epileptic more or less disguised" (ibid.: 87). Dellepiane acknowledges that epilepsy is "a factor in crime" in some cases, but he strongly rejects the notion that "all criminals are epileptics" (ibid.: 89). He points out that many of the similarities observed between epileptics and criminals arise from studies conducted in prisons and hospitals—"places undoubtedly little frequented by the better-off classes of society"—implying that observed traits could be due to "conditions peculiar to the lower classes of society" (ibid.: 90). Dellepiane concedes that Lombroso only asserts "the perfect identity between the epileptic and the born delinquent," while other criminals are considered "epileptoids" and divided into different groups or degrees, all sharing "vestiges of the epileptic temperament." However, Dellepiane dismisses this view as a "way of torturing the facts to make them fit the theory," noting that it "has met with the most lively resistance among the learned" (ibid.: 91). After citing the criticisms of Lacassagne, Tarde, and Colajanni, he concludes: "The brand new Lombrosian hypothesis is therefore an unacceptable generality" (ibid.: 92).[10]

In response, Dellepiane proposes a different approach to understanding crime, one that investigates its social and psychological causes. He advocates for a "criminal sociology," drawing on the work of Quetelet, Colajanni, Garraud, Lacassagne, Tarde, and Ferri. However, he criticizes Ferri and the Italian Positive School for their "determinism," which denies the existence of "free will" (ibid.: 106). For Dellepiane, it is possible to construct a scientific discourse on the causes of crime without negating individual "free will" (ibid.: 103, 127–8).

While acknowledging that "circumstances," "conditions," and "factors" "influence voluntary activity," Dellepiane insists that they do not arrive at "the point of annihilating it," "turning man into a mere result of the play of natural forces" (ibid.: 113, 126). He argues that even if the "regularity of human actions is a constant and general fact," this does not imply, as proponents of the Positive School claim, "the complete destruction of free will," since it cannot impose on "a given individual, the necessity of an action, of any crime" (ibid.: 129–30). Furthermore, he points out that "statistical investigations have shown that such regularity of social phenomena is not as constant as was at first believed following Quetelet" (ibid.: 132). He uses this observation to argue that "social laws" differ fundamentally from "physical or physiological laws," which present "the character of fatality" (ibid.: 133). Dellepiane therefore concludes that:

> The fundamental differences which have just been pointed out demonstrate the error in which the advocates of determinism fall when they confuse the manner of operation of both classes of laws, and attribute to social science the same character of positive certainty which is offered by the physical or natural sciences. Men are

> not governed, in the relations they maintain, by laws of an absolute and inflexible character. (ibid.: 134)

This leads Dellepiane to assert that "the sociological explanation of crime is insufficient." While acknowledging that social and biological influences contribute to the production of crime, he contends that they "are not irresistible." According to him, "Man does not go fatally to crime by virtue of these influences like the stone that falls when abandoned to the action of gravity" (ibid.: 139). Dellepiane argues that there is no morphological or physiological difference between delinquents and honest people, nor is there any psychological difference rooted in the absence of a moral sense. Citing Tarde, he claims, "The psychology of the murderer is basically the psychology of the whole world and, to descend to his heart, it is enough for us to probe our own." He concludes that, "psychically considered," the criminal does not constitute "a species within the species" (ibid.: 146–7). For Dellepiane, crime is ultimately the product of "decay," "perversion," "depravity," and "degradation," which may be stimulated "by influences of the physical and social order" but is for the most part "a product of the free will of the individual" (ibid.: 148). This, he asserts, is the only explanation that "can be admitted, in our concept, in the present state of science" (ibid.: 152).[11]

As illustrated, Dellepiane initially positions himself as a supporter of the "positive method," yet he fundamentally rejects Lombroso's perspective on the etiology of crime. In this sense, his rejection of Lombroso is radical and involves explicitly discarding the project of a "criminal anthropology" and distancing himself from the strong sense of causality associated with "determinism." For this Argentine author, the exploration of the causes of crime does not invalidate the existence of individual free will. Instead, he articulates an explicitly weak version of causality in his discourse, in the name of science relating to the criminal question. His critique opened the door to a series of intellectual exchanges with Catholic and liberal approaches in this field of criminology.

Dellepiane's rejection of Lombroso's ideas involves incorporating concepts and arguments from other authors from the central countries, and then carefully selecting and emphasizing alternatives to the Italian's theories. Unlike Drago, Dellepiane's critique does not rely heavily on empirical information from the local context, though such information plays a role, albeit less as a source for the elaboration of counterpoints to Lombroso than as an a posteriori illustration of such statements developed in other ways and in other places.

Conclusion

In this chapter, I have examined the role of Lombroso's concepts and arguments in the birth of positivist criminology in Argentina. While Lombroso undeniably played a central role, this influence did not result in a single, unified response from local intellectuals involved in the process of cultural importation. Instead, three distinct attitudes toward Lombroso's ideas emerged, which I have explored here.

The first attitude is that of *adoption*, where Lombrosian concepts and arguments were transplanted into the local context and an effort was made to leave them untouched, even after crossing borders and languages. However, this process of adoption inevitably involved a process of selection—deciding what ideas to import and emphasizing their relevance. This selection was a creative act in itself, as intellectuals like Ramos Mejía chose which of the concepts and arguments generated "there" to adopt for "here"—the local context—depending on the problems and questions deemed most important. Nevertheless, even when the intention was to leave these ideas unaltered, the attitude of adoption could never fully avoid the fact that when put into circulation "here," concepts and arguments from "there" precipitate a series of effects shaped by the dynamics at play in the place of reception. There is always an array of historically and spatially situated communicative exchanges that differ—at least partially—from those generated in their context of production. As a result, even in adoption, these imported ideas inevitably undergo a certain (minimum) level of change, reflecting a "dialectic of the same and the different" (Sozzo 2006: 375–9).

The second attitude is that of *transaction*, in which the importer adopts important elements of Lombroso's vocabulary while simultaneously rejecting others of equal importance. In this process, the local intellectual's selection and deployment of opposing operations become clear. Drago, for instance, does so without totally compromising the bond between his own intellectual production and that of the Italian intellectual, as evidenced by the mutual praise he garnered from both sides of the Atlantic. In this way, Drago reproduces an effect also observed in the attitude of adoption.

Crucially, this transactional response enables a reversal in the flow of ideas, as seen in the translation of Drago's book into Italian, and its publication with an introduction by Lombroso himself. From Lombroso's perspective, as we have noted, this does not undermine the hierarchical division between the *creators* and *cultivators* of scientific knowledge on the criminal question, which is mapped onto the spatial relationship between the center and the periphery. For this reason, Lombroso must carry out his own selection of what he considers important in the translated book from the periphery.

Drago's critiques of important aspects of Lombroso's work are in some cases based on empirical information from the local context, whether first- or second-hand. However, they are also made by importing other voices critical of these elements, many of which rely on empirical observations or theoretical arguments generated in the central contexts. In any case, this transactional attitude demonstrates a more explicit openness to local inventiveness and innovation, and reveals a clear metamorphosis of culturally imported elements. Through this dynamic, the shared discursive matrix between center and periphery is both affirmed and rendered more sinuous and flexible.

The third attitude is that of *rejection*, in which local texts primarily repudiate the core elements of Lombroso's vocabulary. Unlike with Drago, the empirical information from the local context does not play a pivotal role in this operation. Instead, the concepts and arguments developed by other authors in the central contexts provide alternatives to Lombroso's ideas. Dellepiane, for instance, selects, emphasizes, and translates these alternative perspectives into his own intellectual work, and here too it is possible to register local creativity and innovation. However, the connection with Lombroso, in contrast to the two previous attitudes, appears weakened, perhaps even severed. However, this does not preclude the vindication of an equally scientific perspective on the criminal question, grounded in the application of the positive method. The approach enables the endorsement from the normative point of view of ideas that open up a whole set of possible articulations from both Catholic and liberal perspectives. Ultimately, Lombroso retains an active influence on these local intellectual productions, but only *in the negative*.

Lombroso's influence on the emergence of positivist criminology in Argentina was polyvalent. As previously noted, this theoretical vocabulary on the criminal question emerges both *thanks to* and *in spite of* his work. The varied uses of Lombroso enabled local intellectuals engaged in these operations of *adoption*, *transaction*, and *rejection* to establish, in the context of this generic intellectual activity, an incipient identity and authority as experts on the criminal question. In addition, these engagements with Lombroso helped to generate, in the local context, the social and cultural prestige associated with Europe and with scientific ideas, which were considered to be sources of "civilized" and "modern" elements. They also formed part of a broader cultural process under way in Argentina (Salvatore 1996: 195; Salvatore and Aguirre 1996: 5; Sozzo 2006: 382–4).

Notes

1. It remains unclear whether they had first-hand knowledge of the book, as no complete Spanish translation was available.
2. Ramos Mejia (1847–1893) was a lawyer, judge, and politician.
3. Drago (1859–1921) was a lawyer, judge, journalist, and politician (a national deputy and minister), and one of the founders of the Society of Legal Anthropology. After publishing this book, he did not write anything more on themes related to the criminal question.
4. He briefly mentions Lombroso sending photographs of the skulls of criminals to the Society of Legal Anthropology of Buenos Aires (Drago 1921 [1888]: 38; see also Salvatore 2016: 2–3).
5. Drago argues for its use as judicial indicia (Drago 1921 [1888]: 44). References to his judicial experience are a fundamental component of his argumentation throughout the book (Salvatore 2016: 3–4).
6. This is something that Ramos Mejía also highlights in his prologue to this book, adding an autobiographical reference when discussing the use of slang (Ramos Mejía 1921 [1888]: 9–12).
7. Marteau is mistaken in stating that Drago takes "as a basis the Lombrosian theory of atavism" (2003: 108). Rodriguez (2006: 65) appears to follow a similar line of thought. However, it is clear that the Argentine author distanced himself firmly from this thesis (Creazzo 2007: 48; Salvatore 2016, 2: 11–12).
8. Dellepiane (1861–1939), a lawyer, became the first professor of sociology of the Faculty of Law of the University of Buenos Aires in 1918. He published another book related to the criminal question in 1894, *El idioma del delito* (The Language of Crime), but thereafter his intellectual production focused on other legal and historical matters.
9. He says of Lombroso that he is "as patient in the observation of facts as he is rash in the generalization of eminently relative principles" (Dellepiane 1892: 87–8).

10. At another point, Dellepiane also discusses the ideas about the predisposition of certain races to crime put forward by Lombroso, pointing out that they involve an "exaggeration" (1892: 157–60).
11. In the second part of his book, Dellepiane uses the theoretical explorations carried out in the first part to account for the "causes of crime in Argentina," emphasizing the "sociological conditions" (1892: 274).

3

Criminal Anthropology in Chile: Origin, Trajectory, and Circulations

Marco Antonio León León

Introduction

The publication of *L'uomo delinquente* in 1876 marked the beginning of what many authors consider the origin of modern criminology. The prevailing view of the criminal world before this work, centered on free will and criminal responsibility, was replaced by a model emphasizing biological determinism. This new approach linked morality more closely to physical appearance and crime to heredity. In Chile, both views were present in the historical and criminological scene from the late nineteenth to the mid-twentieth century, but the rise and circulation of positivist criminology—or criminal anthropology, as it was also known—was particularly significant. Its ideas, and the figures who propagated them, thus formed deep direct links to disciplines such as medicine and law, and to specialisms—like psychiatry and criminal law—with strong claims to autonomy.

Like any system of ideas and beliefs, positivist criminology (and the nuances and divergences it gained from Cesare Lombroso and his followers) generated support, resistance, and adaptations to a historical and sociocultural context that, while different from the European one in several respects, was undergoing modernization. This involved processes in which identifying, defining, classifying, and regulating differences in the population became crucial for the construction of the state and the nation.

Positivist criminology, which drew on earlier racist, classist, degenerative, and phrenological ideas, provided a "scientific" validation for a range of prejudices, stereotypes, and individual and collective stigmas. These were prevalent not only among the general population but also within the authorities. For this reason, positivist criminology quickly became intertwined with various fields of knowledge, as well as with common perceptions of criminal figures such as delinquents and criminals. This becomes evident when reviewing the documentation from the period between 1890 and 1954, which serves as the focus of this study. The starting point of this chapter is the first publication referring to the new Italian penal school, and its endpoint is the enactment of the *Ley de estados antisociales* in 1954. This law made prominent use of positivist criminology, incorporating concepts such as pre-criminal dangerousness and social defense against groups classified according to the probable or potential harm they posed to the established social order.

After discussing the beginnings of criminal anthropology in Chile and its potential routes of entry, we will review its diffusion through specialized journals from the first half of the twentieth century to illustrate the circulation of these ideas across national and cultural boundaries. The pages of the *Revista de ciencias penales* (*RCP*) and the *Revista de psiquiatría y disciplinas conexas* (*RPDC*), alongside opinion pieces and research produced by physicians (psychiatrists) and lawyers (penalists, criminologists), presented ideas, criteria, and diagnoses focused on maintaining social order and defense. However, positivist criminology also influenced the actions of the Chilean police in the twentieth century, as will be explored in the final section. We will examine both the uniformed police, the Carabineros de Chile (established in 1927), and the civilian police, the Policía de Investigaciones de Chile (founded in 1933). Like the aforementioned academic disciplines, these institutions had their own widely distributed magazines—*Revista de los Carabineros de Chile* (1927), *Detective* (1934), and *Revista de criminología y policía científica* (1937–1955)—which helped spread criminological ideas to a broader audience, extending beyond specialists and police officers.

Origins and Entry of Lombrosian Thought in Chile

The origins of Lombrosian criminology in Chile can be traced back to the publication of Luis Barros Méndez's work on the "new Italian penal school," which appeared in the *Revista forense chilena* in 1890 (Barros Méndez 1890b: 241–50). Prior to this, Dr. Augusto Orrego Luco's article on the "cerebro de los criminals," published in the *Revista médica de Chile* between 1879 and 1880, represents the closest precursor to this new approach to the study of criminality and criminals. While it did not cite Cesare Lombroso, Enrico Ferri, or Raffaele Garófalo, as the influence of the phrenological theories of Franz Joseph Gall is more apparent, this article can be considered the first work to shift the focus onto the figure of the criminal. It focused particularly on his morphology or organic constitution rather than on his criminal acts, an aspect to which criminal anthropology would apply itself soon afterward. In this context, we know that many of Lombroso's works were translated into Spanish in the 1890s, so it is quite likely that Chilean doctors and lawyers, many of whom belonged to the professional and intellectual elite and often traveled to Europe, had acquired copies of these works and circulated them upon their return.

By the end of the nineteenth century, travel and the exchanges of ideas, experiences, and publications—in addition to their actual purchase—had given the works of Lombroso, Ferri, and Garófalo greater visibility, both in their original form and in translation. Works such as those of the lawyer Ricardo Escobar Cerda (1900: 723–30) and Dr. Manuel Segundo Beca played a key role in popularizing this new criminological perspective in Chile. Their dissertations, later reworked, spread what Beca described as a "science of observation" whose mission was "solving social problems and working towards the study and implementation of an adequate and universal legislation that, while preserving society, combats and punishes crime, and prevents the injustices that may be committed from failing to recognize those responsible in time" (Beca 1898: 16). While this approach was already being questioned because of its biological determinism, which raised concerns about individual responsibility and personal freedom, it was gradually integrated into medical and legal discussions. It was seen as synthesizing the observations, studies, and experiences of those who had been in direct contact with the criminal world up to that point (Becker and Wetzell 2006; Pick 1989: 146–7).

Studies that retrace the transmission of this body of ideas to Latin America (Salvatore, Aguirre and Joseph 2001) tend to emphasize that the most receptive countries were Mexico, Brazil, and Argentina. Regarding Argentina, a significant historiography has been devoted to evaluating the real extent of Lombroso's influence, both in terms of criminal ideas and practices, as well as his influence on measures taken in prisons following the establishment of criminology laboratories. It is difficult to establish a precise date for the exchange of this knowledge between Chile and Argentina, but geographic proximity and advancements in communications undoubtedly facilitated it (Levaggi 2006: 757–65).

The influence of these criminological ideas remained significant until the mid-twentieth century, as noted by Raúl Carnevali (2008: 1–19). However, they had no bearing on either the Penal Code (1874) or the Code of Criminal Procedure of 1906, which both adhered to the classical model. Instead, the impact was more evident in legal debates and in certain medical specialties, and was particularly noticeable in the press. To paraphrase the Argentine historian Lila Caimari (2007: 9–21), "learned" or specialized criminology ultimately influenced a "profane" and media-driven form of criminology, visible in numerous discussion articles published in magazines and newspapers.

The circulation of Lombroso's ideas among Chilean physicians was also helped by the arrival of Dr. Luis Gambara, the self-styled "General Delegate of the Positive Penal School in the Spanish-American republics." Gambara delivered a course on positive penal law at the Santiago Medical Society, which was later published in the same city (Gambara 1906).[1] The influence of positivist criminology was also evident in less specialized publications, such as the *Revista Contemporánea*, edited by writer Pedro Prado, which printed several articles directly related to the subject (García 1910; Hermansen 1911). However, the most pronounced reception was among jurists, with figures like Professors Valentín Letelier and Raimundo del Río playing a leading role (Matus 2007: 175–203). Letelier, through his teaching, research, and publications, was instrumental in promoting positivist criminological ideas, though he recognized that Lombroso's propositions could not encompass all of criminal law, but rather only a part of it (Del Río 1916).

According to Jean Pierre Matus, the spread of Letelier's teachings, and those of other proponents of positivism, is made clear by the fact that "more than 60% of the monographs written between 1875 and 1920 corresponded to texts referring to the Positive School of criminal law" (Matus 2007: 179). After the 1920s, figures such as Valentín Brandau, Samuel Gajardo, Gustavo Labatut, and Rafael Fontecilla, among others, came to the fore. On the other hand, Lombroso's ideas were used to explain the criminal language of the underworld, which caught the attention of the scholar Julio Vicuña Cifuentes. In keeping with the Italian doctor, Cifuentes was convinced that the approach to this subject provided access to the "most precious psychological and sociological documentation for the study of criminal man" (Vicuña 1910: 17). The interdisciplinary character of Lombrosian criminal anthropology would compensate for its criticized determinism.

Heredity and Social Environment

In 1890, a miner named Antolin Manzano, who had a history of acute alcoholism, was involved in a violent incident that resulted in one person being injured and another killed. His case highlighted the convergence of differing medical and legal opinions on the issue of criminal responsibility, during a time when positivist criminology was gaining traction. Although the diagnoses did not reach a consensus, hereditary factors were considered significant contributors to Manzano's actions. Doctors Joaquín Castro Soffia and Carlos Sazié suggested that the cause could be traced to:

> the alcoholism of the father and brother, an epileptic condition in the sister, and the convict's early inclination to drink. This degenerative chain would lead to a predisposition to insanity, manifesting a delirium of persecution, rendering Manzano an irresponsible subject before the criminal law. (Brangier 2008: 2–3)

As a result, Manzano was declared insane and sent to the Casa de Orates (insane asylum). This case, among others, illustrates how degenerative and deterministic theories gradually gained traction, not only through texts and proponents in medical-criminal institutions but also within judicial processes. The growing emphasis on biology over the social environment thus made significant inroads in the discourse surrounding several criminal trials, whether or not there was an explicit reference to the Italian school.

However, the notion of degeneration was not confined to specific vices like alcoholism—often linked to social factors and heredity—but extended to any behavior deemed incompatible with the prevailing social-political order. Anarchism, for instance, which questioned the governments of both the old and new continents, provoked reprisals and led to its proponents being classified as dangerous individuals. In *Il delitto politico e le rivoluzioni* (1890), cowritten with Rodolfo Laschi, and in *Gli anarchici* (1895), Lombroso outlined how perpetrators of political violence were identified and categorized according to deterministic theories (Fernández 2008: 91–119).

In Chile, these ideas were applied to cases such as those of anarchists Efraín Plaza Olmedo and Antonio Ramón Ramón (Harambour 2004: 137–93; Goicovic 2005). In the first case, Plaza Olmedo, who was accused of murder in Santiago in 1912, supposedly for political motives, was immediately labeled by the capital's press as "sour," "degenerate," "a reflection of evil," and "repugnant as a poisonous reptile" (*El Mercurio*, July 15, 1912), as well as "crazy" and "mentally ill" (*El Diario Ilustrado*, July 14, 1912). However, his psychological evaluation revealed that, aside from some emotional deficiencies, he was a "normal man," demonstrating how these preconceived ideas failed to offer an accurate model for his behavior. In March 1925, Olmedo received a pardon and was released from the penitentiary, only for his body to be discovered a month later on the side of a country road. The case demonstrates how, as knowledge of criminals became less confined to specialists, it increasingly became a matter of public interest, aided by the proliferation and modernization of the written press. The addition of photographs further enhanced this dynamic, giving a new visual dimension to stories.

A similar story unfolded with Antonio Ramón Ramón, who was also branded an anarchist and madman. He was imprisoned and tried after attempting to assassinate General Roberto Silva Renard in Santiago on December 15, 1914. Silva Renard had commanded the regiment that opened fire on workers gathered at the Domingo Santa María School in Iquique, in the northern Chilean saltpeter region, in December 1907. Seven years later, Ramón Ramón, whose brother Manuel Vaca had been among the victims, tried to assassinate Silva, but only succeeded in wounding him. Witnesses to the event brought about Ramón Ramón's capture and subsequent prosecution. The case attracted such significant public interest that there was talk of an "anarchist conspiracy linked to the spirit of revenge," along with labels implying insanity and degeneration, and references to "low moral background" and "social scum." Anarchist gatherings were depicted as "focal points of criminal conspiracies and dens of corruption for the race and society" (*El Mercurio*, February 10, 1911).

The argument of insanity played a significant role in the judicial decisions that followed. Attributing Ramón Ramón's actions to a hereditary problem undermined his initial motive of revenge, generating other considerations that led to him being treated as a sick person rather than a criminal. Initially, he was sentenced to eight years in prison due to the lack of evidence for his supposed insanity. This ruling was appealed, but after several arguments, the plea of insanity was deemed inadmissible. On November 19, 1917, Ramón Ramón was sentenced to five years in prison. However, with time already served, he regained his freedom in December 1919.

Both cases highlighted the clear differences between the ideas of Italian criminology and the approach of alienist medicine. While for positivist criminology, morphological anomalies were clear signs of historical atavism, identifying the individual as a criminal undergoing evolutionary regression, alienist doctors viewed these anomalies as indicative of a sick person—a madman, rather than a criminal. However, both perspectives considered hereditary transmission as crucial, since both anthropologists and physicians sought explanations for the defendant's present actions in his past. This genealogical approach shaped many of the diagnoses and considerations related to the need to develop policies to defend and preserve society from denaturalized, barbaric, and amoral enemies, as criminals from the urban underworld were portrayed.

Circulation and Interrelation between Specialties

In twentieth-century Chile, criminal anthropology circulated and intersected with various disciplines, such as criminal law, criminology, and psychiatry. The latter two were specialties striving for autonomy from law and medicine, respectively. In this process, the establishment of a distinct disciplinary identity was crucial for both professional performance and the social engagement of its protagonists. While documents from the period do not indicate that physicians frequently integrated Lombrosian ideas into their professional practices, it was psychiatry where these ideas had the most explicit influence. Professional publications, often under the auspices of institutions such as the University of Chile and the Institute of Criminal Sciences (a private body with partners in the public sphere), facilitated the circulation of ideas linked to positivist criminology among specialists. These publications also helped to strengthen the discipline's ties to other branches of knowledge. Journals such as the *Revista de ciencias penales* (*RCP*) and the *Revista de psiquiatría y disciplinas conexas* (*RPDC*) (both established in 1935) helped to define and strengthen a professional and disciplinary identity, fostering their respective national and transnational academic and intellectual communities.

Psychiatry's discourse on the dangerous nature of individuals was featured in the pages of the RCP, where it was complemented by Lombroso's criminology, which was adopted with considerable fluency and conviction. Although discussions about criminality and the definition of criminals were supported, there was caution in applying value judgments that could influence law and public policy. In the interpretative framework of criminal anthropology, less emphasis was placed on responsibility and free will—concepts central to the classical view—along with penalties. In contrast, security measures aimed at correcting and reeducating deviants gained prominence. This shift was evident in the discussion of the law of antisocial conditions published in the RCP, which were tied to debates regarding the reformulation of the Penal Code (1929, 1938) and early proposals for a new law (1941). This illustrated how a new model of criminality was incorporated into the classical framework (as found in the codes on the subject), eventually manifesting in the text and spirit of the law finally approved in 1954. This criminalized individuals deemed dangerous, primarily vagrants and beggars, drunks and drug addicts, or promoters of homosexuality.

The ideas of Italian, German, and Spanish penalists therefore underpinned the development of a Chilean criminal law, driven by academic dialogue, congresses, conferences, and the exchange of publications and books from abroad. Although it is argued that "already in the 1930s in Chile—and in Italy a few years earlier—there was serious questioning of the postulates of the Positive School, which became more pronounced in the following decade" (Carnevali 2008, 10), references to Lombroso and his followers did not disappear completely (Matus and Carnevali 2007: 1–138). While the influence of German doctrine on criminal law became apparent in the middle of the century, this shift did not result in a complete replacement of one criminal paradigm by another (Rivacoba y Rivacoba 1991).

The dangerous individual that criminal law, criminology, and psychiatry sought to identify (Campos 2021: 98–138) was part of this line of interpretation. This subject—man or woman—came to be identified as someone lacking self-awareness or moral control, displaying antisocial tendencies (by committing crimes), and, due to specific personal or environmental factors, possessing a high likelihood of committing further antisocial acts (Huertas 1991: 157–99).

In the early years of the *RCP*, being criminally dangerous was understood through the lenses of eugenics and psychoanalysis. While these interpretations, especially that of eugenics, lost prominence over time, much of the determinism underlying them persisted. Throughout several issues of the *RCP*, medicolegal reports and criminological profiles documented several cases, frequently appearing in the journal until the early 1960s. These not only provided specialists with theoretical reflections and updates on the latest authors and topics but also demonstrated that the definitions, characterizations, and classifications used in the journal's other sections had a clear correlation with real-world cases.

The field of psychiatry also sought to define and catalogue this issue. The *RPDC* considered people to be ill if their behavioral pattern diverged from the norm established by political, social, and medical authorities. Throughout the journal there was a growing emphasis on the idea that the symptoms of behavioral problems, psychopathologies, and mental illnesses were most prevalent among the poor. A review of the journal's articles reveals that its subjects and objects of study were predominantly from the urban popular classes, and occasionally from a sort of middle class closely connected to the working-class world. Meanwhile, its contributors—physicians and psychiatrists—also wrote for other contemporary publications, such as the *RCP*, highlighting the connection between disciplines.

The defense of society, for its part, sought to legitimize itself as a theory that was both scientific and sociological (Bustos 1983: 17), thus justifying preventive surveillance and control on the basis of rational neutrality or objectivity (Mallereal 2012: 249–74). According to this logic, psychiatry assumed an important role because, as the journal stated, it was responsible for "the mission of social defense by removing dangerous or antisocial elements from its bosom; and on the other hand, [treating] such elements in their capacity as mentally ill" (Vivado, Larson and Arroyo 1939: 160). Although the view of criminal abnormality faced increasing criticism and complexities over time (León 2015: 133–68), this deterministic outlook was not discarded, officially or unofficially, by either psychiatry or criminology, despite their growth and interrelation. Rosa del Olmo, in her evaluation of criminology education in Latin America through various manuals published from the 1930s onward, highlighted this. She noted that these manuals continued to be dominated by

> a conception of society divided into the normal (those who comply with the law) and the "others," who must be abnormal because they do not abide by the norms of society, specifically the law. This conception of the delinquent as abnormal fulfils an important ideological function, justifying the repressive or "curative" intervention of the state as a "defense" against these "other" abnormals. (Del Olmo 1981: 244)

The Police Perspective

The *Revista de los Carabineros de Chile* (*RCCh*), which began publication in August 1927, was dedicated to promoting the activities of Chile's uniformed police, while publishing the opinions and reflections of its leaders as well as guest writers. Through its pages, one can trace the persistence of ideas like those mentioned above. Despite biological determinism appearing to have been discredited on the international stage, and the magazine emphasizing the renewal of content and forms for presenting police information, the essentialist view of certain people categorized as dangerous remained in force.

By the end of the 1950s, the magazine continued to present a classification of criminals intended as a guide for action, still evoking the criminological tradition of Lombroso, Garofalo, and the International Union of Penal Law (1913). Three categories were recognized: occasional, habitual, and abnormal criminals, as outlined in the anonymous article entitled "Clasificación de los delincuentes" (1957: 15). This continued adherence aligned with a body of ideas and beliefs that weighed hereditary, anthropological, moral, mental, economic, social, and even territorial factors as causes of criminality. These ideas formed a frame of reference that made it easier to understand the enactment, in the middle of that decade, of the aforementioned law of antisocial conditions.

The "abnormal" classification of delinquents was not only rooted in a hereditary justification, which had largely been discredited after the Second World War and the consequent fall of eugenics, but also in a social and economic context that helped explain the persistence of such dangerous figures in the mid-twentieth century (Sánchez 1956: 9–10). There was, therefore, a need to emphasize the changing forms of this social phenomenon and to rethink the terminology used to describe it, in order to warn how to protect public and private spaces. The constant concern for younger generations remained a key criterion for combating vices such as alcoholism. Alcoholics had to be made aware of the need to change their ways, as Enrique Ugarte, third doctor of the Carabineros, made clear: "Do not forget that if you are married and drink too much, you will beget decrepit, stupid, stunted, and useless children, which, naturally, in your condition of dignified and balanced men, and as good Chileans, you have the serious obligation to avoid" (Ugarte 1947: 80). A similar point was made by Dr. René Miranda, a retired Carabineros polyclinic doctor, who argued that alcoholism was a factor in the malnutrition and degradation of the population (Miranda 1947: 79–83).

Meanwhile, publications from the Service of Investigations, Identification and Passports, such as *Detective* (1934–7) and the *Revista de criminología y policía científica* (*RCPC*) (1937–55), featured editorials, reports, and chronicles that depicted delinquent criminals in much the same way, remaining under the influence of positivist criminology. Although criminological studies abroad had become more sophisticated, following various epistemological models that sought to move beyond the positivism and determinism of criminal anthropology (Fausto 2001; Fernández 2003), even in the 1930s and 1940s police magazines continued to propagate these ideas rather than encouraging a paradigm shift or overcoming old prejudices.

There were few references to criminology approaches that considered social rather than biological influences—models that accepted multiple causality and sociological conditioning. While police publications did take the social environment into account when identifying the causes of crime and delinquency, class-based stigmas persisted. The social environment under analysis continued to be limited to one social group: the poor.

These writings perpetuated the idea that the delinquent-criminal could easily be identified by his shabby and dirty appearance and unsettling mannerisms—such as a lost gaze and grimaces of displeasure and perversion—to which was added the telling use of nicknames and specific forms of language. Crime was seen as the manifestation of an imbalance between individuals and their environment, and punishment aimed to restore balance and prevent further harm. The offender, an abnormal person determined by biology and the unchecked force of atavistic instincts, was believed to lack free will, although at times his behavior was attributed to his "social environment." This environment, in turn, was thought to carry many hereditary effects, forming a degenerative chain originating in immoral or vicious family backgrounds that led individuals into the criminal world.

Women were considered inferior to men within the evolutionary framework and, for this reason, were seen as less capable of committing crimes—supposedly explaining their lower representation in criminal statistics (Barros 2009). However, women were depicted as more cruel than men, associated with the primitive, and thus as contributing greatly to blood crimes. Moreover, they were more adaptable to circumstance, allowing them to combine the worst traits of their nature—cunning, rancor, and deceit—with those of male criminals—planning, violence, and force. They were also said to possess strong behavioral skills when facing justice (Klimpel 1962: 65).

Women at this time faced great discrimination and had few political, economic, or social rights (Palafox 2021: 265–86). Police magazines often portrayed their crimes as circumstantial rather than premeditated, and as driven by pressing circumstances. They were never depicted as masterminds behind grand thefts, robberies, or swindles, although when a woman carried out a well-executed swindle, it generated admiration from men. Several of the published works maintained a similar line of interpretation.

Conclusions

This chapter has sought to illustrate how the core concepts of criminal anthropology, as a new form of criminological knowledge, found early reception in Chile. These ideas took hold in a more specialized form, linked to the medical and penal spheres, and in its popularized version, as reflected in the press and police journals. Various publications embraced biological determinism and the association of physical appearance with criminality to construct and define the contemporary image of the delinquent. The circulation of these ideas can be traced in the writings of doctors, lawyers, jurists, and policemen, and to various publications, which further amplified their reach. They then influenced public acts, such as Ferri's conferences, and played a role in specific judicial cases.

This new body of knowledge did not emerge in a vacuum. Its "scientific" character served to validate it while reinforcing a series of prejudices linked to race, class, and ethnicity. The result was a type of "creole criminology" that complemented and reinforced Italian criminology without ever being particularly original. Publications such as the *RCP* and the *RPDC*, along with police magazines, helped to spread Lombrosian ideas and other deterministic theories, constructing dubious notions about the supposedly anomalous figure of the delinquent and criminal. Even though criminal anthropology was already being called into question by the middle of the century, it is understandable that these ideas, beliefs, prejudices, and assumptions continued to support stereotypes of dangerous figures and identities, and to maintain a permanent shadow of suspicion over them that influenced the development of a law which remained in force until its repeal in 1994.

Note

1. It is necessary to point out that Dr. Luis Gambara, of whom there are no major biographical references, despite his self-designation as "General Delegate of the Positive School," never published in the *Archivio di psichiatria*, nor did he exchange correspondence with Cesare Lombroso, as has been claimed.

4

The Impact, Uses, and Vicissitudes of Lombroso's Theories in Bolivia

Françoise Martinez and Pablo Quisbert

At the end of the nineteenth century, Bolivia's intellectual and political elites identified several national weaknesses they sought to address. After losing its coastal territory in the War of the Pacific (1879–83), the nation was perceived as an amputated body, fearing the loss of other regions coveted by neighboring republics. However, the most concerning vulnerability that began to be diagnosed was the significant ethnic component of the Bolivian population. The rural, Indigenous population, larger than in neighboring countries, was viewed as a major contributor to the nation's problematic backwardness. When the results of the General Census of the Republic, launched in 1900, confirmed the decline and probable disappearance of this part of the population, its authors almost expressed satisfaction, suggesting that the "backward cause" of civilization lay in "the indigenous race, essentially resistant to all innovation and progress" (Oficina Nacional 1904: 25–9). Everything seemed to indicate that if Bolivia hoped to survive in the global struggle for existence among human societies, its modernization could no longer be delayed. Only through modernization could the perceived issue of the "degeneration of the race" be addressed.

To understand the circulation and reception of the ideas of Cesare Lombroso and the Italian positivist school in this context—and to assess how Lombroso's theories, or those of his disciples, were used to identify Bolivia's "degenerates"—we must first examine the competing intellectual currents at the end of the nineteenth century. We will demonstrate how, paradoxically, a pronounced anti-Lombrosianism developed in academic institutions before the broader success of Lombrosianism. We will then show that it was during the two-decade liberal rule, beginning in 1899, that Lombrosianism found its greatest expression and application. Finally, we will examine the post-Lombrosian period, when, after the 1920s, certain events led to opposition and distancing from Lombroso's theories, while simultaneously preserving elements of the Italian school's theories and principles.

The End of the Nineteenth Century: Anti-Lombrosianism Before the Success of Lombrosianism

The Case of Rodolfo Soria Galvarro's Professorship

In January 1893, Rodolfo Soria Galvarro, a candidate for a professorship in the first year of free instruction at the Law School of the University of La Paz, passed his examination by citing Lombroso and other members of the Italian positive school, aligning himself with their theories, even "denying volition and free will" ("Informe" 1893: 2).[1] However, on January 17, 1893, President Mariano Baptista's conservative government intervened, issuing a supreme resolution ordering the examining board to investigate Soria Galvarro's application.[2] The board's report concluded that the result should be disregarded.

The conservative press defended the intervention, arguing that it was necessary to control and contain "the propaganda of deleterious doctrines" that undermined the courts' ability to punish offenders by suggesting that "the delinquent is a sick person who must be cured and not punished." Such a view, they claimed, was a "doctrine that destroys the foundation of criminal law." The verdict of the newspaper *El Comercio* was implacable: "As of today, a precedent of high discipline has been established. Galvarro, like all those infatuated with the errors of the moment, is unfit to hold a teaching position" ("La moral" 1893a: 2).

But what motivated this rejection among elites otherwise eager to embrace progress and theories circulating in a Europe deemed more civilized? As the press pointed out, Lombrosian theories not only dismissed free will but also denied "the existence of eternal or natural law and its author, or at least questioned its existence" and rejected "the theological notion of law" (ibid.: 2). This was a boundary that Baptista's conservative government could not allow to be crossed.

Soria Galvarro attempted to defend himself, but he faced powerful enemies in the academic world, particularly Fernando Velásquez Valencia, known as "Weimar," a priest and professor of theology. Despite Soria Galvarro's arguments—and despite the fact that Agustín Aspiazu, rector of the university from 1883 to 1892 and president of the examining tribunal, had initially congratulated him—the Ministry of Justice and Public Instruction ruled against him. On February 6, 1893, it stated that: "the functionary … not only attacks the doctrine and organization of Catholicism with variable and hurtful concepts, but denies the very foundation and significance of Christianity, which are the Gospel and the other scriptures" ("Ministerio" 1893: 2).

This episode demonstrates a certain rejection of Lombrosian discourse, at least within university circles, during the final decade of the nineteenth century. It was a clear attempt to purge Italian positivist ideas that had entered Bolivian academic life. The case also highlights the dilemma faced by conservative governments between 1880 and 1898: while they recognized the need to modernize the country by incorporating new ideological currents, they sought to do so without compromising Bolivia's Christian and Catholic foundations. Moreover, this instance of anti-Lombrosianism within Bolivian academic and political structures challenged the Italian criminologist's claim that there was a clear opposition between a "generous America" that readily accepted his theories and an "ungrateful Europe" that did not (Caimari 2009: 193).

However, this resistance did not prevent Lombroso's ideas from continuing to circulate through scientific conferences and, above all, the press—particularly the newspapers sympathetic to liberal and positivist thought. Between 1888 and 1897, *El Imparcial* published eight articles mentioning Lombroso, whether in reference to legal cases in neighboring countries ("El cura" 1888: 2), discussions of Guy de Maupassant's supposed madness ("Opinión de Zola" 1892), announcements about Lombroso's or his disciples' books being available for sale ("Libreria" 1895: 1),[3] or in articles written by Soria Galvarro himself. In the latter, Soria Galvarro continued to defend the positivist school, urging the minister of instruction to abandon theological approaches and instead read: "*The Criminal Man, The Man of Genius, Criminal Anthropology of Four Hundred Venetian Criminals*, and … *Criminal Anthropology and its Recent Progress*, without forgetting the book cited by Ferri [*New Horizons of Criminal Law*], so that he can appreciate the scope of the positive school in criminal matters" ("La moral" 1893b: 2).

Toward a Growing Legitimacy of the Italian School

One of the most enthusiastic proponents of Lombroso's ideas in the 1890s press was Belisario Díaz Romero, a physician and professor of natural sciences who taught in high schools and at the University of La Paz. His references to Lombroso were consistently laudatory, describing "the special work of Professor Lombroso," "the authoritative word of the sage," and "the never sufficiently praised book of César Lombroso." His admiration reached its peak in the article "Genius and its Psycho-Pathological Determinism," published in 1897 (Díaz Romero 1910), a commentary on *El hombre de genio* (The Man of Genius),[4] in which Lombroso drew parallels between genius and madness. Díaz Romero's commitment to Lombroso and the Italian positivist school was so strong that he not only urged his readers to study their writings but also encouraged them to follow Italy's example in criminology: "Modern Italy marches today with progressive steps and outstanding zeal towards the reform of penal institutions, laying with its Positivist School the foundations of a new criminological and social science. We, as nations, like her, derived from the Latin race, should follow her noble example" (Díaz Romero 1910: 137).

Díaz Romero approached Lombroso's work not only from a medical perspective but also in relation to Bolivian political history. Lombroso had coined the term "mattoids" to describe a typology of individuals in whom madness and genius seemed intertwined, and he referred to artistic, literary, religious, and political mattoids (Lombroso 1894d: 392). Díaz Romero did not hesitate to apply this label to the so-called *caudillos*, the military strongmen who dominated nineteenth-century Bolivia. These *caudillos* had shaped a political model that the conservative and liberal elites sought to dismantle after 1880, establishing the republic that later became known as "oligarchic." According to Díaz Romero: "In Bolivia, we have not ceased to possess them, and we still do—for where [except here] are these fanatical Belcistas, Melgarejistas, Corralistas

…? We have had mattoids in abundance, especially political and literary ones" (Díaz Romero 1910: 133).[5]

Lombroso himself encouraged the application of his theory and terminology to the so-called *caudillista* period of Bolivian history. In fact, not only did he believe that his analysis of geniuses and genius could be applied to historical, artistic, and literary criticism (Lombroso 1894d: 646) but he also praised José María Ramos Mejía's *Las neurosis de los hombres célebres en la historia Argentina*, which analyzed the behavior and mental conditions of *caudillos* and dictators such as Argentina's Juan Manuel de Rosas and Paraguay's José Gaspar Rodríguez de Francia (Ramos Mejía 1878–82). The rejection of the *caudillista* period was one of the major points of consensus between the liberal and conservative groups in Bolivia.

At times, even in death, certain figures became unintended promoters of the Italian positivist school. When the respected lawyer and scholar Agustín Aspiazu died in March 1897, the liberal newspaper *El Imparcial* managed to link Lombroso and his theories to his intellectual legacy. Although there is no evidence that Aspiazu applied Lombroso's ideas, the newspaper suggested this was merely due to a lack of time:

> If he had lived a little longer, the reforms to our legislation—particularly in criminal matters—would have hastened, because Aspiazu found in the latest scientific advances the foundation of an evolution already making history in the judicial annals of old Europe: the atavism of race, the physiological study of man in relation to his acts, Lombroso and Paul Bert. ("La muerte" 1897: 2)

Through such endorsements, Lombroso and the Italian positivist school gained recognition and legitimacy. If Lombroso's ideas offered a framework for confronting troublesome figures from Bolivia's past, by the early twentieth century, they would prove equally useful in addressing the most uncomfortable element of the present: the Indigenous population.

The Liberal Period and the Influences of the Positivist School (1898–1920)

The struggle between liberals and conservatives culminated in armed conflict between the north and the south of the country. The northern army, known as the federal army, was supported by contingents of Aymara and Quechua Indians, who were mobilized with promises of the return of community lands that had been expropriated from them since 1880. The war ended in April 1899 with the military victory of the federal forces.

When the liberals came to power, the fear of an Indian revolution was already widespread, as were rumors of a possible "race war" (Martinez 2021: 132). The federal war itself had sparked Indian uprisings, led in particular by Pablo Zárate, known as Willka, a *cacique* (tribal leader) from the province of Sicasica and leader of the Indians in their struggle to regain confiscated lands. During the conflict, reports of brutal massacres of the conservative army at Peñas, Corocoro, and Ayoayo deeply unsettled the elites. The most shocking attack occurred on March 1, 1899, in Mohoza, where

Indigenous fighters, who had ostensibly been supporting the battalion of José Manuel Pando, turned against it. Without considering the conditions that had driven them to kill, defend themselves, or seek revenge, the very idea that the Indians could shift from being allies to ruthless enemies, capable of brutally exterminating soldiers from both sides in cold blood, solidified the perception that uncontrolled violence permeated their very being. This perception reinforced the belief that Indians, by their very nature, were not only savages but also criminals.

Criminal Indian or Criminal "indiada"?

The Liberal Party's seizure of power brought with it an urgent need to exert control over what was already perceived as the "Indian danger" (ibid.: 132–7). In 1900, the National Office of Immigration, Statistics, and Geographic Propaganda published *Judicial Statistics*, a report on work carried out by Bautista Saavedra—a liberal jurist and sociologist who would later become a Republican president. Informed by the Italian school of thought, Saavedra suggested a correlation between violent crimes, primitive societies, and the "Indigenous race." He claimed, "Blood crimes, the most cruel and inhuman, are therefore the most common crimes of savage societies and the embryonic stages of humanity. This sociological principle, accepted by all positivist criminalists, finds precise application among us in the case of criminality within the indigenous race, which accounts for 90% of all criminals" (Saavedra 1900: 2).

Saavedra compared data from all of Bolivia's departments, pointing to higher numbers of criminals among Indigenous people. He highlighted cases of particular "savagery and barbarism," such as cannibalism in Carangas, a province in the Oruro Department. He claimed that criminality there reached "an extraordinary maximum in the case of attacks and violence against the white race, having presented several cases of anthropophagy" (ibid.: 30). In this way, the long-forgotten nightmares of the Spaniards were reawakened.

Saavedra's observations of Indigenous women prisoners in La Paz appeared to further confirm these racial statistics. After visiting the part of the prison housing women convicted of homicide, he remarked: "We have had occasion to visit this department, and all the criminals turn out to be Indians or cholas [*mestizas*]. The same racial anthropological factors of savagery and barbarism that we have indicated in blood crimes are at play in this group of women criminals" (ibid.: 24).

Based on the scientific criteria of the time, the notion of the "Indian danger" appeared to be validated. However, the key debate over whether Indigenous people were inherently criminal arose in the context of the infamous "Mohoza Trial." While members of the Corocoro or Ayoayo communities, who had risen up against conservative soldiers during the federal war, had been granted political amnesty, the Mohoza community faced punishment for attacking the liberal Pando squadron. The newspaper *La Industria* claimed that the conflict had been exploited by this "ferocious and degenerate class" as a pretext to rise up against the white race ("Tendencias" 1899: 1). Were these rebels innocent and exploited Indians who had reason to rise up against historical abuses? Or were they "criminal Indians" whose innate perversity was tied to their natural environment? This was the crux of the debate.

Throughout the trial, Lombroso's theories were mobilized by Saavedra himself, who agreed to defend the Mohoza community members. His intention was to demonstrate that the massacre was the result of the Indigenous rebels' "atavistic" violence, and was thus a collective crime committed by "overflowing crowds," not attributable to individual responsibility (Saavedra 1903).

Elena Bovo has emphasized the Italian-French debate on psychology and collective crimes, underscoring the undeniable influence of Lombroso, Ferri, and Sighele[6] on Le Bon and his *Psychologie des foules* (Bovo 2021). Olivier Bosc also recognized the importance of Pasquale Rossi and Scipio Sighele, praising their ability to connect the theory of imitation with the biological and Lombrosian theory of atavism to formulate an early theory of crowd psychology (Bosc 2003). Saavedra, in his essay "La criminalidad aymara en el proceso Mohoza" (included in *El ayllu*, published in 1903), made two laudatory references to Professor Sighele, quoting from his works translated into French—*La contagion du meurtre*—and Spanish—*El delito de dos* and *La muchedumbre delincuente*, the latter being his most influential (Saavedra 1903: 76, 200).

In his pioneering defense, Saavedra depicted the Mohoza massacre as a collective crime perpetrated by a "morally atrophied race, or else one degenerated to the point of dehumanization" (ibid.: 171). Given this, and the collective nature of the crime, he argued that the individuals could not be held accountable, and that "in spite of the horrifying cruelty and viciousness with which the Indigenous class fueled their hatreds against the whites, they could not be tried as simple murderers" (ibid.: 209). A clear consistency in Saavedra's adherence to Lombrosian thought, augmented by the Ferri-Sighele influence, can be observed in his application of these ideas to Bolivian society. His views aligned with the elites' fear of not only individual Indians, who could be controlled, but also of the uncontainable *indiada* (Indigenous masses). Ultimately, though, his advocacy failed. Several members of this dangerous collective were sentenced to death.

Uses and Abuses of Lombroso in Court Cases

The theories of the Italian school became ingrained in the cultural fabric of the elites in early-twentieth-century Bolivia, with the term "born criminal" in regular use. Given the context and how frequently Lombroso and his followers were invoked, both in the press and in the justice system, one could speak of the many uses—and abuses—of his ideas. The latter can be illustrated through three key cases from the first decade of the century, which demonstrate Lombroso's ubiquity in Bolivian trials.

In 1903, a well-to-do man named Manuel Zuazo was found dead in his bed in La Paz, shot twice in the head with a revolver. Despite the two gunshot wounds, the authorities initially assumed it was a suicide. However, Zuazo's mother, through her lawyer José Manuel Maldonado, challenged this conclusion by publishing a briefing that placed the blame for a possible murder on the deceased's wife (Torrelio 1903). Maldonado supported his argument by referencing Lombroso's *Medicina legal*, though not verbatim.[7] In response, the wife's attorney, Isidoro Viderique, immediately published his own pamphlet citing Lombroso's *Forensic Medicine* to demonstrate that

Zuazo could indeed have shot himself. Viderique went further, accusing Maldonado of misquoting Lombroso (Viderique 1903: 28–9).

Maldonado responded with yet another pamphlet, this time omitting the earlier reference to Lombroso. Instead, under the premise that "crime is not a hereditary fatality," he distanced himself from Lombrosian ideas, if he had ever truly adhered to them, and launched a sharp critique of the Italian positivist school, dismissing "the fantastic theories of Lombroso, Tailor [*sic*], Ferri, Garofalo and other apostles of the positivist-Italian school" (Maldonado 1903: 3).

A similar dispute over the correct application of the theories of Lombroso and the Italian positivist school arose during the trial of Leonor Collazos in the mining city of Oruro. Collazos, a woman of local elite status, had been subjected to beatings and mistreatment by her husband, Roberto Pelaez, yet it was she who faced trial for adultery, a charge brought against her by her husband. Pelaez's lawyer, Abelardo Renjel, a well-known jurist and founding professor at the University of Oruro, employed questionable tactics in the case, subjecting Collazos to intense pressure and intimidation. On January 7, 1907, while in court, Renjel attempted to have her arrested. In response, Collazos shot the lawyer twice with a revolver, killing him instantly.

During the subsequent murder trial, José Quintín Mendoza, the defense attorney, argued that Collazos suffered from neurasthenia, an ill-defined nervous condition, and thus could not be held responsible for her actions (Mendoza 1907). This defense provoked a strong reaction from Rodolfo Soria Galvarro, the same lawyer whose frustrated candidacy for a professorship at the University of La Paz in 1893 is described above. Representing the plaintiff, Soria Galvarro issued a pamphlet harshly criticizing Mendoza's defense, implying that his knowledge of the Italian positivist school was superficial. Soria Galvaro argued that this led his opponent to make a very serious error: "Those who have barely leafed through some positivist propaganda book have believed that the Italian school, headed by the brilliant Lombroso, tends towards impunity for the criminal. That is a grave mistake" (Soria Galvarro 1907: 24). This case demonstrates that Soria Galvarro remained a staunch Lombrosian, and, as in the 1893 debate, the question of free will played a fundamental role in his insistence on the correct application of Lombroso's ideas and those of the Italian positivist school.

Lombroso's ideas on female criminality, as outlined in his work *La donna delinquente, la prostituta e la donna normale*,[8] also played a significant role in the case of Luis Aruviri's murder. Aruviri, an Indigenous man, had been tasked with transporting remittances for a commercial company from La Paz to the mining town of Corocoro. In April 1908, Carlos Candia, an employee of the same company, devised a plan to ambush Aruviri and steal the money. Moisés Fuentes Villanueva, a railroad employee, and María Caballero, a prostitute suspected of having a sexual relationship with Candia, assisted in the plot. While Villanueva faced judicial proceedings in the absence of Candia and Caballero, the court eventually determined that Candia had masterminded the plan and that Villanueva, with Caballero's help, had carried out the murder.

What stands out in this case is the way that Lombroso's work was used to portray Caballero not only as a criminal prostitute but also as a born criminal. She was described as:

> the principal agent of instigation ... who, by her quality as a prostitute, embodies the outstanding traits of cruelty, as Cesar Lombroso classifies the criminal prostitute when, in dealing with the physical characteristics of this kind of women, he states that prostitution is the equivalent of criminality in women., that is, the specific form under which the degeneration of this sex is manifested. In the same way, those who, according to Lombroso, exhibit exaggerated and continuous lasciviousness are born both criminals and prostitutes, in whom lust manifests itself with ferocity. (Gaceta Judicial 1911: 11–12)

This paragraph illustrates the direct influence of *La donna delinquente* on the case, not only in the reference to Lombroso's well-known assertion that "Prostitution is ultimately the feminine side of criminality" (Lombroso and Ferrero 1893: 571) but also in the attempt to show that Caballero had many of the traits that the Italian criminologist saw as characteristic of the criminal woman. These included refined cruelty, excessive lasciviousness and lust, and greed. In fact, it was argued that Caballero consistently displayed a "greed for money," making continuous demands on Fuentes and allegedly instigating the Aruviri murder out of financial motive.[9]

Criminal Anthropology and Indigenous Delinquency

At the start of the twentieth century, criminal anthropology—or criminology[10]—was gaining prominence in Bolivia. Expectations were high that this new science would provide definitive answers about Indigenous criminality, which was considered an unquestionable reality. The supposed vices and inherent conditions of the Indigenous population—such as barbarism, alcoholism, and physical degeneration—were common topics in the press and popular pamphlets. The only thing required was a scientific confirmation of these assumptions.

Although Bautista Saavedra touched on this subject in his *Estadística judicial* and later in *El ayllu*, he never produced a comprehensive study on Indigenous criminality. Nonetheless, three scientific missions undertaken during these years revealed a clear intent to pursue such a study. These were undertaken by Créqui-Montfort in 1903, Georges Rouma in 1911, and Fructuoso Carpena in 1914.

In 1903, the French scientific mission led by Georges de Créqui-Montfort and Sénéchal de la Grange visited Bolivia to gather data, later published in Arthur Chervin's *Anthropologie bolivienne* (1908). The mission sought to measure and photograph Bolivian Indians (Zamorano 2011), but while they showed particular interest in the prisoners at La Paz prison—including several individuals accused in the Mohoza case—the photographs taken by Chervin's assistants were not always deemed valid or representative of the Indigenous population.[11]

The anthropometric mission undertaken by Georges Rouma in 1911, accompanied by three assistants, was a very different case. Rouma, a Belgian pedagogue hired in 1909 to direct Bolivia's first teacher training school, organized this mission under the auspices of the liberal government of Eliodoro Villazón and the *Sociedad Antropológica* of Sucre. His goal was to study the Indigenous people of the *altiplano* (the Andean Plateau). Rouma managed to obtain photographs and anthropometric measurements of Aymara, Quechua, and Yungas Indians in their home environments. He published his findings in Brussels in 1913 in his French work *Les indiens quitchouas et aymaras des hauts-plateaux de la Bolivie*. The primary focus of his research was simply to compare the supposedly "pure" types (Aymara-Quechua) with their mixed counterparts, seeking evidence of degeneration in mixed and displaced groups. Indicators of this included smaller stature, diminished physical vigor, and even altered female body forms. Rouma's study did not aim to measure criminality but rather sought to evaluate the Indigenous peoples' predisposition to work and better themselves, as well as to demonstrate the supposed benefits of keeping them within their "natural environment" (Martinez 2021: 314 *et sqs*).

A comprehensive study of Indigenous criminality—similar to work undertaken by José Antonio Encinas in Peru (1919)—was required. The task would have entailed combining statistical data analysis like Saavedra's 1900 study with anthropometric measurements like those taken by the Créqui-Montfort and Rouma missions, all in an effort to establish links between physical characteristics and criminal behavior. To fulfil this ambition, the Bolivian government turned to a Spaniard, Fructuoso Carpena, who carried out an expedition in 1914.

Little is known about Carpena's journey in Bolivia. A notary and lawyer, he had published a book titled *Antropología criminal* in Spain in 1909. His assignment in Bolivia was arranged through Luis Salinas Vega, the Bolivian ambassador to Germany, who later served as minister of public instruction and agriculture in the second government of Ismael Montes (1913–17). Carpena's mission was to conduct a study on criminality among the Indigenous population. His findings were never published in Bolivia, but in May 1915, the Spanish magazine *La Esfera* declared that Carpena had found "admirable sources of observation and study that prove the theories of atavism and regression" (Pérez 1915: 29).

Although no evidence was ever published linking criminality with Indigenous peoples, it clear that during two decades of liberal rule, the doctrines of the Italian school were widely used—and abused. The ideas of Lombroso, Ferri, and Sighele gained such popularity that in Armando Chirveches's 1908 satire *La candidatura de Rojas*, the protagonist, a parliamentary candidate named Enrique Rojas, is advised that even though he is standing for the Conservative Party "the doctrines you hold must be new doctrines, the doctrines of D'Aguano [*sic.*], Tarde, Gumplowicz, Fiore, Ferri, Lombroso, Sighele, Pérez Oliva, and Posada" (Chirveches 1998 [1909]: 32). This intellectual influence persisted for some time. Lombroso's death in 1909 marked the necessary renewal of his theories.

Post-Lombrosianism: Rejection and Revival of Lombrosian Theories

From the 1920s onward, Bolivia witnessed the emergence of new discourses, criteria, and positions that may be considered manifestations of a post-Lombrosianism. This phase oscillated between outright rejection of Lombroso's theories (anti-Lombrosianism) and adaptations or reinterpretations of them (new Lombrosianism).

The Case of Apolonia Méndez: Anti-Lombrosianism of a Particular Brand

In late November 1920, the city of La Paz was shaken by the case of Apolonia Méndez (or Polonia, as some referred to her), a young woman from the emerging middle class who fatally stabbed her lover, Fernando Granier, a wealthy member of the elite. With its overtones of a crime of passion, the case captivated public attention. Several lawyers offered to defend Méndez, but in the end, her primary defense attorney was Cleto Cabrera, who had paid a heartfelt tribute to Cesare Lombroso upon hearing of his death in 1909 ("Sociedad" 1909: 2).

The case also attracted the attention of Arthur Posnansky, an Austrian engineer who had studied anthropology in Europe. Posnansky was fascinated by the pre-Hispanic ruins of Tiwanaku and wanted to demonstrate that they were the work of a superior race, which he believed were the ancestors of the contemporary Aymara people (Quisbert 2005). As part of his studies, he made several anthropometric and craniometric analyses of Indigenous people.

In early 1923, Posnansky, who was also interested in criminology, published *Impulsos atávicos. El caso de Polonia Méndez*, a book that opened with a clear declaration of principles that revealed his distance from both Cesare Lombroso and Franz Joseph Gall: "Most of Lombroso's theories and those of Gall were relegated to oblivion some time ago by modern research" (Posnansky 1923: 5). But what, in his view, constituted "modern research"? Posnansky's answer was clear: "Modern criminal anthropology [considers] first and foremost the *milieu* of the criminal." However, he did not fully reject Lombroso, as he still considered his theories on atavism to be relevant: "The main thing that remains immovable from the multiple theories of Lombroso and others of his school is the importance of the signs of degeneration that make us assume certain atavistic characters" (ibid.: 6).

Posnansky emphasized the importance and influence of the social environment and the role of atavistic traits in the manifestation of delinquent behavior. On this point, his approach aligned with Lombroso's theory that some criminals exhibited signs of atavism or hereditary regression. Under this premise, Posnansky analyzed the case of Apolonia Méndez.

After taking her anthropometric measurements, Posnansky searched for signs of atavism. He ultimately concluded that Méndez was a normal young woman, except for one detail: her unusually long arms, similar to those of other women in the La Paz prison, whom he had also measured. Since this arm length had not developed due to physical labor or sport, he interpreted it as "a backward jump" in her development (ibid.: 68). To this Posnansky added the influence of the environment in which Méndez grew up, ultimately concluding:

> Polonia Mendez … is the prototype of the girl "*of to day*" [*sic*], the one who … carries the fatal germ engendered by the pleasures of her predecessors, a germ that the present neuropathic atmosphere and … the morally unhealthy impressions of the cinema favor … awakening sinister instincts and atavistic impulses that would have remained dormant, perhaps forever. These coefficients were the primary

ones that prepared Polonia for crime; the secondary ones are not so important. (ibid.: 48)

In his book, Posnansky affirmed that while the environment plays a significant role in the development of criminal behavior, acting as a catalyst, it is ultimately atavistic impulses that predispose an individual to crime—hence the title *Impulsos atávicos*. In this way, Posnansky curiously distanced himself from Lombroso's proposals, only to arrive at a position strikingly similar to them.

Theories Debated up to the 1940s: José Medrano Ossio vs. Manuel López Rey

Years later, the dispute between José Medrano Ossio, author of *Responsabilidad penal de los indígenas*, and Manuel López Rey exemplified the lingering presence of Lombrosian discourse in Bolivian legal and intellectual circles during the 1940s. Medrano Ossio argued that the Indigenous people in Bolivia lived in a state of "psychological prostration," rendering them unaware of their actions and the crimes they committed. He attributed this condition to social factors that, in his view, had produced Indigenous people who were racially, congenitally, and hereditarily inferior.

Medrano Ossio's position echoed Lombrosian ideas, particularly the notion that congenital anomalies led to a biological predisposition for delinquency. At the same time, he integrated positions more aligned with Enrico Ferri, who emphasized the role of environmental and social factors in shaping criminal behavior. In his text, Medrano Ossio portrayed Indigenous people as abnormal and savage, unintegrated into any society, and offering no guarantee of good behavior—thus framing them as potential born criminals. This perspective justified a shift from a criminal law of social defense to one focused on protecting the criminal (Medrano Ossio 1940; Villegas Díaz 2021).

Medrano Ossio's theories were criticized by Manuel López Rey, who argued that a regime of protection and tutelage would not be enough to bring about a general improvement or penal reform of the Indigenous population. Medrano Ossio found himself having to defend against the charge of being a "backward" disciple of the "today superseded" "primitive positivism" of Lombroso and Ferri—suggesting that even in the 1940s, accusations of this sort could still carry weight (López Rey 1945: 264–73).

By the 1920s, the methods of Lombroso, Ferri, and the Italian positivist school had already fallen out of fashion, and anyone employing them risked being seen as "backward." However, until 1940, the theories of both schools continued to be debated in law courses and criminology conferences, stirred controversy in the press, and reappeared in publications like the *Revista de la Policía Boliviana*—the official journal of an institution whose reform and modernization received the support of a delegation of Italian *Carabinieri*.[12]

Conclusions

Criminal anthropology in Bolivia contributed to the "scientific" support that reinforced many prejudices that stigmatized Indigenous populations as "enemies" or "dangerous elements" against which Bolivian society—particularly its conservative and liberal elites—needed protection. A review of contemporary writings, trials, and legal cases reveals how this new criminological knowledge was embraced by authorities and professionals during Bolivia's liberal period, though it did not follow the traditional trajectory of growing recognition followed by gradual abandonment.

During the conservative period, such ideas faced rejection, largely due to religious opposition. In contrast, the liberal period saw not only their acceptance but also their adaptation to address specific societal concerns, particularly in relation to delinquency and Indigenous populations. Even as these theories came under criticism, they continued to find echoes and advocates, further complicating our understanding of the impact and vicissitudes of Lombrosian theories in Bolivia.

Notes

1. The report mentions: "The questions that gave subject matter to the examination that is recalled were those of the penal system and principles of Natural Law, in which the acting judge exposed the doctrines of Lombroso, Ferrari [*sic*], Gazofalo [*sic*] and others of the positive school." The mistaken spellings of the names of Ferri (written as Ferrari) and Garofalo (cited as Gazofalo) in the reproduction of the attestation of the *vocales* reveals that at the end of the nineteenth century newspapers like *El Comercio* did not yet mention these thinkers particularly frequently.
2. Following Bolivia's withdrawal from the War of the Pacific in 1880, the so-called "conservative" period began, characterized by the consolidation of a parliamentary regime with a civilian presidency and a government dedicated to supporting the mining sector, the country's main export industry. The conservatives adopted a pacifist stance, enabling an end to the war, negotiating indemnification for the lost territories, and investing in projects like the construction of a railroad to facilitate large-scale mineral exports. As Bolivia's first and only party in the early 1880s, unlike countries such as Ecuador, it had less need to defend the Catholic Church, which did not yet feel threatened, except in cases when theories like those by Lombroso questioned its potential for redemption.
3. The article mentioned that Ferri's book (*Antropología criminal*) and those of Lombroso (*Escuela criminológica* and *Hipnotismo*) were for sale in the bookstore of José M. Farfán.
4. The work was known until its third Italian edition as *Genio y Locura*. Belisario Díaz Romero used the second French edition (Lombroso 1896), which was a translation of the sixth Italian edition (Lombroso 1894d). Díaz Romero also advised his readers to consult *El hombre criminal*.
5. It is striking that Díaz Romero lumps together such politically opposite figures as Presidents Isidoro Belzu and Mariano Melgarejo, united only by the *caudillista* character attributed to their governments a posteriori.
6. Sighele was a student of Ferri and his *La folla delinquente* (published in 1891) is a clear homage to *L'uomo delinquente* and a first theorization of collective psychology. According to Sighele (1892), man, already a victim of his own instincts, can also fall prey to external influences, such as the suggestion exerted by a crowd. Such

circumstances can then motivate individual actions, and those involved in this type of collective crime resemble criminals of opportunity.

7. Maldonado used the Spanish version by Pedro Dorado (*Medicina legal*, 1900), the translation of *Sulla medicina legale del cadavere* (Lombroso 1890b).
8. The first Italian edition dates back to 1893, but in Bolivia it was the French translated version that circulated: Cesare Lombroso and Guglielmo Ferrero, *La femme criminelle et la prostituée* (1896).
9. Speaking of the consequences of greed and avarice manifested by born female criminals, Lombroso and Ferrero comment that: "they consequently attempt or instigate crimes, hoping to collect large sums of money or valuables" (1893: 446).
10. The concept of "criminology" is the one that Latin American authors have used the most, since it was disseminated by Garófalo, according to Huáscar Cajías, who used it as the title of his compendium, which became a key text for law students in Bolivia (Cajías 1997 [1955]).
11. The mission managed to photograph only 208 individuals: 103 in the mining center of Pulacayo, apparently workers of the mining company that operated there, and the remaining 105 in the prison of La Paz (Zamorano 2011: 649).
12. An example of his influence on the Bolivian police is Lombroso (1938) (actually an excerpt from *El hombre delincuente*) and also Landa (1940).

5

The Indian as a "Born Criminal"? Lombroso and the Italian School of Positive Anthropology in Peru (1889–1930)

Gabriella Chiaramonti

Toward the end of the nineteenth century, following the dramatic events surrounding the War of the Pacific (1879–83), Peru was experiencing a period of relative political stability—the so-called "Aristocratic Republic"—and economic growth. Crime, however, was widely regarded as a persistent threat to the country's modernization, often associated with the poorest segment of society. These groups, largely made up of Black people, Chinese, and Indigenous peoples, were frequently considered inherently dangerous and unsuited to progress.

Concerns about crime had already surfaced in the mid-nineteenth century, sparking a two-pronged effort to address the problem: in January 1863, a new Penal Code was introduced, inspired by the principles of classical criminology, and between 1855 and 1862, a new prison was built in Lima, considered a decisive step toward rehabilitating criminals (Aguirre 1996: 55–63; Aguirre 1998: 73–4; Aguirre 2004: 309–29; Aguirre 2005: 17–39). However, the reforms of the 1860s largely fell short; the new prison system, limited to the capital, proved particularly ineffective in its attempt to reform criminals (Aguirre 1996: 63–8; Aguirre 2005: 91–5; Morón Ponce 2021: 38–43).

By the close of the nineteenth century, this situation created a favorable environment in Peru for the reception of the ideas of Lombroso and the Italian positive school, which were presented as a new tool for analyzing crime and crafting more effective social protection policies.

The "Exaggerations" of Lombroso

Javier Prado y Ugarteche was the first to introduce the ideas of the positive school into the Peruvian academic environment. In 1889, he defended a thesis titled *El método positivo en el Derecho Penal* at the University of San Marcos in Lima to earn a bachelor's degree from the Faculty of Law.[1] Prado valued the experimental method as the only legitimate approach to all sciences, including criminal science. He criticized the classical school of penology and its claims to be founded on absolute and eternal laws. Following the postulates of the new school, he argued that criminology needed radical reform: its focus had to shift from the abstract concept of crime to the criminals themselves, examining their physical and moral constitution and the influence of natural and social environment on their character.

Citing Ferri, Prado wrote that, just as ancient medicine studied diseases without considering the patient, so criminal law studied crimes as abstract entities, leaving the criminal in a secondary role. Although Prado accepted that an individual's organic and biological constitution could influence their spiritual and moral condition, he distanced himself from the extreme biological positions of Lombrosian criminology. Lombroso, he noted, had described in *El hombre delincuente* the meticulous details of physical and moral traits that connected the "born criminal" to the "savage." However, penetrating critiques by figures like Gabriel Tarde and Alexandre Lacassagne contested this view, arguing that by depicting the criminal as a "neo-savage," Lombroso's theory made atavism into a kind of original sin that left no room for remedy. Prado acknowledged that Lombroso had later modified this theory, and that the criminalists of the Italian school had sought to refute the accusation of having given insufficient weight to the social element. However, he maintained that the criticism remained valid, since, with the exception of Ferri, they had been almost entirely captivated by the biological factors of crime and studied social factors only superficially (Prado y Ugarteche 1985 [1889]: 132, 146, 170). As Aguirre observes, Prado's references to Tarde and Lacassagne indicate that by the late 1880s, criticisms of the Italian school were already circulating internationally, so when its ideas arrived in Latin America, they had to compete with theories that stressed the social environment's impact on crime from the beginning (Aguirre 2005: 44–7).

Nevertheless, the Italian school was gaining ground. In 1891, Manuel C. Barrios, a professor at the Faculty of Medicine, argued in his speech at the opening of the academic year for the need to move beyond the grand canon of metaphysical pseudosciences—namely the notion of free will—and to reform the Penal Code of 1863 based on advancements in criminal science. As a physician, Barrios was particularly concerned with imputability and criminal responsibility in cases of insanity or alcoholism. He proposed that the study of law should be accompanied by criminal anthropology and forensic medicine.

While some conclusions drawn from criminal anthropology appeared premature and exaggerated, Barrios believed that valuable lessons should still be drawn from it. He credited Lombroso and his school with highlighting the importance of incorporating scientific data, particularly biological data, into the analysis of delinquency. However, he maintained that other factors of crime, including social and cosmic influences, should also be given their due importance. Barrios did not intend to dwell on the popular theories regarding the etiology of crime, such as its connections to atavism, infantilism, degeneration, or madness, nor did he seek to address the notion of a "criminal type" or a "born criminal." Instead, he declared himself an eclectic, asserting that while he did not endorse a type in the anthropological sense, he acknowledged the existence of types in the anatomical and psychological sense. He emphasized that both social and individual influences play a role in the genesis of criminality (Barrios 1891).

Barrios's concerns about the accountability of the insane were well-founded. On this issue, lawyers and judges often clashed doctrinally and in the courtroom with doctors. The most notable case, referenced by both Barrios and Prado, was that of Lorenzo Macchiavello, a serial murderer. Initially sentenced to death, his sentence was commuted to fifteen years in prison after lengthy debates, following conclusions reached by a commission of three doctors who declared him afflicted with "impulsive madness" (Ulloa et al. 1890).[2] During the proceedings, prosecutor Manuel Atanasio Fuentes controversially argued that modern phrenologists and philanthropists did not recognize the existence of criminals, as human actions were merely the effects of "cranial prominences or depressions," which could not be altered by education or science. Therefore, he asserted that "penal codes and panopticons should be completely eliminated and replaced by schools and hospitals" (Ulloa 1890a). In the end, José Casimiro Ulloa, one of the commission members, wrote that the light of science had saved a victim from the gallows. He noted that Macchiavello was "the best portrait that Lombroso could have found for his Criminal Man" (Ulloa 1890b).

Between 1889 and 1910, as far as I could verify, more than twenty theses discussing topics related to Lombroso and the Italian school were defended at the University of San Marcos in Lima. During this same period, journals such as *El Diario Judicial*, *La Gaceta Judicial*, *El Derecho*, and *El Ateneo* published articles, essays, and conference proceedings on the same subject.

Most of these theses are rather modest works that, albeit sometimes critical, revisit the ideas of Lombroso, his followers, and his detractors.[3] The more extensive and detailed ones demonstrate a solid understanding of the topic, enriched with references to Italian scholars—primarily Lombroso, Garofalo, and Ferri—as well as to French, English, German, Belgian, and Spanish scholars. They also reference the major congresses where Lombrosian theories were presented and debated, namely those held in Rome in 1885 and Paris in 1889.

Almost all the authors of the analyzed writings shared an awareness of the radical changes brought about by Lombroso's theories in criminal law and recognized the credit due to them for introducing the research methodology of experimental sciences into social and legal studies. This approach dismantled the a priori conceptions of the old codes, developed a new understanding of the criminal, and introduced an innovative theory of crime and punishment. However, some believed that the new school was still in its infancy and that one should be cautious before accepting claims that were not sufficiently proven (Guinassi y Morán 1894; Portella 1905).[4] But even those, like Augusto Rios, who in his doctoral thesis presented to the Faculty of Law at San Marcos stated that he did not share the boldness and exaggerations of the Italian positivist school, acknowledged that it was provoking a healthy debate (Rios 1898: 116).

Beyond these shared beliefs, however, differing positions began to emerge. Some, like Manuel A. Muñiz (1891) and Jesús S. Salazar (1903), fully embraced the new ideas, arguing that there could be no doubt that the root of a criminal's behavior lay in his very nature, in "*something* inherent in the individual."[5]

More numerous were those who did not agree with Lombrosian theories. According to Luis Barros Méndez, a Chilean lawyer and politician, as well as the aforementioned Rios, the Italian positivist school was fundamentally flawed and lacked scientific rigor. They claimed that its "sectarians" employed statistical data and physical and physiological sciences to draw the "most adventurous" conclusions, ultimately destroying moral sentiments in many and undermining the role and importance of laws and the judicial apparatus (Barros Méndez 1890; Rios 1898: 75–6).

Echoing the arguments of Prado y Ugarteche and Barrios, critics feared that Lombroso's doctrine, by denying freedom of conscience and affirming the predominance of anatomical and physiological elements, would undermine the fundamental principle of responsibility for human actions. They argued that this perspective would replace accountability with an empiricism lacking a truly scientific basis. Andrés Menéses, a lawyer, wrote that this view reduced man to a "locomotive," making it inappropriate to punish or reward him for his actions—good or evil—since he acted solely under the impulse of the specific arrangement of his organs (Menéses 1892).

Regarding the notion of the born criminal, which "repulses our reason [because] we believe it impossible that there are people condemned to be devoured by the lair of crime," critics contended that this theory was neither scientifically nor practically substantiated. They viewed it as a product of exaggerations, generalizations, errors, and contradictions, such as that inherent in the very definition of an organic criminal (Jiménez 1898: 117; Portella 1905).[6] Its defenders had to concede that in many cases reality had disproved their conclusions, which were based on isolated and thus insignificant data. Enrique Eco-Aguirre, a student of criminal law, argued that by attempting to establish a correlation between anthropological characteristics and the psychic nature of the criminal, those authors effectively revived the phrenological theories of Franz Joseph Gall, which contemporary science had already discredited (Eco-Aguirre 1898: 342).

In an essay titled *El tipo criminal* Mariano Ignacio Prado y Ugarteche, brother of the aforementioned Javier, devoted considerable attention to Lombroso's observations regarding the skull and brain structure of alleged criminals. He particularly emphasized the significance that Lombroso attributed to the median occipital *foseta*, although he did not report, as Lombroso did, that this was typical among the Aymara. Years later, Carlos Morales Macedo would dedicate his doctoral dissertation in Natural Sciences to this topic (Morales Macedo 1911).

However, Prado did not share the importance that the positivist school attributed to such elements. He argued that there were no fixed or determined physiological or anatomical characteristics that could reveal an individual's criminality a priori. In his opinion, the theory of the anthropological type of the born criminal represented an exaggeration of the system, stemming from an absolute emphasis on anatomical and physiological elements over psychological and social factors as determinants of crime. This, he maintained, could not be accepted as a scientific criterion. Therefore, he concluded that it was appropriate for the positivist school to abandon this fantastical theory in favor of adhering strictly to the positivist method, through which it had revolutionized criminal law. While the school might lose some of its brilliance and novelty, it would gain in scientific truth (Prado y Ugarteche 1899–1900). On the other hand, according to Plácido Jiménez, since Ferri believed that born criminals constituted only 5 percent of the total number of delinquents, it was necessary to acknowledge that social factors held primary importance in the production of crime (Jiménez 1898: 184).

The issue of the death penalty frequently resurfaces, with most authors declaring themselves against it, arguing that it was repugnant to human conscience and should not be included in any legal code. Furthermore, drawing on data provided by Ferri and Garofalo regarding Italy and Spain, they noted its limited effectiveness, observing that crimes had not increased in countries where the death penalty had been abolished (Jiménez 1898: 122–32; Chaves 1898: 75, 106; Pineda Iglesias 1899: 65–86; Eco-Aguirre 1898).[7] Only Oscar Miró Quesada, the first professor of criminology at the University of San Marcos,[8] expressed strong support for the death penalty. He analyzed the case of what he defined as a born criminal (not coincidentally an Indigenous person) responsible for aggravated murder. He believed that, since life imprisonment did not exist in Peru, the death penalty was necessary. Miró Quesada shared the views of the positivist school, which based the right of repression on social defense: "Tigers," he wrote, "are not killed because they are responsible, but because they are tigers; criminals are not punished because they are guilty, but because they are criminals, that is, harmful and antisocial to the community" (Miró Quesada 1916: 283).

The concept of social defense, however, raised significant concerns for Augusto Rios. He argued that reducing the criminal to an abnormal being—insane, sick, or mentally retarded—conditioned by anatomical and physiological defects, and thus almost never punishable, was a mistake. He also believed it erroneous to adopt the idea that humans and society were organisms governed by laws similar to those that ruled the animal and plant worlds, as described in the theories of Darwin and Spencer. This interpretation led to a denial of the ethical reality of crime and moral responsibility, which was replaced by social responsibility and the concept of *temibilidad* (persistent dangerousness).

If crime, according to Garofalo's definition, was the violation of that part of the moral sense derived from the average level of fundamental altruistic feelings existing in a community—feelings essential for an individual's adaptation to society—then punishment was no longer a means of correction and redemption. Instead, it became the reaction of society itself against the person responsible for the violation. This could result in the individual's elimination, with no consideration for their dignity and rights. For Rios, invoking social defense to impose punishment meant introducing a concept that served as a justification for force, the ultimate and supreme reason of evolutionary philosophy. Therefore, he concluded that "the positivist theory led to the despotism of society and the negation of the higher aims of correction and morality that every good penal system must consider" (Rios 1898: 83–4, 106–8).

In summary, few authors of the analyzed texts adhered to the theories of the positivist school. Even those who praised its constructive aspects highlighted the unreliability of the data provided by Lombroso and expressed strong doubts about excessively biological determinism, the theory of the born criminal, and the death penalty. Conversely, even the most critical authors made some concessions. For example, M. I. Prado y Ugarteche admitted that "it was common for some criminals to have the characteristics of delinquency imprinted on their faces." And he emphasized, citing Darwin, Spencer, and Ernst Haeckel, how the Peruvian Indian was the irrefutable proof of the strength and intensity of heredity, as he "continues to be dominated by the weight of an unfortunate inheritance, which was perpetuated in his customs, his type, his characteristics with invincible persistence" (Prado y Ugarteche, M.I. 1900).

Indians and Criminality

The Peruvian population was ethnically diverse, comprising whites, Blacks, Asians, Indigenous people, and *mestizos*. Issues related to race and its impact on criminality were subject to constant scrutiny, primarily focusing on ethnic groups deemed inferior and dangerous—namely, Blacks and Chinese people but especially Indigenous people. The latter, according to the census conducted in 1876, constituted 57.69 percent of the total population, and in certain Andean departments, such as Ayacucho, Huancavelica, Cuzco, and Puno, they exceeded 70 percent and even 80 percent (*Censo* 1878, VII: 6–7).

Peruvian criminologists of that time rarely conducted original research, and when they did, the scientific rigor of their work was questionable, even by the standards of the era. This is evident in the works of Abraham M. Rodríguez, a future physician and professor at the School of Medicine of the University of San Marcos, and Paulino Fuentes Castro, a lawyer and the founder and director of *El Diario Judicial*.

Abraham Rodríguez conducted a study in the Lima penitentiary to analyze the physical and physio-psychological characteristics of inmates, aiming to identify born criminals. By examining photographs of the three hundred inmates,[9] he became convinced that about 10 percent exhibited signs of being born criminals, a belief he later confirmed through individual analyses. These evaluations also led him to establish a series of connections between types of crimes and the size of the cranial cavity. Drawing on Lombroso's observations, which suggested that the cephalic index tended to increase among criminals, Rodríguez noted that some of the inmates identified as born criminals exhibited marked brachycephaly, leading him to conclude that they belonged to the native race in Peru.[10] He also observed that the majority of inmates, including all the born criminals, exhibited a form of plagiocephalic deformation, the prevalence of which might seem excessive. However, if in Italy, according to Lombroso's observations, plagiocephaly characterized 20 percent of normal individuals and rose to 42 percent among criminals, Rodríguez inferred that "in our race … the proportion is extremely exaggerated in those who are predisposed to crime" (Rodríguez 1899: 5–15). As Aguirre notes, this association led to plagiocephalic deformation being identified as a sign of innate criminality among Indigenous people.[11]

In 1890, Paulino Fuentes Castro published several articles describing criminals in his magazine, which he intended to send to Lombroso to assess whether his own judgments aligned with those of the Turin professor (Fuentes Castro 1892b).[12] Notable among these were the cases of Manuel Peña Chacaliaza and Pedro Laredo, both Indigenous individuals whom Fuentes Castro unequivocally labeled as born criminals. Peña Chacaliaza, a serial killer, was described as a genuine moral anomaly, a contradiction to the laws of nature. He killed purely for pleasure, which Lombroso identified as a defining trait of the born criminal. The clear asymmetry of his face and various visible anomalies marked him as the perfect representation of a born criminal, driven to crime by inherent organic imbalances, an inevitability likened to gravitational force (Fuentes Castro 1892a). Pedro Laredo, also an Indigenous murderer, had similarly killed "for pleasure"; his hollowed face suggested idiocy, bordering on the simple-mindedness of an imbecile. An alcoholic with no moral education, Laredo's work as a cattleman forced him to live in isolation, which, Fuentes Castro argued, stifled intelligence and plunged him into "an atrocious state of savagery of which the Indians of the Puna, that is, the inhabitants of the high regions of the Andes, are worthy examples" (Fuentes Castro 1892c).

Although, as mentioned, positivist criminology was increasingly employed to analyze criminals, when it comes to Indigenous people and their definition, the impression is that late-century intellectuals and politicians did not need to rely on the questionable research of Lombroso's most devoted followers to develop their views on their inferiority. Scholars and political figures had absorbed the lessons of social Darwinism, but more importantly, the enduring colonial discourse provided them with a substantial basis on which to construct prejudices and stereotypes. Essays and speeches from the period circulating among the educated circles of the capital, such as those by Luis Carranza, Clemente Palma, Javier Prado y Ugarteche, and Mariano H. Cornejo, underscored this point. Notably, none of them mentioned Lombroso or the Italian school; instead, in his thesis presented to the Faculty of Letters and Human Sciences at the University of San Marcos, Palma cited Gustave Le Bon, as did Cornejo in his 1899 speech for the opening of the university (Palma 1897: 5, 8, 12, 21; Cornejo 1900: 33).[13]

A negative assessment of Peru's racial composition was widespread, with racial groups seen as locked in a perpetual struggle that stifled the development of a "collective soul": Blacks and Chinese were considered decidedly inferior; Blacks were regarded as strong, though akin to draft animals, while Chinese people were viewed as weak and degenerate. Cornejo depicted Indigenous people unfavorably by contrasting them with the white man, whom he considered the highest manifestation of the planet's vital energy. He wrote that Indigenous people lived in a sort of paralysis, akin to certain inferior animals that still retain organic forms but replace the mobility of living matter with the fixity of crystallized matter (Cornejo 1900: 32).

Carranza and Palma recognized that Indians were the main ethnic component of the nation, but they nonetheless described them in extremely negative terms. Carranza, a physician and founder of the Geographic Society of Lima in 1891,[14] asserted that "psychologically, the Indian of our time is, in the moral order of types, what the mammoth preserved in the Siberian sea ice is in the order of organic types." He added that "neither his education nor his nature allows him to serve as a solid foundation for a democracy, in the European sense of the word" (Carranza 1888: 81; 1892: 30). Palma viewed Indigenous people as physically weak, describing them as "men who cannot be called such … unfit for education." He envisioned a future where the useless elements would somehow disappear, leaving the Creole race to thrive—provided it joined with another race capable of making up for its deficiencies, namely the virile Germanic race. Javier Prado y Ugarteche shared a similar view, arguing that since the Indians did not see the homeland as their own and Black people were indifferent to their fate, the entire burden of nation-building fell on the Creoles. However, Prado insisted that the country's racial profile required transformation, advocating the spontaneous immigration of superior races while opposing the influx of inferior ones (Prado y Ugarteche, J. 1980 [1894]: 330–4).

Returning to the texts discussed earlier, mentions of the issue of race are frequent, albeit made up mostly of brief and entirely descriptive references in which, following Lombroso's teachings, it is indicated as a fundamental element in the biological classification of criminals. However, Ladislao Graña diverged from this view, arguing that race was not a biological factor, but rather a social one, since society could mitigate or even eliminate the negative characteristics of race by combating poverty and moral degeneration. Nonetheless, Graña also advocated for the unification of the diverse Peruvian race, envisioning the formation of a superior one that would instill the nation with the character and progressive ideas it lacked (Graña 1899: 727).

Hermilio Valdizán's thesis prevents a more extensive treatment of the theme of race. As a future psychiatrist, he sought to apply Lombroso's etiological factors to Peruvian delinquency, meticulously following the categories of analysis used by the Italian criminologist. Valdizán relied on data from the Section of Statistics and Anthropometry of the Lima Police Department, founded in 1892, allowing him to compile a series of tables and graphs exploring crime in relation to factors like climate, terrain, nutrition, alcoholism, opium and tobacco use, education level, age and sex, and economic conditions. His analysis paid particular attention to the link between race and criminality.

Analyzing data on individuals incarcerated by the Lima police over the previous eight years, he concluded that Indigenous people made up the largest proportion of inmates (43.29 percent of the total), followed by *mestizos*, whites, Blacks, and Chinese. This was understandable, he noted, since Indigenous people were the majority of the population. In his view, Indigenous criminality was the unavoidable result of external factors, especially the harsh conditions of their environment, where they lived "under a regime of incessant oppression [in which] violent reactions are easily explained." Since these conditions, rather than easing, were persisting and even worsening, the crime rates among the Indigenous race increased, further exacerbated by poverty, alcoholism, and coca use, which, Valdizán hypothesized, was responsible for "the painful inertia of a race that seems to sleep the dream of past greatness" (Valdizán 1910).

Years later, in 1919, José Antonio Encinas—a politician and educator, and prominent figure in the indigenist movement—revisited Lombroso and Garofalo's criminological categories, along with ideas from other scholars, from Tarde to sociologists like Alfred Fouillée and Charles Letourneau. This time, however, the aim was to refute them. In a text filled with tables and graphs, Encinas presented findings from interviews and criminal psychology tests with around a hundred inmates, concluding that Indigenous people were not lacking in moral sense, nor were they prone to suicide, laziness, vagrancy, or incompetent. Encinas argued that their inability to adapt to modern life was not due to inherent deficiencies but rather to centuries of neglect and contempt for their development since the time of the conquest. He saw Indigenous people as deprived of freedom due to the oppressive *gamonalismo* (exploitation of natives by large landowners) and the estate system, which had stunted their mental development. They certainly did not exhibit criminal traits rooted in atavism, as they had been guided by moral codes not only during the Inca empire but also in pre-Inca civilizations. In short, excluding murders committed under the influence of alcohol or driven by passion, "there were few indigenous people whose criminality could be encompassed within the formulas of absolute Lombrosianism" (Encinas 1919: 197–9, 202, 215).

In the 1930s Lombroso's ideas resurfaced briefly in the criminal sociology writings of Víctor Modesto Villavicencio. Villavicencio viewed the behaviors often deemed as vices in Indigenous people as a natural defense against the economic, political, and social oppression they endured. He suggested, however, that they continued to live as they had during the Colonial period, without aspirations, and that the crimes they committed fell into what Lombroso defined as violent and primitive delinquency (Villavicencio 1930: 65; 1933: 63).

Over time, however, extreme positions like those of Clemente Palma were gradually excluded from the official narrative, as they threatened to deny the possibility of a national destiny for Peru. Instead, a tendency was slowly prevailing that identified the poverty and conditions of semi-slavery that Indigenous people experienced as the root causes of their perceived "inadequacies."

In the debates of the early twentieth century, both in Peru and other Latin American countries, the question of nation-building and the role of the Indigenous people became increasingly unavoidable. "We need them," wrote Jorge Polar, while José Antonio Encinas stressed that true nationality resided in Indigenous people, as they were historically the rightful owners of Peruvian land, having worked and defended it: "If the Indigenous people were eliminated," he concluded, "the fields would not be plowed, the lands would not be cultivated, the mines would not be exploited" (Polar 1900: 167; Encinas 1932: 57–67).[15]

However, in 1895 and 1896, Peruvian rulers had approved a constitutional amendment and a new electoral law limiting voting rights to literate citizens, effectively disenfranchising the majority of the Indigenous population, who, under a prior indirect voting system, had previously been able to participate. This redefined the country's political geography, favoring the coastal areas and the cities populated by whites and *mestizos*. The decision to exclude a quantitatively and culturally significant portion of the population from political participation reflected a blend of positivist theories and colonial concepts of identity based on the georacial divide between the coastal and the Andean region (Huertas 2016: 51–2). This exclusion took the shape of institutionalized racism, which would become the implicit ideology of the modern oligarchic state, as Portocarrero suggests (Portocarrero 2004: 219), and persisted well beyond the era of the *república aristocrática*, as illiterate citizens would not regain the right to vote until the 1979 constitution.

Conclusions: The Legacy of Lombroso's Disciples

In Italy, following Lombroso's death, some of his followers shifted their focus from solely analyzing physical anomalies as signs of mental deviance to incorporating psychological aspects into their studies. This movement toward what Gibson defines as the "psychologization of positivism" had, in part, been initiated by Lombroso himself (Gibson 2002: 211–23).

A similar trend emerged in Peru between 1910 and 1927, marked by the establishment of three new journals: *La Crónica Médica* (1910), *Revista de Psiquiatría y Disciplinas Conexas* (1918), and *Boletín de Criminología* (1927). These were founded by doctors and psychiatrists Hermilio Valdizán, Carlos Bambarén, and Honorio Delgado. They featured articles centered on clinical-criminological observations, examining the relationships between crime and various factors, including epilepsy, alcoholism, psycho-sexual perversions, mental alienation, and the correlation between somatic constitution and forms of manic-depressive and schizophrenic psychoses. Bambarén, in particular, but also Valdizán, frequently referenced Lombroso and his disciples—especially Mario Carrara, Salvatore Ottolenghi, Enrico Morselli, Mariano Patrizi, and Sante De Sanctis—in their writings (Valdizán 1918: 166–76; Bambarén 1930: V–VII, 1–55).

In 1929, Bambarén became the first director of the Instituto de Criminología, modeled on a similar institution founded in 1907 in Buenos Aires by José Ingenieros. The institute struggled throughout its existence due to a lack of funding, ultimately condemned to languish without achieving its objectives (Aguirre 2005: 99–100). Its establishment was one of the innovations envisioned by the new Penal Code, which was drafted by a commission that included Víctor M. Maúrtua, a lawyer, diplomat, and professor at the University of San Marcos, after whom the code would later be named.

The new code came into effect in July 1924 and incorporated many principles championed by the positivists. These included the individualization of punishment and broad discretion for judges, a system of parallel penalties to differentiate between habitual and ordinary criminals, provisions for conditional sentencing and freedom, the development of criminal records, the establishment of specialized juvenile courts, specific measures for Indigenous populations, and the abolition of the death penalty.

The norms introduced concerning the Indigenous population represented an unprecedented effort in republican legislation. The living conditions—both material and cultural—of Indigenous individuals were considered mitigating factors that suggested alternatives to imprisonment. Those identified as "savages" living in the Selva (the eastern region of the country) and those defined as "semi-civilized or degraded by servitude or alcoholism," living in the Andean area, could be placed in agricultural penal colonies. Members of the latter group who led a disorderly and idle life could also receive work education treatment (Hurtado Pozo 1979: 25–9).

Members of the *Société Générale des Prisons* in Paris positively evaluated an earlier version of the project presented by Maúrtua in 1919. Luis Jiménez de Asúa, a highly esteemed Spanish jurist, described the Peruvian code as a modern law that could be ranked among the most advanced legislative texts ("El Código Maúrtua" 1919: 64; Jiménez de Asúa 1926: 32, 57–8). In many respects, the text drew inspiration from codes and projects from several countries, including Spain, Switzerland, Germany, and Argentina (Hurtado Pozo 1979: 21–4, 50–6). However, Jiménez de Asúa noted that its underlying ideology closely resembled the Italian project by Garofalo and Ferri, which emerged from the recent legal trends established by the positivist school. The concept of social defense, particularly the notion of "dangerousness," one of the most significant contributions of penal sciences, was fully embraced by the Peruvian code. The terms "danger," "dangerousness," and "dangerous state" frequently appeared in its articles, indicating the criteria judges should use to determine the appropriate measures, with a wide range of punitive options that was essential for the individualization of punishment (Jiménez de Asúa 1926: 47–50).

Several years later, the potential developments and serious implications of the concept of "dangerousness" would be made explicit in an essay by Susana Solano, published in Lima in 1937. As Bambarén noted in the introduction, this essay had initially appeared two years earlier in the *Archivio di antropologia criminale*, a journal founded by Lombroso and then directed by Mario Carrara. Solano, referencing Garofalo, Jiménez de Asúa, and many other Italian positivists (including Ferri, Filippo Grispigni, Salvatore Ottolenghi, Benigno di Tullio, Giacinto Viola, and Nicola Pende), emphasized the need to recognize dangerous states outside of crime that still disturbed social harmony and constituted noncriminal dangerousness. Examples of such conditions included prostitution, homosexuality, drug use, alcoholism, vagrancy, and begging (Solano 1937: 1, 5, 54). As Aguirre points out, the inclination to evaluate even noncriminal or pre-criminal dangerousness would eventually lead to the surveillance and scrutiny of entire segments of the population, particularly Indigenous peoples, who were often associated with coca use and alcoholism (Aguirre 2005: 53–5).

In conclusion, the most significant and enduring legacy of Lombroso's theories and the Italian school of positive anthropology in Peru lies in the fields of criminology, forensic medicine, and particularly in the legal and penal systems, rather than in debates related to race, particularly Indigenous race, and the relationship between race and criminality. The 1924 Code faced resistance from Peruvian judges, who deemed it utopian and difficult to implement due to a lack of adequate institutions. Nevertheless, the Maúrtua Code remained in effect until 1991, albeit with notable modifications, including the introduction of the death penalty and anti-terrorism laws that partially contradicted its fundamental principles (Zuñiga Rodríguez 1991: 515–16).

Notes

1. Javier Prado y Ugarteche and his brother Mariano Ignacio belonged to one of the most powerful families in the country. Both were lawyers and held very important positions in academia, politics, and the economy.
2. The full documentation relating to the trial is reproduced in *El Diario Judicial*, I, 1890, September 9–November 22.
3. Many of these theses are analyzed in Aguirre (2005: 40–64).
4. Guinassi and Morán defended his doctoral thesis at the Faculty of Law in Arequipa. Portella was "a medical student": see Aguirre (2005: 51).
5. Italics in the original. Salazar read his bachelor thesis at the Faculty of Law of the University of San Marcos; Muñiz was a physician specializing in psychiatry.
6. The central objective of the doctoral thesis that Jiménez defended at the Faculty of Law of the University of San Marcos was the study of the social causes of crime. See Aguirre (2005: 44–5, 51–2).
7. Chaves and Pineda presented their doctoral dissertation and bachelor's thesis, respectively, at the Faculty of Law of San Marcos.
8. In 1922, O. Miró Quesada published *Breves apuntes de Mesología Criminal Peruana*, in which he presented a broad summary of Lombrosian theories, emphasizing how crime should be studied "with mesological criteria" (1922: 54).

9. In 1892, the *Sección antropométrica y fotográfica* was created at the *Intendencia de Policía* in Lima, at least partially as a result of the spread of Lombrosian ideas: see Morón Ponce (2021: 164–7).
10. In a previous thesis (1898: 400), he had concluded that brachycephaly was the most pronounced and general characteristic of the entire Peruvian race.
11. Aguirre (2005: 43–4). See also Sansone (2022: 97), and Caimari (2009: 197).
12. In the letters available in the ACLM (http://www.museolombroso.unito.it/info/archivio-storico), I found no trace of correspondence between Fuentes Castro and Lombroso.
13. Mariano H. Cornejo was the first professor of Sociology at the University of San Marcos.
14. About Carranza and the Geographic Society, see López-Ocón (2001).
15. On the ambiguities of indigenism, see Aguirre (2005: 48, 9).

Part II

Criminal Anthropology and Racisms

6

How the Median Occipital Fossa Became Aymara

Maria Teresa Milicia

> *On a gray and cold morning in December 1870, while anatomizing the skull of the brigand Villella, I found there a whole long series of atavistic anomalies; and among them an enormous median occipital fossa that corresponded to a great hypertrophy of the Vermis, so as to form a true median cerebellar hemisphere, as in the lower vertebrates.*
>
> *At the sight of that skull, which from that day forth I considered to be the totem and the fetish of criminal anthropology, I seemed to see all of sudden, lighted up as a vast plain under a flamed sky, the problem of the nature of the criminal—an atavistic being who reproduces in our times the characteristics of primitive man, extending all the way back to the carnivores.* (Lombroso 1907a: 501–2)

Cesare Lombroso's famous account of "how criminal anthropology was born" positions the discovery of the anomalous median occipital fossa as the cornerstone of his theoretical elaboration on the born criminal and its atavistic nature.

This final retelling, which followed several earlier versions, was published a few years after the scientist's death in 1909. While the founding event acquired a mythic quality, Lombroso never questioned the scientific value of the "discovery." His attempt to prove that the fossa was indeed a result of atavism became an obsession, beginning with his initial writing on the subject, "Existence of a median occipital fossa in the skull of a delinquent" from January 12, 1871. In this chapter, I aim to trace the most significant stages of the ensuing debate surrounding the atavistic interpretation of this anatomical feature. The literature produced was vast and highly specialized, and the timeframe considered here spans the most intense phases of the controversy over its significance, from 1871 to 1876 in Italy, and from 1883 to 1895 internationally.

The primary goal of my reconstruction is to clarify Lombroso's theoretical and methodological design, which culminated in his decision to name the median occipital fossa typology—found in the skull of Calabrian "brigand" Giuseppe Villella—after a South American people, the Aymara. In May 1883, "La fossette aymarienne chez les criminels et dans la race humaine" appeared in the *Bulletin de la Société d'Anthropologie de Paris* (Lombroso 1883b: 409–10). An important clue to understanding the feverish research leading to the decision to use the ethnonym Aymara emerged from a letter sent in 1882 by the anthropologist Paolo Mantegazza, founder of the Italian Society of Anthropology and Ethnography, who was a colleague and friend of Lombroso.

By examining the median occipital fossa from this perspective, I uncover the deep substratum of Lombroso's Darwinism, a topic that, while certainly not new, remains worthy of further study.[1] In the critical edition of *Criminal Man*, Mary Gibson and Nicole Hahn Rafter emphasize the crux of Darwin's influence on Lombroso, engaging with the then-pioneering studies of Renzo Villa (1985) and Delia Frigessi (2003), which tended to downplay his importance (Lombroso 2006: 462–3). Lombroso's response to the criticisms regarding the Darwinism of his theory, expressed in the preface to the fourth edition of *L'uomo delinquente* (1889: XLVII–XLVIII), stands in stark contrast to what is embodied in the atavistic genesis of the fossa.

Due to the limits of this chapter, I have been unable to address the complex relationship between Mantegazza, Lombroso, and the figure of Darwin, which surfaced while following the fossa, and which, in my view, adds a small but significant piece to the constellation of early Italian Darwinism. Despite the sheer breadth of the thematic issues covered, I have endeavored to present a persuasive picture of the deep connection between the Italian reception of evolutionism and the development of criminal anthropology.

The interest Lombroso's discovery garnered in the scientific community would be incomprehensible if the mystery of man's origin could not be glimpsed in the heart of the fossa. An analysis of the specialized literature reveals that the outcome of the research was not unanimous, and the question of the atavistic nature of the alleged anomaly remained unresolved. The chapter concludes with the return journey of the Aymara fossa to its country of origin, which coincided with the spread of Lombroso's theories to South America. The "criminalidad aymará" had already made its way there with Bautista Saavedra (1903: 171–209), a jurist and future president of Bolivia, when the *fosita aymará* was referenced by Carlos Morales Macedo, a physician and naturalist and member of the Geographical Society of Lima, in his dissertation on the anatomical anomalies of Peruvian skulls (1911). The new research benefited from the impressive number of skulls collected over more than a century from the burial grounds and ruins of the great Inca empire, a resource that was not available to Lombroso.

The Aymara ethnicity today unites indigenous peoples who share the same language and a collective historical memory of colonial oppression and resistance, primarily located in the border territories between Peru, Bolivia, and Chile (Mamani Yanqui 2021). I would like to caution the reader that the historical approach of this text involves quoting expressions that may be upsetting or offensive to Aymara people. My heartfelt intent is to contribute to the knowledge of the material and symbolic despoliation and exploitation suffered by the Aymara people over time.

In Darwin's Shadow: The Latent Germ in Lombroso's Theory

The notion of atavism first emerged within eighteenth-century plant breeding practices. Antoine-Nicolas Duchesne, a botanist and gardener at Versailles, grappling with the spontaneous reversion of the cultivated pansy to its original wild form, coined the French term *atavisme*, derived from the Latin *atavus*. While the underlying causes remained obscure, this empirical notion of atavism was well established by the time Darwin's theory of evolution revolutionized the natural sciences in the 1860s—precisely during the formative period of Lombroso's scientific interests. *On the Origin of Species* was first published in Italy in 1864, translated by Giovanni Canestrini and Giovanni Salimbeni. In the chapter on the Laws of Variation of Species, Darwin explains the principle of reversion or atavism: "Distinct species present analogous variation; and a variety of one species often assumes some of the characters of an allied species, or reverts to some of the characters of an early progenitor" (1859: 157; 1864: 125).[2]

The Variations of Animals and Plants Under Domestication (1868) soon followed, the work in which Darwin's emphasis on the importance of the law of reversion comes through most strongly. Systematic analysis of millennia-old practices in plant and animal crossbreeding, alongside ongoing experimental observations, confirmed the clear presence of laws of biological inheritance: "Reversion, in the ordinary sense of the word, comes into action so incessantly, that it evidently forms an essential part of the general law of inheritance" (Darwin 1868, vol. 2: 400).

Reversion, most significantly, lent empirical support to evolutionary theory by tracing characteristics of present-day beings to their extinct progenitors. In particular, the second volume of *Variations* foreshadows Darwin's eventual treatise on the human species. Extraordinary parallels in embryonic development between humans and animals, along with rudimentary organs like the human coccyx (a remnant of a tail), suggest a permanence "written with an invisible ink" of traits dating back to ancient progenitors that may emerge after only a few generations, or "a wonderful fact," even after hundreds and thousands of years (ibid.: 50).

In this concise exploration of atavism, the impact of Darwin's theories on the founding ideas of criminal anthropology becomes evident. The roots of Darwin's influence on Lombroso's early academic and scientific development can be traced through select excerpts from his correspondence, which are significant considering that most of his letters have been lost. Even before the Italian translation's release, Lombroso was familiar with Darwin's celebrated volume (Lombroso 2006). In a letter dated September 15, 1863, addressed to Jacob Moleschott—a Dutch physiologist then teaching in Turin—Lombroso proposed including a passage from *The Origin of Species* in the Italian version of *Kreislauf des Lebens*, which he was working on at the time.[3] In that same year, he was in charge of a private course in the Clinic of Mental Diseases and Anthropology at the University of Pavia, while also directing the hospital department and the anthropological-psychiatric cabinet (Cenno Storico 1873: 111–16).

In 1866, Lombroso delivered a series of public "lectures for ladies" on the origins of humankind and human races, later consolidated in *L'uomo bianco e l'uomo di colore* (UBUC) (1871c). The structure of the volume and the circumstances surrounding its elaboration further underscore Darwin's influence on Lombroso's ongoing research. On May 13, 1871, Lombroso wrote to Angelo De Gubernatis, lamenting "the cruel publishing conditions" that had delayed the book's publication by three years, "which is a century for this subject." The work had in fact been "written when the Huxley, the Canestrini, and the Darwin had not yet appeared … and now I have to largely redo the work so as not to appear with so much tail and … [*sic*] beard [i.e. out of fashion]."[4]

In reality, the evolutionist framework of Lombroso's work was already established, and it drew extensively on Darwin's major works available at the time. When *The Descent of Man* began appearing in July 1871 in fourteen installments—edited by Michele Lessona and translated by his wife, Adele Masi (Forgione 2018: 379)—Lombroso's concern for further updating UBUC is apparent in a lengthy footnote (Lombroso 1871c: 121–2). Here he notes: "At the moment of correcting the proofs Darwin's new work appeared, before which these poor lines will seem like an attempt of pygmies." In the same footnote, Lombroso also reflects on the crucial assumption of the "pithecoid theory," namely the tendency of variability whereby "the anomalies … are almost as frequent as the rule … This variability sometimes depends on the arrest of development, on a regression to the primitive pithecoid characters, on the disuse of some organs, on the increased use of others."[5]

The Aymara people serve as a representative population for examining the variabilities related to the use and disuse of organs: "the Aymaras, who live in the highest regions of the world … have a longer trunk and shorter arms than the European and Negro, and the humerus is indeed shorter than the forearm, the femur than the tibia" (ibid.: 122).[6] With these words, quoted from Darwin, the *Aymará* entered Lombroso's sphere of interest for the first time.

The Middle Cerebellar Fossa and the Trilobate Cerebellum

In the horizon inflamed by Darwinism, something decisive had happened in December 1870: Lombroso discovered an anatomical anomaly "unique in the natural and pathological history of man" (Lombroso 1871a: 37) that anchored the young scientist to the theory of atavism, ultimately propelling him toward the future science of criminal anthropology. Immersed in evolutionary thought and eager to update his "treatise on races," Lombroso noticed the "existence of a median occipital fossa in the skull of a delinquent," which had been resting undisturbed in Pavia's anthropological cabinet for at least six years. The skull belonged to Giuseppe Villella, a Calabrian convict who had died in Pavia's San Matteo Civic Hospital on November 16, 1864.

The median occipital fossa is located internally at the occipital base of the skull, which houses the cerebellum. The cerebellum, consisting of two hemispheres, includes a central formation that extends downward with an appendage called the *vermis*.

In his two nearly identical articles on the median occipital fossa published in 1871, Lombroso introduced the scientific community to the embryonic form of criminal anthropology. Based purely on conjecture, he declared that the median occipital fossa in the examined skull was an imprint on the bone created by a development of the *vermis* so abnormal that it constituted a true third lobe of the cerebellum. Without having performed an autopsy on Villella—"I, however, cannot vouch for anything other than the skull I have under my eye" (ibid.: 38)—the young scientist interpreted the anomaly through the lens of evolutionism, envisioning a trilobate cerebellum resembling those of species far removed from humans. In describing the anatomical features obtained from the cast of the brain, he introduced the hypothesis of the "arrest of development," a familiar concept to specialists that referred to the embryological origin of a malformation:

> The shape assumed by the wax cast in the cranial cavity, from which results a very regular trilobate cerebellum as in five-month-old fetuses, make us certain that that fossa served for the receptacle of a median lobe in the cerebellum. (ibid.: 39)

This precise passage marks the "quilting point" where Darwinian ideas are directly tied to the fossa, which otherwise would hold no atavistic significance. The presence of a trilobate cerebellum in the anatomy of a fully developed adult follows the law of reversion, aligning precisely with Darwin's assertions in *The Descent of Man*, specifically in the chapter "On the manner of development of man from some lower form."[7]

As we will see later, Lombroso would rely on this line of reasoning to counter critiques of his atavistic interpretation. According to Darwin's gradualism, the law of reversion disregards standard taxonomic boundaries, as "the embryo of man closely resembles that of other mammals" (Darwin 1871, vol. 1: 16). Furthermore, "the marvelous fact that the embryo of a man, dog, seal, bat, reptile &c. can at first hardly be distinguished from each other" can only be explained if one assumes an ancient common progenitor (ibid.: 32).[8] The entry of lemurs into Lombroso's discovery should be understood in this perspective:

> The only trace of a median occipital fossa along with the clear development of a median cerebellar lobe is beginning to be seen in some platyrrhine monkeys and Lemurids … which many would now exclude from quadrumans [primates] and classify among rodents. (Lombroso 1871a: 40)

Aware that he is trespassing into the realm of "natural philosophy," Lombroso reveals an ambition that his median occipital fossa may be used as evidence to support the gradual nature of evolution in the controversy surrounding the pithecoid theory:

> [It] serves to support that theory, so ably trickled down to us by Canestrini, that man [would be] a transformation of an animal progenitor simultaneously of bimans and quadrumans, [a concept] which already rests on anatomical analogies with one and the other. (ibid.: 40–1)

This decisive step places the discovery at the center of the evolutionism debate, legitimizing the circumstantial method to which positivist scientists were forced to resort to in the absence of empirical proof for the existence of a trilobate cerebellum. Most importantly, it underpins the "bold gesture" of creating a new paradigm for the study of the nature of the criminal man:

> Important, however, to note that this cranial anomaly, like others which I hope to expound, was discovered in that unhappy variety of man, which I believe to be more pathological than the alienated: criminal man (ibid.: 41)

> It is important, however, for natural philosophy that this more-than-pithecoid anomaly should have been observed in that species of man, the criminal, that departs more from our type than that of the Negroes and Yellows. (Lombroso 1871b: 65)

The variants of the two closing sentences in the early articles on the median occipital fossa reveal the ambivalent core of Lombroso's criminal anthropology. Atavistic anomaly, viewed as the effect of natural law, coexists with anomaly as a pathological degeneration within the original fabric of his theoretical construction. The two components were revealed to be in tension only when faced with the mounting criticisms from various fronts, prompting the founding father to defend the "anomalies" of his creation. The criminal species and unfortunate pathological people emerge from the same embryo, incubated in the median occipital fossa.

In Pursuit of the Elusive Third Lobe

The news of the discovery of a trilobate cerebellum in the skull of a criminal immediately made headlines. Andrea Verga, considered the father of Italian *freniatria* (an archaic term for psychiatry, not to be confused with phrenology), entered the debate by pinpointing the weak point of Lombroso's discovery. In his observations, Verga had already noted a slight depression in some skulls, which he termed the "median occipital dimple."[9] Lombroso's description of an extraordinarily wide fossa, he acknowledged, could be "the finest example described" (Verga 1872: 275), an exceptional variant of the dimples he had identified in the skulls of an epileptic and a demented pellagra sufferer. Nevertheless, Verga was unwilling to conclude that this feature was an imprint of a trilobate cerebellum:

> So certain is he [Lombroso] shown to be that this median occipital fossa contained a middle lobe of the cerebellum, that in some papers he was naturally spoken of more for having found a middle lobe of the cerebellum than for having found a median occipital fossa. But the presence of a middle cerebellar lobe would represent such a regression in the scale of animal formation that it would make a man in whom it occurred more monstrous than one with two horns or a tail ... To find such a structure developed to the extent supposed to be in Villella, one would have to descend as far as the rodents. I cannot venture to admit that a third lobe of the cerebellum is nested there; I would need Prof. Lombroso and Prof. Zoja to assure me that they have seen this third lobe, or middle lobe of the cerebellum, with their own eyes. (ibid.: 275–6)

The unresolved question of the autopsy—in which he had not only never participated but which had left no trace of any cerebellar anomaly in the autopsy notes[10]—continued to haunt Lombroso, who could only reinforce the Darwinian point of reference to defend the fragility of his fossa. The wax cast reproduced a clearly visible protuberance, yet it said nothing about its intrinsic pathological or atavistic nature. It might have been a congenital cyst, a tumor, or a venous varix.

Lombroso responded with a dense article in which he addressed, with a rigor not typical of him, all the "useful and fruitful" objections of the esteemed psychiatrist (1872: 1058–65). In it, he defends the conjectural approach fundamental to advancements in paleontology, but above all, he insists on the plausibility of reversion, referencing the same cases of "monstrosity" cited by Darwin—without, however, ever naming the British naturalist. This omission was likely related to the context of the debate with fellow colleagues, who were grounded in "autoptic empiricism" and uninterested in the "metaphysics of naturalists." However, to defend the trilobate cerebellum hypothesis, Lombroso cites Ernest T. Hamy, president of the *Société d'Anthropologie de Paris* (ibid.: 648), who, in fact, reiterated Darwin's argument on how to recognize true atavism:

> Whenever a structure is arrested in its development, but continues growing until it closely resembles a corresponding structure in some lower and adult member of the same group, we may in one sense consider it as a case of reversion … and it is hardly credible that a part arrested at an early phase of embryonic development should be enabled to continue growing so as ultimately to perform its proper function, unless it acquires the power of continued growth during some earlier state of existence, when the present exceptional or arrested structure was normal. (Darwin 1871, vol. 1: 122)

Lombroso's brigand, in fact, had not manifested pathologies or teratologies that would have prevented him from living to the age of sixty-two, and he might have lived even longer had he not fallen victim to the prison diseases prevalent at the time. That third lobe could have been, and for Lombroso certainly was, a congenital condition of an atavistic organ directly influencing criminal behavior. The main issue, however, could not be circumvented:

> There always remains, however, that final objection: to be so bold as to conclude and suppose the existence of a median lobe that has not first been touched with the hands or seen with the eyes. It is an objection to which it is impossible to respond with absolute certainty, for in our science, nothing is absolutely certain but what the evidence of sight or touch confirms. (Lombroso 1872: 1064)

This final subtle objection also applied to Verga. Nothing conclusive could be asserted until a comprehensive experimental study, with a large case series, yielded reliable results. The search for *fosse* and *fossette* mobilized anthropologists, anatomists, and zoologists. Numerous autopsies during this period were conducted with maniacal attention, in the hope of finally touching and seeing at least a hypertrophic vermis, if not the third lobe of an ancient progenitor (Lombroso and Bizzozero 1873; Lombroso and Bergonzoli 1874; Foà 1874; Tamassia 1874).

In 1876, Verga concluded his research after a series of autopsies he personally conducted. The presence of numerous hypertrophic vermis, both with and without fossa, led him to inject a plaster solution "with a funnel" into the arachnoid canal of four fresh heads to map the empty spaces between the soft tissues and the cranial vault.

The experiment revealed that subarachnoid fluid forms a cushion between the occipital bone and the vermis, which prevents sufficient pressure from leaving an impression. Thus, he concluded that the existence of a trilobate cerebellum could not be inferred from examining a dry skull alone (Verga 1876: 13).

Contrary to what one might expect, the fossa with its supposedly atavistic features was by no means discredited. Despite increasingly specialized investigations and conflicting findings, the possibility of a median cerebellar lobe was never entirely dismissed. Canestrini unambiguously included the median occipital fossa as evidence for humanity's animal origin (1877: 215). Lombroso and his collaborators examined hundreds of "dry" skulls and "fresh" cerebella, as did independent anatomists (Lombroso 1876). However, the impossibility of proving the regressive origin of Villella's paradigmatic case persisted. Once again, Lombroso invoked Darwin to bolster his obsessive pursuit. He sought recognition for the connection between the middle occipital fossa and the law of reversion, drawing a parallel with the malar bone in the two-month-old human fetus, which Canestrini described and Darwin cited as a prime example of arrested development or reversion (1871, vol. 1: 124–5). Research, Lombroso argued, should extend to different human races, especially ancient races who, as Darwin put it, "stand somewhat nearer in the long line of descent to their remote animal-like progenitor" (ibid.: 120).

La fossette Aymarienne

"I would very gladly do your errand, but I could not read in your letter the most important words, what do you want me to look for 'occipital' in the skull of savages?" So wrote Mantegazza on October 24, 1882, in response to his friend Lombroso's request for data on the presence of the median occipital fossa in exotic and ancient specimens within the extensive craniological collection of the Museum of Anthropology in Florence. Anyone aware of the amount of research triggered by the median occipital fossa since 1871—from the article that appeared in the first issue of Mantegazza's journal to the others that followed, including increasing citations in anatomy textbooks—will grasp how malevolent the question must have sounded to Lombroso's ears. Mantegazza pressed on:

> I understood, however, that you also want to know something about the extraordinary development of the mandibles. I have 2,000 skulls, you know? It is perhaps the third-largest, and in terms of culture, the second collection in the world. (Mantegazza 1882)

Lombroso was well aware of the fact that in those years his friend had the most interesting collection of human craniums (Mantegazza 1871). Mantegazza, who aside from being an anthropologist was also a member of parliament, had a great reputation and a robust network of connections. As early as 1871, the collection had been enriched by a donation from Dr. Enrico Mattei, an ophthalmologist who had emigrated to Chile and, like many other compatriots, was traveling to the "new world" in search of treasures to acquire for his distant homeland (Comunicazioni 1884: 390–1).

On November 26, Lombroso wrote to Luigi Pigorini, director of the National Prehistoric and Ethnographic Museum in Rome, to ask for help in his search for data on the median occipital fossa. After expressing dissatisfaction with Mantegazza's unjust denial, he inquired about American, Papuan, and prehistoric skulls: "I suspect that this anomaly is more frequent than in moderns but I have but few figures on the subject."[11]

In 1883, the article "The median occipital fossa in human races and criminals" (1883a) was published, in which Lombroso presented the results of his recent research. He had finally found the perfect "ancient and semi-civilized race" to substantiate his thesis of atavism. On May 17, 1883, at a meeting of the *Société d'Anthropologie de Paris*, a translation of the article was read with a new and intriguing title: "La fossette aymarienne chez les criminels et dans la race humaine" (Lombroso 1883b: 409–10). His observation of ten Aymara skulls revealed a 40 percent occurrence of the *fossette*, allowing him to assert, "From the data table, it's clear the name Aymarian fossa I gave to this anomaly stands unchallenged."

The appropriation of the Aymara ethnonym can be seen as a genuine international branding operation. Throughout the nineteenth century, the interests of racial craniology had focused on the populations inhabiting the territory of the Inca empire destroyed by the *conquistadores*. Three centuries earlier, vast burial grounds—known as *huacas* or *aya-huaci*—had been raided in search of the fabled riches of the New World. Scientific explorations in the late eighteenth and early nineteenth centuries unearthed new archaeological and anthropological treasures—human remains. In burial grounds and *chullpas*—the burial towers mentioned by Ludovico Bertonio in *Vocabulario de la Lengua Aymara* (1612)—ethnographers extracted specimens of skulls variously modified through infant head compression techniques.

Scientific journals announced sensational discoveries, such as those made by the naturalist Joseph Barclay Pentland (Remarkable 1834). The invention of the "Ancient Peruvians," which Christopher Heaney considers "America's racial baseline" (2023, 110), was part of a racist project aimed at classifying native peoples, as seen in *Crania Americana* (1839). Similarly, the "Aymara Nation" identified by Alcide D'Orbigny in *L'Homme Américaine* (1839: 306–29) spurred new interest in collecting Peruvian skulls and mummies, which became highly sought-after anthropological relics.[12]

The *fossette aymarienne* quickly captured interest. On November 26, 1883, Paul Albrecht, an expert in embryology and comparative anatomy, presented a paper titled "Sur la fossette vermienne du crâne des mammifères" at the Anthropological Society of Brussels. The contribution provided a thorough reconstruction of the Italian debate, focusing on the comparative examination of specific anatomical details of the "interesting fossa" across various animal species—details that he believed had been overlooked in previous studies (Albrecht 1884). Albrecht confirmed Lombroso's atavistic interpretation:

> Among the Aymara … it is undeniable that inferior races, the insane, and criminals may possess savage characteristics, which closely resemble those of lower mammals today and likely also those of the wild ancestors of the human species. (ibid.: 152)

However, as indicated in the title, Albrecht preferred to refer to it as the "vermian fossa," aligning more with anatomical morphology. His study elicited a response from Giulio Chiarugi, chief editor of the *Monitore Zoologico Italiano*, who offered a markedly different perspective on Lombroso's discovery. For Chiarugi, the concept of atavism could not be applied to all *fossette* without first considering the embryological development of the occipital bone, which is not merely a passive container (Chiarugi 1885: 341). In conclusion, he identified two distinct varieties of fossae: the "vermis fossa," proposed by Albrecht, which corresponds to the imprint of the third lobe on the bone and is a normal feature in animals, in rare cases manifesting as an atavistic phenomenon in humans; and the *fossetta del Lombroso*, named in honor of the scientist who first described it, which is much more common in humans and corresponds to a bony depression of variable size, independent of the development of the vermis. Therefore, it is irrelevant to comparative morphology and lacks atavistic significance (ibid.: 343–4).[13]

The *fossetta del Lombroso*, devoid of atavism, is merely an empty shell—an original emptiness stemming from the irretrievable loss of Villella's cerebellum. On the other hand, since no one has ever "seen and touched" that precious organ, no one can conclusively disprove Lombroso's hypothesis with empirical evidence. In this sense, the empty fossa continued to symbolize an open gateway to the abyss of human origins, serving as an inexhaustible resource for the proliferation of fetish objects within the scientific imagination of the time. Lombroso remained firmly convinced of the atavistic significance of his fossa. Beginning with the third edition of *L'uomo delinquente* (1884) and in all subsequent publications, up to his last article on the fossa (Lombroso 1903b: 34–56), the Aymara became part of the fetish of criminal anthropology.

Conclusions: *Desde los tiempos de Lombroso la Fosita Aymará*

Lombroso eventually abandoned the term *fossette aymarienne*, even in *L'homme criminel* (1888b). The term did not fare well in Italian either, appearing only sporadically in French (Debierre 1895) and as "aymara fossa" in English (Russel 1900). Lombroso's coinage remained largely dormant for over two decades.

In 1911, Carlos Morales Macedo, a natural sciences student at the University of Lima, wrote his thesis on the anatomical variations of Peruvian skulls, inspired by the renowned fossa, which became *fosita aymará*. In his study, however, the original atavistic-racial connotation was reshaped to fit the framework of Peruvian nationalism.

As a member of the new generation of scientists trained after the War of the Pacific (1879–83),[14] Macedo actively participated in the revitalization and modernization of a Peruvian nation that had suffered the humiliation of Chilean occupation. This period witnessed cultural policies aimed at reclaiming archaeological heritage, countering rampant collecting practices, and promoting the nationalization of anthropological and geographical knowledge. The establishment of the *Sociedad Geográfica de Lima* in 1888 epitomized this transformation (Riviale 2002: 37–59). The ongoing tensions with

Chile over territorial boundaries reverberated through scientific disputes concerning the interpretation of the pre-Columbian and pre-Incan past, with a pronounced emphasis on asserting territorial primacy in the origins of Andean civilizations.

Macedo drafted his thesis during the years between the First Pan-American Scientific Congress in Santiago de Chile (1908) and the XVII *Congreso Internacional de Americanistas* in Buenos Aires (1910). This period was marked by intense discussions among Chilean scholars and Max Uhle, director of the *Museo Nacional de Lima*, who advocated for the recognition of Peruvian Inca influences within Chilean territories (Crow 2022: 146–50). Macedo examined a substantial number of skulls, utilizing the archaeological classification proposed by Uhle. Many specimens were sourced from the Museo Nacional collection (Macedo 1911: 126). The theoretical approach and research method remained consistent, as the purpose was to verify the validity of Lombroso's data and the investigations that followed the discovery of the *fosita*.

Macedo's examination of 912 skulls from the Museo Raimondi, the *Museo Nacional de Lima*, and his own collection revealed significant inconsistencies in the 40 percent figure that Lombroso calculated based on just ten skulls of uncertain provenance. As expected, Macedo's statistics were accurate, and he precisely indicated the origins of the skulls. He expanded the nomenclature of the median occipital fossa, including variants such as *clásica*, *en boceto*, and *especial*, while criticizing the *Aymará* designation for imposing "on our race the stigma of criminals" (ibid.: 14).

The scientific conclusions of the study, however, align with Lombroso's thesis. Macedo found that various *fosites* undoubtedly exhibited an atavistic character, with ancient Peruvian races displaying a 10 percent occurrence of this "anomaly," which was higher than in all other races. Consequently, "the exaggerated frequency of this anomaly in the skulls I have examined," Macedo argued, "constitutes a character of inferiority for the ancient races of Peru" (ibid.: 42). Furthermore, his analysis of another anomaly enabled him to position ancient Peruvians within the general hierarchy of human races: "somewhat inferior to the white race and far superior, certainly, to the Mongolian, Malay, Australian, and Negro races" (ibid.: 201). In the concluding lines of his thesis, Macedo expressed hope that the scientific data presented would help support the view of "the autochthonous origin of American man or his descent from races that lived in very remote ages" (ibid.: 202).

In conclusion, the arrival of the *fosita aymará* on the American continent illustrates the agency of the symbolic *dispositif* as it is emptied and filled with new meanings. In the search for the remote foundations of the Peruvian nation, the atavism associated with the *fosita* becomes a chronotype of the autochthony of a very ancient race. The stigma of the "criminal race"—*our* race Macedo emphasized—had no foundation. Ancient races exhibit atavistic traits not because of the law of reversion but because they exist at a lower stage of human evolution.

The *fosita* must expel the atavistic connotations of criminality while reinforcing the deep amalgamation of race and nation at its core. However, in the nationalist project, the tension remains between the inclusion of the ancient Peruvian race and discrimination against the living descendants of the same race, who are deemed "somewhat inferior" to the colonizers' race. *Desde los tiempos de Lombroso la fosita Aymará* continued its journey.

Notes

1. After the final draft of this chapter, Paolo Mazzarello published a volume that examines in depth, for the first time, Lombroso's controversial debt to Darwin (2024).
2. Darwin prefers the term reversion. Atavism is recalled only in *Variations*, in reference to the usage prevailing in botany.
3. The epistolary exchange with Canestrini during his translation of *The Origin of Species*, if it ever existed, is now lost. On Moleschott in Turin and his relations with Lombroso, see Forgione (2018: 275–84). LP, Letter of C. Lombroso to Jacob Moleschott, September 15, 1863.
4. LP, Letter of C. Lombroso to Angelo De Gubernatis, May 13, 1871.
5. Use and disuse is a cardinal principle of the Lamarckian conception of the heritability of acquired traits. On the reception of Lamarckism, see the historical overviews from the perspective of contemporary neo-Lamarckism (Ward 2018: 23–33).
6. "It is here seen that the extended arms of the Aymaras are shorter than those of Europeans, and much shorter than those of Negroes" (Darwin 1871: 119). The source is David Forbes (1870), with whom Darwin had an assiduous correspondence.
7. Lombroso draws on it for the footnote in UBUC, mentioned above.
8. I discussed the influence of the post-Darwinian recapitulation theory enhanced by Ernst Haeckel in Milicia (2014: 61–74).
9. It is worth noting that in this early debate Lombroso used the Italian term *fossa* and Verga the diminutive *fossetta*.
10. I have previously reconstructed the autopsy affair, attributable to Giovanni Zanini, who had already passed away when Lombroso discovered he possessed Villella's skull (Milicia 2014). ACLM, Registro dei pezzi del Gabinetto antropologico di Pavia (1864–6), 477.
11. LP, Letter of C. Lombroso to Luigi Pigorini, November 26, 1882.
12. See Heaney (2023) for a comprehensive overview of scientific collecting and burial spoliations in the Inca territory. On D'Orbigny, see also Riviale (2002).
13. Lombroso did not like the honorific designation at all. In the review note to Chiarugi's article, he omits to mention the "fossetta del Lombroso" (Lombroso 1885: 535–6).
14. See Chiaramonti's contribution to this volume.

7

Prisons, Laboratories, and Museums: Cesare Lombroso and His Presence in Mexico in the Late Nineteenth Century

Laura Cházaro García and Gerardo García Rojas[1]

Introduction

Cesare Lombroso (1835–1909), as widely recognized as he was controversial, extended his presence far beyond Italy, with his criminal anthropology penetrating many countries, including Mexico. Studies have highlighted how his work influenced discussions among physicians, lawyers, and anthropologists in Mexico, many of them amateurs, particularly in relation to theories of "dangerousness." This characteristic was believed to be inherent in certain individuals, and was debated by certain specialists in jurisprudence in the 1910s, culminating in 1929 with the *Código Penal del Distrito y Territorios Federales* (Penal Code for the Federal District and Territories). Although this legislation was revoked only two years later, the debates on the "dangerousness" of certain sectors of the population, and the potential for identifying them using Lombrosian concepts, persisted among Mexican jurists. In the 1940s, a group of exiled Spaniards, including Mariano Ruiz-Funes (1889–1953) and Constancio Bernaldo de Quirós (1873–1959), added their voices to those debates, inspired by their keen interest in the writings of Lombroso's school of criminology (Speckman 1992; Urías 2000; Piccato 2001; Buffington 2001; Caimari 2009; Sansone 2022).

Lombroso's presence in Mexico can, however, be traced back several decades earlier to practices associated with the collection and measurement of crania and skeletal remains, aimed at determining the character of the Mexican population. These practices were carried out in particular by physicians working in museums, hospitals, and prisons toward the final decade of the nineteenth century.

To better understand the effects of Lombroso's criminology, this chapter explores the medical, anthropological, and prison practices, as well as the material objects, that his theories produced or were associated with. How can we interpret Lombroso's late-nineteenth-century works in relation to the collection of crania and anthropometric studies in Mexico? This question arises because his writings were never applied uniformly or comprehensively. Beyond juridical debates, Lombroso's works were read in conjunction with French medical and anthropological theories, many of which arrived in Mexico during the French military intervention in support of Maximilian of Hapsburg, which lasted from 1861 to 1867 and enabled the establishment of the *Commission Scientifique du Méxique* (Mexican Scientific Commission) (García 2016).[2] This historical connection explains how and why certain practices associated with the so-called "Italian school of criminal anthropology" were implemented in prisons, medical laboratories, and museums.

This text thus explores the material practices, objects, and subjects that reflect Lombroso's fleeting presence in Mexico (Latour 1995). Assuming that the spaces and places of science shape a differentiated production of ideas and objects, we examine three settings to elucidate the varied influences of Lombroso's theories, while highlighting certain discontinuities and contradictions (Livingstone 2003: 7). These spaces are the anthropology cabinet at the State Penitentiary of Puebla (1891–1900); the physiology laboratory at Mexico's *Instituto Médico Nacional* (IMN, National Institute of Medicine), adapted for anthropometric research on behalf of the *Ministerio de Instrucción Pública y Bellas Artes* (Ministry of Public Education and Fine Arts, 1907–1915); and the anthropology salon at the *Museo Nacional* (National Museum, 1874–1915). Our aim is to demonstrate how Lombroso's ideas took material form in these places, where concepts of degeneration and criminality were translated into practices and objects with distinct methods of production and circulation.

As we will see, crania and body measurements, taken from infant and adults, were used to generate statistical tables that recorded the frequency of certain traits. These tables were based on Lombroso's belief that criminals could be identified by anatomical characteristics, thought to reveal innate predispositions to delinquency. This theory triggered a significant shift in ideas about criminality and punishment.

We also emphasize that the boundaries created by these settings were porous. The skull collections from the Puebla penitentiary eventually found their way to the *Museo Nacional*, acquiring new meanings and destinations along the way. Similarly, measurements taken in the physio-anthropometry laboratory at the *Instituto Médico* were incorporated into tables exhibited at the *Museo Nacional*, later serving to classify children in schools managed by the Ministry of Education. In this way, ideas from Italian jurisprudence were received in Mexico and took root in unexpected places like laboratories and schools (Buffington 2001: 79).

The Anthropology Department at the State Penitentiary of Puebla (1891–1900)

In the final decades of the nineteenth century, under the federal government of General Porfirio Díaz (1830–1915), several new juridical, educational, and scientific institutions were established as part of public policies that emphasizing hygiene. Among these initiatives was the creation of a penitentiary in the city of Puebla in 1891, based on the administrative model of the Auburn State Prison in New York. The new prison was innovative, organizing activities in schools and workshops during the day, while at night confining the inmates to individual cells (Cruz Barrera 1999: 75). This approach reflected a growing concern with criminality, its causes, and methods of punishment.

These priorities were reflected, for example, in the establishment of an infirmary and an Anthropology Department responsible for analyzing inmates' anatomical characteristic and their possible links to criminal behavior. The Anthropology Department was divided into a laboratory, a statistics office, and a museum, and was directed by Dr. Francisco Martínez Baca (*c.*1850–?), assisted by Dr. Manuel Vergara (1862–1948). Both physicians treated patients in the infirmary,[3] which also served as a "laboratory" and attracted jurists interested in "penal law and forensic medicine," many of whom saw prisons as ideal places for field research (Martínez Baca and Vergara 1892: 5).

In the laboratory, inmates' bodies were measured, and their data recorded on paper. Photographs were also taken, mostly of their naked torsos and their faces captured from both the front and profile. Such practices were not entirely new in Mexican prisons. In the capital, for instance, photographs and anthropometric measurements were ordered by judges in order to aid the identification of repeat offenders, but these were primarily kept for administrative purposes and were not collected consistently from all inmates, and thus frequently became obsolete.[4] The Anthropology Department in the Puebla penitentiary transformed this practice into a standardized and systematic process. It not only gathered anthropometric and medical data of convicts but, later, also of the wider Mexican population.

In addition to mandatory records detailing the birthplace, religion, crime, age, occupation, race, biography, and education of inmates (Starr 1897: 14), penitentiary staff also recorded physical measurements. Doctors utilized several instruments, including a Jacquart goniometer built by the *Escuela Politécnica* in Puebla, a Stein cephalometer, a Broca stereograph, a Morton craniometer, and a Mosso plethysmograph and ergograph. Once the data were collected, they were sent to the statistics office, where they were compiled and analyzed using statistical methods. The resulting tables were representative of criminality in Mexico, considered as a collective issue.

Martínez Baca and Vergara's studies were rooted in the research of Paul Broca (1824–1880), who believed that humanity could be classified into distinct racial groups, each identifiable and categorizable through physical measurements. Like many of his followers at the *Société d'Anthropologie de París*, Broca believed that the identification of populations inherently implied hierarchies, though he did not argue for the superiority of any specific group. Instead, he saw racial diversity as stemming from distinct responses to different environments (Cryle and Stephens 2017: 157). This theory echoed late-nineteenth-century debates among Mexican physicians and scholars regarding people identified as "indigenous," and the potential for advancing their development through education (García Rojas 2021). If Broca's assertion that race depended on environmental factors was accurate, then it followed that it was possible to stimulate racial evolution.

Lombroso, in his *L'uomo delinquente* (1876), stated that criminality was an exceptional human condition, more akin to the behavior of children and animals than to that of the general population (Lombroso 1887c: 7). Seen in this light, the racial differences posited by Broca diminished in relevance, as Lombroso's criminal anthropology focused on distinguishing the anatomical features of only two types of individuals: the "normal" and the "criminal" (Cryle and Stephens 2017: 181). The criminal category was further subdivided, with specific morphological traits being associated with particular crimes, such as homicide, rape, or robbery (Lombroso 1887c: 422–8).

However, since no consensus could be reached on the definition of "normality"—a dilemma similar to the challenge Broca and his disciples faced in defining race—Lombroso's criminal anthropology gained practical significance in discussions about criminal responsibility (Lombroso 1892b). According to Lombroso and some of his contemporaries, including jurist Enrico Ferri (1856–1929), this problem could be solved by identifying hereditary and atavistic deviations that, according to their theory, were characteristic of criminals (Lombroso 1887c: 276).

Like Lombroso, doctors in the Puebla penitentiary used anthropology to identify traits of Mexican criminals, contributing to debates on punishment during a period when "progressive" industrialization, hygiene initiatives, and urbanization schemes were implemented by federal and local governments. These changes attracted mixed responses from economically marginalized sections of the population (Piccato 2001: 53). To these concerns, the penitentiary physicians added their focus on Mexico's Indigenous people and their capacity—or lack thereof—for "progress" and "civilization" (Urías 2000). From this perspective, Martínez Baca and Vergara determined that many of the inmates they studied, most of whom were identified as Indigenous, exhibited certain criminal "deviations," as all the races in the world did. In contrast to Lombroso who, as mentioned, made a binary distinction between criminals and normal people, the Puebla penitentiary doctors devised a racial classification system more in line with Broca's approach. Their work oscillated between identifying the distinctive characteristics of the "Indigenous" race and those associated with criminality (Martínez Baca and Vergara 1892: 59).

In addition to recording information from live inmates, the penitentiary doctors also studied osteological remains. Martínez Baca and Vergara, like Broca, believed that the brain provided the primary indication of an individual's or a race's "degree of civilization and perfection." However, as was common among their contemporaries, they faced practical challenges in preserving organic tissues that obliged them to focus on more durable "containers; that is, crania and other bones, objects that endured without any extensive treatment after criminals died, and so could be measured with great facility" (ibid.: 10).

The Anthropology Department's third hall housed a museum where the skulls and brains of deceased inmates were displayed alongside other osteological and anatomical specimens, as well as confiscated weapons, photographs, signature records, and items crafted by prisoners in the workshops. It is likely that the museum was open only to other physicians and experts in criminology, and its establishment was characteristic of the approach to Mexican criminality in this period, focusing mainly on taking anthropometric measurements and conducting statistical analysis.

In 1892, a year after the penitentiary's establishment, Martínez Baca and Vergara published *Estudios de antropología criminal* (Studies in Criminal Anthropology), a book presenting the measurements from the first collection of crania examined in the Anthropology Department. This collection consisted of twenty-six subjects, categorized as "Indigenous," "mestizo," or "of the Mexican, Totonaca, and Mixtec-Zapotec family" (ibid.: 40). The doctors measured cranial weight, volume, and several angles, then compared these findings with anthropometric data from the German physician Moritz Benedikt (1835–1920) (1881). Among the most important measurements was the facial angle, an index popularized by Broca's anthropometric work in the 1880s (Blanckaert 1987: 442). Lombroso considered this angle a vital marker for distinguishing different classes of criminals. To take these measurements, Martínez Baca designed a new instrument, the metapogoniometer, modeled after Broca's goniometer. The device was positioned on the nose in such a way that it formed an angle with the depression in the forehead.

The average angle reported for twenty-six crania measured with the metapogoniometer was 23° 47′ for nineteen Indigenous subjects, and 24° 8′ for seven *mestizos*. The highest and lowest readings corresponded to inmates who had committed murder—36° and 15°, respectively—while measurements for thieves ranged from a maximum of 26° to a minimum of 24°. Martínez Baca and Vergara noted that these findings diverged from Lombroso's, who associated a more pronounced forehead depression with delinquents who had committed crimes against property rather than crimes against persons (Martínez Baca and Vergara 1892: 66). Like their observations of live inmates, Martínez Baca and Vergara's cranial measurements followed Lombroso's typology, although their subsequent analysis integrated a racial classification, introducing a spectrum of normality and, thus, of criminality:

> We believe that the normal or regular is not to be understood as that which is perfect, symmetrical in form but, rather, the form of crania that is common to the race studied. It [involves] asymmetries, protuberances, and depressions, so the majority reflect the same features, except for the natural modality and those related to age, sex, climate, or environment, from which one can extract very important factors that mark changes over time in new generations. (ibid.: 59)

The book *Estudios de antropología criminal* was presented at the World's Columbian Exposition of 1893, where it came into the hands of Lombroso (Monroy, 1893; Cruz Barrera 1999: 70), who initiated a brief correspondence with the Puebla doctors. Lombroso acknowledged their research as the first contribution to criminal anthropology by non-Italian experts in ten years, a view that led to the publication of an Italian translation (Martínez Baca and Vergara 1894). Their relationship lasted a few more years, during which Martínez Baca published *Los tatuages. Estudio psicológico y médico-legal* (Tattoos: A Psychological and Medical-Legal Study, 1899). As the title suggests, this work marked a departure from the approach based on anthropometric measurements, attempting to establish a psychological link between tattoos and the evolutionary status of the minds of their bearers (Martínez Baca 1899: 5). Lombroso praised the book as "the most perfect of those composed up to now in the scientific world," promising to have it translated and published in book form in his *Archivio di psichiatria* (Lombroso 1900d: 12).[5]

Lombroso received his most enthusiastic response in Mexico from the physicians at the Puebla penitentiary, though his work was not without critique. While Martínez

Baca and Vergara accepted his criminal typology, they adapted it by incorporating a racial variable linked to the Indigenous population. In this context, and through the material convergence of live bodies, crania, and instruments, the Anthropology Department produced intertwined conceptions of criminality and Indigeneity.

The National Institute of Medicine and the School Hygiene Inspection Office of the Ministry of Public Education (1907–15)

In 1907, nearly concurrent with research at the Puebla penitentiary, Dr. Daniel Vergara Lope (1865–1938)—unrelated to Manuel Vergara—began gathering anthropometric measurements of school-age children at the public hospice in Mexico City. A physiologist at the *Instituto Médico Nacional* (1889–1915), Vergara Lope undertook his project at the behest of the *Inspección de Higiene Escolar* (School Hygiene Inspection Office, founded in 1888), an agency within the *Ministerio de Instrucción Pública y Bellas Artes* (Ministry of Public Instruction and Fine Arts) responsible for overseeing the physical and mental health of pupils and teachers.

From 1890, Vergara Lope had been conducting research at the Experimental Physiology Laboratory of the *Instituto Médico Nacional* (IMN), focusing on high-altitude respiration. His goal was to demonstrate that inhabitants of Mexico's high central plateau (1,200–2,250 meters above sea level) breathed "normally." French physicians who settled in Mexico after the French military intervention—contemporaries of the well-known physiologist Claude Bernard (1813–1878)—had concluded that Mexicans, both Indigenous and *mestizo*, suffered cerebral anemia due to the thin air at such altitudes. Dr. Dénis Jourdanet (1815–1892) termed this condition "anoxyhémie barometrique," asserting that the rarefied air predisposed Mexicans to anoxemia, thereby condemning them to live as "a miserable race" (Jourdanet 1861: 65–6).

Lombroso himself, who was interested in how climate and geography affected the lives and pathologies of different racial populations, engaged with Jourdanet's work but rejected his conclusions. He argued that the physical and moral condition of Mexicans—compared to others subjected to the same geographic circumstances—could not be reduced to physiological factors. In his view, these did not impose limits on intellectual or muscular function, as demonstrated by the achievements of Mexican civilizations throughout history (Lombroso 1878: 120–1).

Vergara Lope was trained in experimental methods and in taking measurements to assess the normal or pathological functioning of live bodies, whether animal or human. Like his colleagues Martínez Baca and Vergara, as well as European anthropometrists, he relied on instruments to eliminate "errors of observation" and the "personal equation" (Vergara Lope 1890). His focus was on obtaining precise "facts" to support an analysis of supposed "Mexican pathologies" and explain the possible causes of criminal and mental disorders (Blanckaert 2009: 154). This issue was considered of great importance, and Vergara was far from the only Mexican physician concerned with the medical and political implications of Jourdanet's theory, which had gained the support of leading Parisian physiologist, including Paul Bert. A disciple of Claude

Bernard (1813–1878), Bert was the author of *Leçons de la Physiologie de La Réspiration profesées au Muséum d'Histoire Naturelle* (Lessons on the Physiology of Respiration, Taught at the Museum of Natural History, 1870).

As we will see, another physician, Alfonso Luis Herrera (1868–1942), also contributed to research aimed at demonstrating the benefits of high-altitude environments for inhabitants of Mexico's central plateau. Together with Vergara, he published *La vie sur les Hauts Plateaux, influence de la presion barométrique sur la constitution et le Dévéloppement des Êtres Organisés. Traitement climatérique de la Tuberculose* (Life in the Highlands: The Influence of Barometric Pressure on the Constitution and Development of Organized Beings. Climateric Treatment of Tuberculosis, 1899), a work that was awarded a prize by the Smithsonian Institution.

The question of respiration, given its implications for people living at high altitude, became a concern in various academic and scientific circles, including the *Sociedad Indianista* (Indianist Society). There, historian and engineer Ricardo García Granados urged professors and jurists to collect comparative data in order to assess "the physical and moral qualities of the young people of diverse races, subjected to the same education" (García Granados 1911: 82).

Vergara Lope acquired a range of physiological instruments, including some devised by the French physiologist E. Jules Marey (1830–1940) and manufactured in France by instrument-maker Charles Verdin. His collection included cardiographs, sphygmographs, and pneumographs. Like Martínez Baca, however, he also designed and built his own instruments, such as the *toracometro* (thoracograph), which was used to take chest measurements. Like other contemporary physicians, Vergara Lope believed that respiratory capacity was related to the width of the chest, making torso measurement crucial. He was also interested in measuring crania to determine reasoning capacities, measured facial angles using Broca's goniometer, and utilized dynamometers and ergographs to assess muscular strength. Additionally, he utilized instruments from the Turin physiologist Angelo Mosso (1846–1910), particularly his ergographs and electrical coils, which he used to test cutaneous and acoustic sensitivity. Due to the interest generated by Mosso's research and inventions, in 1902 Dr. Fernando Altamirano (1889–1907), then director of the IMN, wrote to Cesare Lombroso and Dr. Edoardo Perroncito, director of the School of Medicine in Turin, inviting them to collaborate as honorary members of the IMN.[6]

Armed with IMN's array of instruments, the laboratory staff conducted extensive measurements on children, assessing the thorax, extremities, chest, and head (including facial and cranial angles), as well as the muscular strength, ocular function, and auditory capacity.[7] Like Lombroso—who believed that children possessed an innately perverse character akin to that of delinquents, but that this could be corrected through education (Guarnieri 2006: 269)—Vergara maintained that maladies caused by deviations and vices could also be cured. If children with criminal or deviant tendencies could be reformed, then his research presented an opportunity to demonstrate that schooling could "rescue" Mexicans (Granja 2009).

One particularly significant outcome of Vergara's studies was the creation of physio-anthropometric cards and profiles in his laboratory. These records reflect a synthesis of methods drawn from Lombroso and Broca, supplemented by the techniques of

Louis Alphonse Bertillon (1821–1883), Martínez Baca, and Manuel Vergara. The cards belonging to each child featured photographs (face and profile) reminiscent of those of registered criminals. They were strictly organized and divided into three columns: the first recorded "personal" data and observations on behavior or "character," the second contained the photographs alongside inhalation and exhalation measurements taken by the thoracograph, and the third documented full-body measurements, including data on hearing and eyesight. The intention appears to have been to progress from the personal or subjective plane to a more precise, statistical approach. Each card also included a profile image reproducing the anatomical geometry of the child's body on graph paper (Cházaro and Rodríguez de Romo 2006: 45–51).

Importantly, these cards were not kept solely by the School Hygiene Inspection Office, as we know that Vergara Lope's team of physicians used them to test theories regarding children's "minds" and "intelligence." This indicates that the federal government sought to shape educational activities through medical precepts based on the technologies of anthropometric measurement. The resulting graphs soon began to circulate and, under the influence of Lombroso, made their way into classrooms, where children were subjected to exercises designed to establish a relation between their physical measurements and their intellectual abilities.

The National Museum of Mexico (1872–1920)

Although it operated only intermittently following its creation in 1825, the *Museo Nacional de México* experienced a period of institutional stability in the late nineteenth century. During this time, archaeological antiquities unearthed in remote regions of the republic were showcased as evidence of the nation's origins, aligning with the cultural project of Porfirio Díaz's government. Those artifacts formed a prominent display in the museum's main salons (Rutsch 2007: 111), but beyond antiquities, the museum housed a Natural History Department dedicated to collecting plant, animal, and mineral specimens. An Anthropology Section was added in 1895 when Mexico City hosted the XI International Congress of Americanists, the first such event held in the Americas.

The newly established section was placed under the direction of the previously mentioned naturalist Dr. Alfonso Luis Herrera, along with Dr. Ricardo E. Cicero (n.d.). In addition to photographs, plaster molds, and ethnographic objects, osteological remains were important exhibits. To expand the museum's collection of crania and other pre-Colombian skeletal remains, Herrera and Cicero turned to archaeological excavations under way in the capital, such as in the Santiago Tlatelolco neighborhood. They also sought loans from other collectors, including the army officer Protasio Tagle (1839–1903) and Martínez Baca in Puebla. The latter was asked to contribute crania from the Puebla penitentiary, along with the statistical tables detailing the results of his research (Herrera and Cícero 1895: 106).

Herrera seized the opportunity to exhibit findings from the aforementioned research on high-altitude physiology he conducted with Vergara Lope. Later, he and Cícero presented statistical charts of their thoracic measurements, arguing that "acclimatation to the altitudes is complete" in the Mexican population, and that "anoxemia does not exist" (ibid.: 105). They had intended to present the results of their original research in the museum, but the hurried planning for the new salon, combined with limited instrumentation, hindered their ability to record the measurements and statistics of the craniological collection.

As these objects, human remains, and statistical tables were transferred to the museum, Cesare Lombroso's influence began to wane, despite his continued significance for physicians in Puebla and those at Vergara's Anthropometry Laboratory. However, traces of his legacy remain in the classifications and typologies used to assess both inmates and children. These classifications were taken from charts and tables that linked the crimes of the former and the behavior of the latter to craniometric and bodily measurements.

The Anthropology Section continued to operate after the Congress of Americanists, though with slight modifications. Dr. Nicolás León (1859–1929) replaced Herrera and Cícero, and was appointed Professor of Ethnology in 1903. After a brief resignation (1907–11), he returned to lead the newly established Anthropology Department following its separation from the natural history collections in 1910. From that point on, Léon concentrated on expanding osteological collections and establishing an anthropometric laboratory to reinforce the discipline's ties to physical anthropology (García Murcia 2013: 148). His work remained connected to that of the physicians in Puebla, where in 1912 Manuel Vergara continued to head the penitentiary's Anthropology Department (León 1919a: 237).

Meanwhile, in 1900, Martínez Baca was recruited by the newly founded Mexico City Penitentiary, to organize an anthropometric identification service.[8] He left the position just two years later for unknown reasons. By 1910, however, he had joined the Anti-Reelectionist Party of Francisco Ignacio Madero, a political opponent of President Porfirio Díaz. The following year, after Madero's rise to power, Martínez Baca was appointed Mexican consul in Los Angeles, California. Likely influenced by Lombroso's view on anarchists,[9] he denounced the activities of Mexican anarchists in the United States, led by the brothers Ricardo and Enrique Flores Magón, whom he described as dangerous and insane (*La entrevista Creelman* 1916: 5; Comisión de Investigaciones Históricas 1966: 307).

In 1908, the *Escuela Correccional para Mujeres* (Correctional School for Women) in Mexico City also introduced an anthropometric identification service, although it followed the methods of the French criminologist Alphonse Bertillon.[10] This institution was short-lived, as its later directors—the physicians Rafael Carrillo (n.d.), Miguel Lasso de la Vega (n.d.), and Manuel Guillen (n.d.)—showed little interest in anthropometric studies, at least compared to Daniel Vergara Lope, Manuel Vergara, and Martínez Baca.[11] Anthropometric measuring systems continued to be implemented in Mexican prisons into the early twentieth century, but without a unified approach. Over time, the focus shifted from identifying criminal traits, as Lombroso had proposed, to the administrative registration of convicts.

When the Mexican Revolution broke out in 1910, major prisons across the country were attacked, leaving their anthropology departments ransacked and in ruins. However, in 1913, from his position in the *Museo Nacional*, Nicolás León reached out to institutions with an interest in anthropology, including the biometry laboratory at the *Escuela Nacional de Altos Estudios* (1910–23), then led by Franz Boas, as well as penitentiaries around the country.[12] In 1916, he successfully arranged for the transfer of 126 skulls from the Mexico City penitentiary to the museum, likely with assistance from Martínez Baca.[13]

In 1919, León reported that the Anthropology Museum at the Puebla penitentiary had been abandoned, with more than half of its collection lost to armed rebellions. Only around 300 crania remained. Despite León's best efforts to have them relocated to the *Museo Nacional*,[14] Puebla's state authorities rejected his proposal, citing their intention to restore their museum. However, this project did not come to fruition until 1939,[15] by which time the collection of skulls had been reduced to just 144 specimens.[16] León's negotiations reflect the *Museo Nacional*'s broader efforts to centralize osteological collections from private collectors and various other sources: by 1922 it housed 1,299 specimens (León 1922). While León took additional measurements of these remains, he always respected the ones taken by Martínez Baca and Vergara (León 1919b), which were highly regarded as graphic representations of the crania of Indigenous groups and their supposed criminality.

Unlike Herrera and Daniel Vergara Lope, Nicolás León did not measure live bodies, even though this approach had been proposed.[17] He distanced himself from the measuring techniques that linked this practice to the creation and classification of criminal typologies. While the crania that came to him from prisons never ceased to be associated with criminality, his interest in the Anthropology Department lay in the racial classification of the population identified as Indigenous.

The Physical Anthropology Office at the *Museo Nacional* collected extensive series of crania from specific geographic areas in an effort to correlate place of origin with craniometric indices. Beyond distinguishing criminal types and identifying pathological characteristics within populations, León used these measurements to classify and define categories of Indigenous peoples, such as the Tarascos, Chontales, and Mayas.

Although the craniological collections were a notable attraction in the museum's Anthropology Department, they never rivaled the importance of the Archaeology Department. The former occupied only two rooms—one dedicated to taking measurements and the other to displaying specimens. Anthropometric studies took place in a marginal area of the museum, and León frequently lamented the lack of proper instruments. Despite these limitations and the secondary status of anthropometry within the institution, he remained tirelessly devoted to taking measurements throughout his life.[18]

Final Considerations

Prisons, laboratories, and museums served as spaces where Lombroso's ideas circulated, leading to the creation of various types of objects—some derived from living bodies, others from crania and bones. Although the instruments used, like the crania and subjects measured, were fragile and have largely disappeared over time, the measurements, charts, and tables have endured. These records established classifications and categories that differentiated specific population groups, such as criminals, schoolchildren with behavior problems, and individuals of diverse racial backgrounds. The sites examined were thus marked by the circulation of bodies and bones, transformed into data through anthropometric measurements.

Marco Galloni (2015) argues that no single instrument defines Lombroso's School. However, in the case of the Mexican physicians connected to the Italian jurist, we know that the tools they employed were widely used. In the Americas, as in Europe, it seemed possible to realize the potential of medical and anthropological knowledge through instruments that ensured scientific rigor. In this way, Lombroso spurred advances in measurement and identification practices. Once recorded in physio-anthropometric tables and cards, those measurements became standardized units that could be compared and interconnected, and eventually emerge in recognizable forms across different times and places. On a global level, records of criminals, the sick, and Indigenous people could be easily transferred and interpreted in France or Italy, in contrast to the crania or bodies of children and adults, dead or alive.

One avenue through which Lombroso's influence entered Mexico was the confrontation between abstract jurisprudence with instruments that systematized measurements and techniques used to preserve crania—an intersection that ultimately facilitated the emergence of a science of criminality. However, variations in climate, geography, and racial differences obliged Francisco Martínez Baca, Manuel Vergara, Daniel Vergara Lope, and Nicolás León to recognize the inherent limitations of drawing broad conclusions from the studies of the earlier figures who inspired them, whether those in France or Italy.

Moreover, this pursuit of generalizations raised fundamental questions: given the numerous distinct races and cranial features, what should be considered the standard of "normalcy"? And how did the crania from the Puebla penitentiary and the bodies of children from the Mexico City hospice become transformed into materials for collections, museum exhibits, and objects for public display? Exhibited in this way, the discourses and practices underpinning typologies of Mexicans—whether defined by race or supposed vices—continue to echo the Lombrosian methods that sought to define "the Mexicans" and determine their place in human history.

Notes

1. We are indebted to Daniel Herrera for his help with the archives consulted. This chapter was supported by the Horizon 2020 MSCA RISE project "SciCoMove," Scientific Collections on the Move (1800–1950)," GA No. 10100757.
2. According to Pablo Piccato (2001: 64), Lombroso's works were read in Mexico in French translations by Gabriel Tarde and Alexandre Lacassagne. For this reason, we referred to those French translations in our research.
3. Both studied medicine and worked together for eight years (1891 to 1899) at the *Gabinete antropológico* in Puebla. After their separation, Manuel Vergara remained in charge of the *Gabinete* until 1902, and published an article titled "Influencia del sexo

en la criminalidad en el Estado de Puebla" (Influence of Sex on Crime in the State of Puebla) in 1904. He was a professor of biology at the *Colegio del Estado* until 1929. In 1900, Martínez Baca was hired to work in the newly established Anthropology Cabinet of the General Prison, known as Lecumberri, in Mexico City, but resigned a few months later.

4. AHCDMX, 1900, Fund: Ayuntamiento/Gobierno del DF, Section: Cárceles, Subsection: Cárceles en general, vol. 505, File: 1150, 3.
5. In 1900, a glowing review of Martínez Baca's book appeared in *APS*, signed by P. Artom (1900: 512–15).
6. AGN, 1902, Fund: Secretaría de Instrucción Pública y Bellas Artes (SIPBA), Box: 124, File: 5, 132–6.
7. Vergara did not work alone. He had a team of two doctors and an illustrator. AGN, 1902, Fund: SIPBA, Box: 132, File: 3.
8. AHCDMX, 1901, Fund: Secretaría de Gobierno del DF, Section: Empleados de la Penitenciaría, Box: 1, File: 49.
9. Cesare Lombroso identified anarchism as a threat, and denounced it as such in his 1894 work *Gli anarchici*.
10. AHCDMX, 1909, Fund: Secretaría de Gobierno, Section: Empleados de la Escuela Correccional para Mujeres, Box: 3, File: 193, 7. In addition, years earlier, in 1903, Dr. Ignacio Fernández Ortigoza, who had studied in Paris with Bertillon, attempted to form an anthropometry cabinet in the old penitentiary of Belén in Mexico City, but this project was never completed.
11. AHCDMX, 1909, Fund: Secretaría de Gobierno, Section: Empleados de la Escuela Correccional para Mujeres, Box: 3, File: 218; AHCDMX, Fondo: Secretaría de Gobierno, Section: Empleados de la Escuela Correccional para Mujeres, Box: 3, File: 231.
12. AGN, 1913, Fund: SIPBA, Box: 174, File: 34.
13. AHMNA, 1916, vol. 22, 178.
14. AHMNA, 1919, vol. 29, 137.
15. AHMNA, 1921, vol. 36, 130.
16. AGEP, 1939, Fund: Penitenciaria, Section: Enfermería, Box: 46, File: 2.
17. AGN, 1903, Fund: SIPBA, Box: 150, File: 26, 4.
18. AHMNA, 1917, vol. 25, 51.

8

Social Sciences, Jewish Public Opinion, and the Jewish Race in the United States of the Progressive Era: American Echoes of Cesare Lombroso's *L'antisemitismo*, 1893–1911

Emanuele D'Antonio

A Limited but Not Irrelevant Reception

In 1894, Cesare Lombroso published *L'antisemitismo e le scienze moderne* (*Anti-Semitism in the Light of Modern Sciences*), the most significant Italian contribution to the debate surrounding the Jewish question in fin-de-siècle Europe. Lombroso's work addressed a political phenomenon of international importance, which, on the eve of the Dreyfus Affair in France, had already undermined the process of Jewish emancipation in Central and Eastern Europe. He framed anti-Semitism as the product of an ancient, prerational hatred of Jews, deeply ingrained among Gentiles—a psychological trait with atavistic roots, passed down through heredity.

Lombroso's socio-anthropological critique refuted anti-Jewish claims of racial difference and inferiority, which were used to justify the exclusion of Jewish minorities from political life across European nations. He argued that the Jews were, in fact, anthropologically equal to the so-called Aryan peoples—socially integrated, and contributing greatly to the progress of European societies. Any socioeconomic or cultural characteristics attributed to them—where these were real and not merely the perception of a hostile or impressionistic gaze—were the result of persecution and sociopolitical oppression, and as such would disappear in the social processes promoted by civil and political equality. His book culminated in a utilitarian defense of emancipation, coupled with the hope for the eventual "fusion" of Jews and Christians, who, liberated from their supposedly anachronistic traditional identities, would unite in a new solidarity emerging from a utopian socialist religion of humanity.

Lombroso's social science delegitimized anti-Semitism as a movement that promoted unjust, unscientific anti-Jewish racism and exclusionary policies harmful to the broader development of European societies. As a figure widely known in Italy and beyond (Forgacs 2003: 99), Lombroso was an Italian Jew who defended emancipation, which he had personally experienced three decades earlier as a supporter of the national Risorgimento and the newly formed liberal state. His hope for assimilation reflected a critical stance toward the historical role of religions, including Judaism, which he criticized in harsh and stereotypical terms (Harrowitz 1994) rooted in his materialistic worldview.

While Lombroso had distanced himself from the Jewish faith and its communal institutions in his youth, this did not make him an "assimilated" Jew—historically defined as someone entirely estranged from their Jewish identity (Stanislawski 2001: 8–9). Throughout his life, Lombroso saw himself as Jewish in biological and racial terms,[1] and retained a "firm ethnic identity" rooted in his Jewish family background (Dolza 1990: 30). These family ties influenced important personal decisions and sustained a Jewish historical self-consciousness that was partly distinct from that of Gentile Italians. Though his research on anti-Semitism was driven by personal and subjective anxieties, he sought objectivity by employing the analytical and interpretive tools of socio-anthropological science.

Lombrosian critique of anti-Semitism should be understood within the context of a new Jewish literary genre, the "scientific apologia" (Efron 1994: 90), developed by Jewish social scientists engaged in the scientific debates surrounding the Jewish question in late-nineteenth-century Europe. Lombroso, in alignment with the international anthropological culture of the era, saw mankind as divided into inferior and superior races, differentiated by psychophysical and moral traits shaped by heredity and environment, which in turn influenced social behaviors (Nani 2009; Montaldo 2018a). His fellow anthropologists shared this racist view of human diversity, reinforced by their academic training, as well as by anthropometric and statistical methods for measuring physical characteristics.

Since the mid-nineteenth century, mainstream racial science had increasingly focused on European Jews, reconceptualizing their distinctiveness in biological terms and attributing it largely to innate and hereditary factors (Stone 2008). However, Jewish race scientists employed this same scientific knowledge to build "a new form of Jewish self-defense" (Efron 1994: 59), countering the anti-Jewish stereotypes often propagated by their Gentile colleagues. Their most common strategy to dismantle essentialist views of Jewish difference—though not their only one—was to advance an environmentalist interpretation. They argued that Jewish diversity was largely the result of their interaction with a hostile environment, one that Gentiles had never experienced (Hart 2000: 11–12).

Lombroso's entry into the "scientific apologia" genre was prompted in the 1860s by the negative impact of the myth of the Indo-Iranian, or Aryan, origins of European peoples on the image of his fellow Jews (D'Antonio 2020–1). The Jews were widely perceived by European culture, including its Jewish subculture, as the "Semites of Europe." In the new bio-anthropological language, this term signified their connection to the Middle-Eastern Semitic racial stock, thereby marking them as racially distinct from the other European populations. Lombroso, while sharing the common belief in the Semitic origins of European Jews, was able to restore the link between them and their Aryan counterparts. He believed that the Jews had undergone a racial evolution after their emigration from Palestine, successfully adapting to the new and challenging historical and natural environment of Europe. He later argued—in a conception developed in depth in *L'antisemitismo*—that Jews embodied an ancient Aryan-Semitic nexus, biologically and mentally.

Lombroso's book was translated into four other languages (Lombroso 1894a; 1899; 1903a; 1906a) and achieved a broad global circulation, though this reception remains historically underexplored. This chapter focuses on the book's reception in the United States between the late nineteenth century and the First World War. The general public paid little or no attention to it, as it was never translated into English and was aimed at a European audience. As a result, it did not engage with the growing anxieties surrounding the Jewish question during the Progressive Era. While organized political anti-Semitism was not prominent in the United States at the time, significant unease persisted regarding the mass immigration of Jews from the Tsarist Empire. This wave of immigration, which began in the early 1880s following the bloody anti-Jewish pogroms of 1881–2 and the 1882 Laws of May that produced severe legal discrimination against Jews, became a central point of tension.

Lombroso supported Jewish immigration as a means to improve the living conditions of his oppressed fellow Jews, but he appeared—perhaps deliberately—unaware of the heated American debates on the subject (Lombroso 1894c: 24–5, 93–4, 106). In Anglo-Saxon cultures, a widespread hostile perception of Russian-Jewish refugees had emerged amidst a broader backlash against migratory processes that were reshaping the socio-demographic landscape of the United States. The recent, massive waves of immigrants from Central, Eastern, and Southern Europe were often viewed as bearers of unassimilable cultural and racial differences, which were perceived as detrimental to the nation's social development and national identity (Jacobson 1998). American nativist movements became the political voice of these sentiments, advocating for a restrictive overhaul of immigration laws, which ultimately led to the passage of the Johnson-Reed Act in 1924 (Higham 1955).

In this context, Lombroso's book on anti-Semitism, with its investigation into the racial identity of the Jews, garnered limited but not insignificant attention among American participants in the Progressive Era's debates on the assimilation and potential assimilation of Russian-Jewish immigrants. This chapter will first examine how two social scientists, one with nativist convictions and the other a supporter of Jewish immigration, utilized Lombroso's thesis. The following section will examine its reception among American Jews, especially in their popular English-language journals.

An Unassimilable, Undesirable Aryan-Semitic People

In 1899, William Zebina Ripley (1867–1941) dedicated a chapter of *The Races of Europe* to the anthropological status of the Jews. The book presented his research on the racial geography of Europe, developed against the backdrop of American social science debates on immigration. Ripley, a professor at the Massachusetts Institute of Technology and Columbia University, was an economist, sociologist, and anthropologist from Boston who took great pride in his Anglo-Saxon heritage and Protestant Unitarian faith. He shared the nativist concerns regarding the impact of mass immigration from non-Anglo-Saxon Europe on American society (Winlow 2006: 126–7).

Ripley's study generated widespread public and scientific attention, attracting interest not only from fellow social scientists but also from cultural and associative circles aligned with nativism and racism (Decker 2014: 167; Spiro 2009: 92–7, 100–3). Using the analytical and interpretive tools of physical anthropology, he identified three European races: the Teutonic in the north, the Alpine or Celtic in the center, and the Mediterranean in the south. The Jews, however, were treated separately. Spread across the entire continent and possessing what he called a "single racial standard" (Ripley 1899: 33), they represented an exception to his geographically based tripartite classification.

Ripley's investigation fits within the prevailing anthropological framework that traced the origins of the Jews to the Semitic races, a view recently reaffirmed in the United States by the authoritative ethnographer Daniel Brinton (1890: 138–9). Ripley asked whether the Jews' "social individuality" in contemporary Europe arose solely from their shared religious faith and, negatively, the effects of social ostracism, or whether it also stemmed from a deeper "physical brotherhood" of race (Ripley 1899: 369–70). His belief that race could be measured solely by a group's physical traits led him to address this scientific question using the methods of bio-anthropological analysis to explore "the problems of Jewish derivation and descent." Ripley examined the skeletons and the physiognomies of European Jews, but assigned a determinative role to cranial morphology. In line with late-nineteenth-century anthropological thought, he viewed the shape of the skull as the only human anatomical feature unaffected by environmental conditions and, therefore, as purely hereditary in nature (Stone 2008: 142).

First, Ripley noted that the international anthropological literature consistently described European Jews as a brachycephalic population (Ripley 1899: 386–92). Their skulls were typically broad and short, in contrast to the narrow, elongated (dolichocephalic) skulls that specialists attributed to Semitic populations. This brachycephaly was interpreted as the most significant marker of Jewish deviation from the supposedly primitive physical type of Semitic races—a deviation produced, he argued, by millennia of interbreeding with other racial groups. Thus, despite popular beliefs and the "opinion" of several of his colleagues regarding Jewish "purity of descent," Ripley considered them a racially hybrid group.

Second, Ripley observed that craniometric studies detected considerable variation in the cephalic index of Jews from different European regions. Jewish skulls were morphologically more similar to those of their non-Jewish fellow citizens than to those of their coreligionists in other nations. He concluded that European Jews were "physically more Aryan than Semitic," and had, through generations of reproduction, "unconsciously" acquired and hereditarily crystallized biological traits resembling those of the surrounding populations. For Ripley, Jewish solidarity was thus a historical-religious phenomenon rather than an expression of racial unity: "The Jews," his treatise concluded, "are not a race, but only a people, after all" (ibid.: 400).

In his discussion, Ripley extensively cited Lombroso, recognizing him—along with the German geographer Richard Andrée (1881) and the French historian Anatole Leroy-Beaulieu (1893)—as a significant contributor to Jewish race science (ibid.: 368). Lombroso's book on anti-Semitism provided Ripley not only with anthropometric data but, more importantly, with the idea that the Jews were "a people much more Aryan than Semitic." The criminologist had borrowed this thesis from a study by the anthropologist and archaeologist Felix von Luschan (1892), structuring his critique of anti-Jewish accusations of racial diversity around it (Lombroso 1894c: 35–42). According to the authoritative Austrian scholar, modern Jews with physical traits distinct from the so-called Semitic type represented living proof of ancient Israel's racial hybridism. Their brachycephalic skulls and/or light complexion suggested that they descended from interbreeding between Israelite tribes and Indo-European groups settled in the Middle East in pre-biblical times. In *L'antisemitismo*, Lombroso extensively quoted a study that, in his view, refuted, "in the light of craniology," the alleged "ethnic antagonism" postulated by anti-Semites. He argued that this Aryan-Semitic *métissage* established a quasi-primordial biological kinship between Jews and the rest of European society. Moreover, the "broad Aryan base" of their blood, he contended, had facilitated their assimilation into European civilization, a process successfully achieved shortly after their initial immigration from Palestine to the European continent (ibid.: 41–2).

Ripley's adherence to Lombroso's anthropological thesis, however, was culturally detached and in opposition to the apologetic framework that structured it. The Bostonian viewed "craniology" as a purely cognitive tool and did not establish any connection between a human group's racial hybridism and its ability to assimilate into a host society. This did not mean that he dismissed the psychological influence of race altogether. However, for him, the Aryan-Semitic *métissage* did not make the Jewish masses fleeing the Tsarist Empire any more assimilable to American society. His analysis of the geography of European Jewry gave him an opportunity to call indirectly for legislation restricting the "ingress" of "[this] great Polish swamp of miserable human beings, terrific in its proportions, [that] threatens to drain itself off into our country" (Ripley 1899: 372).

Ripley's stance possibly reflected the anti-Jewish prejudices common among the "old stock patrician families in Boston" (Dinnerstein 1994: 52). His aversion to Russian-Jewish immigration, however, was not directly legitimized by negative stereotypes about the Jewish body that were crystallized in international anthropological literature (Gilman 1991). While he acknowledged the widespread "physical degeneracy" of the Jews, he attributed this primarily to historical conditions rather than inherent racial inferiority. In his view, their generally healthy lifestyle and ritual practices mitigated these deficiencies, and—at least in theory—improving their living conditions could alleviate them (Ripley 1899: 381–5).

Nevertheless, Ripley expressed deep concerns about what he saw as an "unalterable characteristic" of supposedly racial origins in "this peculiar people": their inclination toward urbanization and intellectual professions, coupled with their demographic growth, seemed to him a future source of destabilization for American society (ibid.: 372–3). To him, the problem mirrored the one facing Germany and Austria, two countries heavily affected by migration from the Tsarist Empire. He believed that the population of Berlin defended the Germanness of the German capital through anti-Semitic claims, fearful of the risk that it would be transformed into "a new Jerusalem for the horde of Russian exiles." The threat looming over Austrian and German cities, he warned, was beginning to cast its shadows over American metropolises as well. The Aryan-Semitic people whose assimilation Lombroso had celebrated, in Ripley's view, remained an unassimilable, undesirable alien group wherever they settled.

Celebrating Jewish Assimilation through Race Science

In 1911, Maurice Fishberg (1872–1934) published *The Jews*, a monographic study that gained wide circulation in international social science circles. The book disseminated the findings of his socio-anthropological study on the Jews, summarizing his extensive research from the previous decade, which was shaped by the ongoing debates in American social sciences on Jewish immigration. Fishberg, a Ukrainian-born Jew, arrived in New York in 1889, earned his medical degree in 1897, and served as chief sanitary examinator for the United Hebrew Charity, a prominent charitable institution (Hart 1999: 290; Goldstein 2006: 110–14). His scientific debut in 1901 aimed to defend Russian-Jewish immigrants against nativist accusations that they carried serious infectious diseases and posed a public health threat to the nation (Kraut 1994: 136–65).

Fishberg's field of inquiry quickly expanded beyond Jewish pathology and hygiene to the crucial study of the physical anthropology of the Jews, gradually incorporating a wide range of social phenomena relevant to Jewish life. Among his other contributions, he published an essay in a miscellaneous volume honoring the renowned anthropologist Franz Boas, who was his friend and a fellow Jew (Fishberg 1906). Despite lacking an academic position, Fishberg was widely regarded as an authoritative scholar by the American scientific community and the foremost American expert on Jewish racial science.

In *The Jews*, Fishberg addressed the broad question of Jewish assimilability and, more generally, their historical fate in the United States and the global Diaspora. His bio-anthropological analysis laid the foundation for an objective answer to this issue, free from both anti-Semitic or philo-Semitic biases. The fundamental question he sought to address was whether the Jews were racially distinct from the populations of the nations in which they lived (Fishberg 1911: VI). Like many anthropologists of his time, he accepted the idea of the Jews' Semitic origins but questioned whether this original racial identity had survived into the present. His research sought hereditary markers of diversity in the biological characteristics of his coreligionists, operating within a theoretical and methodological framework strongly influenced by Ripley's study (Goldstein 2006: 111). However, unlike Ripley—who relied on anthropometric data from international scientific literature—Fishberg collected thousands of anthropometric measurements himself, in New York, North Africa, and Central and Eastern Europe.

Despite the large volume of data he gathered, Fishberg did not produce particularly original scientific conclusions. He largely refined the arguments of Ripley and Lombroso, asserting that Jews were a racially mixed Aryan-Semitic group. According to Fishberg, extensive crossbreeding with different racial groups over millennia had led the Jews to undergo anthropological changes wherever they lived. As a result, they had lost their primitive Semitic physical traits and developed a new organic constitution identical to that of their non-Jewish fellow citizens. After establishing that Jews were racially equal to Aryans, Fishberg constructed a rigidly environmentalist interpretation of the biosocial characteristics that seemed to distinguish Jewish minorities worldwide. Since any differences between Jews and Aryans were not innate, he argued that such specificities were merely the product of social factors—namely, the conditions of the Jewish milieu. In other words, any differences in Jewish physiognomies, health-demographic trends, economic-professional structures, and criminal behaviors compared to the Gentiles were, in his view, simply legacies of centuries of persecution.

For Fishberg, this meant that Jewish diversity was nonessential, ephemeral, and hopefully transitory in modern times. In a strong rebuke of Zionism, he contended that the historical fate of the Jews was not to reconstruct their national political unity in Palestine, which he deemed anachronistic. Instead, he argued that the similarity between the bodies and behavioral attitudes of the Jews and Gentiles demonstrated—both to scientific observers and, by extension, the world—that Jews would naturally assimilate into American and European societies.

In *The Jews*, Fishberg extensively cited *L'antisemitismo*, which he had read in its German translation early in his career, along with other works by Lombroso (Fishberg 1901: 581–2; Lombroso 1887a). He did not engage with its general theoretical framework but focused on the anthropometric and socio-statistical studies presented in its appendix. Among these, Lombroso had examined the "oldest Jewish skulls" known to anthropologists—five Jewish skulls from the second century CE found in the Roman catacombs of San Calisto, which were housed in the Academy of Sciences in Turin. He was the only scholar in the world to have questioned the racial status of the ancient people of Israel on the basis of such a rare set of its biological remains (Fishberg 1911: 47). The criminologist noted the brachycephaly of two of the skulls, and argued that this supposed hereditary trait, foreign to Semitic physical characteristics and in line with Luschan's theory of Aryan-Semitic mixtures, indicated "the little Semitism of the Jews even in ancient times" (Lombroso 1894c: 141–8). Although Fishberg acknowledged that Lombroso's conclusions were not definitive due to the small sample size, he deemed them "of great scientific interest," as they challenged "the opinion" that ancient Hebrews were a "pure dolichocephalic race" (Fishberg 1911: 47–8). In other words, the process of hybridization that transformed the Jewish bio-anthropological constitution could, he suggested, have begun in a remote epoch of human civilization.

In his treatise, Fishberg primarily used *L'antisemitismo* as a source of quantitative data on the biosocial characteristics of contemporary Jews, though he frequently questioned both the reliability of these data and their interpretation (ibid.: 239, 304, 309, 330). While Lombroso shared the view that Jewish diversity was a product of "the peculiarity of the Jewish milieu" (ibid.: 289), he must have struck Fishberg as a somewhat non-rigorous social scientist, lacking methodological accuracy and prone to unfounded generalizations. The statistical-demographic research in the appendix of Lombroso's book—which was, in fact, an undeclared republication of his earlier study on the mortality of Veronese Jews (Lombroso 1867)—systematically refuted racial explanations for the differences in Jewish mortality rates (Lombroso 1894c: 123–39). However, while such socio-historical explanations may have seemed plausible to an observer in mid-nineteenth-century Italy, they likely appeared less convincing to one living in early-twentieth-century America.

For instance, Lombroso argued on statistical grounds that Jews exhibited relative immunity to respiratory diseases, attributing this to their predominance in non-strenuous, indoor commercial professions, which shielded them from "sudden chills" and inclement weather. Fishberg acknowledged that this immunity was well-documented in European health statistics, but he strongly refuted Lombroso's interpretation. While it was true that Jewish proletarians in American cities, London, and in the cities of the Tsarist Empire did not work outdoors, the physical strain of the sweatshop system and the unhealthy condition of their workshops should, in theory, have made them "more liable" to tuberculosis and other bronchopulmonary diseases, rather than making them more resistant (Fishberg 1911: 288–9, 302–4).

For Fishberg, explaining the advantageous differential in respiratory health required a deeper hypothesis than Lombroso's. He proposed that Jews had been an urban population for centuries, forced to live long in ghettos in overcrowded conditions, where they were exposed to massive inhalation of dust and other harmful particles. Over time, he argued, Jews had adapted to these unsanitary environments, which facilitated the proliferation of germs responsible for several deadly respiratory diseases, developing an organic resistance to them. This resistance, he suggested, had eventually become hereditary, ensuring their survival both individually and collectively (ibid.: 293).

Fishberg's Jewish social science was influenced only indirectly by Lombroso's socio-anthropological work on Jews, primarily through the filter of Ripley, a hostile yet respected scholar. Lombroso's theories on the benefits of Aryan-Semitic *métissage* and the causes of anti-Semitism left Fishberg even more perplexed (ibid.: 210, 449), though his objections were formulated only incidentally and in extremely general terms, making them difficult to discuss in detail here. Nonetheless, Fishberg was aware of the profound affinity between his own and Lombroso's scientific conceptions of the Jews—both ultimately converging in the celebration of their racial equality with Gentiles and their assimilation into non-Jewish society.

Lombroso's name, therefore, could be used instrumentally by Fishberg in his anti-Zionist polemics. He deployed it, for instance, to discredit Max Nordau, a Hungarian Zionist leader who professed to be—and in fact was—a fervent Lombrosian. Nordau, a social Darwinist intellectual well known in the United States, had championed the idea of Jewish racial purity, provocatively declaring the observations of a "street loafer" more convincing than the uncertain hypotheses of anthropologists (Nordau 1909: 474). Fishberg seized on this claim, remarking maliciously that it cast doubt on whether the Hungarian *Kulturkritiker* was truly an "avowed disciple of Lombroso"—a remark aimed at exposing the unscientific character of Zionist ideology (Fishberg 1911: 474). Lombroso, however, was not merely an emblem of modern scientific thought, useful only in delegitimizing Jewish opponents of assimilation.

In the concluding pages of his book, Fishberg examined the factors that continued to hinder the full assimilation of Jews into non-Jewish societies (ibid.: 552–5). He noted that conversion to Christianity, a centuries-old phenomenon, had led many Jews to become "champions of Christian ideals, of 'Aryan' culture and civilization" (ibid.:

552), demonstrating that no insurmountable resistance to assimilation existed on the Jewish side. Citing Lombroso, Fishberg argued that if "all the Jews" were eventually baptized, their descendants would lose "any peculiarities" within a few generations. Lombroso had borrowed this hyperbolic statement from an important sociological study by the aforementioned Leroy-Beaulieu (1893: 183), using the French historian's words to encapsulate his theory on the exogenous origin of the biosocial specificities of European Jews. Their distinctive traits, he suggested, would fade and eventually disappear completely in proportion to the degree of Jewish "assimilation" into the social body that the "surrounding population" allowed them (Lombroso 1894c: 45). "Lombroso was right," Fishberg agreed (1911: 552). The "differences between the Jews and the others" were not due to racial diversity—now defunct—nor to the (supposed) exclusivism originally inherent in the Jewish religion. Modern Jews had abandoned their most separatist dogmas and rites, which for centuries had prevented them from fully adopting the cultural practices and traditions of the non-Jewish world. The primary obstacle to their full assimilation, he argued, was not internal but external: the sociopolitical resistance of the Gentile world. This resistance manifested itself in two key forms: the anti-Jewish legislation enforced in Eastern European states and the informal discrimination practiced in Western societies. According to Fishberg, Jews continued to look slightly different only because of the hostile attitudes and exclusionary policies of non-Jewish authorities and populations. If he had wished to return the American's generosity, Lombroso would likely have remarked that Fishberg was right.

The "Great Jewish Criminologist" and a Polemic on Jewish Criminality

In 1893, the *Menorah*, a New York-based monthly journal of the important American Jewish lodge *B'nai B'rith*, printed an English translation of an article by Lombroso on anti-Semitism. Originally published in the *Neue Freie Presse*, Vienna's most authoritative newspaper (Lombroso 1893a; 1893c), the article drew on socio-anthropological knowledge to defend Jewish emancipation, which was under attack from anti-Semitic "political Pseudo-Anthropologists" amidst rising anti-Semitism in Austrian society. Lombroso's arguments, which anticipated those he would later develop more fully in his book, sparked a heated debate among the Viennese public. This debate did not go unnoticed by German-origin American Jews. A reform-oriented weekly periodical published in Chicago commented that the article spared "neither friend nor foe" and was "candid, frank, and above all, truthful" ([Literary Notes] 1893).

However, *Menorah* softened Lombroso's harsh judgment on Judaism and on religion in general by appending remarks from one of his most authoritative Viennese critics, Rabbi Adolf Jellinek (J[ellinek] 1893). Jellinek argued that the struggle against anti-Semitism did not require a new humanist religion. Rather, the "old religions," when true to their biblical and evangelical moral principles, already taught universal love for one's neighbor, regardless of religious belief.

Despite his vehement hostility to religion, Lombroso maintained that Jews and Gentiles, though different in racial origins, were now racially equal and bound by a shared bio-anthropological identity shaped by history. For American Jews in the 1890s, Lombroso's thesis may have been useful in defending against the growing nativist political opposition to Russian-Jewish immigration (Dinnerstein 1994: 43, 45).

Lombrosian science, for American Jews, was seen as a potential "instrument of truth," as defined by another Jewish journal ([Das Wesen] 1901), in the fight against anti-Jewish prejudice. However, its limited use in the context of apologetic articles does not suggest that Jews were leaning toward a defense based on a conception of human diversity inspired by cultural relativism—a perspective that would not become dominant until later in the twentieth century (Jacobson 1998: 199). On the contrary, the bio-anthropological foundations of Lombroso's work resonated with the self-understanding of a religious group that also defined itself in racial terms. Racial characteristics provided "a sense of stability [of the] Jewish identity," which had been eroded by the modernization and secularization of mentality and lifestyle (Goldstein 2006: 11).

While Lombrosian socio-anthropological knowledge seemed to offer an effective theoretical response to anti-Jewish racism, it was less useful in addressing the concrete challenges emerging from public debates on Jewish immigration. Nativist attacks against Russian-Jewish immigrants focused on accusations of immoral and antisocial behaviors which, though rooted in a racist mindset, had to be refuted on the basis of an accurate understanding of the local context. Lombroso was regarded as a "competent and reliable" interpreter of Jewish biosocial phenomena (Are Jews 1901; Arnold 1893; [Why are the Jews] 1900), but had not studied the Jewish question in the United States. As a result, his contributions in this regard were limited.

Nevertheless, Lombrosian science was employed by the American Jewish press in an apologetic role during a major public controversy fueled by a shocking anti-Jewish declaration emerging from nativist culture. In 1908, New York Jews faced an accusation of criminality that was particularly dangerous due to the institutional authority of its source and the national attention it garnered. Police Commissioner Theodore Bingham, in an article on foreign criminality published in the *North American Review*, claimed—allegedly based on statistical data—that "perhaps half of the criminals" in the metropolitan area were "of [Hebrew] race" (Bingham 1908a: 383–4). The nativist police officer argued that crime was naturally attractive to a population of one million, mostly Russian immigrants, who were often unable to assimilate due to being "ignorant of the language" and/or "physically [unfit] for hard labor." Bingham further claimed that Russian-Jewish criminals specialized in property crimes and were often children or adolescents "brought up to lives of crime," before moving on to discuss other ethno-national groups.

New York Jews were outraged by Bingham's article, viewing it as overtly anti-Semitic. The accusation against the morality of the entire "[Hebrew] race" united various national and religious factions, leading to an intense and multifaceted protest. Jewish journals in English, German, and Yiddish published a flood of articles rejecting the charge, using a wide range of arguments (Ribak 2014: 13). In *The Independent*, Francis Oppenheimer, speaking on behalf of his "race" to the general public, challenged the police commissioner to provide evidence that half of New York's criminals were Jewish and urged him to retract his previous statement if he were unable to do so (Oppenheimer 1908). Several months earlier, the Jewish activist continued, Metropolitan Jewish organizations had conducted a rigorous quantitative analysis, for internal purposes, of the criminality of their coreligionists, which disproved Bingham's slanderous portrayal of Jews as an "impossible [and] criminal race." This analysis showed that, in 1907, New York Jews had a proportionally lower rate of criminal convictions than the rest of the population, and juvenile delinquency rates among them were only slightly "above the average."

Forced to retract, Bingham denied harboring anti-Jewish prejudice and claimed to have been misled by inaccurate prison statistics provided by his office ([Bingham] 1908b). The case was officially closed following a meeting between the police commissioner and a Jewish delegation (Halitvak 1908), but it left lingering anxieties within the Jewish community ([The Evil] 1908).

The New York Jewish press continued its campaign against Bingham, celebrating the triumph of truth over defamation and reason over prejudice. In this context, the popular *Hebrew Standard* republished comments on Jewish criminality from a longer interview with Lombroso, originally published in the London-based *Jewish Chronicle* and widely circulated in the Jewish press across multiple countries ([Attraverso la stampa] 1908). During the interview—conducted while Lombroso was vacationing in Sandown, a village on the Isle of Wight (Lombroso Ferrero 1921: 422; Dolza 1990: 153–6)—the criminologist described the Jews as a "special people" who, by surviving millennia of persecution, had undergone a kind of Darwinian selection that culled weaker members while fortifying the survivors of the massacres. This painful process of artificial selection had not, however, turned them into an "abnormal" people immune to the degenerations common to all human groups. Lombroso asserted that the Jews demonstrated a strong predisposition toward both madness and what he regarded as its opposite, genius, but displayed only a modest inclination toward crime.

As he had already done in *L'uomo delinquente* and *L'antisemitismo*, Lombroso questioned the reliability of judicial statistics, while acknowledging that they showed that Jews made a minor contribution to the overall European criminal population (Lombroso 1876: 125–6; Lombroso 1894c: 100–1). Regardless of the uncertainty about the extent of Jewish criminality, Lombroso asserted that it was socially insignificant and not particularly dangerous, as it was oriented toward "getting rich quick" and thus nonviolent property crimes. He attributed this to sociocultural factors: Jews were impelled to abstain from harassment, brawling, and murder by their bourgeois "[repression of] criminal instincts," their serene family life, their focus on child-rearing, and their sober lifestyle free from alcohol abuse.

While publishing an excerpt from the interview with Lombroso, the *Hebrew Standard* launched a scathing attack on Bingham's morality. The "great Jewish criminologist"—remarked a brief editorial note sarcastically—did not share "such a high opinion of the Jewish criminal" ([Evidently] 1908). In contrast, the American Jewish public regarded Lombroso as a celebrated figure in international social science and modern Jewry, and he had recently been honored with the inclusion of his bio-bibliographical entry in the *Jewish Encyclopaedia*, an important editorial project initiated by a committee of Jewish scholars based in New York (N[ordau] 1906; Schwartz 1991). His authoritative judgment, grounded in criminological knowledge, reminded the Jewish public of the "recent outburst" provoked by an unnamed slanderer—clearly identifiable as Bingham—who had raised a loud alarm against Jewish criminality. Lombrosian science effectively silenced this accusation, countering Bingham's malevolent prejudice and reaffirming, through modern scientific discourse, an age-old moral truth: "the libels—as taught by the Bible (Pss. 7.16)—will be hurled at the head of him who put it forth." The interview with the "great Jewish criminologist" was reprinted and discussed by other American Jewish periodicals for an extended period (Montague 1908; Echoes from Europe 1908; Scientific Notes 1913), providing Jewish readers with comfort, dignity, and hope, though it had little impact on nativist beliefs regarding Jewish criminality.

Lombroso's death in 1909, one year after the Bingham case, garnered significant attention among American Jews. Jewish journals published numerous commemorative articles, celebrating his global fame—as they did with any coreligionist who had achieved success in the public sphere—as a source of pride for the entire Jewish community (Goldstein 2006: 20). According to the *Hebrew Standard*, which published one of the more detailed and accurate obituaries, Lombroso had been a scientific innovator but, most importantly, a good Jew (The Death 1909). He had taken pride in his ancestry and race, and had defended his "oppressed brethren," also showing a late and largely unexpected interest in the Zionist cause.

However, his biological determinism drew criticism from several American rabbis, who rejected a criminological perspective that they felt deliberately disregarded the moral truths of Judaism (Sale 1900). The *Hebrew Standard* preferred to remember Lombroso's scientific contributions, recalling his book on *Anti-Semitism*, which delegitimized "the enemies of the Jews" and showcased the scientist's "abhorrence of the dreaded disease of racial prejudice" (The Death 1909). The Zionist Socialist Party of America (Poalei Zion) expressed its condolences to Lombroso's widow, with the Party's secretary, Baruch Zuckerman—a New Yorker of Lithuanian origin—writing that the "Jewish people" had lost one of their "[noblest] sons," the social sciences one of their most courageous scholars, and mankind a "great fighter … against every form of oppression."[2]

Conclusion

This chapter has reconstructed three significant episodes in the reception of Lombroso's *Antisemitismo* in the United States during the nineteenth and twentieth centuries. The analysis suggests that while the echoes of this work were limited, they were far from irrelevant in the social sciences and in Jewish public opinion across the Atlantic. Commentators and interpreters made selective use of the text, disregarding Lombroso's interpretation of political anti-Semitism—a phenomenon they considered entirely "European" and non-American. On the other hand, Lombroso's theories on the racial status of the Jews generated scientific insights that were considered useful to American society, particularly as it sought to reestablish the notion of Jewish difference in relation to the possibility of Jewish assimilation.

Lombroso's social science celebrated the Jews' ability to assimilate, presenting them as having a complete anthropological identity with other racially distinct populations within the nation. His thesis that Jews were the product of an ancient Aryan-Semitic *métissage* was widely embraced by American anthropological culture, which, however, did not necessarily subscribe to his apologetic intent. Jewish social scientists like Maurice Fishberg faithfully interpreted Lombroso's vision of racial equality, using it to argue that Jews were entirely capable of being assimilated into American society. This theme was also embraced by the English-speaking Jewish press, which sought to popularize it among its readers. Lombroso was thus legitimately perceived as a "defender of the race" in Jewish circles.

However, the anthropological depiction of Jews could also be adopted by hostile interpretations that simply ignored its original purpose of challenging anti-Jewish racism. The idea that Jews were Aryan-Semitic was in fact also accepted by the sociologist William Zebina Ripley, a Gentile with ties to nativist political and cultural currents. Ripley, however, believed that the Aryan blood flowing through Jewish veins did nothing to improve their ability to assimilate into Aryan society, and he did not think it made such assimilation desirable.

Notes

1. Archivio di Stato di Torino, Archivio Loria, 10/24-1.1., Letter of C. Lombroso to Achille Loria, Turin, July 31, 1890.
2. ACLM, Letter of B. Zuckerman to N. Lombroso, New York, November 3, 1909.

9

Imagining Southern Italians as Undesirable Aliens: How North American Social Scientists Adapted, Adopted, or Rejected the Views of the "Italian School of Criminology" while Debating Mass Immigration (1890–1924)

Alessandra Lorini

Introduction

In the late nineteenth century, American public opinion portrayed Southern Italians migrating to the United States as "inborn criminals" and inferior to "white" people. Was Lombroso's influence a factor, especially considering that by this time the Italian criminologist had published numerous articles in popular American magazines? It can be argued that whether his writings garnered significant followers, as Nicole Hahn Rafter asserts, or whether criminal anthropology sparked skepticism, as Lucia Zedner contends (Zedner 1991; Rafter 1992), European scientific theories responded to an unresolved American need for scientific legitimation of a society fixated on racialization—a society where a focus on skin color and institutionalized racial segregation were already deeply entrenched. In the United States, this racial prejudice had seeped into scientific paradigms, and the concept of "race," despite being a social construction, was erroneously perceived as hereditary and immutable (Lorini 1999, 2013, 2019). The new immigrants from Southern and Eastern Europe were classified according to a perceived distance or proximity to people of African descent. In this transatlantic exchange of ideas about inborn criminality and atavistic regression, North American social scientists selectively embraced views from the "Italian School of Criminology"—in which they included the founder Cesare Lombroso, anthropologist Giuseppe Sergi, sociologist Alfredo Niceforo, and a few others—and adapted them to a preexisting classification of races dating back to the era of slavery. These views were subsequently reconfigured and adopted by the new system of racial apartheid of the Jim Crow era. In other words, professional and amateur scientists in America *adapted*, *adopted*, or *rejected* Lombrosian concepts of inborn criminality and atavism in order to classify their internal "others"—namely, people of color and new foreign immigrants.

Between 1880 and 1924, some twenty-four million immigrants entered the United States, of whom over four million were Italians. Between 1900 and 1910, half of the arriving Italians had fled rural poverty in Southern Italy. In contrast, prior to 1870, just over 25,000 Italians had entered the United States, followed by some 55,000 in the following decade. Unlike these earlier small migratory waves from the northern and central Italian regions, by the end of the nineteenth century, the great majority of migrants were from Southern Italy. The number of Sicilians, for example, increased from only ninety in 1879 to more than 10,000 in 1892, and almost 110,000 in 1913.

Perceptions of Italians shifted dramatically in parallel to this influx. In the nineteenth century, Italian exiles from the Risorgimento had assimilated without difficulty; some became citizens, and a few even fought in the American Civil War, on one side or the other. In fact, during the mid-nineteenth century, Italy was generally viewed positively by American intellectuals and politicians, who admired the nation's struggle for liberty. The unification movement, from 1848 to 1870, was seen as the realization of democratic ideals shared by the American revolution.

However, by the end of the nineteenth century, the view had shifted from admiration to contempt. Southern Italian peasants, now crowding into Little Italies, speaking their dialects and preserving their traditions, were blamed for the urban degeneration in which they lived with their large families, with the American public unwilling to consider the social conditions that led to their plight. To many observers who visited the impoverished neighborhoods of industrial cities, Southern Italians appeared to carry with them an inherent degradation, which kept them at the lowest rung of American society (Luconi 2010: 2–4).

The "Blackness" of Southern Italians

Embedded within the North American modernity that Lombroso described in *Delitti vecchi e delitti nuovi* (1902), the reader may encounter several forms of atavistic regression:

> It is well to note that even in a civilization as highly advanced as North America, when harmful influences of race and immigration intervene, bloody crime continues to increase rapidly. The very means of repression against this, such as lynching, constitutes a new form of collective bloody crime. (Lombroso 1902: 57)

At the turn of the twentieth century, extremely active "lynch mobs" brutalized the segregated South. Crowds of white citizens would gather, as if at a festival, to take part in the collective murder of Black individuals, many of whom were accused, without solid evidence, of sexually harassing or raping white women, or else simply failing to show deference to white people.[1] Crowds of men, often in the presence of women and children, tortured, killed, and burned Black bodies in what were referred to as "Negro barbecues."

By defining lynching as an extreme remedy to the harms caused by "legal subtleties and police insufficiencies," Lombroso echoed views expressed in the North American press. However, he also highlighted the dangers of the practice, which he argued often provoked a new type of crime, "perhaps more serious than the effects, because it accustoms the most civilized people in the world to blood, to the most ferocious spectacle, to collective murder and, by accustoming them, it then makes them more inclined to murder for other causes." Lombroso thus established a relationship between lynch mobs and those who watched them, noting that "the honest are not only spectators, but also actors of the killing," and that they enjoyed seeing victims "die prematurely, renewing the old medieval torture" (ibid.: 21).

One might find it odd that Lombroso's brief discussion of lynching in the United States makes no mention of the famous case that occurred in New Orleans in March 1891, involving not African Americans but eleven Sicilians accused of murdering the local chief of police. These Sicilians, having been found innocent by a jury, were taken from jail by a large mob and killed in the city streets in horrific ways. Lombroso would certainly have been aware of the case, given that the Italian government came close to breaking off diplomatic relations with the United States because of it, and it was widely reported in the Italian papers. Why, then, did he remain silent?

Lombroso had high regard for several Sicilian men of "letters, science, and politics"—including Sergi, Crispi, La Farina, Pitré, Amari, Paternò, Cannizzaro, Verga, and Capuana—whom he considered examples of a successful mix of Norman, Greek, and Semitic blood (Lombroso 1894c: 56). But were these Sicilian immigrants, largely illiterate unskilled laborers, to be considered entirely different? As mafiosi and inborn criminals who had somehow provoked their collective murder by the lynch mob (Gambino 1977; De Cristofaro 2023)?[2]

Southern Italians, particularly in former Confederate states, were not accepted as white ethnics. They occupied a racial middle ground in an otherwise binary system of "white-over-black." Although they were white enough for naturalization and voting rights, they were racialized as "white niggers" (Jacobson 1998: 57). After the Civil War, Italian newcomers in Louisiana replaced emancipated Black laborers, often living in crowded Sicilian neighborhoods where they spoke their dialect and preserved their customs. In some cases, Sicilians developed successful businesses serving African American customers, with whom they fraternized and even married. Because of their proximity to "Blackness," white Southerners viewed Sicilians as not fully white and, therefore, subjected them to forms of persecution typically reserved for Blacks, including lynching.

The stereotype of Southern Italians as inborn criminals circulated widely in the national press. In 1880 the *New York Times* described them as "links in a descending chain of evolution," as bandits and members of the criminal classes—poor, unskilled, and destitute. Two years later, an editorial in the *Times* referred to Italian immigrant children as "utterly unfit—ragged, filthy, and verminous as they were—to be placed in the public primary schools among the decent children of American mechanics." In 1887, the northern newspaper reported a story about a Mississippi lynching of a man named "Dago Joe," described as a "half breed" of "a Sicilian father and a mulatto mother," with "the worst characteristics of both races in his makeup." He was said to be "cunning, treacherous, and cruel, and he was regarded in the community where he lived as an assassin by nature." This was the cultural context in which the New Orleans massacre occurred.

A witness on the scene, where the police chief—of Irish descent—was killed, claimed he had heard the chief saying that he had been shot by "dagoes." However, a lack of solid evidence led the jury to acquit the accused, prompting a vigilante raid. A large mob, including members of the White League (a post-Civil War terrorist organization similar to the more famous Ku Klux Klan [KKK]) (ibid.: 57) took the prisoners from jail and executed them (Staples 2019). The following day, the *New York Times* editorial reported the bloody details: "Chief Hennessey Avenged: Eleven of his Italian Assassins Lynched by a Mob" composed "mostly of the best element" of New Orleans society. Two days later, another *Times* editorial dehumanized the victims and explicitly justified their lynching:

> These sneaking and cowardly Sicilians, the descendants of bandits and assassins, who have transported to this country the lawless passions, the cutthroat practices ... are to us a pest without mitigations. Our own rattlesnakes are as good citizens as they. Our own murderers are men of feeling and nobility compared to them. (ibid.)

The editors concluded that it would be difficult to find a single individual in the country "who would confess that privately he deplores [the lynching] very much." They may have exaggerated, but even future president Theodore Roosevelt, then serving as a high-ranking secretary in the Harrison administration, wrote to his sister that the lynching in New Orleans was "a rather good thing" and that it was time "someone gave the race what it deserved" (Roosevelt 1891). For Roosevelt's friend and Harvard companion Henry Cabot Lodge of Massachusetts, a powerful anti-immigrant patrician who would soon join the US Senate, the real issue in New Orleans was not the mob violence but the lack of confidence in juries. In Lodge's view, the lynching had been a reasonable response by good citizens to horrific secret immigrant organizations like the Mafia and their deplorable influence. He believed lynchings would become common if immigration was not restricted (Jacobson 1998: 60; Martucci 2014: 118).

However, due to pressure from the Italian government, led by the Sicilian marquis Antonio di Rudinì, and from the Italian-American communities, the New Orleans massacre did not go uncontested, as was often the case with lynchings of African Americans. One year after the New Orleans carnage, the New York Italian community inaugurated a monument to Columbus in Manhattan, which still stands at Columbus Circle. This was an important step in transforming Christopher Columbus from a figure of American iconography into that of the first Italian immigrant. By making Columbus a symbol of Italian glory, Italian Americans sought to ascend the social ladder of mainstream American whiteness (Lorini 2023). However, there was still a long way to go, which may explain Lombroso's silence on the matter.

How an Obsession with "Race Suicide" Became a Scientific Paradigm

In 1908, Guglielmo Ferrero—Lombroso's son-in-law and the coauthor of *The Female Offender* (1895), the first of the criminologist's works to appear in English[3]—visited

President Theodore Roosevelt. An authority on ancient history, Ferrero had just completed a highly successful lecture tour of major American universities. Roosevelt, who had read the French translation of Ferrero's latest volume, *Grandezza e decadenza di Roma* (1902–6), sent the Italian scholar a very enthusiastic letter inviting him to the White House.

Ferrero found Roosevelt an ideal embodiment of the American characteristics he would later explore in "The Riddle of America" (*The Atlantic* 1913). "I'm a barbarian, *Signor* Ferrero," the president said after showing his guest an extensive collection of guns from his hunting trips in Africa. Ferrero later described his impressions: "The man finds a keen delight in violent exercise, in dangerous sports, in savage nature," and "in all that seems most completely opposed to the refinements of civilization." Yet that self-proclaimed "barbarian" was a voracious reader—an "intellectual, as they say in Europe; a scholar as they say here." For Ferrero, Roosevelt exemplified the contradictory forces of American society that fascinated and shocked European visitors, as well as the relentless belief in progress that defined early-twentieth-century American culture (Ferrero 1908).

Born in 1858 into an old New York family of Dutch ancestry, Theodore Roosevelt was a shrewd politician, a progressive reformer, an amateur historian, a naturalist, a big-game hunter, and a man committed to reinvigorating the mythical pioneer spirit of the American West. He viewed the harsh life of the old frontier as the antidote to the "racial degeneration" threatening American society—a decline he believed echoed the decadence of late imperial Rome. Industrialized cities, crowded with foreign immigrants, had eroded the Western values of courage, honor, shrewdness, independence, self-control, and leadership forged in the pioneers' struggle against "Nature" and the "Savages."

In 1898, Roosevelt saw the war against Spain as an opportunity to rekindle these values. The conflict, which targeted a "decadent" Latin empire, aimed to expand North American influence to Cuba, Puerto Rico, Samoa, and the Philippines, inaugurating the "mission" of the new "benevolent" American empire. Roosevelt chronicled his war exploits, portraying himself as a mythical hero, and soon afterward became the governor of New York, then vice president, and, in 1901, the youngest president in US history following the assassination of President William McKinley.

Throughout his career, Roosevelt was deeply preoccupied with the threat of "race suicide"—the idea that the "better races" of Americans who built the country could be replaced by inferior ones, whose higher birth rates outpaced those of Old Stock Americans. In 1901, he wrote an admiring letter to sociologist Edward A. Ross, who had coined the term "race suicide" to explain that "the higher race quietly and unmurmuringly eliminates itself rather than endure individually the bitter competition it has failed to ward off by collective action" (Ross 1901a: 88).

Ross, a proud Scottish-Irish American who taught at the universities of Stanford, Nebraska, and Wisconsin, gained popularity for his support of labor unions in their struggle to defend American wages from cheaper immigrant labor.[4] Like Roosevelt, Ross believed that American identity had been forged in the wilderness of the Old West. But by 1890, with the entire North American continent colonized, the US Census marked the end of the frontier era. No longer was there new land to claim, and with that, the incorporation of large numbers of foreign immigrants was no longer desirable. Immigration restrictions and eugenic policies were the assured antidotes to the inexorable "race suicide" of Old Stock Americans.

In his bestselling book *Social Control: Survey on the Foundation of Order* (1901), Ross made a forceful argument that the native Old Stock, biologically suited to rural life in the Midwest, was less equipped to living in industrial cities filled with masses of foreign immigrants. In his view, Latins, Slavs, Asians, and Hebrews, although "inferior races," adapted more easily than Americans to low wages and miserable living standards. These "inferior races," being naturally prolific, would outbreed the "superior" Anglo-Saxon race. After three centuries of dominance—taming the wilderness, conquering new lands, and expanding American civilization—the courageous and aggressive Anglo-Saxon breed was now failing to breed, exhausted by the stresses of modern urban and industrial life. Meanwhile, immigrant groups were multiplying at an alarming rate, threatening American democracy (Ross 1901b; Lorini 1980: 54–7).

Building on similar arguments, in 1905 President Roosevelt addressed the National Congress of Mothers, harshly admonishing white women for prioritizing self-fulfillment at the expense of their primary roles as wives and mothers: "The existence of women of this type forms one of the most unpleasant and unwholesome features of modern life." The president blamed women for the decline of the original American stock family, arguing that their reluctance to bear children threatened the survival of the nation. According to the eugenic model supported by Roosevelt, the ideal (white Anglo-Saxon) family required more than two children; otherwise this most gifted racial group would soon face extinction through "race suicide." The arithmetic was simple: if Roosevelt's wealthy New York neighbors had only one child—or none at all—while "inferior" Jewish and Southern Italian immigrants in the city's poor neighborhoods had an average of eight to ten, "racial replacement" would become inevitable (Lorini 2023: 112–13). By the 1920s, these anxieties had crystallized into policy. Positive eugenic programs—encouraging the production of the "best" races—coexisted with negative eugenic measures, such as forced sterilization and the potential elimination of so-called degenerates, which were codified into law in twenty-seven states.

From Racial Prejudices to Law: The Monumental Work of the US Immigration Commission

In 1907, President Roosevelt proposed the creation of a federal investigative commission to examine the impact of new immigration, a measure swiftly approved by Congress. From 1907 to 1911, the so-called Dillingham Commission—named after the senator who led its nine-member panel—produced forty-two volumes of reports (some 27,000 pages), granting scientific legitimacy to preexisting racial prejudices against foreign newcomers with different religions and cultural values. The commission reinforced the notion that immigration was "a problem" requiring federal intervention. Conducting research across forty-six states and several US territories, it represented an unprecedented collaboration between government and social scientists, with a staff of more than three hundred researchers in economics, sociology, law, political science, and anthropology (Benton-Cohen 2018).

Among its many lasting impacts, the Dillingham Commission significantly narrowed the interpretation of "whiteness" as a prerequisite for citizenship. It also proposed a literacy test designed to exclude the majority of illiterate Southern Europeans. The first naturalization law of 1790 had included the phrase "white persons" as a qualification for American citizenship, a criterion that had historically applied to nearly all European-born migrants. However, after 1911, not all European-born individuals were considered eligible.

The Commission's reports cited Giuseppe Sergi and Alfredo Niceforo as scientific authorities to justify restrictive immigration measures and to reinforce a distinction between Northern and Southern Italians—a form of racialization that excluded Mediterranean people from the category of "whiteness." At the same time, this distinction facilitated the inclusion of "Celtic" Northern Italians within the "old" immigrant groups of the "Nordic" type (Jacobson 1998; Guglielmo and Salerno 2003). In fact, the *Dictionary of Races or Peoples*, volume 5 of the US Immigration *Reports*, noted in the entry for "Italians":

> The Bureau of Immigration divides this race into two groups, North Italian and South Italian. These two groups differ from each other materially in language, physique, and character … The Apennine chain of mountains forms a boundary between two distinct ethnic groups, the north inhabited by a very broad-headed and tallish people. All of Italy south are occupied by a long-headed, dark "Mediterranean" race of short stature. The foremost Italian ethnologist, Sergi, traces their origin to Hamitic stock of North Africa, not Negritic or true African, although there may be some traces of an infusion of African blood in this stock in Sicily and Sardinia … An Italian sociologist, Niceforo, has pointed out that these two ethnic groups differ as radically in psychic characters as they do in physical. He describes the South Italian as excitable, impulsive, highly imaginative, impracticable; as an individualistic having little adaptability to highly organized society. The North Italian is pictured as cool, deliberate, patient, practical, and as capable of great progress in the political and social organization of modern civilization. Most of the immigration to the United States is recruited from the farming and laboring classes of Italy … Niceforo shows from Italian statistics that all crimes, and especially violent crimes, are several times more numerous among the South than the North Italians. Gambling is common. The Mafia and Camorra are institutions of great influence among the people, which take the law into their own hands and which are responsible for much of the crime. (*Dictionary of Races or Peoples* 1911: 57, 81, 82)

The Commission, however, selectively extracted from Sergi's works only those elements that aligned with preexisting American racial views. By 1901, an English translation of his *The Mediterranean Race: A Study of the Origin of European People* was available. In this work, the Italian anthropologist—who shared Lombroso's views on atavism—traced the history of the peopling of Europe during the Neolithic period. According to historian Peter D'Agostino, Sergi's narrative directly challenged "the central contention of Indo-Germanism that the civilization of classical Greece and Rome derived from Aryans, that the Latin language was not a German import as it originated in Italy" (D'Agostino 2002: 325). Sergi "browned Europe," something that Americans, obsessed with racial purity and skin color, could not accept. Why, then, would mainstream WASP North American social scientists cite Sergi as an authority? Presumably because while he argued that the Mediterranean race had once been superior to the savage Aryan invaders, he also contended that it had since degenerated, stunting Southern European cultural and social development.

American social scientists also embraced Sergi's suggestion that Aryans—the groups of North America's "old immigration"—possessed strong organizational capacities, believed in order and discipline, acted for common interests, and venerated freedom. Italics, by contrast, were rebellious, undisciplined, and incapable of being properly educated, as the Southern Italian immigrants demonstrated (Teti 2011: 179–83). No education or social improvement could make them assimilable into American society, leading to their classification as "undesirable aliens." The names of Sergi and Niceforo were thus cited rather superficially, serving to reinforce preexisting prejudices (Cerro 2017: 128).

With the publication of the monumental US Immigration Commission reports in 1911, the division between "old" and "new" immigrants became institutionalized. Northern Europeans were separated from any association with Mediterranean and African peoples, while Southern and Northern Italians were now regarded as having distinct racial origins. However, the Mediterranean's once-glorious past was stripped of any African influence; unlike Sergi, North American researchers attributed Roman classical culture to Aryan origins (D'Agostino 2002: 331). Yet, among the forty-two volumes, one challenged this rigid racial framework. Authored by Columbia University anthropologist Franz Boas, volume 38, *Changes in Bodily Form of Descendants of the Immigrants* (1911), challenged the framework and purpose of the Dillingham Commission by presenting strong evidence that the children of "new immigrants," after years of living in the United States, exhibited measurable alterations in their body shape. How did Boas reach this groundbreaking conclusion?

Franz Boas's Challenge to Racial Prejudices and Mainstream Eugenics

In the late 1880s, the German-Jewish immigrant Franz Boas chose to make the United States his adoptive country. Having grown up in a household where "the ideals of the revolution of 1848 were a living force," Boas studied physics, geography, and physical anthropology in Germany. He conducted fieldwork among Indigenous tribes of the Northwestern Pacific Coast and was responsible for anthropological exhibits and anthropometric laboratories at the Chicago World's Columbian Exposition of 1893. Boas then embarked on a career as a citizen-scientist, challenging racial prejudices and prevailing ideas on inequality. He became a central figure in New York's intellectual and public life, serving as curator of anthropological exhibits at the American Museum of Natural History, founding the Department of Anthropology at Columbia University, and collaborating with the National Association for the Advancement of Colored People (having met NAACP founder W. E. B. Du Bois at Atlanta University in 1906). In addition, he wrote scientific articles published in major journals and magazines, and was an extraordinary researcher and teacher (Lorini 1999: 76–102; Lewis 2001; King 2019).

By the time Jeremiah Jenks, a member of the Dillingham Commission and an academic at Cornell University, accepted Boas's proposal to measure immigrant children and their parents, the Columbia University anthropologist had already built a strong reputation in his field.[5] With his research team, Boas examined around 18,000 "new" immigrants living in New York neighborhoods. His findings, by producing evidence that human bodies could change in new environments, challenged mainstream views of racially fixed types. Anthropometric measurements showed that immigrant adaptability was greater than previously thought, and that children born in the United States shared more traits with Old Stock American children than with their parents. Living conditions exerted a rapid and measurable effect even on head shape, which was previously thought to be inherited and unchangeable. Boas concluded that "races were unstable," and there was no evidence to suggest that individuals from a particular racial category or nation created more problems, were less assimilable to society, or were more inclined to crime. It was what a person *did*, not what a person *was*, that made the difference (Stocking 1974: 202–18).

In 1911, Boas published his most famous work, *The Mind of Primitive Man*, in which he argued that the human mind worked the same way regardless of latitude and demonstrated that the notion of inherited racial traits was a prejudice of hegemonic Western culture. In 1912, while leading the large Italian delegation to the First Congress of Eugenics in London, Giuseppe Sergi rejected Boas's findings on the basis that they relied on erroneous statistical methods. Sergi forcefully reaffirmed his position that craniums could not be changed by external factors (Cerro 2017: 121; Piasere 2020: 40–70). His attack on Boas was not an isolated case. In the transatlantic exchange of racial ideas among early-twentieth-century social scientists, Boas became the focal point of a new chapter in the titanic dispute between proponents of heredity and those emphasizing environmental factors.

The most ferocious attack on Boas, however, came not from Europe but from his powerful enemies in New York (Boas 1917). In 1916, New York patrician lawyer, amateur zoologist, and leading eugenicist Madison Grant published his acclaimed book *The Passing of a Great Race: Or, the Racial Basis of European History*. The "great race" in question was the "superior" white Anglo-Saxon Protestant group, which Grant warned was on the verge of being replaced by "new" immigrants. A close friend of Theodore Roosevelt, Grant was also a conservationist and a promoter of national parks.

With ancestors tracing back to the Puritans and a law degree from Columbia University, Grant considered it unsettling that a foreign-born, Jewish anthropologist like Franz Boas—an American by naturalization—could hold a full professorship at his alma mater. Despite Boas's doctorate from the renowned University of Kiel and his extraordinary fieldwork for major European and North American institutions, Grant and his elitist circle refused to recognize his work as legitimate science. They therefore used all their influence to block Boas and his students from accessing research funds (King 2019: 121–3; Spiro 2009). In *The Passing of a Great Race*, Grant makes a sarcastic attack on an unnamed "expert":

> Recent attempts have been made in the interest of the inferior races among our immigrants to show that the shape of the skull does change, not merely in a century, but in a single generation. In 1910, the report of the anthropological expert of the … Immigration Commission gravely declared that a round skull Jew on his way across the Atlantic might and did have a round skull child; but a few years later, in response to the subtle elixir of American institutions as exemplified in an East Side tenement, might and did have a child whose skull was appreciably longer; and that a long skull south Italian, breeding freely, would have precisely the same experience in the reverse direction. In other words, the Melting Pot was acting instantly under the influence of a changed environment. (Grant 1916: 17–19)

For Grant, Boas was an irrational egalitarian who failed to grasp that social order needed to be maintained by morally superior elites. Grant also vehemently opposed racial mixing, which he believed had turned Southern and Eastern European neighborhoods in New York into a "cloaca gentium,"—a "sewer of races" (Spiro 2009: 204). In his beloved New York, Grant saw "old stock" Americans "literally driven off the streets" by "swarms" of immigrants who could "adopt the language of the native American … wear his clothes … steal his name; and they are beginning to take his women, but they seldom adopt his religion or understand his ideals" (Grant 1916: 80–1).

Grant devised a simplified hierarchy of three European "races": Nordic, Alpine, and Mediterranean, drawing freely from the works of the Lombrosian school. Although he cited Sergi as the primary authority on the Mediterranean race and the racial composition of Italy, he ignored the Italian anthropologist's argument that the Nordics had been contaminated by Mediterranean races of African origins. Obsessed with Nordic racial purity, Grant could not accept such a claim. Instead, he followed the reports of the Dillingham Commission, which had cleansed Europe of any African origin by "revising" Sergi's arguments. Grant placed the Nordics at the center of European history, asserting their unique racial purity and crediting them with the development of classical Roman civilization. Unlike Sergi—who maintained that the Latin language and civilization were Mediterranean and Italian accomplishments—Grant asserted that Rome's efficient legal system, military organization, and commitment to family life, loyalty, and truth stemmed from "a northern rather than a Mediterranean origin" (Grant 1916: 167–79; D'Agostino 2002: 336–7). Given his obsession with racial purity, Grant could not accept that the Sicilians and Neapolitans infesting New York might carry traces of ancient Roman heredity.

Grant's book became a bestseller, received positive reviews in journals like *Science*, and went through multiple editions and many reprints. Buoyed by its success, Grant took steps to advance his anti-Boas and anti-immigration agenda. In April 1918, he founded the Galton Society, an exclusive organization dedicated to the study of races and explicitly opposed to Boas's cultural anthropology. Alongside eugenicists Henry F. Osborn and Charles Davenport, Grant ensured that the Galton Society remained an aristocratic association, open only to native-born Americans "who are anthropologically, socially, and politically sound … no Bolsheviki need apply" (Spiro 2009: 305).

The Society wielded enormous influence, directing fundraising efforts for large-scale eugenic sterilization programs and helping to make eugenics a mainstream subject across academic disciplines. Its sixteen members, all prominent members of scientific associations like the National Academy of Sciences, the American Philosophical Society, and the American Association for the Advancement of Science, were very influential figures and used their elite status to promote bigoted prejudice as science (Okrent 2019; Spiro 2009: 306). Nativist eugenicists—highly educated upper-class white Protestant men—had nothing to fear from new immigrants yet promoted sterilization programs targeting the "unfit," and propaganda events aimed at people with "goodly heritage" from the "Nordic" Old Stock of American citizens.[6]

In the battle of science against science, some academic social scientists, emboldened by the aftermath of the Dillingham Commission reports, used popular magazines to stoke fears about a mass invasion of inferior immigrants and the "race suicide" of Old Stock Americans. Sociologist Edward Ross, for example, spent three months in New York in 1912 interviewing immigrants, immigration officials, and settlement workers for a series of articles published in the magazine *Century*. These were later collected together in the book *The Old World in the New* (1914). As the most influential contributor to nativist thought at the time, Ross catered to a public predisposed to support highly restrictive immigration laws (Lorini 1980: 5–78, 153–7; Martucci 2014: 116–18).

In his book, Ross, citing Niceforo as an authority, revived the idea of Southern Italian atavism: "Professor Niceforo shows that blue eyes and fair hair occur twice as often among the North Italians as among the people south of Rome." He argued that Southern Italians belonged to a different race, stating, "the figure of Niceforo show that the provinces that contribute most to our immigration *have been utterly sterile in creators of beauty*" (Ross 1914: 98). He appeared to indicate that there was no hope for artistic production from a population he portrayed in the most degrading physiognomic terms:

> Steerage passengers from a Naples boat show a distressing frequency of low foreheads, open mouths, weak chins, poor features, skew faces, small or knobby crania, and backless head. Such people lack the power to take rational care of themselves; hence their death-rate in New York is twice the general death-rate and thrice that of the Germans. (ibid.: 113)

Ross warned his readers to expect an early decline in the frequency of good looks among the American people: "It is unthinkable that so many persons with crooked faces, coarse mouths, bad noses, heavy jaws, and low foreheads can mingle their heredity with ours without making personal beauty yet more rare among us than it actually is." He described Southern Italians as ugly and filthy, and said that among "3,000 desperados" from Southern Italy, a figure that he took from a former New York police commissioner, there were "as many ferocious and desperate men as ever gathered in a modern city in time of peace—medieval criminals who must be dealt with under modern law" (ibid.: 109). A proud nativist from the Midwest, Ross portrayed Southern Italians as atavistic criminals—an inferior and immutable human waste polluting American society.

Conclusions

The immense efforts deployed by those obsessed with eugenics and immigration restriction to combat "race replacement" culminated in the passage of the Immigration Act of 1924 (The Johnson-Reed Act), designed to halt "a stream of alien blood." The KKK strongly supported the legislation, claiming that it was God's will to preserve America as a white Protestant nation. Named after US representative Albert Johnson, a eugenics advocate backed by the KKK, and Senator David Reed, the Act remained in effect until 1965 and was used to justify the refusal to accept refugees from Nazi Germany. In the 1930s, Hitler made Grant's book his "Bible," and Nazi racial laws cited the American Immigration Act as a model for Germany.[7]

Most Southern Italians were hard workers striving to become "white Americans." Some were radicals, union members, or held anarchist or socialist views—ideologies considered "un-American" and sometimes leading to punishment or deportation under the Espionage Act of 1917. Ironically, though, under the Italian Fascist regime, the long-standing stigma of Southern Italians as "inborn criminals" was lifted, particularly within Italian diasporic communities in the United States (Jacobson 1988; Luconi 2011). By invoking heroic figures like Columbus, the Fascist regime crafted a mythically superior "Italian identity" that made poor immigrants proud of the Roman Empire and of having brought civilization to the New World.

The introduction of Columbus Day as a national holiday in 1937 marked a crucial moment in the process by which Italian Americans became "white ethnics." How did this decision come about? It was largely the work of Generoso Pope, who had arrived in New York in 1906 as a poor fifteen-year-old from a small town near Benevento. By the early 1930s, he had risen to become the king of the building industry, one of the ten wealthiest men in New York, and a leading figure in the Knights of Columbus.

A powerful businessman with strong political connections, Pope offered his services to Benito Mussolini while also courting President Franklin Delano Roosevelt. In exchange for a national holiday honoring Columbus, he promised Roosevelt the Italian-American vote in New York for the Democratic Party. Controlling key media outlets, including radio stations and *Il Progresso Italo Americano*, Pope effectively spread Fascist propaganda, promoting a sense of racial pride within the Italian-American community.[8] Supporters of the Fascist regime hailed Mussolini as "the modern Columbus," viewing him as a leader who could restore Italian-American dignity in the face of the anti-Catholic WASP racism of the 1920s.

Fascist rhetoric on Italian racial superiority incorporated aspects of Sergi and Niceforo's views while rejecting Lombroso's theories as "Jewish science." This narrative resonated with Italian immigrants who had found success in the American business world and were eager to "act white" by distancing themselves from African Americans, socialists, and anarchists. Little by little, by the 1930s, many Italian Americans opposed African American rights as a means of assimilating into the American mainstream. Meanwhile, citizen-scientist Franz Boas continued his battle for racial equality and cultural pluralism. In 1933, in front of the university in Kiel, Germany—where he had studied—Boas's books were burned alongside those of Marx, Freud, Trotsky, and Einstein.

Notes

1. A total of 4,500 people were lynched in the United States between 1880 and 1930 (Lorini 2019: 221–46).
2. The mayor of New Orleans issued an official apology for this act of anti-immigrant violence 130 years after the lynching.
3. On the complex story of the translation of this book and the tumultuous relationship between Lombroso and the young scholar at that time, see Montaldo (2019: 189–97).
4. Ross is often depicted as a champion of academic freedom due to his dismissal from Stanford University for expressing publicly his opposition to the cheap Asian laborers who were used by the university's owner to build Californian railroads (Lorini 1980: 53–4; Frezza 2007).
5. Boas had already completed a pilot study of schoolchildren in Worcester, Massachusetts (Stocking 1974: 59).
6. By 1924 twenty-seven states had enacted pro-sterilization laws, and some 3,000 people had been sterilized. Additionally, Virginia passed the Racial Integrity Act, which required individuals to declare their race ("white" or "colored") on their marriage licenses.
7. The law prevented immigration from Asia and set limited quotas on the number of immigrants from Eastern and Southern Europe.
8. A staunch anti-communist, Pope quickly reinvented himself during the war as an anti-Fascist and later emerged as a strong supporter of the Christian Democratic Party from the United States.

Part III

Transnational Debates on Art, Prison, Anarchism, and Blackness

10

Beautiful Poems and Dirty Literature: Criminological Readings of Mass Culture in South America

Diego Galeano

Introduction

During a visit to Italian prisons at the beginning of the twentieth century, the criminologist José Ingenieros spoke with several detainees, and one thing in particular caught his attention. He used the concept of "criminal vanity" to describe what he observed: namely, that the criminals were highly concerned with their public reputation, with how their names circulated in the press, and with the possibility that some of this fame might outlive them.

Born in Sicily in 1877 as Giuseppe Ingegneri, Ingenieros migrated to Argentina with his parents as a child. There, he earned a degree in medicine and became the director of the Institute of Criminology at the National Penitentiary of Buenos Aires, where he began to build a career that would make a pillar of South American criminological science (Ben Plotkin 2021: 19–41).

In one of his tours of Italian prisons, Ingenieros met a Calabrian prisoner who implored him to publish his picture in one of his forthcoming books. He also encountered a Neapolitan *camorrista* who sent his writings to newspapers that frequently published critiques of the police, a murderer preoccupied with writing his autobiography, and an endless stream of detainees eager to share their stories, "show off their exploits," and, not infrequently, fabricate "imaginary misdeeds." Ingenieros concluded that the offenders who wrote poems, sought to inscribe their names in some criminal pantheon and yearned for the recognition of posterity that could have "numbered in the millions" (Ingenieros 1907: 15). "Lombroso mentions many similar cases," he noted, briefly referencing the Italian's earlier observations on the relationship between vanity and prison writings.

Ingenieros dedicated an extensive work to the study of the "simulation of talent" and interpreted vanity as a by-product of the excessive quest for fame in mass society. Although the problem extended beyond the criminal world, he conceptualized the obsession with fabricating stories inside prison walls as a manifestation of deviance. Like Lombroso, the Italian-Argentine criminologist interpreted these writing practices as "illnesses of vanity" and as indicative of "morbid types." The mediocre quality of the literature produced by prisoners—whose identity as authors mattered little—served to confirm medical assumptions concerning their personality and the immoral nature of places of incarceration.

By the end of the eighteenth century, prison writings had already established themselves as a genre focused on the brutality and inhumane conditions of confinement (Schorn and Williams 2017). However, it was only in the second half of the nineteenth century that diverse disciplines such as forensic medicine, psychiatry, criminology, and pedagogy began to make these writing practices the subject of a broad field of inquiry into the normal and the pathological. Like hieroglyphs to be observed and decoded, the written work of prisoners (along with those of the suicidal and mentally ill) became objects of scientific scrutiny and a gateway to understanding the mysteries of crime. The proliferation of studies on prison writing, slang, and tattoos belonged to a movement that tended to interpret them as symbols revealing a profound truth about the nature of delinquency (Artières 2013: 45–55).

Before embarking on a systematic critique of Lombroso's criminology, Ingenieros defended a theory about the relationship between culture and crime.[1] In an article published in a Uruguayan literary magazine, he attributed to crime an important "intellective function," claiming that it inspired the "geniuses of art" in their task of intuiting phenomena that would later be transformed into rational theories by the "geniuses of science." Starting from this law of the progressive integration of knowledge, Ingenieros advocated a bottom-up epistemology. He argued that throughout history, human knowledge moved closer to truth by emerging first from "embryonic manifestations" originating in an "instinctive and nebulous understanding by part of the popular mass that crystallizes it in their daily speech or in the form of proverbs." Next, great artists "filter and synthesize this diffuse knowledge," transforming it, for example, into works of theater and novels. Finally, science arises to produce theory, which is how the truth about crime is uncovered. Without prison poetry, and lowbrow popular literature, there would have been no Shakespeare, Dostoevsky, or Balzac, and without them there would have been no Lombroso. Thus, the "genius ideas of the sage of Turin" and his entire criminological edifice had their distant origin in this plebeian criminal literary production, which included prison writings (Ingenieros 1899).

Ingenieros's reading took place within a broad, varied, and at times critical South American reception of Cesare Lombroso's work on vanity and prison literature (particularly several chapters from *L'uomo delinquente* and *Palimsesti del carcere*). This corpus offers a criminological perspective on the effects of the massification of culture. Scholars have made significant strides in understanding the effects that Lombroso's work had *on* the mass culture of his time, from the dissemination of his ideas in the commercial press to their influence on *fin-de-siècle* literary production. However, there has been less focus on the criminological interpretations *of* mass cultural consumption.[2] By examining the connections between literary production in prisons and the circulation of scientific knowledge between Southern Europe and South America, this chapter delves into the effects of these interpretations.

The very concept of "mass" played a central role in the language used by the criminologists, with Ingenieros himself referring to the cultural production of the "popular mass." This perspective followed the path laid out by crowd psychology, with its insistence on the collective phenomenon of criminal contagion.

This chapter begins by analyzing Argentine and Brazilian appropriations of Lombroso's theme of "prison literature," reconstructing the interpretations and translations of Cesare Lombroso's work, along with the essays of Enrico Ferri and Scipio Sighele on this topic. It also discusses the reception of French criminology (including the work of Pierre Valette, Émile Laurent, and others) and its role in the international dissemination of the theory of "herostratism," which denounced the modern practice of committing crimes in order to become famous. Furthermore, the chapter reveals the significant contributions made by South American criminologists and police officers to the transatlantic dialogue surrounding the concepts of criminal "vanity," "suggestion," and "imitation." It explores how, by the 1910s, this debate acquired new meanings amid emerging anxieties about cinematography. Many of the specialists involved, including Ingenieros, were descendants of immigrants and participated in the tensions experienced by their societies as a result of geographical, economic, and social mobility. These conversations were therefore not limited to scientists, but included the voices of journalists, police, and judicial officials, all of whom were concerned about what they saw as the pernicious effects of mass cultural consumption in the early 1900s.

Literature in prisons

In late 1913, the popular magazine *A Ilustração Brasileira* released a series of four articles under the heading "The Literature of the Prisons." They discussed jailhouse poetry, prisoners who wrote songs or works of prose, and the preferred reading material of detainees. The author, Elisio de Carvalho, was the director of the police's Bureau of Identification. He was a highly unusual police officer—not a beat cop, but rather a man of letters from the Brazilian Northeast who, from his post in the state bureaucracy, sought to make a name for himself among the elites of Rio de Janeiro, the capital of the young Brazilian republic (Galeano and Rodrigues 2017).

Carvalho's attempt to position himself as a sort of tropical Alphonse Bertillon and align with the global wave of innovation in the field of scientific policing proved rather dynamic. In 1907, he founded a magazine called *Boletim Policial*, in which he translated essential criminological and criminalistic texts. He also produced a series of pamphlets containing both his own works and translations of global luminaries in criminal science: from Ferri and Sighele to Edmond Locard and Rudolph Reiss, the Swiss-German criminalist whom Carvalho brought to Rio in 1913 to speak at a series of conferences (Carvalho 1913a).

The stories about prison literature were illustrated with photographs of the authors and readers, along with excerpts from writings collected from the municipal jail (*Casa de Detenção*). Although Carvalho also published specialized works in the field of scientific policing, these accounts were aimed at the broader audience of illustrated magazines popular at the time. They were made possible in part because of Carvalho's position as a civil servant familiar with the jail and its records. The identification bureau he directed was located in a police office adjacent to the jail and was responsible for photographing and registering the convicts. He thus included numerous cases of prison writers from Rio de Janeiro, who were often well known to the local press. However, the stories' narrative structure and subject matter, along with references to other criminals of letters whose work gained notoriety in the international press, suggest that Carvalho' work owed as much to his library research as to *in situ* observations in the local jail.

Carvalho opened his first instalment with the assertion that "Criminals have always been obsessed with writing" (1913b: 369). The series as a whole followed the path trodden by other experts on crime, from the reference to the French murderer Pierre-François Lacenaire (writer of poems and an autobiography) to the citation of the well-known memoirs of Vidocq (Lejeune 1986; Kalifa 2005: 67–102). In addition to the signals that such names conveyed, the text presented a dual problem that was also present in earlier criminological works. First, Carvalho analyzed a "literature that emanates directly from the prisoners," suggesting it should be read less for its aesthetic virtues than as a "manifestation of a mentality." Its value was eminently scientific: jailhouse literature was best viewed as a window into the criminal soul. Second, as the author ironically and disparagingly insinuated, reading these texts required considerable effort: "We aren't dealing with great poets, nor with great authors of prose: almost all of them lack talent, are mediocre at best and, to summarize, are nothing more than mere graphomaniacs."[3] Through this notion of written culture as an expression of the criminal mind and a field of scientific observation, the connection to the discipline of criminology, in which Lombroso held a central position, becomes evident.

Like the theoretical lineage upon which he based his work, Carvalho connected prison writing to a literary practice of "ordinary" and "mediocre" men both within and outside the prison walls. He used the French term *colportage* to refer to the street sale of popular verses and short stories, which in Brazil were known as *literatura de cordel* (Curran 2001: 43–8). According to Carvalho, this popular reading material consisted of "the recounting in prose or verse of the most famous happenings of the criminal universe" and was known to "more or less everyone" (Carvalho 1913b: 369). The slim pamphlets containing this literature were hawked in the streets and public squares by an army of vendors who loudly proclaimed their content. As in Europe and elsewhere in the Americas, in Rio de Janeiro, crime was one of the *colportage* market's favorite topics.

Carvalho was somewhat vague when it came to crediting his sources. Nevertheless, he did acknowledge them indirectly in a passage about prose writers referring to Carleto, a famous criminal who was serving a long sentence for the "crime of Carioca Street," a brutal murder in 1906. "A true archetype of degeneration," Carleto's face resembled one "of those faces that illustrate the atlases of Lombroso and Ferri" (Carvalho 1913c: 406).[4] According to the press, Carleto was an Italian immigrant in Buenos Aires who fled to Brazil at the start of the twentieth century to escape the police, who were pursuing him for a series of robberies. His case received a great deal of attention in Brazilian newspapers and periodicals, popular literature, and specialized criminological publications (Dias 2010: 51–98, Porto 2010). Carleto also stood out as one of the few prison authors in whom Carvalho recognized some literary talent, in addition to highlighting that he read Virgil and Dante and was familiar with "various Italian works of criminal anthropology" (Carvalho 1913c: 406).

Embedded within these words—and indeed within Carvalho's entire series of stories about jailhouse literature—was a tension between the cognitive and aesthetic value of prisoners' writings. To historicize this dynamic, it is necessary to analyze the textual networks that, both directly and indirectly, shaped the interpretations of South American specialists in criminology and scientific policing. While Carvalho's stories were neither unique nor original, they serve as a guiding thread for examining the processes of reading and translation that constituted this detailed investigation of prison writing.

Carvalho's account drew on the French critique of criminal anthropology—particularly the work of Émile Laurent—to challenge the very notion of "prison literature." He argued that the inmates, who had no appreciation for reading, were vain and cynical souls who wrote obscene and repetitive texts lacking any "elevation of style" (a judgment that also applied to their drawings and plastic arts). For Carvalho, the expression "literature by criminals" was an oxymoron because literature, like any art form, presupposed masterpieces, originality, aesthetic virtue, and, above all, well-defined "moral ends." He noted that the prisoners lacked all of these qualities in the same measure as they possessed an excess of "criminal vanity" (1913b: 406–407).

Carvalho must have read the passages in Laurent's book discussing vanity, the "literature of the inmates," and the "artistic aptitude of the inmates" (1908: 81–109). This section was, strictly speaking, a gloss on the ideas of another French author, Pierre Valette, a disciple of Alexandre Lacassagne, who five years earlier had defended his doctoral thesis in Lyon on "herostratism and criminal vanity."[5] The name of Herostratus, known for setting fire to the Temple of Artemis to gain notoriety, was appropriated by French legal medicine to refer to crimes motivated by the modern obsession with gaining public recognition. Lacassagne and Valette were also the sources for José Ingenieros's article on this topic, in which he accused the crime columns in dailies, gazettes, and illustrated magazines of having become "an entire system to foment criminal vanity." For Ingenieros (1907: 17–21), reading and vanity constituted "the psychological pairing of modern herostratism."

As Ingenieros acknowledged, the topic of literature written by prisoners had been present from Cesare Lombroso to Scipio Sighele. However, Carvalho, who was less proficient in Italian than his Argentine counterpart, approached the question of criminal vanity by studying the works of Lacassagne, Valette, and other French authors. This was not simply an issue of language. The French approach, in addition to adopting a more moralistic and censorious tone, emphasized sociological factors external to the criminal. It highlighted in particular the role of crime reporting in the press and the "publicity" it gave to crime, along with the influence of a "dirty literature" that fueled the reader's imagination by glamorizing the lives of thieves and murderers.[6]

Born and raised among ordinary people, modern criminals, in their vanity, committed crimes in pursuit of glory and to boast of their exploits. It was no coincidence that jails were the main laboratory for all this written and oral imaginative expression, recounted in prose and verse. Following the lead of his French sources, Carvalho (1913d) even took the trouble to discover what materials the prisoners read, dedicating the final instalment of his series to this topic. Unlike Carleto, most of them consumed popular adventure novels and crime-themed literature, which circulated in the form of *cordel* pamphlets. Filled with blood, obscenity, and vice, these readings, Carvalho concluded, did not improve the convicts' souls but instead exacerbated their worst tendencies.

Criminal Suggestions

"It would be like looking for a diamond in a sewer," Émile Laurent (1908: 84) remarked, dismissing the possibility of attributing any aesthetic value to the literature produced in prisons. This outright rejection of any literary ability among prisoners had an indirect interlocutor: Cesare Lombroso. The point of departure for the discussion was the chapter on prison literature in *L'uomo delinquente*,[7] which Lombroso expanded upon in 1888 in *Palimsesti del carcere*, a monumental collection of writings, autobiographies, letters, poems, paintings, and other prison works that he had gathered among his personal papers.

Lombroso, however, was more ambivalent than his French and South American counterparts regarding the artistic merit of criminal art. In *L'uomo delinquente*, he referred to criminal literature as a "sort of anonymous library that is of very little benefit to the people and, indeed, often harmful." He warned about the damage this criminal culture could cause, pointing out that thieves were "avid readers of these texts that unfortunately produce more thieves." In his collection of prison poetry, presented in both prose and verse, Lombroso claimed that prison writing "denuded the soul of the habitual offender," with its demonstrations of cynicism, impulses toward greed, and thirst for vengeance. Still, despite these critical observations, he was not entirely scornful of the literature emanating from the minds of prisoners. He occasionally recognized the existence of "beautiful poems" and even admitted that "an aesthetic sense is not totally lacking in criminals" (Lombroso 1889: 508–18).

Lombroso's prison songbook was characterized by laments over lost freedom, fits of vengeance, and rage directed toward judges and the police. His personal collection had grown significantly since the first edition of 1876, bolstered by his tours of Italian prisons and public squares, but also by admirers who, from an early date, sent him material from across Europe and the Americas (Leschiutta 1996; Montaldo 2015: 127–44). In fact, in one section in which Lombroso allowed for the possibility that the poetry might have a degree of aesthetic merit, he referred to two poems sent from Brazil by a "Dr. Ferriere," who had "carried out excellent studies of the topic," and he devoted considerable effort to translating these into Italian for the fourth edition of *L'uomo delinquente*. One was the lyrics of a bitter song dictated by a murderer just days before his execution; the other, a poem written by a seminarian who had murdered a prostitute.

The original Portuguese versions of the poems had been sent from Recife, capital of the state of Pernambuco, whose law school—the oldest and most traditional in the country—pioneered the dissemination of Lombroso's work in Brazil (Álvarez 2003: 72–82). Although "Dr. Ferriere's" letter was not preserved in Lombroso's archive, the *Diário de Pernambuco* offers some intriguing clues. In an issue published shortly after the release of *Palimpsesti del carcere*, a letter from Lombroso appeared in response to a series of articles by Pernambuco's leading criminologist, João Vieira. Lombroso wrote, "The influence of his voice in his School [of Law of Recife] has certainly had the effect of attracting convicted and active supporters to us," adding that "Dr. Ferrer sent me a beautiful work that I have wanted to thank him for."[8]

Another issue of the same newspaper helps clarify the identity of Lombroso's Brazilian interlocutor: it was most likely Vicente Ferrer de Barros, a lawyer who, also in 1888, produced an early Portuguese translation of two chapters of *L'uomo delinquente*. These were published as separate pamphlets—one focusing on the religion of criminals, the other specifically on their literature. It seems plausible, therefore, that Ferrer also sent him the two poems as well as his own work on the subject.[9]

This transatlantic circulation of prison letters and artifacts formed part of an early network of communication between Lombroso and Latin American criminologists in the 1880s. In addition to adding legitimacy to the careers of doctors and legal scholars striving to establish themselves as local authorities in criminal science, these contacts were a major impetus for successive new editions and translations of Lombroso's own work (Caimari 2009; Petit 2010; Sozzo 2017). As a result, the constant rewriting of his books produced textual palimpsests, within which traces of the international discourse on the relationship between crime and mass culture were inscribed.

It is therefore necessary to understand this criminological corpus as existing in a state of constant flux, which in turn prompts reflection on the historicity of the debate and the specificity of its reading contexts. At the turn of the century, a second wave of South American interest emerged, focusing on the chapters concerning criminal literature in *L'uomo delinquente* and *Palimsesti del carcere*, as well as on works like *I delinquenti nell'arte* by Enrico Ferri (1896) and *Letteratura tragica* by Scipio Sighele (1906).[10] In this period, which included the contributions by Ingenieros, the debate was dominated by an issue that Sighele dubbed "literary suggestion"—the risk of contagion and imitation associated with cultural consumption. At that time, not only had theater and literature fallen under this concern, but so too had crime writing, which had already gained prominence in illustrated weeklies, blurring the boundaries between crime reporting and detective fiction.

These ideas circulated amid heated discussions in South America about the detrimental role of the mass media. Since the late nineteenth century, criticism had mounted regarding the excessive interference of journalists in fields properly belonging to specialists in crime, such as the police, judges, prosecutors, and forensic doctors. Sensationalist reporting and the relentless pursuit of scoops were repeatedly condemned for hindering investigations, disrupting the production of briefs and expert reports, and complicating trials. As if all this were not enough, newspapers and weeklies enabled detective novels, serialized in instalments, to reach an expanding working-class readership (Caimari 2004: 169–71).

In August 1914, Celso Vieira, a Brazilian legal scholar teaching at the police school founded by Elisio de Carvalho, delivered a public lecture in Rio de Janeiro. His topic was the relationship between the publicizing of crime and the preventive work of the police. Vieira reviewed criminological works on the "phenomenon of imitative propagation," tracing their evolution from Lombroso, Tarde, and Lacassagne to more contemporary works by Sighele, and did so with a critical eye toward their theoretical legacy. Speaking to a diverse audience packed in the auditorium of the police department, Vieira acknowledged the problem of "direct contagion" through the glorification of crime in society. This phenomenon, he argued, infiltrated daily life, spreading an unrelenting incitement to crime that reached the "bosom of families" and wreaked havoc on the social development of the youth. He noted that young people also absorbed this unhealthy influence in schools and bars and were directly exposed "to conversations in which the exploits of criminals are praised, and the advantages of crime are touted amid the disastrous promiscuity of prisons" (Vieira 1915: 182).

Beyond acknowledging the serious harm caused by these spaces of direct contamination, Vieira was more skeptical about the phenomenon of indirect contagion through literary and journalistic consumption. He disagreed with the axiom that "bad reading" was equivalent to "bad company." Vieira's divergence from this interpretation was not rooted so much in theory, but rather in the realities of police surveillance. In South America, the threat of criminal suggestion among readers and theatergoers was less severe than in Europe, as its effects on impressionable minds were kept under control by market dynamics. With theater tickets and books being so expensive, criminal-themed cultural production did not "attract crowds" and instead became "a kind of cocaineism or literary morphinism, cultivated in the performance halls or the bedrooms" (Vieira 1915: 215).

Since Vieira assumed that the elites were less susceptible to suggestion than the lower classes, he saw no need to increase censorship of printed materials or police persecution of sellers of popular books, as was happening across the Atlantic. Using the same argument, he emphatically defended the freedom of the press, even while acknowledging the problematic role of police journalism. He argued that exaggerating the "maleficent role of publicity" was unnecessary in the South American context of widespread illiteracy, which had its roots in the same poverty that underpinned crime. However, Vieira's benevolence reached its limit when confronted with a new development: cinema. He saw this as capable of inciting criminal suggestion among audiences gathered in front of the big screen. Unlike reading, he believed that the "heroic remedy" of state control over popular consumption was necessary in this new realm of mass culture. Municipalities should regulate minors' access to movie theaters, and the police should oversee film censorship.

The years leading up to the First World War saw a third wave of interest in criminological discourse surrounding crime and mass culture, particularly regarding the potential for criminal suggestion in cinema and the need to suppress "scandalous films" (Kalifa 1995: 199–219). Along with the arrival in South America of the series *Zigomar*, *Nick Carter*, and *Fantômas*—which in Europe were accused of glorifying crime and corrupting youth—early crime films also included some local productions. It is in this context, which differed somewhat from the criminological view of written culture at the turn of the century, that Vieira's references to the "hypnotic zone" of criminal contagion must be understood. The criminologist Rudolph Reiss dedicated a lecture to this topic during a stay in Rio de Janeiro in 1913 (Reiss 1913), while Elisio de Carvalho, the promoter of Reiss's visit, published articles around the same time discussing the influence of the film industry on the criminal world.

The impetus for Carvalho's writings came from a feature film about a bloody episode that had captivated readers of Brazilian newspapers: *Um crime sensacional* (1913), which dramatized a grisly double homicide solved shortly before the movie's theatrical release. Depicting real criminal cases on screen was not a novelty; one of the first titles of the emerging national film industry had been *Os estranguladores* (1908), which portrayed the aforementioned Carioca Street crime that led to Carleto's imprisonment. While these productions enjoyed public success, they were also subjected to police scrutiny, resulting in bans on screenings and the seizure of film reels (Navitski, 2017: 123–66). However, Carvalho refrained from criticizing the film, as doing so would have required him to admit to having mingled with an audience he despised. Instead, he directly analyzed the "corrupting nature of cinema" (Carvalho 1913e), which had reemerged as a subject of interest in works on criminal suggestion.

In most literary genres, it was difficult to draw a clear line between entertainment and incitement to crime, but the film industry seemed to eliminate any ambiguity. From Carvalho's perspective, its ability to "make an impression on the imagination of the vulgar" rendered it a living manual of crime, detailing how to plan offenses and evade police detection and capture. The cinema was a veritable "school of crime and immorality," possessing an exceptional ability to awaken the worst latent tendencies in vulnerable spirits. The "primitive ferments of theft, homicide, and lust" that Lombroso had observed could be ignited through suggestion, contagion, and imitation of the scenes displayed on screen (Carvalho 1913e). The solution to this emerging problem, Carvalho argued, was to follow the example of several European countries and nearby Argentina by implementing police control over film reels and prohibiting screenings. Like Vieira, he called for extending the police censorship apparatus already in place in Rio de Janeiro for theater to the burgeoning film industry (Carvalho 1913f).

The fact that these texts were published in mass-circulation newspapers, rather than being confined to journals specializing in criminology, should be understood within its immediate context. Amid legal debates and pressure from various Catholic organizations—who criticized cinema for its supposed immorality and potential influence on juvenile delinquency—police surveillance of mass culture continued to escalate in South America in the years that followed. Consequently, a contextual and strategic interpretation of the criminological theory of suggestion became integral to the heated debate surrounding the role of state agencies in regulating cultural consumption.

Conclusions

In his article on vanity, José Ingenieros noted the emergence of a field of knowledge coming into its own at the beginning of the twentieth century: "scientific policing." This focused less on explaining the etiology of criminal behavior and more on developing specific techniques to combat its effects and support the criminal justice system. Ingenieros described how, at Salvatore Ottolenghi's Scuola di Polizia Scientifica in

Rome, police officers were taught to exploit the vanity of suspects to gain an advantage in criminal investigations. During interrogations of professional thieves, officers would play on their obsession with fame, praising their criminal skills and treating them as masters of their craft. This tactic encouraged suspects to "confirm that honorable reputation" by revealing details of their own "criminal biography" and that of their accomplices. Ingenieros (1907: 18) claimed to have witnessed this technique in action at the Buenos Aires police investigation bureau and opined that this confirmed "an old claim of Lombroso": that professional vanity in criminals was stronger than in artists, writers, elegant women, and even doctors—which was quite a statement.[11]

This passage from *L'uomo delinquente* was widely cited in contemporary criminological literature and sparked a prolonged and varied transatlantic conversation about criminal vanity, art, and literature produced by criminals. This conversation unfolded over time and encompassed various waves of interest in the work of Lombroso, his disciples, and his detractors: the first wave in the 1880s, which involved correspondence between experts and the circulation of prison writings along the same Atlantic routes that brought the first books of criminal anthropology to South America; the second wave at the turn of the century, featuring a debate on literary suggestion, heavily influenced by the voices of Ferri and Sighele; and the third wave in the 1910s, marked by a reinterpretation of earlier theories in light of the emergence of cinema as a new form of cultural production. Given this context, it is not surprising that moralists concerned about the potential repressive implications of these ideas proliferated along the Atlantic coast of South America, which was home to a thriving publishing industry, numerous variety theater companies, and the region's main film productions.

The conversation was also varied because it extended beyond the spaces typically reserved for discussions among specialists in forensic medicine and criminology—such as university professorships, doctoral theses, laboratories for observing prisoners, and scientific journals. The impact of these ideas on other areas, such as reports in high-circulation illustrated weeklies, daily police work, and, above all, life in prisons, warrants further investigation. The prisoners themselves, who—like Carleto—were familiar with "several Italian works of criminal anthropology," were ultimately writing to add their voices to the chorus of interpretations about the effects of mass culture on the world of crime (Galeano 2016).

The diversity of voices and perspectives led to distinct styles of argumentation. Criminologists discussed the nuances between the "suggestion" affecting fragile spirits ("degenerates" and minors) and "contagion" as a broader phenomenon that could also influence "normal" (albeit unscrupulous) subjects. Police publications, more concerned with negotiating the boundaries of state intervention in entertainment markets than with the etiology of deviance, tended to stress the need to distinguish between the right to amuse and the detrimental effects of publicizing crime. They highlighted concerns about "imitation" inspired by news reports or movie scenes, as well as the potential obstruction of investigations and the administration of justice. Despite these differences, both groups shared a fundamental distrust of mass culture and began to cultivate a common outlook that associated the circulation of news, literature, and, later cinematography with the rise of modern forms of crime.

Notes

1. On the critiques José Ingenieros made of Lombroso in his criminological work of the 1910s, see Salvatore (2006) and Creazzo (2007: 150–61).
2. Rafter and Ystehede (2009). On the massification of writing, see Lyons (2012).
3. Carvalho (1913b: 369). Attention to the "ordinary" writing of "mediocre men" was also central to the work of Ingenieros (Mailhe 2013).
4. The Ibero-American Institute in Berlin preserves a catalogue of Carvalho's personal library, but there are no works on criminology and scientific policing. A note clarifies that "the catalogued books represent one-twentieth of the library, the rest having been sold by a worthy bookseller-publisher" when Carvalho was still alive (Paiva 1926: 2).
5. Valette himself acknowledged in his thesis that he owed to his teacher Lacassagne the authorship of the concept of "herostratism" (Valette 1903: 8). On the use of the concept of herostratism in the criminological discourse on anarchism, see: Albornoz (2021: 16).
6. Carvalho also cited the work of Raymond Hesse (1912). The French expression "*littérature ordurière*" (dirty literature) appears in Valette (1903: 28).
7. This was chapter 9 of the first Italian edition (1876) and, in an enlarged and revised version, chapter 12 of the 1889 edition, one of the most widely circulated in South America, along with the French translation of 1887 (Sansone 2022: 82–8).
8. Lombroso concluded by explaining that he could not locate Ferrer, since the postal service had returned his letter of appreciation, which he included in his reply to João Vieira in the hope that it would reach its intended recipient: 'Honroso' (1888), *Diário de Pernambuco*, Recife, December 19: 3.
9. 'Biblioteca provincial' (1888), *Diário de Pernambuco*, Recife, May 9: 3. These exchanges of letters can be pinpointed with some chronological precision, since the reference to Ferrer and the poems of Recife do not appear in the French edition (1887) but do appear in the *Palimsesti* (Lombroso 1888b: 88, 115).
10. Ferri's and Sighele's works had partial and complete translations into Portuguese and Spanish; see: Ferri (1899); Sighele (1908; 1910).
11. The original sentence by Cesare Lombroso (which, in contrast to Ingenieros, did not include doctors) is in Lombroso (1889: 386).

11

"Exaggerations of the Truth": Cesare Lombroso, Criminology and Anarchism in Argentina

Martín Albornoz

Introduction

The news that broke on the morning of October 20, 1909, caused a stir across South America. The day before, the renowned doctor and criminologist Cesare Lombroso had passed away in his sleep at his home in Turin at the age of seventy-four. The press was unanimous in paying tribute. In Buenos Aires, a prominent daily captured the prevailing sentiment, declaring that "universal science" had lost "one of its princes."[1] In the major cities of South America, state and cultural institutions interrupted their routines to honor Lombroso. In Rio de Janeiro, the Senate declared an official day of mourning, while in Santiago de Chile, various civil groups quickly organized a "funeral wake" in his honor.[2] Distinguished Argentine criminologist José Ingenieros spoke at the University of Buenos Aires to improvise a eulogy for Lombroso, whose passing, he said, "grieves contemporary science and merits the respectful homage of every educated person. Friends and adversaries may raise their voices in unison to express their most heartfelt condolences."[3]

Ingenieros was not wrong about the scope of the mourning. It is not surprising that Argentine socialists echoed the mainstream press, as they regarded Lombroso as one of their own.[4] What might be more surprising, however, is that, despite some reservations, the anarchist press reacted in a similar manner. In São Paulo, *La Battaglia* remarked that although Lombroso "was wrong on many occasions," they felt compelled to honor the "memory of this great worker."[5] In Buenos Aires, *La Protesta*, the leading anarchist publication in South America, suggested suspending critical judgment in order to appreciate Lombroso's work: "This is not the time to dispute his theories; it is enough to say that he contributed to the intellectual progress of his time, was a master of his subject, and as such, we lament his passing. With Lombroso, the scientific world has lost one of its leading lights."[6]

Anyone familiar with the historiography of criminology and anarchism in Argentina and elsewhere might be surprised to see left-wing militants lamenting the death of a man often remembered as a steadfast opponent. Overlooking the more nuanced views expressed in his other texts, Lombroso's relationship with anarchism was often reduced to his one work addressing anarchists specifically, *Gli anarchici*, from 1894, which marked an unofficial rift between the Italian criminologist and the radical movement. Scholarship has generally depicted criminology as a tool primarily intended to reinforce state power (Zimmerman 1994; Suriano 1990; Salessi 1995; Ansolabehere 2012), overlooking the significant interest anarchists took in criminal science. With few exceptions, this reductive interpretation—which also appears in studies on anarchism—omits important aspects, including the voices of the anarchists themselves. Although they believed that Lombroso "as often happens with learned men, exaggerated the truth," they nevertheless recognized his positive contributions to the science of sociology.[7]

This chapter aims to examine this ambiguity and contribute to recent studies suggesting that there was, in fact, considerable common ground between anarchists and criminologists, including in the work of Lombroso himself (Girón 2002; Bass 2019). Patricio Geli (1992) pioneered this analytical approach in the Argentine context, observing the productive ways some Buenos Aires anarchists engaged with Italian criminology. Building on this argument and considering the enormous circulation of Lombroso's texts in South America, I intend to conduct an in-depth examination of events in Argentina where both anarchism and criminology had an international impact. I hope to demonstrate that the relationship between these fields was marked by a dynamic and sustained exchange, challenging the notion that it can be characterized as simple antagonism.

A Great Contemporary Thinker

In South America, the spread of Cesare Lombroso's ideas on anarchism was not driven by local realities. By the end of the nineteenth century, in countries where anarchism was not yet seen as a pressing concern, interest in the movement arose largely due to news about the situation in Europe, which filled the pages of the leading local newspapers. Even before the publication of *Gli anarchici* in 1894, readers of the popular press in South American cities were already familiar with the exploits of celebrated anarchists such as Ravachol, Émile Henry, Vittorio Pini, Auguste Vaillant, and Sante Caserio, all central characters in the anarchist drama that Lombroso would later portray (Albornoz 2021; C. Leal 2006).[8] Thus, one might argue that Lombroso was not the first writer to address the subject but rather built upon an international phenomenon that, according to one Argentine observer, had become the "subject on everyone's lips."[9]

These discussions were fueled by telegrams, correspondence, editorials, and opinion pieces that, reflecting more fascination than fear, attempted to understand what anarchism truly was and what might drive someone to set off a bomb in a bar or assassinate a president in public. Leading this chorus of amazement were major international writers who sought to answer these questions from very different perspectives. Portuguese writer Eça De Queiroz, a regular correspondent in Paris for the Rio de Janeiro newspaper *Gazeta de Noticias*, frequently focused on the actions of French anarchists in his chronicles (1892; 1894). Meanwhile, Nicaraguan writer Rubén Darío, contributing to *La Tribuna* in Buenos Aires, wrote an essay entitled "Dynamite," in which he praised Ravachol as "an exquisite artist" (1893). Cesare Lombroso was another of these distinguished voices.

When *La Nación* of Buenos Aires reported in 1894 that the "celebrated criminalist" had just published a book dedicated to studying anarchist "characters," the news drew considerable attention.[10] This interest stemmed not just from anarchism's notoriety, but also from Lombroso's own fame; he was already a *bona fide* celebrity in cultural circles. His contributions to the press, duly remembered by *La Nación* upon his death, along with the potency of his narratives, the versatility of his contributions, and his attempts to provide scientific explanations for crime, made him an object of fascination in his own right—even if his theories were met with caution and criticism within the local scientific community (Sozzo 2017). That such a celebrated thinker, equally at ease writing on topics as varied as spiritualism, crime, and antisemitism, had taken an interest in anarchism was something that could only enhance both his renown and the tragic, spectacular aura surrounding the anarchists themselves.

Globally, *Gli anarchici* became a true bestseller, capitalizing on the media and intellectual fervor surrounding the anarchists.[11] An initial modest print run was soon followed by an expanded, illustrated second edition the next year. The interest generated by its controversial subject matter explains why it was swiftly translated into French (1897b), as French criminologists had already written extensively on anarchism as well as into Spanish (1894e) and German (1895a). In this international context, Argentina stood out as an exception as the first edition was not released by a major publishing house or motivated by an interest in criminology. The individual responsible for expanding the reach of the "Lombroso galaxy" (Sansone 2022) was the well-known anarchist printer Pedro Tonini. Born in Venice, Tonini oversaw publications at the Elzeviriana publishing house. His bookshop and printing press, located in the heart of the city, was a leading source of left-wing literature (Cunha 2018: 146–51) where anyone interested could purchase the edition of *Los anarquistas* (1895c).

Why, in 1895, would an anarchist publisher include in his catalogue a text that, even today, is often viewed as a vehement expression of anti-anarchism? Elsewhere, the publication of *Gli anarchici* did not provoke much controversy in literary circles. Gina Lombroso, in recounting her father's life, noted that, despite warnings from his friends, he was never a target of anarchist attacks. In fact, she even recalled an occasion when he was invited by an anarchist group in Milan to a "kind of debate," which turned into a peaceful exchange of ideas (Lombroso G. 2009: 212). In Spain, the Galician anarchist Ricardo Mella published a refutation of Lombroso's views on anarchism. However, alongside his critique, Mella's text reveals a measure of respect and admiration. Disappointment, rather than hostility, seemed to be the dominant emotion in his eminently respectful response (Mella 1896).

In Buenos Aires, Tonini's edition included no warnings to readers, nor any indication that this was the work of an adversary that they should approach with caution. On the contrary, the book's foreword made it clear that the goal was to offer "the best texts by the great contemporary thinkers" to the public at an affordable price (Lombroso 1895c: 3). We lack information on whether Tonini achieved his stated aim of rescuing "the great majority of the public" from "old sources of superstition." However, aside from muted complaints from some local anarchists, the publication did not stir any controversy, which aligns with Gina Lombroso's recollections. This could have been because the book went largely unnoticed or because its content was not perceived as particularly provocative.

Overall, Lombroso's account of the history of the anarchist movement was not deemed offensive. In fact, some of his positions bore a resemblance to anarchist criticisms of contemporary society. In the first ten pages, he argued that anarchism could be explained—if not justified—primarily by social and political conditions. His sharpest criticisms were aimed at parliamentary governments, economic injustice, and religious fanaticism, leading him to acknowledge the "validity of some anarchist ideas":

> In this regard, it is possible not to justify, but rather to explain how anarchism arose, how the idea of protest in a sincere or agitated soul is kindled by lies and injustice that humiliate and demean the honorable and the hardworking. (Lombroso 1895c: 12)

Lombroso's economic perspective (though he himself considered anarchist beliefs unrealistic and regressive) gave prominence to the work of Piotr Kropotkin, Élisée Reclus, and Francesco Saverio Merlino—none of whom, of course, he regarded as insane or criminal. The problem, in his view, lay in the rest of the anarchists. However, he did not base his examples on the anonymous mass of union activists or the more moderate statements of sympathizers; instead, he focused on those who had gained global notoriety through sensational attacks. In this respect, Lombroso may have been influenced by media accounts that transformed certain anarchists into veritable global celebrities. This is evident not only in his selection of case studies, but also in his choice of sources: newspapers, illustrated magazines, and widely circulated articles of the time, such as *Le Péril Anarchiste* by Félix Dubois (1894) or *Les coulisses de l'anarchie* by Flor O'Squarr (1892).

It was when analyzing criminal anarchists that Lombroso applied his full analytical arsenal: biological interpretation, morbid inheritance, degeneration, and nervous diseases. However, even when these analytical approaches were central, nuances and variations appear in *Los anarquistas*. For example, Ravachol is depicted as a clear and inexorable example of the born criminal, while Auguste Vaillant, whose physical characteristics were unremarkable, required a more subtle analysis. Finally, Sante Caserio, the assassin of French president Sadi Carnot, is characterized as a "passionate criminal," with biological and anatomical explanations given little emphasis.

Overall, Lombroso's text presents a disorganized accumulation of information, blending elements typically associated with crime—such as slang and tattoos—with positive traits like altruism, honesty, and disdain for wealth. Amid this tangled array of arguments, where theory takes pride of place, it is difficult to extract a single, universal model for the anarchist, even though the title suggests an attempt at a general theory. Finally, in the section dedicated to the prevention of anarchism, Lombroso criticizes the use of the death penalty, special laws, and lengthy prison sentences, arguing that these repressive measures only exacerbate the problems they are designed to prevent. His recommendations instead emphasize curtailing the root causes of the anarchist epidemic through extensive and profound social, economic, and educational reforms.

Neither Insane, nor Criminals

Around the time *Gli anarchici* was published in Argentina, the Cordobán legal scholar Cornelio Moyano Gacitúa released a brief paper titled *Sobre el anarquismo* (On Anarchism). Responding to the worldwide shock following the assassination of French President Sadi Carnot, Moyano sought to examine "the causes of this human monstrosity." However, this proved no easy task. Due to its radical novelty, anarchism confounded the explanations offered by international criminologists at the time. Moyano Gacitúa, therefore, presented an eclectic array of readings, allowing him to diverge significantly from Lombroso's view, noting that it "is not possible to attribute purely individual or organic factors to this criminality; it is not a hive of born criminals" (Moyano Gacitúa 1894: 8). In his view, anarchists "are not Lombroso's morally insane or Ferri's innate criminals, as they are disinterested, not cowardly, overflowing with enthusiasm, and hold no regard for their lives. They are not epileptic criminals, because such individuals do not associate or organize to commit crimes, but act on blind and senseless epileptic impulses" (ibid.: 18). In these unsettling circumstances, the causes should be sought in a "morbid social state" rather than in individual idiosyncrasies. Moyano Gacitúa concluded that the "remedy is not in the execution chamber" or the "penal code," but in fostering a spiritual renewal, the specifics of which he left somewhat vague.

Moyano Gacitúa's pamphlet anticipated several of the issues that would later preoccupy criminological circles in Argentina in their analysis of anarchism: critiques of biological reductionism, the need for multicausal explanations (and thus an eclectic range of references), critical distance from Lombroso, and an explicit rejection of repressive persecution. Some of these concerns also surfaced in the analysis of a leading Argentine criminologist, Dr. Francisco de Veyga. The founder and inaugural head professor of a degree program in Criminal anthropology at the University of Buenos Aires (Weissmann 1999), de Veyga wrote an extensive study on anarchism in 1897, departing from any assumption of an inherent tendency toward criminality within the movement. On the contrary, "we believe anarchism to be a system of elevated and sincere moral principles with reasoned, practical, albeit idealistic, objectives whose essence lacks any criminal intent or, we believe, delinquency" (de Veyga 1897: 437).

Like Lombroso, from whom he distanced himself, de Veyga approvingly included anarchist texts in his study and criticized political repression. After a lengthy digression on the historical aspects of anarchism, he concluded that "members of the anarchist sect" who committed crimes did not deserve different treatment from other "innate criminals." His proposed solution was to identify targets selectively, thereby preventing the authorities from responding with indiscriminate crackdowns, as had happened previously. In summary, he stated, "the authorities must round up vagabonds and parasites regardless of the circumstances, keep career criminals detained, and separate the unbalanced with a tendency for political mysticism … but leave untouched true anarchists and not consider anarchism to be a criminal motive in itself" (ibid.: 455).

Francisco de Veyga's motives were not philanthropic. The severity of his words has led most historians to view his stance as a clear example of stigmatization and authoritarian exclusion. However, this assessment does not hold for his specific consideration of anarchism as a political and cultural phenomenon. In fact, de Veyga was influenced more by the French anarchist criminologist Augustin Hamon than by Lombroso. Hamon, whom he described as "a writer who displays great talent," led de Veyga to define a psychological profile shared by all anarchists that went beyond purely biological and social determinism.

The dedicated publisher Pedro Tonini released a Spanish translation of Hamon's *Psychologie de l'anarchiste-socialiste*, the book that had so captivated Francisco de Veyga, in the same collection in which he had published Lombroso's *Los anarquistas*. Hamon's goal in this work was twofold: to demonstrate that anarchists worldwide shared a similar psychological makeup and to challenge the broad application of the "anarchist" label to individuals who did not exhibit these traits. Having surveyed anarchists from several parts of the world, including Argentina and Uruguay,[12] Hamon argued that his analyses should not include individualists demanding absolute freedom or those labeled "anarchists" merely for rebelling against oppressive social structures. Nor should it include those who tried to disguise immoral acts with an air of altruism. The latter, he argued, were "simple criminals who bear no relation with the anarchist-socialist doctrine other than the name." He also excluded from the category those who shouted the slogan "¡Viva la anarquía!" solely to justify personal hatred and resentment (Hamon 1898: 34).

Hamon engaged in the international debate over the causes of the anarchist movement, though he took a different approach from Lombroso's. He noted that anarchists came from very diverse backgrounds: they could be Chinese, Lap, Scandinavian, Breton, American, or Argentine. They worked in a wide range of professions, including academia, journalism, sales, artisanal trades, the arts, industry, engineering, law, and literature. Others were landlords, public officials of all kinds, and even soldiers. Beneath their ideology, Hamon observed a distinctive psychological profile that emerged when subjected to secondary stimuli. Rather than seeing biological or social factors as fully determinative, he sought to identify certain emotional and subjective traits common to all anarchists: rebelliousness, a love of freedom, compassion, altruism, a sense of justice, logic, curiosity, and an urge to proselytize. Hamon regarded these elements, some of which also appeared in Lombroso's analysis, as uniquely virtuous collective qualities.

The publication of Hamon's book in Buenos Aires generated predictable excitement among local anarchists, who had already published excerpts in their newspapers. However, it was a young José Ingenieros, then an influential social activist well-versed in the local anarchist circles, who undertook a detailed critique in a lengthy essay for *El Mercurio de América*. Ingenieros's familiarity with the anarchist ecosystem in Argentina set him apart from the positions of Cornelio Moyano Gacitúa and Francisco de Veyga, who had taken a more global approach. His goal was to depart from the study of hypothetical anarchists in favor of real-world examples, and this formed the foundation of his criticism of Hamon, which he considered flawed due to its narrow scope. By excluding various "sub-species" of anarchists for their perceived lack of purity, Hamon constructed an "ideal type" that failed to capture the movement's distinctive character. Without those advocating violence, whom he dismissed as mere political criminals; without those protesting the political system under the anarchist label; without the "mattoids" who misunderstood the doctrine; without common thieves justifying crimes with anarchist rhetoric; and without artists identifying as anarchists in their disdain for mediocrity and the bourgeoisie—anarchism, Inenieros argued, was reduced to an empty shell (Ingenieros 1898: 36).

Ingenieros saw himself as well positioned to address these shortcomings by offering his own interpretation of the anarchist spirit. His first major contribution was to attribute suggestibility and a tendency toward "psychological unity" to the anarchist profile. These traits, he argued, explained why many activists formed strong allegiances with a few individuals, whom he referred to as "bosses"—a phenomenon "made more interesting by how at odds it seems with one of the essential principles in whose name the sect is fighting: the suppression of authority" (ibid.: 40). A second defining trait was what he saw as anarchists' excessive emotionality, a factor that eluded physiological and social explanations, thereby introducing a psychological dimension into the discourse.

Beyond Ingenieros's rhetoric, which veered into social psychology, Ingenieros distinguished himself from Lombroso, who in fact had focused exclusively on anarchist criminals, as well as from de Veyga and Moyano Gacitúa, who analyzed anarchism without reference to its empirical manifestations. Ingenieros dismissed the idea of a "model anarchist" as a construct of literary or journalistic imagination. Instead, he argued that anarchism encompassed an endless variety of individuals shaped by highly diverse backgrounds and influences. Compared with the seamless, homogeneous world depicted by Hamon, Ingenieros's complex view of anarchism better represented the social diversity of a city such as Buenos Aires, where anarchism was attracting a growing following. This included elders, troublemakers, intellectuals, militants, spiritualists, drunks, thieves, socialites, misanthropes, and the uneducated.

Uproarious Laughter

Ingenieros's view of anarchism was shaped not only by the European situation described in the international media, which influenced the studies of Cornelio Moyano Gacitúa and Francisco de Veyga, but also by his personal interactions. In 1903, he claimed to speak "with the authority of someone who has personally known almost all the anarchists who have set foot in Buenos Aires, from the intellectuals Malatesta and Gori to the lowest prison thug who calls himself an anarchist" (Ingenieros 1903b). The mention of Pietro Gori is noteworthy. This Italian anarchist, a lawyer and criminologist familiar to Ingenieros, had founded the journal *Criminalogía Moderna* shortly after his arrival in Buenos Aires. The journal has been described as the first systematic attempt to introduce criminology to Argentina (Creazzo 2007; Rotondo 2014). Gori's arrival was also considered a watershed moment in the history of Argentine anarchism. His talent for organization, persuasive rhetoric, and marked preference for evolution over the violent polemics typical of anarchism distinguished him as a key figure in the movement's growth, which had become clear by the time he left the country in 1902.

During the four years that Pietro Gori spent in Buenos Aires (1898–1902), Cesare Lombroso's contributions to the local press became increasingly frequent. In one article, he sought to explain the reasons behind the assassination of the empress Elisabeth of Austria by Luigi Lucheni in Geneva on September 10, 1898. This piece exemplified the analyses of anarchist crime that Lombroso aimed at the general reader. It included extensive details, an analysis of Lucheni's handwriting, physiology, family background, epilepsy, and shyness. While these characteristics meant he could easily be mistaken for a common criminal, Lucheni could not be regarded as such because he also possessed the qualities of honor, sensitivity, and altruism. Lombroso further urged readers not to overlook social causes, such as nationality and poverty, noting that the former explained why there were more Latin than Anglo-Saxon anarchists (Lombroso 1898a).

Lombroso's article was countered by the journal *Criminalogía Moderna*, where Lombroso was also a staff writer. An unsigned article, likely written by Pietro Gori, argued that Lombroso, the "illustrious contributor," had exaggerated the anthropological and political motivations behind Lucheni's actions. However, it also acknowledged that this was merely a matter of emphasis and did not fundamentally disagree with Lombroso's view. It suggested that the assassination of the Empress of Austria resulted from a "combined effect of psychological and physical temperament under the provocation of the environment in which he lived."[13]

Gori's efforts to reconcile academic rigor with anarchist theory and practice, along with the diverse audiences that he attracted, elicited a mix of perplexity and distant respect from some of his ideological comrades (Albornoz 2014). Undoubtedly, his career exemplified the intersection of anarchism, Lombrosian ideas, and criminology in South America (Quinta 2018), although he was not the only figure to navigate this complex terrain. The anarchist press frequently invoked Lombroso's name for various reasons. On some occasions, for instance, his opinions were considered compatible with the movement and were even cited to lend scientific credibility to aspects of its doctrine. For instance, the anarchist newspaper *Tribuna Libertaria* in Montevideo published a lengthy article by Lombroso discussing the dangers of Jesuit influence in France (Lombroso 1900a). Similarly, other anarchist publications referenced his work when denouncing issues such as alcoholism, antisemitism, and excessive patriotism among workers.[14] They also invoked *Los anarquistas* to oppose the enactment of anti-anarchist legislation in Europe.[15]

The strategic appropriation of excerpts from Lombrosian texts was just one way anarchists engaged with his work. While he lent legitimacy to certain issues, in other contexts he was viewed less favorably. According to anarchist supporter Eduardo Gilimón, Lombroso's widespread success stemmed from his ability to reinforce the ignorant beliefs of the masses through the mass-market press, offering scientific validation for their superstitions (Gilimón 1902). Gilimón argued that Lombroso's supposed major discoveries in criminal science were merely simple prejudices already prevalent in popular society. He also inadvertently highlighted another dimension of Lombroso's work, illustrating how some aspects of it were treated frivolously and mocked by detractors. As Paul Knepper convincingly argues, anarchists laughing at Lombroso may have inadvertently enhanced his celebrity (Knepper 2018b).

In the anarchists' arsenal of defamation, Lombroso became a target for personal attacks, with repeated accusations of being delirious. When Pedro Tonini decided to publish *Los anarquistas*, the newspaper *El Perseguido* described him as "Lombroso the lunatic." Meanwhile, the sophisticated magazine *Questione Sociale* published a letter from Europe suggesting that Lombroso had spent so much time studying madness in others that he had ended up losing his own mind: "The obsession with seeing madness and degeneration in other people's heads has ended up undermining his own sanity."[16] In a similarly ironic tone, "Altair," a pseudonym for Mariano Cortés, claimed that reading Lombroso's article in *La Nación* about Gaetano Bresci, the assassin of Italian King Umberto I (Lombroso 1900b), had triggered an epileptic attack and recommended that "we laugh uproariously in Cesare's face." He concluded that the best response was not to take Lombroso seriously: "let it be known that when a *professore* tells a joke, we know how to take it as such."[17]

This irreverent approach allowed the label and notion of the "born criminal," attributed to Lombroso, to be used mockingly against countless targets. The profanation of Lombroso's work aligned seamlessly with its widespread circulation in newspapers and magazines, where readers often relished comic takes on the news. Anarchists enthusiastically adopted the practice of ridiculing other people's skulls and physical traits, linking them to negative connotations. For example, in the case of Ramón Falcón, the Chief of Police of Buenos Aires, who had been assassinated by a young Russian anarchist the previous year, anarchists boldly claimed that "in Lombroso's hands, Falcón's head would not have provided much cause for criminological meditation: his physiological characteristics revealed widespread physical degradation; his entirely and exemplary antisocial and bloodthirsty idiosyncrasy showed him to be the embodiment of the born criminal."[18]

Such invocations of Lombroso were common. For instance, when anarchists in Montevideo discovered a spy in their midst, they published the following description to ensure he would be recognized: "sunken forehead, excessively pronounced zygomatic arches, a wary, alert gaze, handle-shaped ears (the kind seen in degenerates and those who fail at their trade), spiky hair, and a simian gait … in short, the kind of fellow who wouldn't last long in Lombroso's clutches."[19] As Lila Caimari has noted, the widespread use of Lombrosian vocabulary helped keep his memory alive long after criminology had debunked most of his theories (Caimari 2004: 191). Three decades after the publication of *Los anarquistas*, his ideas and example continued to be used across various fields, such that an anarchist newspaper in Brazil confidently declared the existence of "born policemen."[20] In 1929, a group of police officers were described as characters "who could star in a Lombrosian gallery."[21] By 1930, a strikebreaker was referred to as "a prototype of the born thug and Lombrosian criminal."[22]

For anarchists in Argentina and across South America, Lombroso was an omnipresent figure, perceived in multiple ways. Respect for a scientist who sought to uncover the practical causes of crime in areas that also interested anarchist thinkers coexisted with a comic and mocking application of his classifications, which anarchists used frequently and for diverse purposes. This enduring influence is reflected in the fact that the next edition of *Los anarquistas*, following Tonini's 1922 version, was again published by anarchists, this time accompanied by critical notes.[23]

Conclusions

At the turn of the twentieth century, Argentina witnessed ongoing interaction and exchange between the work of Lombroso, the anarchist movement, and criminology. These debates involved agreements and disagreements, which, even at their most ambivalent, could not be described as entirely indifferent or antagonistic. Anarchists did not perceive criminology as stigmatizing; rather, they engaged with criminological literature with scientific interest, identifying areas of overlap between the field's arguments and their own movement. This interaction also had a strong comic element, which was employed in various ways.

José Ingenieros, Cornelio Moyano Gacitúa, and Francisco de Veyga saw anarchism as a unique opportunity to address one of the great issues of their time: the spectacular terrorist attacks that received widespread coverage in the international media. While they adopted various approaches and interpretative arguments, they shared reservations about Lombroso's theories. They also remained open to other influences, such as Augustin Hamon, drawing creatively from their theoretical references and empirical studies. However, a central question persisted: how could an apparently normal person commit such explosive acts of violence?

The issue took on a new urgency on August 11, 1905, when the young Catalan anarchist typographer Salvador Planas y Virella attempted to assassinate Argentine President Manuel Quintana. According to press reports, there were no prior indications that the attempt was imminent (Albornoz 2021: 156–69). The perpetrator was a dedicated worker leading an ascetic life and, like many young people in Buenos Aires, attended anarchist meetings. At most, he was considered an eccentric—a fruitarian—but not a danger. The prosecutor took a different view, demanding a harsh sentence with no consideration for mitigating circumstances. During the course of the two-year trial, one key question returned: to what degree was he responsible for his actions?

A year later, Francisco de Veyga, by then a renowned criminologist, was invited to provide expert medical testimony for the defense. His report, which he chose to publish in the journal *Archivos de Psiquiatría y Criminología*, became fundamental not only for understanding the context of the trial, but also as a document showcasing the sensitivity and nuance that criminological studies of anarchism could possess (de Veyga 1906a).

De Veyga, who a decade earlier had identified the flaws in most assessments of the issue, refuted the connection between anarchism and crime to such an extent that he now declared that political ideology had not significantly motivated Planas y Virella's failed attack. Instead, he attributed the primary trigger to an emotional disorder stemming from family issues and unrequited love. Under this pressure, "an abnormal state of the spirit" had taken hold that, saturated with anarchist literature, led to the idea of assassinating the president. De Veyga concluded that Quintana had become a mere object onto which the would-be assassin could vent his frustrations, rather than the source of his distress. He further argued that, at the time of the attack, Planas was not in full possession of his faculties and thus could not be held responsible. On this point, he was explicit: "medical and legal criteria do not always agree."

This argument was proved when Salvador Planas was sentenced to thirteen years in prison. The lengthy report, written in vivid detail, cast an empathetic eye on the criminal, depoliticizing the assassination attempt considerably. As Hugo Vezzetti has noted (1985: 221), this revealed a humanitarian aspect to criminology that drew on references beyond the usual Lombrosian canon. Anarchists, who avidly consumed everything written about them, showered praise on de Veyga's report. In an article published in *La Protesta*, Fag Libert, a pseudonym of Federico Gutiérrez, asserted that the "excellent psychiatrist" had acted as a defender of science against a dubious penal system intent on condemning Salvador Planas y Virella regardless of his actual responsibility (Fag Libert: 1907). Given the facts outlined above, this harmonious confluence of criminology, assassination, and anarchism should not come as a surprise.

Notes

1. "Lombroso," (1909), *La Prensa*, Buenos Aires, October 20. Newspapers in Brazil and Uruguay had similar reactions: "Cesar Lombroso. Fallecido ayer en Turín" (1909), *El Siglo*, Montevideo, October 20; "A morte de Lombroso" (1909), *Correio da Manhã*, Río de Janeiro, October 20.
2. "Telegramas" (1909), *La Nación*, Buenos Aires, October 21.
3. "Cesare Lombroso" (1909), *La Nación*, Buenos Aires, October 20.
4. "Cesare Lombroso" (1909), *La Vanguardia*, Buenos Aires, October 20.
5. "Cesare Lombroso" (1909), *La Battaglia*, São Paulo, October 24.
6. "Césare Lombroso" (1909), *La Protesta*, Buenos Aires, October 22.
7. Ibid.
8. From 1890 onward, based mostly in Paris, anarchism captured the public imagination through a series of varied and shocking attacks that culminated with the assassination of Sadi Carnot in 1894. See Merriman (2016); Jensen (2014).
9. "El asesinato de Carnot. Impresión en la ciudad" (1894), *La Nación*, Buenos Aires, June 25.
10. "Lombroso" (1894), *La Nación*, Buenos Aires, August 15.
11. Uri Eisenzweig calls attention to this fact by noting the few works dedicated to the study of anarchism in the 1880s compared to the "hundreds of studies and essays dedicated to anarchism by outsiders from 1894 onward" (2004: 23).
12. "A los anarquistas" (1895), *La Anarquía*, La Plata, January 27; "A los anarquistas" (1895), *El derecho a la vida*, Montevideo, March 17.
13. "El regicidio de ginebra" (1898), *Criminalogía Moderna*, Año I, N°1, November 20: 13.
14. "Maravillas de la civilización" (1894), *El derecho a la vida*, Montevideo, June 18; "Gori en Salta" (1901), *El Rebelde*, Buenos Aires, July 27; *La Barricata. Periódico anarchico* (1912), São Paulo, September 22.
15. "Sobre esa ley" (1897), *La Protesta Humana*, August 19.
16. "Carta desde Europa" (1895), *La questione sociale*, Año II, March 18: 23.
17. Altäir (Mariano Cortés), "Las zangamangas de un sabio" (1898), *La Protesta Humana*, November 6.

18. "En pleno día" (1910), *El Obrero gráfico*, Buenos Aires, February 1.
19. "Un complot chingado" (1901), *Tribuna Libertaria*, Montevido, May 12.
20. "L'obbedienza" (1910), *La Battaglia*, São Paulo, February 6.
21. "De Temperley" (1929), *La Protesta*, Buenos Aires, September 15.
22. "Sobre el conflicto agrícola" (1920), *La organización obrera*, Buenos Aires, February.
23. "Los anarquistas" (1922), *El Trabajo*, Montevideo, July 1.

12

What Remains? Finding Losses and Retracing Presences: The Misplaced Photographs by Lewis Hine in the Cesare Lombroso Museum of Criminal Anthropology

Nadia Pugliese

Introduction

In 2014, the management of the Lombroso Museum reported the loss of eight photographs from its archive to the Archival and Bibliographic Superintendence of the Regions of Piemonte and Valle d'Aosta. These photographs were created by Lewis Wickes Hine, an American sociologist and photographer widely regarded among the fathers of modern photojournalism. Evidence that Hine's pictures were part of the museum's holdings can be found in the 1978 book *Wanted!* by Ando Gilardi (Gilardi 1978). Gilardi, an Italian photojournalist and historian, visited the museum in the 1970s when it was directed by Sergio Tovo, a professor in Forensic Medicine and Insurance. During his visit, Gilardi photographed several of Hine's images, later publishing one of them in his book. Among his own photographs, now catalogued in the *Fototeca Gilardi*, are eight reproductions of Hine's images, labeled "Photographic prints included in the collection of the Cesare Lombroso Museum of Criminal Anthropology." Gilardi also notes that, at the time, there were as many as fifty pictures attributed to Hine in the Lombroso Museum. However, none of these original photographs are in the museum's current collection, nor were they found during the first cataloguing campaign conducted in the 1990s.

This chapter seeks to uncover the lost legacy of Lewis Hine's photographs: fifty images focused on the phenomenon of immigration in New York State, captured in 1909 and missing from the museum's collection since the late 1970s. To trace the path of these images, it is necessary to address some seemingly straightforward questions: Where exactly did these pictures originate? Who commissioned them, and how did they come into the museum's possession? Who were they intended for, and what purpose did they serve? What was the circulation of this material over time, and where was it published?

The methodological framework of this study is an interdisciplinary history of the photographic medium, constructed in dialogue with the history of science and the history of media studies. This approach is grounded in the understanding of photographs as both material and social objects (Edwards 2012). To this end, I have searched for evidence in national and international magazines and journals such as the *New York Times*, *L'Illustrazione Italiana*, *The Monist*, *Charities and the Commons*, and *The Survey*. I have also examined correspondence preserved in the museum's historical archive, Lombroso's books, articles published abroad, and letters from notable American political figures addressed to Lombroso's daughter Gina and her husband, Guglielmo Ferrero. Additionally, I reviewed a series of images in the museum's archive from various parts of the United States. In particular, I studied the portraits of George Engel, Adolph Fischer, Louis Lingg, and Michael Schwab—German anarchists who emigrated from Europe to North America and were tried and convicted for the 1886 Haymarket Square bombing in Chicago. I also examined a photograph of an eleven-year-old murderer from 1892, sent to Lombroso by the governor of Colorado. Ultimately, my research has focused on the circumstances that led not only to the creation of Hine's photographs but also to their circulation within a network of criminalist anthropologists and advocates for the theories of the Lombrosian school.

This study also aims to address a series of interrelated questions regarding archival absence and photographic heritage. Could the missing photographs from the museum's archive also be absent from critical discourses on the dissemination of Lombroso's theories in the United States? How can we engage with photographic objects and histories that have been forgotten, suppressed, excluded, or misplaced?

These questions form the starting point for this research.

The Museum's Photographic Collection

In 1907 the *New York Times* published an article by Cesare Lombroso titled "My Museum of Criminal Psychology" (Lombroso 1907b). This was the English version of a piece he had written a year earlier for the popular Italian current affairs and cultural magazine *L'Illustrazione italiana* (Lombroso 1906b). The Italian article was published just a few weeks before the Sixth International Congress of Criminal Anthropology, held in Turin in 1906. Both the Italian and English versions were the first written accounts of Lombroso's criminal museum, which had been housed in the Anatomical Institutes Building at the University of Turin since 1898. These articles outline the history of the scientific collection that Lombroso began assembling during his medical studies and gradually expanded to encompass a range of research fields related to criminal anthropology, such as forensic medicine and psychiatry.

The fact that the English version was published in one the most prestigious newspapers in the world demonstrates the American public's interest in the Italian criminologist and his work. The article included two lithographs based on images from the original Italian piece, depicting various rooms of the museum and a selection of objects in their original display cases. Among these, we can clearly see how drawings, photographs, artifacts, and anatomical specimens were integral to the exhibition.

Today, the historical archive of the Lombroso Museum (Valentino 2011; Cilli and Montaldo 2024) preserves photographs, paper positives, glass negatives, drawings, lithographs, and various prints. Dating from the late 1850s to the late 1930s, these materials reflect the scientific exchange and collaboration between Lombroso, his student and son-in-law Mario Carrara—who took over the museum's direction after Lombroso's death in 1909 (Capozzi 2022)—and other criminal anthropologists, psychiatrists, and forensic doctors with whom they corresponded. The prominence of the father of criminal anthropology helped with the collection of these materials, which were frequently sent to him by public and private institutions in Italy and abroad seeking forensic and psychiatric assessments. Lombroso required material evidence to support his theories and thus considered all the items in his personal collection—not only drawings and photographs, but also skulls and anatomical specimen, bodies of evidence, and artifacts created in prison and in mental institutions—as equal expressions of the "criminal world." Through these objects, he believed he could discern "signs" that might clarify the psychological state of offenders (Villa 1985).

Many of these materials were commissioned directly by Lombroso from local photographers and painters. He used this visual content extensively in his scientific publications, university lectures, conferences, and exhibitions at national and international congresses. The majority of the photographs and drawings depict human faces (Leonardi and Pugliese 2024) and primarily originate from medical-scientific and judicial contexts.[1] The former includes portraits of psychiatric patients, while the latter, extensively adopting Alphonse Bertillon's photographic anthropometric model, features some of the most famous images of nineteenth-century criminals, alongside portraits of common delinquents.

There is a considerable overlap between these two domains, as many of the prisoners depicted also suffered from psychiatric disorders, and numerous photographic medical records document criminal histories. Lombroso used this diverse iconographic material to support his belief that criminals could be identified by specific physical stigmata. His theory of the "atavistic criminal" suggested that these characteristics signified a regression on the evolutionary ladder to a "subhuman" or "primitive" type.

Recent studies have shown how Lombroso used different types of media as scientific "evidence," particularly photography (Leonardi 2015). Due to its specific optical, chemical, physical, and mechanic properties, photography was regarded by late-nineteenth-century scientists as the elite medium for its perceived objectivity, and thus viewed as a "scientific object," despite emerging from the mass visual culture of the era (Edwards 2009).

Among this extensive collection are several images from the Americas, particularly from the island of Cuba (Pugliese 2023). Although Lombroso never visited the Americas, he established connections with numerous American scholars and Italian émigrés. Fernando Ortiz, one of Cuba's most influential intellectuals, met Lombroso between 1905 and 1906 (Montaldo 2023), while John Henry Wigmore, an American legal academic at Northwestern University, visited Turin in 1908 and invited the father of criminal anthropology to lecture in the United States (Rafter 2009). Lombroso also encountered many other Americans at the International Congresses of Criminal anthropology, and his theories were widely disseminated by the criminologist Enrico Ferri, his daughter Gina, and his son-in-law Guglielmo Ferrero, who delivered numerous public lectures during their travels on the continent.

Images from North America

The first set of images from the United States includes a series of four photographs (Figures 12.1–12.4) depicting George Engel, Adolph Fischer, Louis Lingg, and Michael Schwab—German Anarchists who had emigrated from Europe to North America and were later tried and convicted for their involvement in the 1886 Haymarket Square bombing in Chicago.

The starting point of the Haymarket affair was a large general strike on May 1, 1886, advocating for an eight-hour workday. On May 3, after three days of protests, Chicago police opened fire on unarmed demonstrators at the McCormick Harvesting Machine Company plant, killing one worker and injuring several others. The following day, a group of anarchists organized a protest rally in Haymarket Square. As a large contingent of Chicago police officers marched on the protestors to disperse them, a bomb was thrown at the police, killing one officer instantly. Six more officers died from their injuries in the following days, and at least three of the protesters were killed in the ensuing gunfire, with many others severely wounded on both sides.

In the wake of the incident, sensationalist newspaper articles fueled the myth of an anarchist conspiracy, stoking popular fears of immigrants and radical labor leaders. Many immigrants were arrested without warrants, and workers' civil rights were openly violated. The eight-hour movement, along with other labor reforms, was effectively halted. That summer, what was then called the "trial of the century" took place. A biased jury delivered a verdict of guilty for eight defendants, and all except one were sentenced to death for allegedly aiding the unknown bomber and attempting to establish anarchism as the dominant ideology. It was without doubt one of the most politically charged trials in American history (Green 2006).

A significant number of anarchists resided in Chicago at the time, most of whom were European immigrants working in the city. Five of the defendants—August Spies, Adolph Fischer, George Engel, Louis Lingg, and Michael Schwab—were German-born immigrants, while a sixth, Oscar Neebe, was a US citizen of German descent. Of the remaining two, Albert Parsons was born in the United States, while Samuel Fielden was born in England.

The trial began on June 21, 1886, and ended on August 11, 1886. On November 10, 1887, Fielden and Schwab were sentenced to life imprisonment. Lingg, who was scheduled to be executed, took his own life the night before the execution. The following day, Engel, Fischer, Parsons, and Spies were led to the gallows, having refused to plead for clemency (ibid.).

Lombroso's interest in extreme political actions was far from marginal, evolving in various ways over his lifetime (Bovo 2024). His views were primarily expressed in his 1890 book *Il delitto politico* (Political Crime) and in the two editions of *Gli anarchici* (The Anarchists, 1894–5). Initially, Lombroso argued that only a specific type of criminal was drawn to anarchism (Lombroso and Laschi 1890). Over time, however, he recognized that morally upright individuals were also attracted to the movement, and he began to classify anarchists into two types: positive figures, who advanced

Adolph. Fischer
Jac. Maul
CHICAGO

Jac. Maul
CHICAGO

Georg. Engel
Jac. Maul
CHICAGO.

Figures 12.1–12.4 Jacob Maul, *Adolph Fischer, Louis Lingg, George Engel, and Michael Schwab*, Chicago Anarchist, albumen print on card, (*c*. 16.7 × 10.8 cm), *c*. 1886. ACLM.

humanity's progress by breaking antiquated laws, and treacherous, deranged figures who triggered violent reactions (Lombroso 1894b).

In his books, Lombroso presented several cases of people from diverse backgrounds who committed brutal acts in the name of anarchism. Despite the violence they committed, Lombroso also noted that many of these individuals turned to extremism only after failing to improve the sociopolitical and economic conditions of the masses due to the corruption of the ruling classes. All three of Lombroso's works relating to anarchism were accompanied by halftones of well-known anarchists, revolutionaries, and political criminals, both male and female. The father of criminal anthropology used these published images to examine the physiognomic traits of anarchists with criminal characteristics and to compare them with those of ordinary felons.

In 1891, Lombroso directly addressed the Haymarket affair by publishing "The physiognomy of the Anarchists" (Lombroso 1891a), an article featured in that year's edition of *The Monist.*[2] Through this article, we learn that Dr Paul Carus, the journal's director, sent Lombroso forty-three portraits of the Chicago anarchists. Among them were those of George Engel, Adolph Fischer, Louis Lingg, and Michael Schwab, which are currently preserved in the museum's archive.

The portraits of the convicted Chicago revolutionists were not new to the public, as many had been published in national and international newspapers during the trial. However, a series of detailed halftones printed two years earlier is particularly noteworthy. In 1889, Captain Michael J. Schaack, a Chicago police captain who investigated anarchist activities during the late nineteenth century, published *Anarchy and Anarchism*. The book provides a detailed account of the events, ideologies, and individuals involved in the anarchist movement during that period. Focusing specifically on the Haymarket affair and its key figures, it offers a law enforcement perspective on the methods and challenges that Schaack faced in dealing with anarchist activities as a police captain (Schaack 1889).

A copy of the book, which includes numerous illustrations depicting the eight convicts from Chicago, was also provided to Lombroso by Dr. Carus. In his article, the father of criminal anthropology noted that he initially preferred to use the halftones from Schaack's book instead of the photographic portraits, since he could not see in them the physical features he needed to sustain his theories: "these characteristics are much less apparent in the photographs that I received from *The Monist* and in which the jaw of Fischer even decreases. Perhaps these photographs were taken some years before the crime, when they were very young" (Lombroso 1891a).

Later in the article, when discussing August Spies, Lombroso amended his original opinion on Schaack's volume in a footnote, stating, "Thus according to the portrait in Schaack's book; but according to information which I later received from General Trumbull of Chicago, this portrait is not true to life. It would seem, then, that the features upon which my opinion is based do not exist." Consequently, the images sent to him as material evidence proved to be completely useless.

It is important to note that photography at the time was considered a scientific medium, albeit an ambiguous one. Unlike the tradition of scientific drawings, which relied on the scientist's eye, the final results of photographs depended on the photomechanical process, raising questions about their objectivity (Daston and Galison 2010).

After Lombroso's article was published in January 1891, Michael Schwab, who had been serving a life sentence since 1887, responded to the professor in *The Monist* the following spring. "A Convicted Anarchist's Reply to Professor Lombroso" is possibly the only response to the renowned criminologist by a convicted anarchist subject to one of his studies. In his reply, Schwab criticizes Lombroso's theories, particularly his use of the information and halftones contained into Schaak's book. According to the anarchist, Lombroso should have relied on the photographs, which he described as "the only true to life pictures":

> The portraits from which he made his deductions are not sufficiently truthful for his purpose. "Schaak's" book is said to be a fictitious "robber story," and I am informed that it contains many untruths absolutely invented for ornament and decoration. It is in the highest degree improbable that such a book should not have caricatured the portraits of the anarchists. In books designed for sale to the masses, the illustrations are not, as a rule, of any value as works of art, even if the persons pictured in them enjoy the author's favor. The only true to life pictures are the photographs which Dr. Carus sent to Professor Lombroso, and these were taken in the county jail. (Schwab 1891)

Another interesting portrait from North America in the museum's collection is that of a young boy accused of murder. The story behind this photograph is recounted by Lombroso in his 1902 book *Delitti vecchi e delitti nuovi* (Old and New Crimes), specifically in the section titled "A criminological consultation across the ocean." Lombroso claims that the original photograph (Figure 12.5) depicting nine-year-old Antonie Woodey and printed as a halftone in the text (1902: 170) was sent to him in 1899 by the governor of Colorado, Charles Spalding Thomas, who was a great admirer of his work. Along with the print, the governor also included two other portraits, a detailed biography of the young offender and some drawings created by Woodey during his time in jail (none of these objects can be found in the collection today).

Woodey's story is significant for the practical applications of Lombroso's theories. Spalding, who supported the death penalty and lynch law—particularly in the cases of Afro-American suspects—was eager to obtain a criminological report on Woodey to counter the jail management's desire to release the young offender due to his good conduct. Flattered by a request from so far away, Lombroso examined the boy's face and handwriting, claiming to identify the typical characteristics of the "born criminal" despite Woodey's exemplary behavior in prison (Lombroso 1902: 169–73).

The theme of juvenile and child crime had previously been addressed by Lombroso as early as 1876 in the first edition of *L'uomo delinquente*. The topic captured the interest of criminal anthropologists, who collected findings and photographs related to it (Guarnieri 2006). In 1913, Mario Carrara contributed to this discourse with an article titled 'Un museo per la criminalità infantile' (A Museum for Juvenile Crime). In it, he described a valuable collection of instruments used by minors in committing felonies, which was on display at the Children's Court of Munich. Carrara noted that

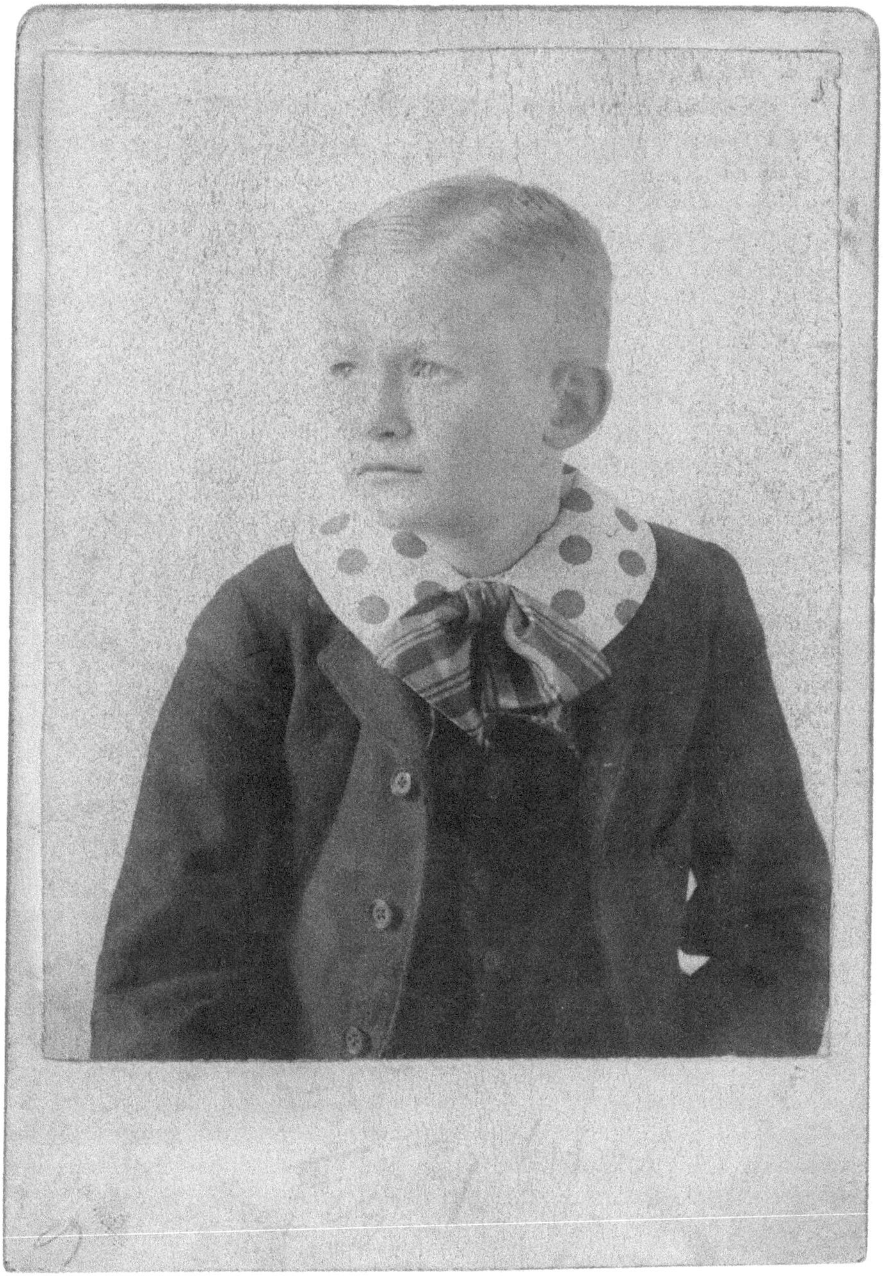

Figure 12.5 Unidentified photographer, *Antonie Woodey*, a young murderer from Colorado, albumen print on card, (c. 16x10,5 cm), 1892. ACLM.

the German example was the first to present a museum dedicated to juvenile crime, a theme widely developed by scholars, journalists, and public authorities. He also mentioned that in Turin, two of his pupils, Camillo Tovo and Anselmo Sacerdote—who would later become professors of Forensic Medicine and had experience on the matter—had begun gathering a collection of such materials for the Lombroso Museum (Carrara 1913).

Regarding this theme, the museum's archive contains many other images depicting young criminals. Additionally, there is an intriguing collection of water jugs from Turin's juvenile jail, La Generala, engraved and painted by the young inmates. This collection can be viewed in one of the museum's rooms (Merlo 2024).

Lewis Hine's Misplaced Photographs

In 1909, Hine published his first credited photo-essay, contributing to "Child Labor in the Carolinas," an article published in the social work journal *Charities and the Commons* (McKelway 1909). Shortly afterward, Paul Underwood Kellogg, the journal's future director, proposed renaming it *The Survey*, a title he felt would better represent the methods and techniques of social work. The name was inspired by the *Pittsburgh Survey*, a journal that investigated Pittsburgh's steel district and was under Kellogg's direction from 1907 to 1909. Kellogg became the editor of *The Survey* in 1912 and held this position until financial complications and worsening health forced him to relinquish it in 1952. His vision for the magazine was to combine creative investigation with quality journalism at the intersection of research, reportage, and public welfare (Chambers 1971).

Shortly after the *Charities* publication, Kellogg hired Hine to work for *The Survey*. He "gave to Lewis Hine, then an unknown teacher and amateur photographer, the assignment of taking documentary photographs of workers, factories, and homes" (Chambers 1971). From 1910 to 1912, Hine's photographs regularly appeared on the covers of Kellogg's publication.

In November 1909, Hine embarked on an automobile tour with Lillian D. Wald, head of the Henry Street Settlement (Lillian Wald Dies 1940), and Frances A. Kellor, director of the Intermunicipal Research Committee (Sicherman and Green 1980b), both members of the New York State Immigration Commission. Accompanying them was also Mary Elisabeth Dreier of the Woman's Trade Union League (Sicherman and Green 1980a). Together, they investigated conditions in immigrant camps along the New York State's New Barge Canal and the New York Aqueduct. Their findings resulted in the article "The Construction Camps of the People," which was written by the two commissioners and accompanied by Hine's photographs. It was published in *The Survey* in 1910 (Wald and Kellor 1910).

The article highlights the industrial and sanitary conditions within the large labor camps where New York City and New York State authorities accommodated thousands of migrant men, women, and children. The Barge Canal project, central to providing the city's new water supply, was a major initiative. Nevertheless, the two female authors condemned the municipality—then a primary employer of migrant labor—for not establishing adequate, modern measures. The article also called for the establishment of a new approach involving contracts specifying sanitary standards and the establishment of a new system of sanitary supervision.

In the same edition of *The Survey*, Hine detailed the dire conditions faced by migrant children living and working in the construction camps and cannery settlements. "Roving Children" denounces, both in words but more powerfully with its images, the harsh realities of lives spent in shacks and company hovels with a complete absence of playgrounds, supervision, schools, or acceptable sanitation (Hine 1910). Among these images, are the eight photographs reproduced by Gilardi, featured in his book *Wanted!* and missing from the Lombroso Museum's collection (Figure 12.6–12.7).

In 1978, Gilardi's book *Wanted!* (Gilardi 1978) included a reproduction of one of Hine's original photographs taken in the migrant camps. Printed alongside the image is its reverse, where typewritten notes confirm its origin and authorship, and handwritten indications give instructions for its editorial use: "Construction Camps. No. 38 Youngster-Halleaur Settlement, Webster, N.Y. Photo Oct/09 by Lewis W. Hine Vignette 3 ¼ high." The image depicts a small child standing in one of the camps and looking directly into the camera. A white brush stroke, added during printing, encircles the boy to isolate him from the background, specifying the desired layout for the journal's publication. Gilardi also states on the same page that there were fifty such photographs in the Hine-Lombroso collection. By reviewing Hine's images published in *The Survey* in 1910 as part of the article on the construction camps, and the related photo insert, this number is indeed confirmed.

But how did these pictures become part of the Lombroso Museum's holdings? Lombroso himself passed away in October 1909 and, as already stated, had never visited the American continent. However, as also mentioned, his daughter Gina and son-in-law Guglielmo Ferrero presented his ideas extensively during their travels across North and South America. It is therefore plausible that they were the ones who facilitated the entry of these images into the museum's collection.

In 1908, President Theodore Roosevelt invited Ferrero to the White House as well as to various cities and universities across the United States (Roosevelt 1908).[3] This led Ferrero to deliver a series of lectures on Roman history (Ferrero and Litt 1909) and on the historical and cultural connections between ancient Rome and modern America (Ferrero 1914). Accompanied by his wife Gina, they visited New York in December 1908. Evidence of this visit appears in a letter dated December 24, 1908, from Mary Dreier to a doctor named Stella. In it, Drier thanks Stella for introducing her to Mrs. Ferrero, whom she had invited to participate in a meeting with two Italian members of the New York Women's Trade Union League. Dreier also asks the doctor to invite Gina to lunch in the following days: "it will be a very small one, as we want to get Mrs. Ferrero's suggestions and help in working with the women" (Dreier 1908).[4]

It is possible that Dreier, who later participated in the social investigation into New York's construction camps, may have sent Hine's photographs for *The Survey* to Gina after their first encounter. Perhaps the two women discussed migrants and labor conditions in the United States, while Gina expressed her political opinions grounded in her father's ideological legacy. Criminal anthropology, as a discipline, was concerned with the evolution of civil society through the application of science and the

ROVING CHILDREN

NOT OF THE STAGE OR THE CIRCUS; BUT OF THE CANNING DISTRICTS, THE CONSTRUCTION CAMPS, THE STONE QUARRIES AND OTHER TRANSIENT OR SEASONAL COMMUNITIES. IS OUR CIVILIZATION MAKING THE MOST OF THEM?

PHOTOGRAPHS BY

LEWIS W. HINE

CONSTRUCTION CAMP CHILDREN.

ROVING CHILDREN

These are not the children who tour the country on the stage or with the circus. Such children have the protection of cruelty societies and child labor laws to guard them from the perils of the road.

These are the children who can be seen scattered throughout the state, wherever there are construction camps, stone quarries and canneries to offer work to their parents. A yearly exodus from the cities begins early in June when whole families move from their winter homes and settle down for the summer's work.

Often the quarters provided by the employer or padrone lack the first requisites of proper housing. Sanitation is neglected and men, women and children are herded together like animals, a whole family, including adults and children, may be given

Figures 12.6–12.7 Front cover and first page of Hine, L. (1910). "Roving Children," *The Survey: Social, Charitable, Civic: A Journal of Constructive Philanthropy*, 23: 480–1.

betterment of disadvantaged social classes. Furthermore, the discipline was interested in the study of infancy and its implications for criminality.

However, notable differences emerge between Dreier's and Gina Lombroso's perspectives on women's rights movements. Dreier was a labor reformer and a suffragist: "she chaired New York City's Woman Suffrage party and headed the industrial section of that party's state organization." Realizing that the attitudes of male trade unionists toward working women contributed to broader social problems, Dreier became an outspoken campaigner for women's rights (Sicherman and Green 1980a). Around 1903, Dreier met Kellor, and despite their different social backgrounds, they lived together for nearly fifty years as part of an influential collective of lesbian activists in the early twentieth century.

Gina Lombroso is often portrayed as living under her father's influential shadow (Dolza 1990). However, recent studies have illuminated other facets of her life, such as her complicated relationship with her husband and her political and intellectual interests (Di Natale 2023). In seeming contrast to her father's misogynistic theories, Gina pursued a liberal education and studied to become a doctor. Working closely with her father, she later became one of only two recognized female criminologists in Europe, alongside the Russian scientist Pauline Tarnowsky. Within the scientific community, she was well known for her contributions to discussions on the female condition (G. Lombroso 1927), though her stance diverged notably from that of Dreier and early women's rights activists. Gina believed that while women were not equal to men, men were not inherently superior either. She stated, "I do not believe that women are equal to men, but neither do I see what man is superior to them. I don't see in him any perfection such that you deserve to propose it as ideal, to try to imitate it" (G. Lombroso 1908). Instead, she viewed the roles of men and women as complementary, suggesting that there was no need for women to replace men in modern society or, for example, for specific laws governing female workers (G. Lombroso 1902).

What exactly Dreier may have wanted from Gina is not clear. Perhaps she was struck by meeting a well-educated, affluent Italian woman of Gina's stature and imagined she could advise the other participants of the Women's Trade Union League on engaging with working-class migrant women from Italy.

Retracing the story of Hine's pictures from the museum archive to their origin sheds light on aspects of Gina Lombroso's life: her interest in the status of women, her connections with prominent figures in American feminism at the turn of the century, and her own position as an educated and intellectual woman despite her father's legacy and her husband's influence. However, in addition to aiding the rediscovery of Gina's character, it is also possible to discern some form of direct relationship between Lombroso's method and Hine's photographic practice.

Conclusions

Born in 1874 to a shopkeeper in Oshkosh, Wisconsin, Hine did not receive formal training in photographic technology or composition (*America & Lewis Hine* 1977).

Between 1900 and 1901, Frank A. Manny, a progressive educator, recommended him for the Parker School in Chicago and assisted him in enrolling as a graduate student. In 1900, at the age of 26, Hine enrolled at the University of Chicago to pursue a teaching career. He took courses in geography, botany, history, and education, studying under influential teachers such as John Dewey, Ella Flagg Young, and Dr. Charles C. Adams, all of whom were associated with educational reform. Around the same time, Frances Kellor, who would later collaborate with Hine on the inquiry into immigrant camps, also began her studies at the same university. Kellor was a significant figure in US feminism and attended criminal anthropology classes taught by Charles Richmond Henderson, where she met William Thomas, one of the founders of the Chicago School of Sociology and an admirer of Lombroso (Montaldo 2019). This coincidence suggests that in his university years Hine may have encountered some of the earliest American proponents of criminal anthropology (Rafter 2009), whose theories possibly influenced his photographic approach.

Hine's interest in photography emerged precisely during this period, coinciding with his visits to Ellis Island, where he photographed people arriving from all over the world between 1904 and 1909, producing over two hundred plates. Opened in 1892, Ellis Island, in upper New York Bay, was the busiest port of entry inspection station for migrants and travelers to America. As a public institution, immigrants passing through Ellis Island were subjected to invasive questioning by state agents, medical inspections, hospitalization, and, in worse cases, detention for deportation. While working there, Hine gradually understood how documentary photography could relate to social justice, a realization that changed his direction in life: "I was merely changing the educational efforts from the classroom to the world" (*America & Lewis Hine* 1977).

Hine's Ellis Island photographs departed from the nineteenth-century iconographic conventions that depicted the poor as simpletons, or, as in the case of Augustus Sherman's portraits of migrants (Sherman and Mesenhöller 2005), sought to appeal to the bourgeois taste for exoticism. Instead, his perspective offered a new interpretation of the life experiences of members of the working class, regardless of their geographical origins, and stood in contrast to the nativists, racists, and eugenicists who were shaping public opinion at the time.

From 1906 to 1918, Hine worked for the National Child Labor Committee (NCLC). Founded in 1904 to eradicate child labor, the committee was "dedicated to surveying and publicizing the ills of child labor" (Schwartz 2022). Its leadership viewed photography as overly sensationalist, unlike Hine, for whom it was a powerful investigative tool with great educational potential. Nevertheless, during the twelve years he traveled between West Virginia and Mississippi, documenting the lives and working conditions of children and producing more than five thousand photographs, the NCLC never gave him public recognition for his work (Lugon 2008).

In 1909, Hine delivered a groundbreaking speech titled "Social Photography: How the Camera May Help in the Social Uplift" to an audience of social workers. Identifying himself as a "public educator," he argued for photography as an essential instrument in "our appeal to public sympathy" (Hine 2022). His images, carefully marked with detailed captions about their subjects, helped raise awareness of the need to end the employment of children in dangerous and underpaid work. However, the law regulating the employment of children under 16 or 18 years did not arrive until the Fair Labor Standards Act of 1938, having been preceded by the 1916 Keating-Owen Child Labor Act. By that time, Hine was long forgotten, with his contributions only formally recognized later due to the efforts of photographer Berenice Abbott and art critics Beaumont Newhall and Elizabeth McCausland, who named him the "Spiritual father of contemporary photography" (Lugon 2008).

Contrasting Hine's style with Jacob Riss's journalistic approach to photography in the late nineteenth century (Riis 1890) reveals how the former focused much more on the *faces* of the children he photographed, aiming to better engage with public opinion on a deeper level (Schwartz 2022). Moreover, the notes on the back of his prints often reveal the date and location of the shot, physical details on the subjects, their personal history, and in some cases his recollections about how he approached them:

> Since he often resorted to tricks in order to get the pictures he wanted, he was careful to document every photograph with precise facts and figures. Hine knew the height of each button on his vest from the floor, so he could measure a child standing alongside him with no one being the wiser. Hidden in his pocket was a small notebook. He used it to record the name, age, hours of work, daily earnings, schooling, and other facts about each child he photographed. "All along I had to be double-sure that my photo data was 100% pure no retouching or fakery of any kind," he wrote. (Freedman 1994)

A formal example of the use of photography linking Lombroso and Hine is the practice of "composite portraits," which had been invented in 1878 by British scientist Francis Galton. The technique involves superimposing a series of photographs of different people on top of each other in order to capture their shared physical features and visualize a synthesis of them in a single image (Galton 1878). Lombroso created two series of composite portraits: the first featured criminal skulls and was published in the *Atlante*, the accompanying publication to the fifth edition of *L'uomo delinquente* (1897a, Figure XXVII), and the second depicted two convicts in Turin at the end of the nineteenth century (Figure 12.8). In 1913, Hine produced a series of composite photographs for the NCLC by rephotographing male and female child laborers on the same photographic plate[5] (Sekula 1986) (Figures 12.9–12.12). For both Galton and Lombroso, the main purpose of the composite portrait was to identify an ideal human type. In contrast, Hine, who never published his composites, likely employed the technique to reinforce his observations about the damaging physical effects of factory labor on the bodies of young workers.

Despite their differing explanations of the causes of crime—biological in criminal anthropology and social in the Chicago School of Sociology—both schools are clearly scientific, deterministic, and systematic in their approach to society. Hine, who may have been exposed to the ideas of the Chicago School during his university years, used photography in his sociological research, creating images influenced by this intellectual culture. It is therefore not surprising that a series of his images eventually became part of the Lombroso Museum's holdings.

Figure 12.8 Giuseppe Vanetti, *Composite portrait*, albumen print on card, (*c.* 10 × 6 cm), *c.* 1888. ACLM.

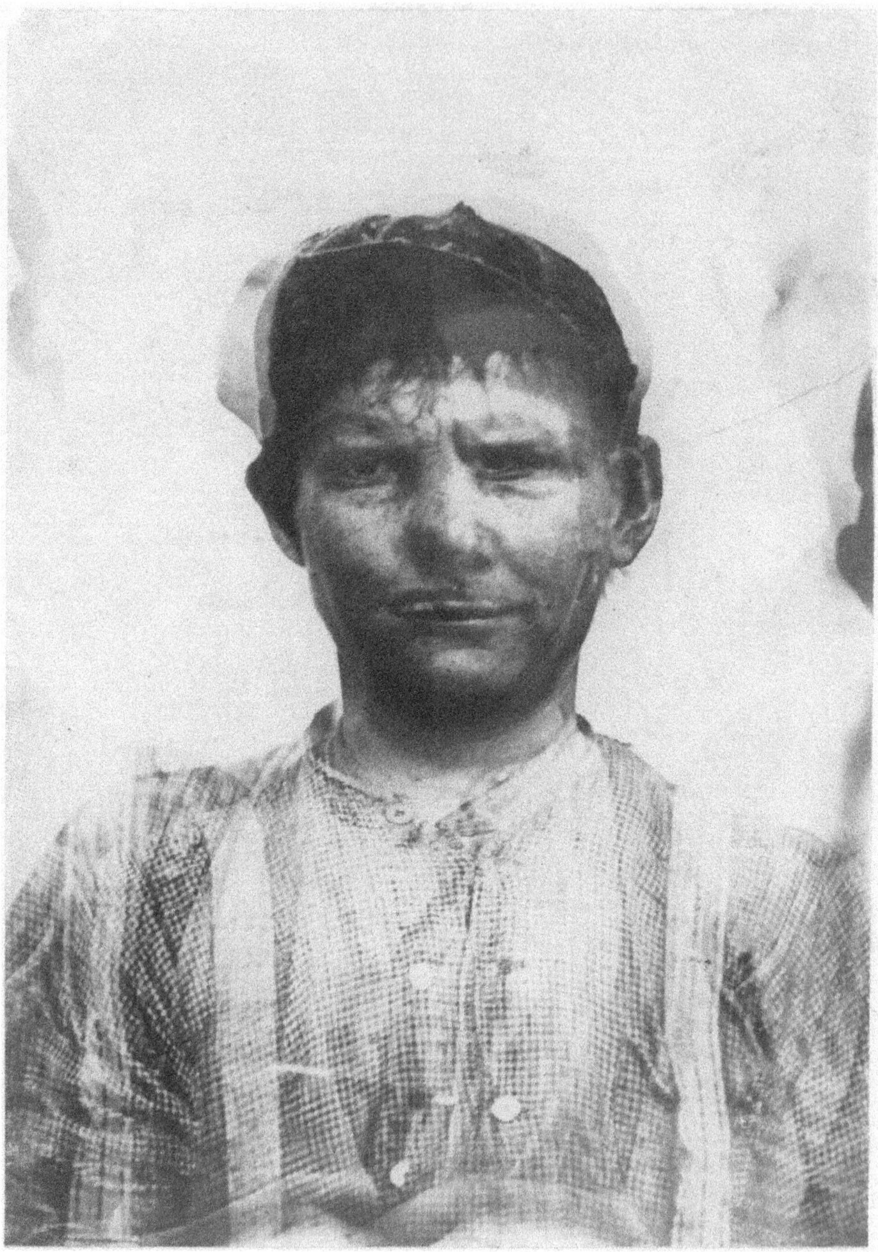

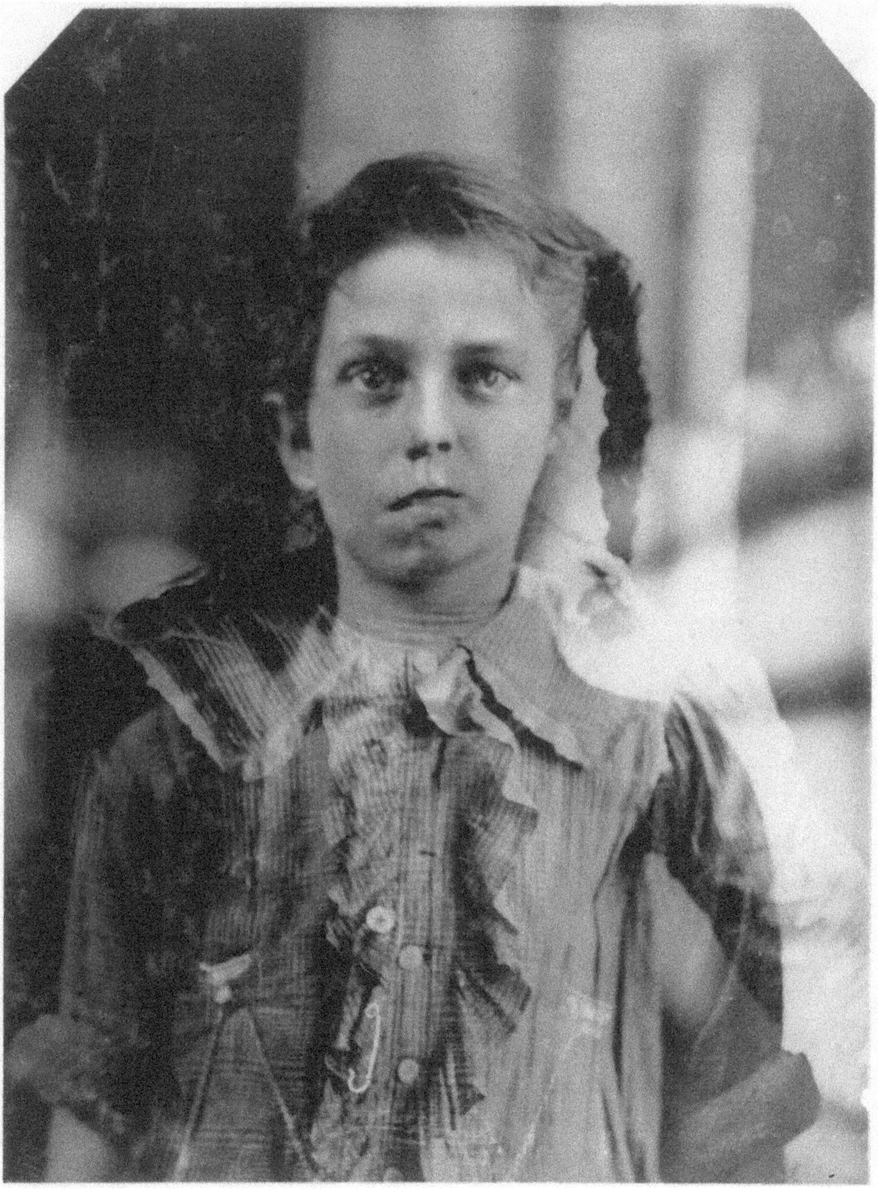

Figures 12.9–12.12 Lewis Wickes Hine, *Composite Photograph of Child Laborers Made from Cotton Mill Children*, silver gelatin prints, 1913. Library of Congress, Washington.

Notes

1. The photographic collection, consisting of approximately 6,500 items, also includes photographs of the Lombroso family, portraits of scientists, views of classrooms and laboratories, tools and objects used by thieves, crime scenes, reproductions of drawings and artifacts made in mental hospitals, and spiritist photographs. Drawings depicting physical anomalies are also present, together with many writings and other images created by psychiatric patients.
2. Founded in 1888 by Edward C. Hegeler, *The Monist* is one of the oldest and most important philosophical journals in the world. Under the direction of Paul Carus (1890–1919) and Mary Carus (1919–36) the publication helped to establish philosophy as an academic discipline in the United States.
3. "Letter from Theodore Roosevelt to Guglielmo Ferrero," November 14, 1908. Collection: Library of Congress Manuscript Division.
4. CURB, Series I: Correspondence, Box 19, Letter from Mary Dreier to Dr Stella, December 1908.
5. "Lewis Hine Composite Photograph of Child Laborers Made from Cotton Mill Children" (n.d.), Library of Congress, Washington, DC.

13

Raimundo Nina Rodrigues, Aurelino Leal, Cesare Lombroso, and the Making of a New Ethnographic Sensibility in Bahia, Brazil (1896–1906)

Livio Sansone

From Slaves to Citizens

In the twenty years from the abolition of slavery in 1888 to Cesare Lombroso's death in 1909, debates among Brazil's intellectual, medical, and political elites centered on the "quality" of "their people." In 1889, Brazil became a republic through a coup d'état, but not an inclusive one: literacy was made a requirement for voting, which meant that fewer people could vote than before. Despite only five percent of the population being literate, Brazil became the first nation to feature a motto in its vernacular language on its flag: "Order and Progress"—a shortened, more authoritarian version of Comte's famous phrase, "brotherhood, order and progress."

With the abolition of slavery, former slaves became citizens, but no special measures were taken to integrate them into society on equal terms. At the same time, mass immigration, mostly from Southern Europe (with Italy being the primary source), radically altered the country's social landscape. As a result, scrutinizing the "quality" of the Brazilian people meant investigating a wide range of issues: hygiene, both old and new diseases, tropical medicine, hunger, rural and urban poverty (and the forms of social deviance they produced), vagrancy (a widespread problem soon after abolition), new mental disorders supposedly exacerbated by a more open society (such as hysteria among women), *metissage*, Africa, the Africanness of Brazilian slums and lower-class religiosity, eating habits, musical tradition and popular culture, and the reorganization of both the prison and police systems. The rise of fetishism became iconic, drawing significant attention: how could a country where so many people believed in magic and fetishes advance toward "Order and Progress"? In response, the courts launched a new offensive against practitioners of fetishism, whom judges believed were harming others. Paradoxically, the republican and positivist courts themselves appeared to believe in the superior power of the fetish (Maggie 1992).

In this heated debate, different positions inevitably emerged. Was the Brazilian "race" weakened by widespread *metissage* and the tropical climate, or was it a sick population further debilitated by malnutrition, hookworm, and poor sanitation?[1]

A pivotal point of reference for this debate took place far away, at the Conference of Berlin (1884–5). This event, which included delegates from many countries, including Brazil, addressed major issues for the future of international relations and delved into obscure ethnographic knowledge. Particularly relevant to Brazil's aspirations of becoming a progressive country—like Australia—was the designation of the Tropics as an inherently problematic climate zone (especially for white people), the identification of African cultures and populations as among the most colonizable for Europeans due to their perceived lack of an inner drive toward progress, and the representation of the *mestizo* as a potentially weakening factor for the four or five so-called "great races."

Most observers at the conference divided African cultures into two main groups: the Sudanese-Nilotic and the Sub-Equatorial Bantu. Given the predominantly black and *mestizo* origins of Brazil's population, many national and international observers predicted a bleak future for the country. On the one hand, speakers from the Brazilian elites regarded their people as "a problem"; on the other hand, a growing minority of scholars, artists, and writers began to advocate for recognizing popular culture and highlighting the unique qualities of the Brazilian people, rather than viewing them as intrinsically weak. This emerging group included both liberals and conservatives, with a general alignment toward Catholicism.

The groundwork for a more positive approach to "the people" had already been laid by Silvio Romero, one of the most respected scholars of the Recife School of Law—a pivotal academic institution and a stronghold of "lombrosianismos"[2] in a country that did not have real universities until the 1930s. Romero, an avid reader of the latest texts on Africa available in Brazil, had, as early as 1879, argued that while Europeans were delving into African studies, Brazilian scholars had thus far neglected the nation's population of African origin and should stop ignoring "Africa in our backyard."[3]

Romero was well-versed in the quasi-ethnographic debates and the most critical texts discussed at the Berlin Conference on Africa's various cultures and ethnic groups, such as those by Alfred B. Ellis and Wilhelm Bleek. He was among the first linguists in Brazil to use the word "Bantu" and the first to reference Bleek's work. While Bleek used the term to describe a family of related languages, Romero expanded it to encompass all sub-Equatorial Africans.[4] The nascent ethnographic curiosity that began as a trickle in the 1900s would eventually grow into the broader movement of Brazilian modernism.[5] Romero's pioneering call to pay attention to what, from the 1930s, would be called Afro-Brazilian cultures did not go entirely unheard, particularly among linguists, and helped foster a new ethnographic sensibility.

In this tragic and contradictory context, fertile for a popular-scientific debate on deviancy, race, and progress, Lombroso's ideas—or rather, a selective reinterpretation of them and those of his close associates—became a compelling source of inspiration. However, Lombroso was never the only influence, as equal attention was given to other European ideas, particularly positivism (Comte and Spencer were frequently cited), evolutionism, and Marxism. Consequently, the incorporation of Lombroso's work into Brazilian social thought was neither complete nor unconditional (Sansone 2022). It is therefore necessary to identify which aspects were directly adopted and which were discarded.

Lombroso's ideas concerning the study of criminals, female offenders, social bandits, the prison system as an instrument of vengeance, the link between genius and madness, prison art (*arte carceraria*), fetishism as a primitive religion, hypnosis, and spiritualism were widely embraced. While some argued that his focus on the born criminal and atavism was excessive, these ideas were nonetheless well received.

Lombroso's ideas on African cultures and *metissage* present a very different picture. Between 1890 and 1920, thanks in part to the growing modernist mood, particularly in Cuba and Brazil (the countries with the largest populations of African origin), black people (*negros*), while still considered a developing "race," began to be accepted as an essential and positive component of the nation and its national-popular culture. However, Lombroso's views on this matter were not what most Cuban or Brazilian scholars expected—or wanted.

It was mainly during the period from the Battle of Adua (1896, fought between the Italian and the Ethiopian armies) to the last years of his life that Lombroso formulated his ideas on *metissage*, Africa, Africans, and the Afro-Catholic cults in Cuba and Brazil—views that are now largely forgotten. According to his daughter Gina, who was also his biographer and hagiographer, Africa and anti-colonialism became two of Lombroso's primary preoccupations during these years. He believed in the perfectibility of all "races," including the African ones, and did not share the common view held by many foreign observers of African societies that examples of civilizations south of the Sahara were the work of people of Mediterranean descent. This perspective was informed by heliocentrism, an old idea that, in the nineteenth century, evolved into a scientific theory suggesting that most if not all development in black Africa revolved around the central star of ancient Egypt (Howe 1998).[6] As I show elsewhere (Sansone 2022), Lombroso was opposed to colonialism in Africa and believed that Africans, particularly the Abyssinians, had the right to choose their own rulers. He also viewed *metissage* as a source of strength for a population, arguing that degeneration in humans—and in mammals more generally—was the result of excessive inbreeding, not *metissage*.

In Salvador da Bahia, one of the cities with the largest black population in Latin America, it is widely acknowledged that the psychiatrist Raimundo Nina Rodrigues (1866–1906) was the only one to study black people and their customs for at least ten years, from 1896 until his death in 1906. Nina took pride in his pioneering role; in the foreword to his book *L'anymisme fetichiste*,[7] he claimed to be the first Brazilian to explore this subject. He was relatively well-known as a researcher throughout Brazil and Argentina and as a result corresponded with journals such as *Archivio* in Turin and *Archivos* in Buenos Aires. His correspondence focused on topics like the relationship between black people and the application of the law, fetishism, the contribution of "African races" to the Brazilian nation, and Afro-Catholic cults. He argued that these cults should no longer be treated as phenomena of depravity and crime by the police but should instead be addressed by psychiatrists.

Nina's ideas about black people were complex, which is why he was described as "a shaky racialist" (Monteiro 2020; Correa 1998) and a "man of his time" (Venda Fortuna 2013), in tune with the "racial religion" (Cavalli Sforza and Padoan 2013) that dominated thought in those decades. He was convinced that black people in Brazil had not yet reached the level of development of white people and that the *mestizos* were not an "ideal race," but simply a historical reality. However, in his first book, *As racas humanas e a responsabilidade penal no Brasil* (The Human Races and Penal Accountability in Brazil, 1894), he argued that slavery had hindered the development of black people and that they deserved fair treatment in courts, with special legislation. He believed that their perceptions of private property and physical violence differed from those of citizens who were born free.

Nina certainly considered Afro-Brazilian religious life to be more primitive than mainstream religiosity, but he argued that Candomblé houses of worship should be tolerated and not treated as a police problem. He was the first scholar to take the position of Ogan, protector of the house, in the famous Candomblé temple Gantois, where several Brazilian and foreign scholars would later take the same position (Sansone 2023). Known by many as the "ambassador" of the Lombroso school in Brazil, Nina was influenced by that way of thinking, although in his foreword to *As raças humanas*, alongside Lombroso, Ferri, and Garofalo he also acknowledged Lacassagne, Tarde, and Corre, and when arguing for special legal treatment of former slaves in Brazil, he drew on literature concerning British colonial rule.

The figure of Raimundo Nina Rodrigues thus combines multiple roles: positivist researcher, psychiatrist, psychologist, sociologist, anthropologist, nationalist, social Darwinist and social evolutionist, historian, philologist, linguist, and folklorist. He was eclectic, much like Lombroso, but, as with most progressive Brazilian scholars of his time, while being a reformist, he lacked the socialist and Jewish imprint that characterized Lombroso and many of his acolytes.

In his books *As raças humanas* (1938 [1894]) and *O Animismo Fetichista* (Fetishist Animism, 2006 [1896]) as well as in articles published in the *Revista Brasileira* and *Kosmos* (posthumously collected in *Os Africanos no Brasil*, 2010 [1933]), Nina established a model for studying religiosity and fetishism among Africans and their descendants in Bahia. These groups had created a set of religious systems that syncretized popular Catholicism, particularly its cult of the saints, with elements, memories, objects, and practices of the religiosity they had brought from Africa. In general, the more the system was created by Africans of Sudanese or Yoruba origins, the purer the cosmogony and practices remained. By contrast, systems linked to people of Bantu origin tended to become less pure through the incorporation of Catholic or Native American religiosity, or even spiritualism.

Nina argued that the majority of slaves transported to Bahia in the later waves were "Sudanese"—a term that gained traction in Brazil after the Berlin Conference—coming from above the Equator and closely related to Africans of Hamitic origin. Nina was particularly influenced by Tylor's references to the Yoruba and, a few years later, especially by Ellis's work on the Yoruba in Nigeria, which described their complex and sophisticated religious systems. The book had been recommended to him by Marcel Mauss. Nina's interpretation of Yoruba religion in Brazil was based on just three foreign sources: the aforementioned work by Tylor and Ellis, and Maurice Delafosse's articles in the French magazine *Nature* on Yuruba-Abome sculptures in the Ethnographic Museum of the Trocadéro in Paris. Nina clearly favored the Yoruba-Sudanese, often portraying them as Apollonian, while depicting the Bantu as Dionysian. This preference would dominate the study of Afro-Brazilian religion until the 1980s.

Nina contended that possession rituals should no longer be a matter for the police but rather monitored by psychiatrists. He argued that protecting African religiosity, particularly in its purest forms, would contribute to the integration of black Brazilians into mainstream society. Regarding *metissage*, early in his career he was convinced that this was a form of degeneration or closely related to it (Nina Rodrigues 1890 and 1899). However, in later essays published in journals, newspapers, and posthumously in *Os Africanos no Brasil* (1933), he shifted toward accepting it as part of Brazilian history. This change in perspective resulted from his shift in focus from the biology of the individual to the social and natural environment as key influences on individual behavior. The same shift also took place in the Lombroso school and among many other scholars in the period from 1890 to 1910.

Nina held a pioneering position, as he was the first to establish a link between black cultural and religious life in Brazil and the African origins of a large part of its population. However, he was not alone in his curiosity about black Brazilians or in advocating for their recognition as an essential component of Brazilian culture.

Also interested in these topics was Dr. Oscar Freire (1882–1923), who succeeded Nina in his academic position after Nina's premature death, as well as Juliano Moreira, the black psychiatrist generally regarded as the first to introduce and adapt Freudian theory in Brazil. Moreira was the only one of the three to meet Lombroso, doing so at the 1906 International Congress of Criminal Anthropology in Turin, which celebrated thirty years of Lombroso's career.[8] Moreira also stood out for his explicit antiracist stance, which became well known a decade later when he moved to Rio to direct the city's main mental asylum, where he gained recognition for his unconventional treatment of inmates.

Among many authors from the Bahia School of Medicine, Moreira and Freire were scholars committed to fieldwork and self-taught ethnography focused especially on the black and *mestizo* populations. Both men shared Lombroso's view that crossbreeding was not the source of degeneration but rather a healthy biological and cultural trend. In 1907, Freire wrote his thesis for the Bahia School of Medicine on the topic of animism among blacks, *Etiologia das formas concretas de religiosidade do negro no Brasil* (Etiology of the Concrete Forms of Negro Religiosity in Brazil). In this Lamarckian work, he argued against the theories of Le Bon, who at that time was very popular at the school. Contending that races and Africans were improving and evolving, Moreira rejected the idea that miscegenation led to degeneration, arguing against any notion that black contributions to mixed heritage were negative (Oda, Raimundo, and Dalgalarrondo 2000, 178).

Voices arguing against the mainstream association of black and mixed-race people with madness and crime did exist, though they were few and overshadowed by the immense intellectual prestige of Raimundo Nina Rodrigues. In Bahia,[9] the debate about the African origin of many cultural traits and "bad" habits found a central stage in the prestigious and historic medical school, founded in 1808 and often considered the oldest school of tropical medicine. This institution, both the primary academic institution of the city and the locus of political and ethnic tension, played a crucial role in these discussions (Castellucci 2023). Every significant decision, such as the selection of the dean, was heavily political, but never made public.

Such debates extended to the law school, the history of which remains largely unexplored. Both it and the medical school were heavily influenced by Lombroso and his followers, though often through a local reinterpretation of his ideas. Despite Lombroso's generally high reputation, his ideas on Africa and Africans were hardly known in Brazil, as they were mostly published in Italian newspapers, which were difficult to access. This led to what could be described as a "truncated influence" rather than a widespread one.

Moreover, Lombroso's ideas on Africans did not reach the western shore of the Atlantic alone, but were joined by those expressed by the "colonial library"—a body of essential books on Africans produced mainly by missionaries, travelers, explorers, and European officials that every colonial administrator was expected to know (Mudimbe 1988). Authors such as Wilhelm Bleek and Alfred B. Ellis were frequently referenced in doctoral theses from the Bahia School of Medicine. However, due to the scarcity of foreign books in local libraries, citations of these authors were often based on short summaries of their works published in widely read academic journals like *Archivio*, *Archives*, and *Archivos* (Sansone 2022). In this context, a key figure in the Bahia School of Law was Aurelino Leal.

Nina, Freire, Moreira, and Leal developed an interest in the character, level of deviance, and religious life of black Brazilians, drawing on criminal anthropology and social psychology—or rather, on reinterpretations of thinkers like Lombroso, Lacassagne, Corre, and Tarde. Unfortunately, research into the first phase of Afro-Bahian studies is challenging, as significant gaps remain in the historical record regarding Leal, Nina, and, to a lesser extent, Freire and Moreira. There is little archival material, and many of the relevant publications and newspapers—particularly those printed in the State of Bahia—have disappeared. Nonetheless, in the following pages, I will focus on the differing views on fetishism and black religiosity in Bahia, which led Nina and Leal to engage in a polite but forthright debate. This exchange highlighted their contrasting perspectives on the integration of the black population into Brazilian society.

Aurelino Leal

Little remembered today in Bahia, despite having a small town in the state's hinterland named after him,[10] is Aurelino Araujo Leal (1877, Rio de Contas, Bahia—1924, Rio de Janeiro), the young jurist, director of the penitentiary, and later police chief and senator. Leal led a short but very dynamic life that spanned the law school, the courts, and local and federal politics as well as the Bahia State and federal prison systems and police forces.

After graduating from the Faculty of Law of Bahia in 1894 after focusing on criminal law, he soon published *Preventive Prison* (1895), *Crime Germs* (1896), *Religion Among the Condemned of Bahia* (1898a), and *Studies in Sociology and Criminal Psychology* (1904). In 1902, following a brief stint as a public prosecutor and a term in the state legislature, he assumed the directorship of the Bahia State Penitentiary and Police Department, eventually becoming secretary-general of the Bahian government.

At just eighteen years old, Leal began his career as the public prosecutor of the small town of Amargosa in 1895, where he initiated his study of the criminal personality. Influenced by the Scuola Positiva, he developed a profound distrust of the popular jury, which he viewed as an institution dedicated to vengeance rather than modern justice. That same year, Leal advocated for the removal of the *pelourinho* (whipping pole) from the main square of Amargosa, seeing it as a symbol of slavery, a stain on Brazilian history (H. Leal 1968: 40).

His career received praise from various local newspapers, such as *O Regenerador*, based in the town of Nazaré (Bahia), which referred to him on August 3, 1902. From the end of 1904 to 1906, he served as the head of the Bahia police, where he successfully separated the military from the civil police, utilizing the latter to conduct investigations. After this, he relocated to the federal capital, Rio de Janeiro, where he assumed political responsibilities within the prison system and police. Following this transition, his publications, in which he presented himself as a law student, historian, and sociologist, centered on the history of the Brazilian constitutions—a topic for which he is still remembered and cited among legal scholars (Leal 2014). In early 1914, he became a permanent member of the Brazilian Geography and History Institute (IHGB), a prestigious national academic institution second only to the Brazilian Literature Academy (ABL). His earlier essays, published in book form, were compilations of articles from Bahian newspapers and are now almost entirely forgotten, despite their popularity at the time of publication.[11]

In his first book, *Prisão Preventiva* (Preventive Prison, 1895), which he claimed to have written in just a week, Leal championed the cause of preventive detention while ensuring reparation for those incarcerated and later declared innocent. His writings indicated that he was already well acquainted with the works of Lombroso, Ferri, Garofalo, and Tarde. A year later, in 1896, drawing on his experience as a public prosecutor, Leal published *Germens do Crime* (Germs of Crime). This work explored "germs" that arise from the malfunctioning of the courts. In it, he urged legislators to "submerge their eyes into the deepest social layers to study hygiene, means, education, mood, and the movements of the psychological world of everyone, for only in this way can we provide our Fatherland with a Good Law that offers the best tools for its strengthening and social order."

Leal also proposed the establishment of the study of criminal anthropology and the creation of correctional colonies and encouraged law students to visit prisons to gain first-hand experience. He later moved to the larger town of Nazaré, where he became a successful lawyer. During this period, he published two books, *O regime penitenciario da Bahia* (The Penitentiary System in Bahia), a compilation of sixteen articles published in the *Jornal de Noticias*, one of the most important newspapers in the state, and *A religiao entre os condenados da Bahia* (Religion Among the Bahia Prison Inmates), a thirty-six-page pamphlet.

In his first work, which was positively reviewed by Cesare Lombroso (Archivio 1900: 299),[12] Leal included a set of recommendations typical of his publications. One of these was the need to incorporate "indeterminate condemnation" in the law for recalcitrant, brutal criminals (a Brazilian version of the US sentence "from one year to eternity," often applied to black men). According to Leal, the criminal needed to be seen as a human being:

> The criminal man does not deserve contempt nor social repugnance: he is an unfortunate human being, sometimes the victim of an organic anomaly or otherwise perverted by mesological [environmental] conditions. He is a prejudicially sick person, and thus society intervenes to uphold the guarantees of freedom and rights, without disengaging from his integrity and being. [Society] is therefore compelled to instill in his soul a respect for the law and morality. (Leal 1898b)

European criminology was referenced throughout the book in relation to penitentiaries, with Lombroso's stance against incarceration as a form of vengeance receiving particular praise. Leal paid homage to Lombroso and his New School, quoting his *Palimsesti del carcere*, while also citing Ferri, Garofalo, and Tarde. In line with these authors, Leal believed that sentencing should be tailored to the individual criminal and opposed uniform penalties. He respectfully quoted Nina's *As racas humanas*.

Leal described his fourth book as "a very original study of criminal psychology" (H. Leal 1968: 51) and claimed that it received positive evaluations from Ferri, Tarde, and Nina.[13] It explored the relationship between crime, religion, superstition, and the *mandinga*[14] and was the result of pioneering fieldwork in the Bahia State Penitentiary, deemed "the worst such institution in the civilized world" (Leal 1898b: 607). Leal was granted permission to organize a spiritual retreat there, assisted by the Catholic chaplain. Despite identifying as a "free thinker," he closely followed the retreat, observing and interviewing inmates while diligently recording everything in his notebook. He stated that the fieldwork experiment required a strong stomach due to the disgraceful scenes witnessed.

Leal observed that the religion practiced during the retreat was thoroughly mechanical, an offshoot of inactivity. Most convicts succumbed to religious superstition, believing in amulets that purportedly protected their bodies and bolstered individual ambitions and plans. With the chaplain, Father Paulino Fugnano, Leal endeavored to collect amulets (called *breves* or *patuás*) that the convicts wore mostly around their necks. Some were unintelligible, while others combined images of Catholic saints with popular creeds and were aimed at offering extravagant protection from diseases, disasters, harm "with iron," and death in prison. Some inmates also carried images and signs, such as the signs of Solomon, which the *mandingueiros* or superstitious believed possessed prodigious powers to protect them from harm. These symbols were usually painted on their arms or tattooed on their chests.

Leal also studied the superstitious practitioners of *mandinga*, known as *mandingueiros* or *cacundeiros*. He believed their beliefs stemmed from an "old background" and a lack of religious education, arguing that to counteract them one had to show the convicts their ineffectiveness. For Leal, *mandinga* was a psychological factor contributing to criminality in the backlands of Bahia. He concluded that proper

(Catholic) faith, religious assistance, and good priests should be available in every prison.

Leal was also deeply struck by what he considered the anthropomorphism of God in its purest form: "The readers have seen that altar objects are highly valued. God is invoked for evil with the same ardor and the same conviction that the true believer puts into invoking Him for good" (Leal 1899: 619). At times, Leal seemed to come very close to acknowledging the presence of fetishism.

During his fieldwork experiment, Leal encountered the usual challenges faced by ethnographers:

> When I wanted to study the degree of religious feeling of the condemned, I found it impossible to make good observations; they knew that their *patuas* had been given to me, and they all remained silent when they were not assuring me of their firm belief in God, assuring me that they did not believe in *mandingas*. The prejudice against me reached the point where the priest, assistant to the administrator, was obliged to defend me during an instruction, assuring them that I did not mean them any harm. (ibid.: 614)

The respondents were extraordinary people: "It is important not to forget that I am not generalizing my assertion. I always speak of the most uneducated, wildest part of the population, I should say, which, however, is very numerous" (ibid.: 624). Although race and ethnicity were not central to the text, there were some references to the *metissage* of most inmates, and to their inferiority and anthropological incapacity, which stemmed from their complete ignorance and lack of contact with civilization (ibid.: 625).

In 1902, Leal published *Estudos de sociologia e psicologia criminal* (Sociology and Criminal Psychology Studies), a celebration of "modern criminology." In the last section, the tone of the book changes, becoming a long response to Nina, who had commented on *A Religiao dos condenados da Bahia*.[15] Much of the discussion revolves around the origin and understanding of *mandinga*. Both authors were also interested in amulets, which for Nina were a core component of fetishism, while for Leal they were mere examples of superstitious Catholicism.

According to Nina, amulets were particularly significant for the small group of Muslims still living in Salvador, remnants of a much larger community deported to Africa after the Malê Revolt of 1835. He explained that these Muslims used *mandinga* as an equivalent to amulets. Leal, however, argued that the term *mandinga* was not uniquely tied to African survival but was used by a broader population, not just in the capital, Salvador, but also in the interior of the state of Bahia. It was understood as a magical practice meant to safeguard a person's body and fortune. In short, Nina contended that what Leal considered fetishism was, in fact, part of a religious system rooted in African traditions. In his reply, while extremely respectful of Nina's status, Leal countered firmly that it was not an African religion at all. He argued that such a religion could not have existed because the (black) Bahian people were already a civilized people. In short,

> African fetishist animism, diluted within the superstitious background of the white race and reinforced by the incipient animism of the aboriginal American, constitutes the subsoil … Catholic beliefs, spiritual practices, cartomancy, etc., all absorb and equally reflect the influence of witchcraft and the fetishist idolatry of Black people. (Nina Rodrigues 1897: 321)

According to Leal, belief in *mandinga* was merely the superstitious expression of poor and illiterate people who put their faith in talismans, amulets, and the evil eye—similar to practices in other Catholic countries. He believed that African religious traditions were remnants of the past and would gradually disappear as the black and *mestizo* majority population advanced to higher levels of civilization.

Comparing Views on Fetishism and the Racial Question

The aftermath of slavery and its abolition in Bahia, as elsewhere in Brazil, gave rise to the creation of folk devils and moral panics. The pressing social question was socio-racial, with scholars and intellectuals across the country concerned with the quality of "their people," especially the large impoverished population (Albuquerque 2009; Fraga 2014). Vagrants and abandoned minors posed significant challenges and in response Leal advocated for the establishment of correctional and criminal colonies. The widespread belief in superstition, particularly though not exclusively among the lower classes, further complicated these societal concerns.

Both Nina and Leal shared a strong Catholic perspective on religiosity. For them, there was a distinction between a proper, well-behaved (Catholic) religion and more primitive religious forms. Leal supported the deployment of priests in prisons, while Nina was a staunch defender of the separation between Church and State. Despite their affinities with the theoretical and professional eclecticism of the *scuola positiva* in Turin, neither Nina nor Leal were atheistic-agnostic or Jewish. Their political involvement, while present, remained in the reformist sphere, and they never became closely aligned with many of the European authors with whom they were associated, including Lombroso.

There was a significant divide between European positivism—often intertwined with socialist atheism and anticlericalism—and the neo-Lamarckian, progressive Catholicism of Latin America.[16] For the former group, religion was a social phenomenon, whereas for the latter, it was the cohesive moral force of society. Brazilian early modernism had both progressive and conservative political strains. The conservative aspect would evolve into what in the 1930s was called regionalism, with sociologist Gilberto Freyre emerging as its most prominent figure. Freyre focused on the virtues of the Brazilian people as rooted in the past, rather than in the future.

Nina, Leal, Freyre, and Moreira faced an excruciating dilemma: on the one hand, following abolition, there was a tendency to downplay racial terms and to implement a color-blind republican ideal, which discouraged any mention of race in public documents (see Mattos 1998). On the other hand, the racial question remained central to determining the future of Brazilian citizenship and defining the ideal qualities of the nation's population.

These Bahian researchers established a joint research agenda focused on the anthropology of black people and the black question, reflecting both fidelity and deviation from Lombroso's ideas regarding *metissage* and the perfectibility of African "races." Unlike Lombroso, Nina and Leal viewed *metissage* as a factor of degeneration and indeed as one of the main reasons for the perceived intrinsic weakness of the "Brazilian race." In contrast, Freire aligned much more closely with Lombroso, considering *metissage* to be a source of vitality for the population and believing that the various African cultures could evolve to achieve higher degrees of civilization. Furthermore, he disagreed with the prevailing notion, later supported and popularized by the German ethnologist Leo Frobenius, that the great civilizations of black Africa were the product of Mediterranean or Egyptian influences. Moreira, a notably dark *mulato*, firmly rejected the association of dark skin with any form of degeneration.

Nina and Leal had two distinct and opposing projects for integrating the black population into Brazilian society, which had theoretically become a society divided into classes of free citizens. Nina emphasized cultural diversity as an asset, arguing that "our Africans," particularly in Bahia, were among the best and most civilized, largely of Yoruba and Hamitic origin, and encompassing various groups then generally referred to as Sudanese. Leal, on the other hand, maintained that "our negros are not Cafres any longer"; they were not savages, even if slavery did not permit their proper education. They inherited habits from Africa (Leal 1898a: 232), but they were Catholic and also superstitious, like many in the lower classes, and had no other religion.

These were two attempts to determine how best to integrate the population of African origin into Bahian society. The half-racialized integrationist projects of Leal and Nina seemed to differ along the same lines that would later distinguish Melville Herskovits from Franklin Frazier's view of emancipation from racism thirty to forty years later in Bahia: is the best way to emancipate the African-origin population from racial discrimination to emphasize their cultural diversity, or is it better to promote universalism, on the basis that blacks deserve equal treatment simply because they are citizens and human beings like everybody else? (Sansone 2023).

Conclusions: A Lasting Research Agenda

The underlying lesson is that Nina was not the only one to address fetishism, despite his claim to be the sole pioneer of research into the religiosity and fetishism of black Brazilians in Bahia. The complex creation of this pioneering field of study emerged within a context of limited intellectual density, where theories approximating those generated by Lombroso's New School were used alongside ideas from other figures in the field of criminal anthropology and psychology, such as Ferri, Sighele, Lacassagne, Tarde, Le Bon, and Corre.

This environment fostered a research agenda that quickly became comparatively international, not least due to Lombroso, who supported a collaboration between the Cuban Ortiz and the Brazilian-Bahian Nina from 1902 to 1906.[17] By the 1930s and 1940s, as anthropology became established within the young Brazilian university system, this agenda ultimately defined the research agenda of Afro-Brazilian studies.

In a way, it is still influential today, as scholars continue to explore the existence of a Bantu-Sudanese polarity in "being African" and examine the cultural and religious forms of black Brazilians. Within this framework, the Bantu is often associated with the Dionysian component, while the Sudanese, sometimes identified as Yoruba, represent the Apollonian one.

Leal, Freire, and Moreira were young and exceptional intellectuals. Together with Nina, they established a distinct field of research—albeit a short-lived one, since Nina died in 1906, and Freire, Leal, and Moreira soon moved to the capital, Rio de Janeiro—within a context characterized by a scarcity of intellectuals and the absence of proper universities.[18] If we acknowledge that a pioneering field of research was being created in Bahia during those years, it is clear that each of these scholars made a significant contribution to it and were in close dialogue with one another. They also established contacts with renowned foreign scholars such as Lombroso, Ingenieros, and Tarde, whom they regarded as sources of intellectual strength.

The Brazilians not only remained on good terms with one another (after Nina's death, Freire took his academic position), but they shared intellectual resources, drawing from the same well of ideas. The authors of the Scuola Positiva, through their writings or often through summaries of their work in the leading journals, became integral to what can be termed the socio-racial library of that era in Latin America.[19] This is supported by an examination of the personal libraries of the famous Rio de Janeiro journalist João do Rio and the Bahian physician Estacio de Lima, who, in the early part of his long career, was regarded as Lombroso's last disciple in Bahia.[20] More so than with scholars from the United States, France, and Great Britain, the association between the Lombroso circle and the socio-racial debate in the medical school and among jurists in Bahia was very much a partnership of convenience. Quoting Lombroso and his acolytes bolstered the credibility of the Bahian scholars, while it also benefited the Lombroso school to promote figures like Nina as its ambassadors in Latin America.[21]

In the two decades after abolition, there was a growing scholarly interest in "the people," which, in Bahia, referred primarily to the lower-class black and mixed-race populations and their cultural habits and traditions. During this period, ethnography began to be deployed by both medical practitioners and legal scholars, though they did not explicitly label it as such. For them, medicine and law were also social sciences—disciplines that required not only technical knowledge but also direct engagement with the people. The populations they studied could no longer be ignored or rendered invisible; they needed to be seen, heard, questioned, and, whenever possible, documented. Scholars set out to photograph and fingerprint them and to collect their cultural artifacts, including amulets, musical instruments, garments, and pieces of craftwork or artistic creation. Most of these scholars were racialists, and some were outright racists. This serves as another example of the fact that the history of ethnography is not exclusive to anthropology. Even before the establishment of formal universities in the late 1930s, firsthand knowledge of "the people" became a methodology used across various disciplines. Moreover, while it is generally understood that an ethnographic sensibility toward populations of African descent arose from cultural relativism and, more recently, racial tolerance, it is important to recognize that ethnography—and an ethnographic sensibility and curiosity—could also develop among scholars who believed in a hierarchy of the races, even before the rise of modern anthropology.

Notes

1. On the Tropics as a "problem" see, among others, Peard (2000). On the debate on social improvement through sanitation or European immigration at the end of the nineteenth century, see Maio (ed.) 2010.
2. Romero and his adversary within the Recife school, Tobias Barreto, both quoted Lombroso and his school. Tobias Barreto is said to have been the first in Brazil to quote Lombroso, but he also quoted Karl Marx.
3. Sílvio Romero, "Estudos sobre a Poesia Popular do Brasil" (1879), *Revista Brasileira*, Tomo 1: 9.
4. The first to use the term was de Antonio Joaquim de Macedo Soares in "Estudos lexicográficos do dialecto brazileiro" (1880), *Revista Brazileira*, Tomo 4: 243–71.
5. The touchstone of Brazilian modernism is generally considered to be the 1922 São Paulo Modernist Biennale. Its mission was to show that the problem of Brazil's failure to make progress could best be resolved by dealing with the needs of "the people" (*o povo*).
6. Two decades later, the influential German ethnographer Leo Frobenius continued to argue in very much the same way.
7. In his effort to communicate with the international community, Nina personally financed the translation of this book into French, as well as the costs of printing and mailing it overseas. This was a practice also followed by other Bahian scholars, such as Aurelino Leal, whose book *A Religiao dos condenados da Bahia* (1898) was published in French just one year later. Despite the potential costs associated with this endeavor, it proved beneficial; these authors are cited abroad primarily because of their French translation. Today, it is much easier to access certain texts in French than in the original Portuguese editions.
8. See the report *Atti del Congresso internazionale di antropologia criminale*, held in Turin in 1906, available in the ACLM.
9. The attention paid to fetishism and religious practices of African origin was not limited to Bahia; it was also evident in other cities, including the federal capital, Rio de Janeiro (Do Rio 1906; Maggie 1992), and Recife (Bivar et al. 2017).
10. Through now an outlawed practice, the State Government used to "immortalize" local politicians by renaming towns (as well as schools, bridges, hospitals, etc.) after them. Before such name changes, towns invariably had either a Tupi-Guarani name or were named after Catholic saints. The tragicomic aspect of this is that the State of Bahia immortalized Leal by renaming the town of Barra do Rio de Contas after him in 1961. However, very few, if any, of Leal's publications have been preserved in the Bahia State Library. I was only able to locate the most influential publication for this text in two libraries of the University of São Paulo (Centro de Estudos Brasileiros and the Oscar Freire Library of Medicine).
11. I have never seen references to Leal in any recent study of race relations in Bahia from 1890 to 1920. The recent exception is Olivia Gomes da Cunha (2020: 157–61)

who commented on the French translation of *A religiao entre os condenados da Bahia* published in *Archives* in 1899.

12. Surprisingly, in his review, Lombroso does not mention nor argue with Leal's suggestion of using Catholic religious education to redeem prison inmates from the creed of fetishism.
13. I was unable to trace such reviews. However, Leal gained international attention after he published in French 'La religion chez les condamnes a Bahia' (1899), *Archives d'Anthropologie Criminelle*, 14 (84): 605–31, and, in Spanish, "El trabajo penitenciario en el Brasil" (1902), in *APC*, 1: 414–19.
14. The word *Mandinga* refers to a language group in Western Africa well-known for the power of their witch doctors, but also to the actual fetish.
15. Possibly in his widely read articles in the Rio de Janeiro daily *Journal do Comercio*, and the Bahia daily newspapers *Journal de Noticias*, *Diario de Noticias* or *Diario da Bahia*. I am almost sure that Leal is responding to the article by Nina entitled "Ilusoes da Catechese no Brasil," published in the *Revista Brasileira* (1897) and again, with a very different title, in the French version of his *L'animisme fetichiste des de negres de Bahia*.
16. The pompous state and Catholic funeral of Nina in Salvador, reported in headlines on the front page of the leading Bahian daily for three days (*Jornal de Noticias*, August, 11–13, 1906), not only underscored the respect he commanded from the Bahian establishment but also reflected the deep devotion he and his family had to the Catholic Church. The newspaper reported that Nina's body, which had been preserved after his death in Paris en route to Milan and Turin, where he had intended to meet Lombroso, was interred in the most prestigious cemetery in Bahia, alongside the tombs of other scholars. Notably, it had not been embalmed, thereby eliminating any suggestion that the body could have been donated to science, as Lombroso and many other positivist—and often atheistic—scholars of this time did.
17. As evidenced by Nina's letter to Ortiz dated August 25, 1903 (Ortiz Papers, Biblioteca Nacional Jose´Marti, Havana), the two began corresponding and exchanging publications shortly before Ortiz moved to Genoa. From there, he made several trips to Lombroso's cabinet and home in Turin. It was in Turin, largely due to Lombroso's emphasis on an international perspective on forms of primitive religion, however, that Ortiz more thoroughly incorporated Nina's work into his own research.
18. In the capital of the State of Bahia there were three faculties: medicine, law, and engineering. The first university, the Universidade Federal da Bahia, was not established until 1946.
19. My point is that, alongside the colonial library for Africa, there existed, for Latin American intellectuals and politicians, a need and desire for a similar library tailored to their own nations—a collection of national and foreign texts deemed essential for understanding the social and racial challenges perceived by intellectual elites. The works of Lombroso and his school were integral to this Latin American (neocolonial) library.
20. The library of Paulo Barreto (1881–1921), who wrote under the pseudonym João do Rio, was donated to the Real Gabinete de Leitura Portugues in Rio de Janeiro. Containing 3,000 books, it was substantial for its time. The personal library of Estacio de Lima (1897–1984) was donated by his family to the Gonzalo Muniz Library, housed in the Bahia School of Medicine of the Federal University of Bahia.

21. In the case of Bahia, which was relatively short-lived and occurred quite early, the relationship between Ortiz and Lombroso should be considered differently from the conclusions drawn by Silvano Montaldo. Montaldo argues that this was more significant for Lombroso than Ortiz (Montaldo 2023). However, it can be more accurately described as a relationship of mutual convenience or a win-win situation, as diplomats might say today.

14

Between Social Transgression and Cultural Integration: Following Criminological Traces in the Work of Fernando Ortiz

Mario Valero

The Ups and Downs of a Criminologist

Historians, anthropologists, and scholars of modern Caribbean and Latin American studies typically approach the vast bibliography produced by the Cuban polymath Fernando Ortiz through his 1940 book *Contrapunteo Cubano* (Cuban Counterpoint), which is widely regarded as foundational for cultural and anthropological studies across the continent. In this work, Ortiz introduced the term "transculturation" to define the methodological strategy he had developed to explain the dynamics of Cuba's historical evolution. From that moment on, the term became central to understanding his encyclopedic account of Afro-Cuban culture. His career is often viewed as progressing organically toward this critical moment, which overshadowed any of his earlier or later critical positions.[1]

From this perspective, the theories developed by Cesare Lombroso and the Italian school of criminology—key influences on Ortiz at the beginning of his career in criminology—are submerged within a wide range of outdated theoretical sources and interpreted as a sort of negative background. These theories are viewed as something Ortiz eventually dissented from to establish his anthropological approach to Afro-Cuban history and culture.[2] However, a closer examination of his work across various fields published during his prolific career reveals how Ortiz, shaped by the racial configuration and history of Cuba, adapted some of the foundational methodological concepts of Lombroso and his followers to suit his own research interests. He reinterpreted criminological principles and categories, transforming their methodology into an anthropological reinterpretation of Cuban history.

Fernando Ortiz spent his formative years on the island of Menorca and studied law in Madrid and Barcelona, graduating in 1902. In 1905, he returned to Cuba and began a multifaceted career in law, anthropology, and politics. Before this, he had served as consul in Genoa, where he came into direct contact with Cesare Lombroso and his associates.[3] His professional relationship with Lombroso reflects a customary social practice within the international criminological community at the turn of the twentieth century: the Cuban disciple and his Italian master exchanged favors, gifts, and correspondence. Ortiz used Lombroso's international prestige to bolster his early career in criminal ethnography,[4] while Lombroso saw Ortiz's work as a validation of the universal relevance of his theories and accepted the Cuban's enthusiastic praise, along with the ethnographic artifacts he sent to expand his criminological collection.

This convenient exchange of letters and gifts acquires added significance when we consider the development of Ortiz's anthropological career (Montaldo 2023). One example is his use of a letter sent to him by Lombroso on September 18, 1905, which Ortiz included as a sort of prologue to the 1906 edition of his book, *Los negros brujos* (The black Sorcerers), the first volume of an ambitious project on the history of crime in Cuba. Ortiz's minor alterations and strategic placement of the letter recast its significance: from a general expression of approval and some comments on the manuscript, it became a sort of dictum and formal encouragement of his future career. While this clever gesture might be interpreted on a purely tactical level, it also demonstrates how some of Lombroso's methodological principles underpinned Ortiz's work, even after the apparent shift from his early criminological phase to the cultural focus of his later anthropological research. Lombroso's criminological method can be seen throughout the multiple, and apparently contradictory, directions Ortiz pursued during his career as one of Latin America's most emblematic anthropologists and the man who coined the term *cubanía* to define the unique cultural identity that, in his view, Cuba owed to its African heritage (Gonçalves 2014; Arnedo Gómez 2022).

The Black Sorcerers was published in 1906 in Madrid as the first volume of a planned trilogy on Cuba's criminological history. At the time, Ortiz was a young lawyer aiming to build a career in criminal anthropology, a relatively new discipline that had become essential for population control and central to the urgent institutional modernization required by the recently established Cuban republic. While studying law in Spain, Ortiz had encountered the Italian positivist school of criminology led by Cesare Lombroso, particularly through his participation in the criminology laboratory supervised by his professor and mentor, Rafael Salillas (Naranjo-Orovio 2016: 3).

A second edition of *The Black Sorcerers*, published in 1917, included a preliminary note by Ortiz stating that an entire section from the original book had been removed and would be included in expanded form in later publications. This section addressed various crimes associated with African slaves and their descendants in Cuba. In keeping with its title, the second edition focused exclusively on Cuban sorcery, while the removed and expanded section had been published in Cuba a year earlier, in 1916, as a large volume titled *Los negros esclavos* (The Black Slaves). The purpose of the expansion was to place Afro-Cuban crime within a comprehensive historical overview of the island's colonial evolution. By emphasizing the racial dimension, Ortiz aimed to advance a hypothesis explaining the country's structural socioeconomic inequalities and criminal profile.

Since the end of the last independence war in 1898 and the subsequent military and political intervention of the United States, Cuba's historical dynamics had intensified, bringing racial contradictions to the fore and revealing the discrimination suffered by blacks and mulattoes (Helg 1995: 193). Likely influenced by these historical circumstances, Ortiz's editorial decisions indicate a shift in his approach to the subject of his anthropological investigations, although his commitment to positivist methodology and criminological theoretical premises remained unchanged.

From this period onward, Ortiz's research increasingly focused on various aspects of Afro-Cuban culture, which he aimed to integrate into the broader history of the island. While his historiographic work and field research remained the cornerstone of his methodology, he began using these approaches to contextualize ethnographic information rather than to explain historical or empirical facts from a strictly criminological standpoint. The hybrid nature of criminological research methods—which lay halfway between deterministic causality and speculative interpretation—allowed Ortiz to establish a complementary relationship between the negative view of the African element, often uncritically accepted by the racialist disciplines of the time, and a historical–cultural framework that positioned Afro-Cuban culture as an exceptional case, challenging a priori categorizations.

In *The Black Slaves* (1916), Ortiz drew on Cuba's unique history of racial development to outline the island's distinct criminal profile, advocating for a discipline with a multidimensional perspective to address what he considered a unique object of inquiry. This essentialist view, which insisted on cultural exceptionalism, would later inform his studies of Afro-Cuban music in the 1930s. It was a position at odds with the epistemological concept of transculturation that underpinned his earlier criminological work, which emphasized the hybrid nature of Cuba's cultural development (Pavez Ojeda 2021: 131).

The vital institutional modernization promoted by the government of the new republic required a reconsideration of race as a categorical variable, not only so the government's interpretation could be imbued with cultural value, but also so that race could be used as a demographic factor in extensive health and police campaigns. For Ortiz, any anthropological approach to the country's racial composition had to be subjected to historical analysis, suggesting that cultural integration had the potential to address the social challenges that racial mixing presented in governing the Cuban population. Anticipating the post–Second World War shift in anthropology, where the notion of race evolved from an objectively scientific category to a subjective cultural concept, Ortiz's understanding of race reveals how Cuban institutional powers developed a narrative presenting the nation's racial profile both as a foundation for understanding structural socioeconomic disparities and as a distinctive element of the nation's cultural exceptionalism (Balibar 2008: 1635).

In *The Black Slaves* (1916), Ortiz expanded the conceptual scope of his earlier criminological research to create "densely contextualized monographs," similar to anthropologist Bronislaw Malinowski's late functionalist approach. This style is characterized by comprehensive works that aim to assemble their subject through a massive inclusion of data without producing cohesive, systematic descriptions (Clifford 1988: 104). Shifting to a cultural anthropological perspective, Ortiz moved beyond the evidence-based focus of his earlier criminological work to embrace a diverse array of historiographic and empirical sources. The extensive compilation of disparate references included in *The Black Slaves* exemplifies this cumulative approach. The book also serves as both a synthesis and culmination of Ortiz's earlier scholarly output, from his ethnological research on criminal behavior to his Durkheimian study on racial suicide, and a comparative manual on different identification systems. These publications can be seen as preliminary studies that Ortiz eventually integrated into *The Black Slaves*, a volume that, over two decades later, would itself be subsumed into *Cuban Counterpoint*.

The criminological topics addressed in Ortiz's earlier essays on black criminal behavior, suicide, and sorcery, published in the *Archivio di psichiatria,* later provided support for his historical analysis of slavery. He interpreted the high rate of suicide among African slaves as an act of rebellion against the commodification of their bodies, akin to the resistance displayed by runaway slaves who escaped their masters' subjugation (Ortiz 1995b: 35). Witchcraft and potentially criminal associations like the "ñáñigos," composed of Black and mulatto Cubans, were presented by him as examples of Afro-Cuban syncretic folklore and as strategies of cultural resistance and resilience.[5] Rather than signaling a turning point in his anthropological career, this shift marked Ortiz's move away from fixed criminological principles and toward a relativistic interpretation of criminal acts—which he increasingly saw as culturally conditioned behaviors influenced by multiple factors that changed over time.[6] Though still informed by criminological principles, reconsidering Afro-Cubans as subjects of scientific study became central to his later transcultural methodological model. His manual on fingerprint identification, created for policing purposes, contributed to the establishment of Cuba's first national identification institution, a project supported by both the United States government and Cuba's conservative republican government at the time. The manual reflected a Lombrosian atavistic notion of crime, associating certain groups—predominantly Black, mulatto, or impoverished white immigrants—with a disruptive potential. In his draft for the work, Ortiz proposed the creation of an "anthropological name" to construct the identity profile of these potential criminals as an aggregate of distinct physical and cultural traits that would allow law enforcement to anticipate future behavior.

In 1923, Ortiz published *Un catauro de cubanismos* (A Basket of Cuban Words), a lexicographic study on the historical evolution of Cuban terms that emphasized their mixed origins. This etymological work aimed to inscribe Cuban popular language, including criminal slang, within the broader field of Spanish American dialectology. Each word's meaning was presented as a contingent mediation between various options, highlighting the difficulty of the lexicographer's task of systematizing this dynamic aspect of Cuban popular culture. Determining the meaning of a word diachronically also allowed one to identify its usage and communicative function, making the dictionary an essential tool for forensic investigation. The book was based on the exhaustive research by Dr. Israel Castellanos, who studied "peculiar speech and linguistic constructions characteristic and widely used among individuals of the populace … words and phrases typical of the vocabulary of the masses" (Castellanos 1914d: 191).[7] Ortiz went beyond a criminological approach, presenting local dialects as symbols of Cuba's hybrid culture. This was a particularly resonant stance, considering that the United States, which at the time was consolidating its role as the new hegemonic power in the Spanish American continent, was endorsing a discriminatory view of the racial divide.

In 1926, *A Project for a Cuban Penal Code*, drafted by a commission led by Fernando Ortiz and published in Havana, revealed his dialectical engagement with the philosophical principles of the Italian school of criminal anthropology. In the prologue to this legal project, he included an enthusiastic letter from Enrico Ferri, then leader of the Italian school, who eulogized Ortiz's approach to adapting positivist criminological principles to Cuba's specific historical conditions. While the code was built on a positivist conception of crime and punishment, rooted in the criminological notion of the criminal type and criminal act, the Cuban project placed more emphasis on sociocultural factors than on heredity in shaping an individual's inclination toward crime.

Ortiz's proposal emerged during a period of social upheaval and labor unrest following the profound economic crisis caused by the steady decline of international sugar prices in the 1920s. General Gerardo Machado had been elected Cuba's president in 1924, as American naval forces withdrew from the island in the midst of the crisis. Both the United States and the Cuban oligarchy viewed Machado as a strongman who, if necessary, would restore order through brute force in a country facing massive unemployment and a sharp rise in crime. The plan for a new criminal code masterminded by Fernando Ortiz was the third produced since Machado assumed power. Although Ortiz's proposal was clearly guided by positivist principles, its sections on prevention and other social defense mechanisms reflected the Cuban government's repressive aims. Aware of his subordinate role as an organic intellectual in the Gramscian sense, Ortiz sought to create a penal code suited to Cuba's specific social and political conditions, thereby helping to secure the consensus between the state, civil society, and political elites needed to maintain the existing order.

The repressive control of a potentially unruly population by a strong state was deemed essential, while the longer process of social assimilation and civil education of the poorest sectors of Afro-Cuban and white immigrant communities required a carefully coordinated strategy of cultural recognition. Ortiz and Lombroso shared a belief in social evolution and the importance of state-led preventive and reformatory measures. However, Ortiz recognized that Cuba's racial demography made it impossible to apply Lombroso's racist juxtaposition of civilization and barbarism as well as his geographic determinism regarding crime. From early in his anthropological approach to crime, Ortiz understood that African sorcery was not merely a "barbarian" trait imported into a "civilized" setting but rather a culturally specific social practice criminalized by a society with a diverse set of values (Ortiz 1995b: 186). In *The Black Sorcerers*, Ortiz theorized that "de-Africanizing" witchcraft would occur by assimilating African culture through a mutual transformation of both host and foreign elements. This instrumental view of cultural exchange, evident throughout Ortiz's work, demonstrates his awareness of Cuba's unique historical context while also reflecting the criminological principle of social defense.

Title VIII, First Chapter, Article 326 of Ortiz's proposed penal code specifies categories of individuals deemed potentially dangerous, along with the corresponding forms of coercion. These individuals included vagrants, abandoned minors, unassimilated foreigners, recidivists, an ambiguous category of low-life individuals, and others "rationally considered" prone to criminal acts. The methods of preventive social control encompassed awards, commendations, persuasions, propaganda, education, public shaming, physical or psychological discipline, threats, corrective treatments, and penalties. According to the code, crime prevention must begin in elementary school and, if necessary, continue through prison or even a mental asylum.

Afrocubanía: Revising the Notion of Transgression

Race, as a defining aspect of Cuba's population, was implicitly embedded in the code's legal provisions. Despite the absence of racial features in the generic description of potentially dangerous individuals, race was reflected in the code's discriminatory socioeconomic assumptions, given that Afro-Cubans overwhelmingly occupied the lowest ranks of Cuban society. Blacks, mulattoes, and, to a lesser degree, immigrants from the Canary Islands were among the poorest and most vulnerable segments of the population. As Ortiz had demonstrated in *The Black Slaves* a decade earlier, one of the major challenges in managing the Cuban population stemmed from the legal vacuum left by the colonial slave regime. During the colonial period, slaves were not granted citizenship, even if they obtained freedom, which explained the constant abuses perpetrated by their former masters. Conversely, this legal gap also permitted a relative freedom for slaves and their descendants to form associations, such as secret societies like the so-called "ñáñigos" or "cabildos" (Kemner 2012). The new penal code was intended to address this legal gap by subjecting Afro-Cubans to the law while acknowledging their distinct legal status relative to their African ancestors. This approach, serving simultaneously as a means of legal control and political validation, illustrates Ortiz's continuous attempt to balance the positivist emphasis on biological inheritance with the sociohistorical evolution of his country. This contrast between biological inheritance and historical evolution recurs frequently in his work, approached from various angles. In *El engaño de las razas*, a collection of his 1944 lessons at the University of Havana on Cuba's ethnic and social formation (published in 1946), Ortiz dissected the historical evolution of the concept of race, assessing various anthropological and sociological theories. He ultimately concluded that racial traits evolve continually, shaped by the dialectical relationship between social and biological factors (Ortiz 2022: 297–321).

Another instance of Ortiz's dialectical approach to race appears in his Introduction to José Antonio Saco's book, *History of the Slavery of the Indians in the New World* (1883), published in 1932 as part of the Cuban Collection of Rare and Unpublished Books and Documents. This project, which Ortiz coordinated, aimed to publish authors whose work contributed to the foundation of Cuban cultural history. Saco, a nineteenth-century Cuban polymath and abolitionist, was highly admired by Ortiz, who saw him as one of his predecessors. In the Introduction, Ortiz describes racial and cultural mixing, or *mestizaje*, as the result of a biological conflagration from which only the fittest survive. In a seemingly anachronistic turn that aligned him with Ludwig Gumplowicz's evolutionary theories of racial struggle, which sought to naturalize every human act,[8] Ortiz emphasized the unpredictability of racial mixing as a historical process. Mixing could ensure a group's social stability, or, conversely, pose a biological threat to its survival. Using a series of war metaphors, Ortiz presented the groups in competition as various subspecies of the genus *Homo* whose "phylogenic osmosis" [*sic*] shaped individual physiological and psychological development, or ontogenesis. Consequently, he saw each individual as a "physiological labyrinth" that explained the instability of the mixed-race type.

Regardless of the scientific inaccuracies in his descriptive analysis, Ortiz transforms a historical reference to Cuba's colonial past into a plea against biological racist preconceptions and a critique of European colonialism during his own time. This assertion could also be interpreted as a warning about the physiological and psychological instability of Cuba's mixed-race population, and, hence, the need for state-sponsored preventive health and policing campaigns. Atavistic traits are presented as indicators of an enduring cultural exchange, irrespective of their seemingly tragic outcomes. Within the dynamics of transculturation, historical events represent just one moment in a continuous process of dialectical transformation. Ortiz historicized criminological premises to uncover their analytical potential, even if this appears to regress to an earlier theoretical perspective. His application of race as an analytical category throughout his work aligned with criminological principles; notable examples emerge from its initial consideration in *The Black Sorcerers* (1906). Significantly, race was among the physiological traits used to identify potentially disruptive behavior in the 1913 fingerprint identification manual for Cuba. In *La filosofía penal de los espiritistas*, his 1915 examination of Allan Kardec's theories, Ortiz connects social practices associated with spiritualist beliefs—such as Afro-Cuban religious rituals and sorcery—to a comparative analysis of spiritualism and criminology (Ortiz 2012).[9]

Beginning with his initial interest in African sorcery and criminal behavior, Ortiz aimed to provide a comprehensive explanation of this cultural practice rather than restricting himself to a narrow criminological interpretation. He utilized the extensive information he had gathered to develop his conceptual framework, wherein racial categories were intrinsically linked to classifying individuals prone to criminal behavior in order to focus on prevention and reformation. This approach ensured that all citizens were subject to the rule of law while promoting the assimilation of potentially dangerous groups through cultural reevaluation. The book's final chapter compares positivist theories, including Lombroso's, with spiritualist perspectives concerning social transgression and crime, suggesting that Kardec's viewpoint offered a less restrictive explanation. As Arcadio Díaz Quiñónez proposes, Kardec's spiritualist proposals allowed Ortiz to relativize Lombroso's biological determinist concept of the born criminal, since the French educator's interpretation of spiritual evolution considered factors such as national culture, material progress, and racial mixing from a historical perspective (Díaz-Quiñones 1997: 75).

This Janus-like approach to racial characteristics, used simultaneously as criminological evidence and cultural assets, allowed Ortiz to recast criminal acts—such as sorcery—as expressions of Afro-Cuban culture. Understanding the historical evolution of such cultural practices proved crucial for devising appropriate methods of crime prevention while also integrating these practices into Cuba's national identity. In *El engaño de las razas*, Ortiz's critique of the misleading role played by race in the interpretation and classification of human behavior draws upon an anthropological understanding of historical data. As an object of scientific inquiry, race contributes to understanding the racist historical underpinnings in human sciences, including criminal anthropology. Using his characteristic method of constructing hypotheses dialectically through the accumulation of historical data, Ortiz achieved his goal through a meticulous and varied examination of racial constructs. By reinterpreting and questioning core criminological principles, such as atavism and regression, Ortiz transformed the idea of a criminal type into an *ideal type* akin to the model developed by the German sociologist Max Weber at around the same time. The ideal type's provisional nature allows the researcher to modify it to fit the intelligibility of the described phenomenon and the chosen analytical perspective (Weber 1949: 90). In this context, Ortiz's anthropological concepts—such as the black sorcerer, black slave, or black *curro* (a vagrant former slave)—were not fixed racial representations but historical formations that served as analytical tools for describing specific cultural configurations, from criminal types to folklore or musical styles.

Back to Lombroso on the Path to Transculturation

For Ortiz, inheritance and atavism—the key variables in defining the concept of the born criminal—were contingent factors rather than essentialist causes. His anthropological approach to history not only challenged the deterministic interpretation of human behavior but also enabled social scientists to propose social defense mechanisms based on cultural integration as a fitting strategy for countries with mixed-race populations. From the start of his career in criminal anthropology, Ortiz's focus on the black sorcerer and his role in Afro-Cuban cultural history revealed his growing aspiration to transcend the notion of race as a reductive marker of identity.

Ortiz understood *mestizaje* in both ethnic and biological terms as the outcome of racial mixing, a process yielding endless new combinations and ultimately fostering "de-racialization," a term he coined to describe the increasing elimination of race as an anthropological category. He envisioned a future in which Cuba's conventional racial divides, inherited from colonial rule, and its hierarchical socioeconomic structures would dissolve into a homogeneous human type with a unified cultural identity, where race would be merely a physical trait, a hereditary consequence devoid of any biological association with specific psychological or cultural characteristics.[10] Regardless of this utopian vision, Ortiz continued to employ racial categorizations in his anthropological view of culture. However, unlike the prevailing racist notion of "whitening," which saw racial mixing as a solution to racial tensions and socioeconomic inequality, Ortiz considered a comprehensive understanding of Cuba's history of slavery essential for explaining the disruptive tendencies presented by specific racial groups in Cuba. Instead of relying on limited biological assumptions, he saw *mestizaje* as a long-term historical solution capable of mitigating potential racial conflicts.

As a Cuban anthropologist, Ortiz viewed Africans and their descendants as fundamental to Cuba's identity, seeing the very fact of being Cuban as the object of his research. This approach differs from that of European and American anthropologists of his time, for whom a certain detachment from their subjects was necessary for the production of ethnographic material.[11] Ortiz's relationship with his subject of study bears parallels to Lombroso's research on Italy's "Southern Question." In newly independent Cuba, Ortiz envisioned his extensive ethnographic undertaking as part of a nation-building project, essential to establishing a hierarchical order within a highly diverse and divided society—much like Lombroso's in post-unified Italy. In Italy, the figure of the *brigante*, where racial mixing was pivotal to explaining potential criminal behavior, posed a challenge for the Italian liberal state. In Cuba, the image of the black criminal threatened the stability of the newly constituted nation, especially since the government's ability to maintain the tenuous stability of the country was closely monitored by the United States, which employed a racialized framework for social control.

Like Lombroso, Ortiz held a positive view of racial miscegenation, opposing Arthur de Gobineau's prevalent notion that racial mixing was degenerative. Given that Cuba's mixed-race population was neither geographically nor culturally isolated, but an integral part of the body politic, Ortiz eventually saw that what might have been considered a drawback in fact offered a potential solution, if considered as a cultural asset. Acknowledging this aspect of the Cuban population, Ortiz began to contextualize African customs previously deemed criminal, expanding and relativizing their supposedly disruptive qualities. Sorcery, for instance, entailed diverse cultural elements, including music, dance, language, religion, and the production of syncretic language and myths.

In the final stage of his criminological research, Cesare Lombroso developed a similarly keen interest in spiritualism and paranormal phenomena, questioning the widespread dismissal of them as unscientific. In his last book, *Ricerche sui fenomeni ipnotici e spiritici*, he shifted his focus beyond criminal potential to the practitioners of these beliefs, their cultural traits, and ancient historical precedents (Lombroso 1909b).[12] Questioning his long-held belief in the contrast between the primitive and civilized stages of human evolution—beliefs that had underpinned his conceptions of atavism and the born criminal—Lombroso came to regard spiritualist practices as a form of empirical knowledge that had been overlooked by the human sciences since the turn of the twentieth century (Knepper 2018a). Criminal anthropology, he argued, needed to consider customs and rituals from popular and primitive cultures to expand and ultimately transform the scope of its analysis: "In physical matters we are very far from having attained scientific certainty. But the spiritistic hypothesis seems to me like a continent incompletely submerged by the ocean, in which broad islands raised above the general level are visible in the distance, and which only the scientific viewpoint can see as coalescing in one immense and compact body of land" (Lombroso 1909a: VI–VII). Lombroso's initial doubts about hypnotic phenomena and paranormal experiences gave way to a kind of conversion, in which he rejected straightforward scientific explanations.

In his 1915 book, *La filosofía penal de los espiritistas*, Ortiz acknowledged this understanding of spiritualism as a sociohistorical phenomenon, assuming a similar position to the one expressed by Lombroso at the end of his career. In this comparative study between two seemingly opposed positions—criminological positivism and spiritualism—Ortiz concluded that these antithetical views ultimately align in their philosophical principles regarding the evolution of the human spirit. Notably, in his dialectical examination of materialistic and idealistic notions of crime, he sought to complement the theoretical principles he had absorbed through his academic training with his own understanding of Cuba's cultural reality. As Arcadio Díaz-Quiñónez suggests, this cultural perspective—one that accepted spiritualist theories as valid explanatory tools—prefigured his later methodological approach, embodied in the notion of transculturation (Díaz-Quiñónez 1997).

In *Cuban Counterpoint*, Ortiz introduces the term transculturation as the essential framework for interpreting the evolution of Cuban culture. He constructs this epistemological model of Cuba's cultural history by bringing together diverse economic, statistical, sociological, ethnographic, legal, linguistic, and literary sources to form complex matrices of knowledge that reflect the island's complex colonial past. Tobacco and sugar, the two pillars of Cuban culture, are represented in his text through a strategic integration of these varied sources, made possible by a skilled dialectical balancing of anthropological narrative and ethnographic data (Clifford 1988: 112). This oscillation between presenting the findings of participant observation and data collected in fieldwork, on the one hand, and interpreting historical information, on the other, was a hallmark of his methodology from the beginning of his career in criminal anthropology. During this time, he learned the rudiments of assembling large amounts of data to construct arguments that he then wove through an elaborate writing style that was often described as baroque or allegorical (Coronil 2019; Pavez-Ojeda 2021). Ortiz's approach bears more resemblance to criminology's cumulative information management or Max Weber's model of comprehensive sociology than to the research procedures followed by Functionalism, the anthropological theory with which Ortiz's method is sometimes associated.

In his Introduction to *Cuban Counterpoint*, Bronislaw Malinowski acknowledged the significance of the concept of transculturation, viewing it as a useful technical term to describe a process of cultural exchanges between distinct, quantifiable cultural elements and aligning it with his own functionalist approach. He saw this process as contingent on the unique natural and cultural conditions in which it occurred, with its results, according to Malinowski, being unpredictable. However, Ortiz underscored the continuous nature of transculturation, which, in Cuba's case, generated unique cultural formations.[13] Even more significant was Ortiz's extensive use of the historical archive—the keystone of his anthropological work—which was at odds with Malinowski's aversion to historical analysis.

In *Cuban Counterpoint*, Ortiz presented Cuban history through the prism of tobacco and sugar, the island's most essential agricultural commodities, personifying them as incarnations of the nation's unique Creole culture and proposing an organic description that placed Afro-Cuban culture at the core of their historical development. Through a recalibration of Afro-Cuban culture within this transcultural framework, Ortiz reaffirmed his initial aspiration to integrate the African component into a hybrid conception of culture that implied an increasing process of de-Africanization resulting from racial mixing. Ortiz essentialized commodities like tobacco and sugar, as he had previously done with criminal types like Black sorcerers, to propose a transcultural epistemology that used hybridity and change to ultimately overcome the racial divide. Ortiz intentionally maintained his explanatory method of Cuban racial evolution as an open and ongoing project (Perez Firmat 1989; Benítez Rojo 2001; Coronil 2019).

This echoes Lombroso's late appreciation of spiritualism, in which he envisioned criminology's ultimate horizon relying on an evolving, hierarchical spiritual order and reconsidered the value of primitive knowledge—a perspective resonant with Ortiz's attempt to essentialize Afro-Cuban cultural practices and artifacts as part of an endless, perennially transient transmigration in both spiritual and cultural terms.

Notes

1. Fernando Ortiz's career can be divided into three phases: The formative phase, from 1905 to 1924, was shaped by scientific positivism, his political commitments with various government administrations, and a prolific output across diverse texts. The intermediate phase, spanning 1924 to 1940, saw Ortiz undertake cultural and scientific publishing projects that appeared to lack overt political motivations. In the final phase, from 1940 until 1969, he focused on Afro-Cuban history, making substantial cultural contributions and engaging in a renewed political commitment (Le Riverend 1995).
2. For Ortiz's transition from criminology to cultural anthropology, see Coronil's Introduction to Ortiz (1995: IX–LVI).
3. See Gonçalves (2014); Naranjo Orovio (2016); Le Riverend (1995); Ortiz (1995).
4. LP, Letter of F. Ortiz to C. Lombroso, June 6, 1906.
5. A perspective that he already assumed in the chapters dedicated to contextualizing historically Afro-Cuban witchcraft in *The Black Sorcerers* and then expanded in *Cuban Counterpoint*: Ortiz (1995): 64–112.
6. See his 1940 prologue to Cabrera, *Cuentos Negros*, 8.
7. The three essays represented a comprehensive compilation of Afro-Cuban dialects from diverse criminal groups in Havana.
8. On Gumplowicz's racist theories see Barnes (2013).
9. The book was dedicated to Lombroso, who had asked him to write an article on the topic for the *Archivio di psichiatria*.
10. At the First Inter-American Congress of Demography held in Havana in 1943, in the midst of the Second World War, Ortiz advocated for the elimination of the term race from any official, legislative, legal or administrative document on the island (Ortiz 1993: XXXI).
11. The notion of "denial of coevalness" as "the persistent and systematic tendency to place the referent(s) of anthropology in a Time other than the present of the producer of anthropological discourse" (Fabian 2002: 31).
12. The English edition was published in 1909, the same year of its original Italian publication.
13. Following a strategy similar to the one that he had pursued when he included a letter from Lombroso as part of the prologue to *Los negros brujos*, the inclusion of Malinowski's introduction to *Contrapunteo cubano* is more of a convenient publishing decision than an expression of professional recognition. See Ortiz (1995a); Coronil (2019).

Part IV

After Lombroso

15

Israel Castellanos and Lombrosian Criminal Anthropology in Cuba

Franco Orlandi

Of all the Latin American countries, Cuba was perhaps the one where Cesare Lombroso's criminological theories found the greatest success in the first half of the twentieth century. The appeal of the Lombrosian criminological paradigm on the Caribbean Island was driven by several factors: pronounced social and racial tensions, Cuba's ambition to be recognized as a modern country, and the elite's ongoing debate over which groups should be included or excluded in the construction of the national state after independence in 1902. Lombroso's doctrine appeared to offer the Cuban ruling class both practical and conceptual tools to address the island's most pressing issues—above all, its fragile social order and its large population of African descent.

One of the foremost advocates of criminal anthropology in Cuba was Israel Castellanos. Despite his modest origins, he ascended to hold prestigious positions within the country's security apparatus and became one of the most authoritative figures in Latin American criminology. His scientific work reveals the remarkable endurance of Lombrosian theories, which, even as they waned in Europe from the late nineteenth century onward, experienced a vigorous revival across the Atlantic.

A Lombrosian "with no teachers or libraries"

The story of Israel Castellanos is one of remarkable social ascent. Born in Havana in 1891 to a family of modest means—the grandson of a Chinese laborer and the son of a tinsmith—he rose to become "Cuba's most powerful criminologist" (Bronfman 2007b: 61). According to his own account, his adolescence was "sad and disoriented" (Castellanos 1917a: 307), marked by a lack of ambition and hope for the future. His life changed forever in 1908, at the age of seventeen, when he first encountered the ideas of Cesare Lombroso. At his father's name day party, a lawyer among the guests delivered an impromptu lecture on crime, vehemently criticizing the theories of the Italian criminal anthropologist. Rather than deterring him, these words had the opposite effect on the young Castellanos, who from that moment resolved to devote himself to the study of criminal anthropology.

Despite his limited formal education, Castellanos quickly grasped the core ideas of Lombroso's doctrine: "After a few months, I removed the dust covering Lombroso's books, I read through their pages, and—with an emotion I will never forget—I realized that I was assimilating his ideas, that I was able to distinguish the stigmata and their atavistic and pathological significance" (ibid.: 309). Even before beginning his medical studies at university, he had started collecting human remains and visiting prisons, asylums, and juvenile correctional centers to study the anthropological characteristics of "madmen and criminals, murderers, and prostitutes" (ibid.). During these years, as he later recounted, he "weighed jaws, measured skulls, looked for and collected photographs, studied tattoos, took fingerprints, and investigated the entire human organism" (ibid.). Crucial to the start of his scientific career were the Cuban doctor Diego Tamayo and Antonio Lecha-Marzo, professor of Forensic Medicine at the University of Granada, who encouraged him to publish his early research in the journals they edited.

Within just a few years, this "self-taught anthropologist" became, in the words of historian Andrés Galera Gomez, "one of the leading figures in twentieth-century American criminology" (1991: 148). In 1914, at just twenty-three—nine years before he graduated—Castellanos was appointed corresponding professor at the Spanish Institute of Criminology in Madrid. A year later, he became an honorary professor at the Institute of Forensic Medicine at the Central University of Madrid (Abascal 1930: 203). Castellanos enrolled in the Faculty of Medicine at the University of Havana in 1917, graduating in 1923. By 1921, however, he was already director of the National Bureau of Identification, an institution founded in 1909 for criminal identification. A close associate of President Gerardo Machado, in 1928 he was appointed as the director of the Central Laboratory of Penitentiary Anthropology, which had been established to study the anthropological characteristics of Cuban prisoners. A staunch supporter of the Fulgencio Batista regime, Castellanos was forced to flee Cuba after the Castro revolution of 1958. He spent most of his remaining years in exile in Puerto Rico, where he worked as a police consultant. He died in Miami in 1977 (Galera Gomez 1991: 150–151).

The Criminal Anthropology of "Inferior Races"

Castellanos's youthful enthusiasm for Lombroso's theories led to an extraordinary outpouring of scientific work. Between 1911 and 1916, he published over 110 studies, nearly all focused on criminal anthropology (Castellanos 1917a: 313–316). In his early research, he sought to identify new somatic and skeletal anomalies in criminals to support Lombroso's theory of atavism.

In 1914, in his first study published in Spain, Castellanos described an "atavistic prehuman" trait that he had observed in some patients at the Azorra asylum and in photographs of criminals provided by the secret police: the so-called "simian mouth" (*boca simiesca*). He argued that the frequent occurrence of this monkey-like mouth among "criminals and idiots" indicated the "marked atavistic significance" of this morphological feature (Castellanos 1914c: 3–4). By analyzing the skull of a white

Cuban criminal, he claimed to have discovered a new variation of the middle occipital fossa, located in a different position from the "classic" one that Lombroso identified in the skull of Giuseppe Villella in 1870 (Castellanos 1914a: 222–5).

Castellanos's work soon made its way from Spain to Italy, where it was warmly received by the Lombrosian school. In 1915, the *Archivio* published its first review of several of his studies, including a "rich and interesting" photographic atlas of Cuban criminals (Carrara 1915: 576–7). Mario Carrara, Cesare Lombroso's son-in-law, scientific heir, and professor of Forensic Medicine at the University of Turin, praised the "diligent and productive" Cuban scholar for his dedication to advancing Lombroso's theories, encouraging him to "continue in his work full of faith and youthful vivacity" (ibid.).

The publication of *A través de la criminología* in 1914—the collection of photographs of criminals praised by Carrara—introduced Castellanos to Cuba's scientific community (Castellanos 1914b). The esteemed anthropologist Fernando Ortiz, who had previously been unaware of him, praised the work and described Castellanos as a promising figure in Cuban social sciences. Ortiz commended the young scholar's dedication to Lombrosian criminal anthropology, a discipline he believed was unfairly neglected in Cuba (Abascal 1930: 204).

The fusion of criminological theory and racialist thought in Castellanos's work is particularly evident in his early craniometric studies. Seeking to demonstrate the atavistic nature of the Cuban criminal—whom he believed embodied the physical and moral traits of both primitive humans and animals—Castellanos highlighted in one study the supposed resemblance between the jaw of a presumed Afro-Cuban criminal and that of a gorilla (Castellanos 1914e). To further validate Lombroso's theory of atavism, he included in the same publication the mugshots of two Afro-Cuban criminals with "enormous jaws," implying a similarity between their features and those of apes. His biological determinism, particularly his belief in an inherent criminal disposition, led him to openly advocate for the death penalty, which he viewed as the only effective means of defending society from its most dangerous elements—while also providing him with human remains for study (ibid.: 8).

Ortiz reviewed Castellanos's study of the criminal jawbone favorably, describing him as not only "a good disciple of the Lombrosian school" but also as the figure destined to revive criminal anthropology in Cuba (Abascal 1930: 204–5). Castellanos lived up to Ortiz's expectations, continuing to study the physiognomic characteristics of Cuban criminals, particularly those of African descent. A notable work in this regard was his *Contribution to the Craniometric Study of Black Delinquents*, first published in Spain in 1916 and republished in Italian in the *Archivio* the following year. Castellanos claimed that his research represented a significant addition to the "criminal anthropology of inferior races," a nearly unexplored field (Castellanos 1917b: 118).

Despite the plural in the title, the study was based on the examination of a single skull belonging to the same Afro-Cuban criminal whose jawbone he had analyzed in his previous work. Castellanos compared its measurements with the skulls of three white criminals. This absurdly small sample size did not prevent him from drawing sweeping conclusions about the atavistic—and therefore criminal—nature of Africans. Among the predominant morphological features of the "black skull," he noted the "protruding supraorbital arches," a "receding forehead," "prognathism," and "hypertrophic" canines. He lazily dismissed the possibility that the large cranial circumference could indicate an overdeveloped brain, attributing it instead to a "greater somatic volume" of the bones (ibid.: 120).

When comparing the skull of the Afro-Cuban criminal with those of white offenders, Castellanos observed that the latter exhibited more severe and pronounced stigmata, indicating "greater signs of inferiority" than Africans. To explain this seemingly counterintuitive phenomenon—"the absence of criminal traits in individuals of inferior race"—he relied on the reasoning used by Italian Lombrosian criminal anthropologists in their studies of African populations. Africans, he argued, belonged to a race so undeveloped that "criminal degeneration" could scarcely push them further down the evolutionary ladder. By contrast, white people had evolved through numerous stages of "organic progress" and could thus fall back on the evolutionary scale, regressing to "more primitive species" (ibid.).

Like Lombroso, Castellanos did not consider race an immutable trait but believed it could evolve under favorable conditions, such as exposure to an advanced civilization like Cuba. This, he asserted, explained why the skull of the Afro-Cuban criminal displayed "some signs of organic superiority" compared with that of a "normal" African from the Congo (ibid.: 123). Having demonstrated that "criminality is physically less marked among the inferior races," Castellanos believed he had also confirmed Lombroso's theory of atavism: "Lombroso's corollary on the nature of criminality, as explained by atavism, thus finds complete confirmation in our comprehensive doctrine. Time will tell us where the rays of truth are heading" (ibid.).

Despite his Chinese heritage, Castellanos included not only Africans but also Asians among the "inferior races." However, unlike Fernando Ortiz, who in 1908 had labeled Chinese immigration to Cuba a "yellow peril," Castellanos regarded Asian criminality as a minor and relatively benign issue (Amador 2016). He argued that Chinese criminals generally exhibited a calm temperament, were not involved in organized crime, and refrained from violent acts (Castellanos 1914f). Unlike criminals of other races, their somatic traits were not particularly distinctive. In his view, the "true representatives of Cuban criminality" were Africans, who, along with their mixed-race descendants, had introduced *brujería* (sorcery) and *ñañiguismo* (membership of an Afro-Cuban secret society) to the island (ibid.). It was precisely on these two criminal phenomena that Castellanos's most famous work focused.

Afro-Cuban Sorcerers and *Mafiosi*

Published in 1916 under the telling motto *Kulturkampf*, Castellanos's book *La brujería y el ñañiguismo desde su punto de vista medico-legal* (Sorcery and Ñañiguismo from a Medico-Legal Perspective) exemplifies how Lombroso's theories were adapted in Cuba to reinforce racial hierarchies and criminalize a segment of the population (Palmié 2002; Bronfman, 2004; Cunha 2020). That same year, the study was awarded the Gordon Prize for the best work in forensic medicine by the Academy of Medical, Physical, and Natural Sciences of Havana. Notably, Castellanos was not even a university student at the time.

The purpose of Castellanos's study was to establish a scientific distinction between what he saw as the two main forms of Afro-Cuban criminality: *brujería* and *ñañiguismo*. According to him, both "criminal" phenomena had been introduced to the island by African slaves, but they were often conflated. Despite their common African origins, *brujería* and *ñañiguismo* were, in his view, fundamentally different.

The *brujo* (sorcerer) was a deeply religious figure whose criminal activities centered on invoking deities, healing, and divination. While sorcerers wielded powerful spells to cast or lift curses, Castellanos characterized them as peaceful and mild-mannered, rarely involved in murder or organized crime. Notably, the Cuban constitution of 1901 permitted all forms of religious practice, so alleged sorcerers were typically arrested on charges of illicit association or the unauthorized practice of medicine.

The *ñañiguo*, on the other hand, was described by Castellanos as a violent and vengeful individual for whom religion held little significance. His defining trait was membership of the Abakuá brotherhood, a hierarchical and secretive criminal association that Castellanos likened to the Italian mafia, claiming its members were "the most violent microbes in the Cuban criminal world" (Castellanos 1936: 33). The delinquency of the *ñañiguo* was "atavistic and regressive," marked by "brutal impulsiveness" akin to that of primitive humanity and frequently expressed through violence.

While Castellanos attributed the *ñañiguo*'s criminal tendencies to evolutionary regression, he saw the *brujo*'s as stemming from an utter lack of evolution. The *brujo*'s psyche, he claimed, remained untouched by the progress of Cuban society, unchanged from that of his savage African ancestors. For Castellanos, the true danger posed by the *brujo* lay in his obscurantism, antisocial behavior, and inability to adapt to the new order, traits that undermined the foundations of the young Cuban republic. He feared that, like a pathogen, sorcery and the "primitive African mentality" could spread unchecked through large segments of the population, jeopardizing Cuba's aspirations to become one of the most advanced nations in Latin America.

However, the *brujo* and the *ñañiguo* represented different kinds of threats. Though the *brujo*'s gruesome rituals and illegal medical practices endangered society, they did not directly threaten individual lives. By contrast, the "instinctive criminality" of the *ñañiguo* spread violence and terror in the streets. The *brujo*, according to Castellanos, acted out of a misguided but genuine desire to help others, while the *ñañiguo* felt no remorse in harming or killing his enemies. In other words, the *brujo* committed crimes "in good faith," while the *ñañiguo* did not (ibid.: 91).

After defining *brujería* and *ñañiguismo* in "sociological" and "psychological" terms, Castellanos sought to identify the morphological stigmata that could distinguish *brujos* and *ñañiguos* from each other and from ordinary Cuban criminals. In his enthusiastic preface to Ortiz's *Los negros brujos*—a key influence on Castellanos—Lombroso had suggested that future studies of Cuban sorcery should include "data on cranial, physiognomic, and tactile sensitivity anomalies in a certain number of delinquents and *brujos*, as well as in an equal number of normal blacks" (Lombroso quoted in Pavez Ojeda 2009: 98). However, Castellanos's attempt to follow Lombroso's research recommendations was frustrated by the almost complete lack of statistical data for comparison and human remains for measurement.

The scarcity of scientific literature and absence of anatomical collections in Cuba forced Castellanos to base his research on limited and unreliable evidence regarding the anatomical, anthropometric, and psychological characteristics of the *brujo*, *ñañiguo*, and ordinary "Cuban delinquent." His sources included only a single skull, a few fingerprints, a dozen photographs, and a couple of secondhand ethnographic reports. This lack of anthropometric and descriptive data drew criticism in Italy from Carrara, who otherwise appreciated Castellanos's work (Carrara 1918: 291–2). Despite this astonishing lack of materials, Castellanos proceeded to compile a list of distinctive physical traits for the *brujo* and *ñañiguo*, which he claimed confirmed Lombroso's theory of atavism.

The *ñañiguo*, he claimed, exhibited "frontal microcephaly," pronounced eyebrow arches, prognathism, and a fierce gaze, regardless of his "race" (Castellanos 1936: 108–13). Like the common Cuban criminal, the *ñañiguo* favored tattoos with "obscene, zoological, and revenge-themed" imagery, often depicting the *diablito*, a masked dancer symbolizing a demon who performed specific functions in Abakuá ceremonies (ibid.: 119). While the description of the *ñañiguo* appeared to echo Lombroso's concept of the "born criminal," the physical traits Castellanos attributed to the *brujo* were quite ordinary: a "broad and sloping forehead," "slightly pronounced frontal sinuses," small ears, a "modestly sized jaw," a humble gaze, and a "white and well-groomed beard" (ibid.: 109–82).

Although Castellanos regarded the Afro-Cuban sorcerer as a "savage" stuck in an ancestral stage of humanity, the data he gathered suggested otherwise. The *brujo*'s fingerprints showed no "primitive or simian shape," his chest was not asymmetrical, as was often thought typical of epileptics, his nose was no wider than those of most members of the "African race," his gaze was gentle, and he had no tattoos. According to Castellanos, only the *brujo*'s very dark skin served as an obvious marker of atavism. Relying on the authority of Lombroso's *L'uomo bianco e l'uomo di colore* (1871), he asserted that when Africans arrived in America and integrated into a more advanced civilization, they tended to lose their regressive characteristics over generations, softening their facial features and lightening their skin. The lack of any sign of "evolution or improvement" in the *brujo*, despite his immersion in Cuban society, was indicative of an evolutionary arrest (ibid.: 107).

In Castellanos's view, the overwhelming absence of atavistic and degenerative traits in the bodies of *brujos* did not disprove Lombroso's theories but in fact validated them. As noted earlier, these theories suggested that physical manifestations of criminality were less pronounced among "inferior races," who could descend further on the evolutionary scale. Additionally, Castellanos argued that the "psychic primitiveness" of the Afro-Cuban *brujo* was revealed by his complete lack of remorse in performing gruesome rituals, his mysterious and incomprehensible language, his barbaric dances, and the crude fetishes adorning his altars, which reflected an "artistic laziness and primitiveness."

Nevertheless, Castellanos was forced to admit that *brujos* and *ñañiguos* could not be distinguished from ordinary Cuban criminals based on physical characteristics alone (ibid.: 159). In this regard, his study was a complete failure, as it ended up demonstrating the opposite of what he had set out to prove: the existence of scientifically identifiable criminal types. Lacking clear anthropological criteria to identify the *brujo*, Castellanos had no choice but to abandon criminal anthropology and turn to other disciplines. Indeed, he ultimately conceded that it was the "ethnographic" and "social" traits of the "born *brujo*," rather than his anthropological features, that distinguished him from his common imitator, the "pseudo-*brujo*" (ibid.: 161).

The born *brujo* consistently exhibited the "anthropological and ethnographic characteristics of the black continent": a neck adorned with necklaces, a head covered with a cloth, and a white beard. He was characterized by his modesty and disinterest in profit, and he was motivated by sincere altruism—even when performing human sacrifices. According to Castellanos, the authentic sorcerer was not a "prehuman criminal" like Lombroso's born criminal, but rather an "African type" (ibid.). The *brujo*'s behavior would not have been considered deviant in Africa, as it fully conformed with the continent's low moral standards. The problem emerged when he arrived in Cuba and was unable to adapt to a society that was too civilized for his "African psyche," leading him into the criminal underworld. The pseudo-*brujo*, on the other hand, was a true criminal in the Lombrosian sense: physically degenerate, this impostor was a mere parasite who exploited the gullibility of the lower classes for personal gain.

Castellanos's study concluded with a warning. He argued for the urgent establishment of a national institute of forensic medicine in Cuba, modeled after those in Belgium or Argentina, to conduct "biometric, anthropological, and clinical investigations" on criminals and abnormal individuals. This research would reveal "their true degree of degeneration and social maladjustment" (ibid.: 183). There was no time to lose, as contact between Jamaican and Haitian laborers on Cuban sugar plantations and Afro-Cuban *brujos* threatened to encourage a form of "fetishism" that was even "more criminal and savage" (ibid.: 185). How could this threat be addressed? Unlike Italian Lombrosian criminal anthropologists, who were mostly fervent socialists, Castellanos argued that universal education alone was not the solution. Instead, he believed that only an effort—which he did not describe in detail—to foster "hygiene" among Cuba's lower classes and rural population would make it possible to develop immunity against "the blinding fever of fanaticism" (ibid.: 186). Unlike Fernando Ortiz, Castellanos continued to defend the validity of his research findings as late as 1937, as I will discuss later.

Female Delinquency in Cuba, a Non-Lombrosian Book

"I received a magnificent publication on criminology from Havana, which is the result of the tireless efforts of a scholar already well-known in the field of Criminal anthropology: Israel Castellanos" (Carrara 1929: 559). So began Mario Carrara's enthusiastic review of *La delincuencia femenina en Cuba* (Female Delinquency in Cuba), a work he hailed as "one of the most remarkable contributions to anthropology in recent years" (ibid.: 562). By the time his study on female criminality was published in 1929, Castellanos had emerged as Cuba's most influential criminologist. Having led the National Bureau of Identification since 1921 and the Central Laboratory of

Penitentiary Anthropology since 1928, he had become a central figure within the Machado regime's repressive apparatus.

La delincuencia femenina consisted of two volumes: the first provided an extensive series of statistical charts and graphs of female delinquency in Cuba, and the second featured mugshots of over 400 women incarcerated in Havana. A third volume, intended to explore the "female in the Cuban zoological world" as well as the biological and psychological characteristics of "normal" and "criminal" Cuban woman in the pre-Columbian, colonial, and republican eras, was announced by Castellanos in the same year but never completed (ibid.: 559).

The fact that Castellanos conducted such a comprehensive study on female criminality was relatively unusual for the time. Criminologists generally considered women less worthy of scholarly attention than men, viewing them as significantly less inclined toward crime and as posing less of a threat to society. Few criminological treatises had tackled female criminality in either America or Europe, with Cesare Lombroso's *La donna delinquente* (1893) standing as the main exception. In this book, the Italian maintained that women were as inclined to crime as men, since he considered prostitution as the female equivalent to male criminal behavior (Montaldo 2019). Castellanos's unusually keen interest in female delinquency stemmed not only from his adherence to Lombrosian doctrine but also from the unprecedented social visibility of women in Cuba at the time. The feminist congresses of 1923 and 1925, President Gerardo Machado's pledge to introduce universal female suffrage if reelected in 1934, and Police Chief Rogerio Zajas Bazàn's campaign to curb prostitution were all factors bringing women to the center of Cuban public and political discourse for the first time (Bronfman 2007b).

It was no coincidence that the first volume of *La delincuencia femenina* opened with a heartfelt dedication to Machado, whose "broad vision as a statesman" had enabled the establishment of the Central Laboratory of Penitentiary Anthropology in Cuba. This institution, located within the *Presidio Modelo* (Model Prison) inaugurated in 1926, was designed to collect data on Cuban criminality and study the anatomical and pathological traits of male and female offenders. Over the years, the Model Prison would house not only common criminals but also political dissidents of the Machado regime.

As the director of the laboratory, Castellanos drew on its criminal statistics to announce a sensational discovery to the scientific community: "Cuban women are, among all women in the world, the least delinquent" (Castellanos 1929a: 39). He supported this "irrefutable truth" with extensive data, noting, for instance, that from 1909 to 1913, the proportion of convicted Cuban women did not exceed sixteen per 5,000 inhabitants (i.e., 0.32 percent; ibid.: 32). Between 1914 and 1915, only 1.78 percent of those convicted of minor offenses and 3.47 percent of those convicted of serious crimes were women (Bronfman 2007a: 77). Castellanos estimated that in Cuba the ratio of female delinquents to law-abiding women was one in a thousand, a figure fifty-three times lower than the male ratio (Castellanos 1929a: 95). But that was not all. Cuban women's crime rates were not only significantly lower than those of other Latin American countries, but also lower than those in the United States and Europe (ibid.: 93–7).

Unlike Lombroso, who considered women to be physically and mentally inferior to men, and often more malevolent and cruel, Castellanos repeatedly celebrated the exceptional "moral strength" and "extraordinary resistance" of Cuban women "to the criminal virus" and "habitual and chronic delinquency in all its variants and forms" (ibid.: 32–9). This conclusion carried both scientific and political weight, particularly in the context of Machado's promise to introduce universal female suffrage. It is therefore not surprising that Castellanos cited, without comment but in implied agreement, Justice Secretary Cristobal de la Guardia, who had stated that granting women the vote would be "the solution to many of our problems" (Bronfman 2007a: 78).

While the main purpose of Castellanos's book was to assert the moral supremacy of Cuban women globally, he did not investigate the causes or provide an explanation for this phenomenon. In fact, as historian Alejandra Bronfman has noted, he appeared more interested in statistics on female crime than in the actual nature of female criminality. This is evident from the opening pages of *La delincuencia femenina*, which did not begin with an examination of the anthropological characteristics of female criminals but with a comprehensive history of judicial statistics in Cuba. The obsessive focus on morphology and psychological traits that characterized Castellanos's book on sorcery and *ñañiguismo* was entirely absent from his work on female criminality. Instead of relying on anecdotal evidence or ethnographic accounts to support his arguments, he now opted for diagrams, charts, and graphs.

Castellanos was not inclined to elaborate an overall theory on female delinquency: "We will avoid any doctrinal debate and do without the rigid ideological frameworks of the different schools, strictly adhering to the data provided by criminal statistics" (Castellanos 1929a: 89). Although his book outlined briefly certain key theories explaining women's lower participation in crime, he refrained from voicing his own opinion on the matter. One of the criminologists he referenced was Luigi Roncoroni, an Italian student and collaborator of Lombroso, who argued that women committed fewer crimes than men due to their evolutionary inferiority and smaller number of cortical centers (ibid.: 90). Lombroso himself was almost entirely absent from the text, with his conclusions about women's physical and intellectual inferiority mentioned only in passing, alongside those of Gabriel Tarde, for whom women were morally superior, and Napoleone Colajanni, who attributed lower female delinquency to economic and social causes (ibid.: 93–4). Castellanos did not dedicate a single word to Lombroso's famous theory that prostitutes were the female equivalents of born criminals. One explanation for this reticence is that he was aware of the substantial criticisms that had arisen in England, France, and Germany, following the publication of English and French translations of Lombroso's *La donna delinquente* (Montaldo 2019). Since the book had never been translated into Spanish, it is conceivable that Castellanos sought to fill a gap in the Spanish-speaking criminological literature of the period by addressing female criminality while conveniently avoiding any explicit references to Lombroso.

In the concluding section of the first volume, Castellanos discussed the relationship between race and female criminality, once again sidelining criminological theory in favor of what he considered the indisputable truth of the statistics. After criticizing the "ethnic puritanism" of North Americans, who persisted in producing statistics on delinquency that did not distinguish between mixed-race and Black individuals, Castellanos established a clear racial hierarchy of female criminality in Cuba: "It is undeniable … that black women are more delinquent than mulattoes, and that mulattoes are more delinquent than whites" (Castellanos 1929a: 104).[1] He further stated: "Delinquency intensifies with increasing skin pigmentation, that is, it increases in relation to the darkening of the skin" (ibid.). However, this conclusion was starkly contradicted by his own statistics. His tables revealed that *mestizas*, and not Black women, accounted for the highest rates of criminality, including sexual offences such as adultery and "corruption of minors." This inconsistently became even more pronounced in his statistics on crimes committed by foreign women, which indicated that white women were the most prone to delinquency (ibid.).

To address this contradiction, which he never explicitly acknowledged in the text, Castellanos suggested that the higher rate of criminality among Black women could largely be attributed to the recent immigration of Black Antilleans. "Our black race," he wrote, "is as good … as no other of its ethnogenetic lineage" (ibid.). However, the same could not be said for other Black Caribbean races, like the Haitians, who were migrating *en masse* to Cuba at the time.[2] This narrative reflected the twin messages of racism and nationalism that permeated both his 1916 monograph on sorcery and this work.

La delincuencia femenina en Cuba was complemented by a second, very different, volume (Castellanos 1929b), the first part of which contained an alphabetical index of the names, surnames, and nicknames of 2,034 women convicted in Cuba between 1909 and 1927. It also included fingerprint records of some female criminals, which Castellanos had collected at the Gabinete Nacional de Identificación. However, the bulk of the volume was devoted to what Castellanos termed the "album identoscópico" (identoscopic album), a photographic atlas of 424 female inmates from Havana's prison, captured from the front and in profile according to the Bertillon method. Each mugshot was accompanied by a brief description detailing age, race, level of education, height, weight, type of crime committed, and notable somatic anomalies such as lower-jaw protrusion, facial asymmetry, and masculine appearance. As Bronfman has pointed out, the fact that the photographs were arranged in alphabetical order rather than according to the inmates' "criminal type" ultimately demonstrated the "inadequacy of [the] criminological categories" developed by the Lombrosian school, which struggled to encapsulate complex realities (Bronfman 2007b: 73–4).

The numerous contradictions in Castellanos's work did not prevent it from being very well received by the international scientific community and achieving great success. The *Revista de Medicina legal de Cuba* hailed it as "a milestone" in criminal anthropology (Tejera 1929), while the French journal *Revue Internationale de Criminalistique* considered it "an admirable work" and a "treasure of documentation." In his review, the editor Edmond Locard wrote: "It would be desirable that all civilized countries produced [works] like this" (Locard 1929: 410–11). The Italian journal *La Giustizia Penale* referred to it as a "wonderful and complete work" ("*Castellanos*" 1934: 110–11).

However, the most prestigious recognition came from Turin, the stronghold of the Lombroso school. As previously noted, Carrara praised Castellanos's work in his review for the *Archivio*, and it was at his suggestion that it was awarded the Lombroso Prize in 1930 by unanimous decision (Montoro 1930). Established posthumously in accordance with Lombroso's last will, the prize—then in its third edition—was intended to honor the most remarkable work in the field of criminal anthropology. When announcing the award, Carrara congratulated Castellanos for having "managed to enrich the anthropological-criminal bibliography with such an important work" (Abascal 1930: 200). Notably, this was the first time the award, consisting of a cash prize and a bronze plaque, was given to a non-European scholar.

Castellanos's achievement was celebrated in his homeland as a significant triumph for Cuban science on the world stage. The *Revista Bimestre Cubana* honored him with a lengthy article detailing the key milestones of his scientific career. In the introductory note, editor Fernando Ortiz referred to Castellanos as "one of the most accomplished men of science in contemporary Cuba" (ibid.: 199). The article's author, Doctor Horacio Abascal Vera, framed Castellanos's prize as a glorious victory for Cuba, the first nation to bring the prestigious Lombroso Prize across the ocean (ibid.: 200–1). Similarly, the *Revista de Medicina legal de Cuba* declared that "the moral and cultural significance of the precious award" obtained by Castellanos was "magnificent and incomparable," representing "a legitimate honor" for the country (*El lauro* 1930: 480). Finally, the life sciences journal *Vida Nueva*, of which Castellanos was codirector, proudly emphasized that for the first time, the prize had been awarded to "a native of the New World," with the decision made by "the most illustrious Masters of Forensic Medicine of our days" (Montoro 1930: XXVII).

The somewhat extravagant reactions to Castellanos's award from the Cuban scientific community reveal the enduring prestige that Cesare Lombroso continued to command in Latin America more than twenty years after his death. Above all, it highlights Cuba's desire and ambition to be recognized by the rest of the world as a modern and developed nation, whose scientists actively contributed to the advancement of global knowledge.

Conclusion

Castellanos's success in Cuba appeared unstoppable. Between 1926 and 1935, his works, including *La talla de los delincuentes en Cuba* (The Height of Cuban Delinquents; 1927), *El pelo en los cubanos* (The Hair of Cubans; 1933), and *El peso corporal de los delincuentes en Cuba* (The Weight of Cuban Delinquents; 1937), were all awarded the Cañongo Prize by the Academy of Sciences of Havana.

Although he largely abandoned criminal anthropology in subsequent years to devote himself to forensic dactyloscopy and hematology, Castellanos remained committed to Lombroso's criminological theories. In the late 1920s he published an ethnographic study in the *Archivos del folklore*, directed by Fernando Ortiz, where he continued to use adjectives like "primitive" and "barbaric" to describe Afro-Cuban festivities and musical practices (Moore 1997: 33). By 1937, he was still defending his earlier studies on Afro-Cuban criminality, which were all reprinted, reiterating his belief in the "innate criminal tendency" of the *ñañiguos* and the atavism of the *brujos* (Castellanos 1937b). In the same year, in his obituary for Mario Carrara, Castellanos proclaimed the "immortality of Lombroso" and the "triumph of Criminal anthropology" worldwide (Castellanos 1937a: 379).

The scientific work of Israel Castellanos demonstrates the lasting impact and extensive transnational and transatlantic circulation of the Lombrosian doctrine, which, despite waning in Europe after Lombroso's death, found renewed vigor in Latin America.

Notes

1. Castellanos estimated that Black women committed 48.3 percent of female crimes, mixed-race women 28.2 percent, and white women 24.4 percent.
2. On the widespread anti-Haitian sentiment in Cuba at the time, see McLeod (1998).

16

The Effects of Lombrosian Thought on Daily Life in Brazilian Prisons

Viviane Borges and Fernando Salla

The Social Context

The ideas of the positivist school of criminology arrived in Brazil in the 1880s during a period of political, social, and economic upheaval. Many aspects of social life were suffering the impacts of scientific and modernizing concepts emerging from Europe and the United States. Economically, the expansion of coffee in international markets revolutionized Brazilian agriculture, generating wealth for the agrarian elites and enabling the introduction of modern developments in various aspects of daily life. Some urban centers, such as Rio de Janeiro and São Paulo, became symbols of modernity, benefiting from public lighting, urban transportation systems, contemporary buildings, and new lifestyle habits. These cities were also home to factories, which attracted a new class of workers to a country that had previously been predominantly agricultural.

The abolition of slavery in 1888 resulted in thousands of formerly enslaved Black workers gaining their freedom without any economic compensation, reparations, or support for social integration. Many left the fields for urban centers, where they continued to face social discrimination, particularly in terms of their employment opportunities. Rather than integrating them into the workforce, the elites promoted the "whitening" of society by encouraging white immigrants, especially from Europe, to fill agricultural and factory jobs.

Politically, the monarchy was replaced in 1889 by a republican regime led by the coffee-producing elite of the state of São Paulo. However, this transition failed to ensure broad political participation or universal rights for citizens. The elites who had overthrown the monarchy and taken over the Republic demonstrated a deep-seated fear of social and political participation from marginalized groups, particularly Black people and the poor.[1]

The positivist criminological currents that captivated Brazilian jurists and a diverse group of thinkers in the decades surrounding the transition from the nineteenth to the twentieth century may have hindered the consolidation of the liberal ideals expressed in the first republican constitution of 1891, particularly those relating to citizenship. The abolition of slavery in 1888 and the proclamation of the Republic in 1889 created, at least formally, the conditions for citizenship to be guided by the principles of a democratic society. At the same time, the opportunity arose to build a social structure characterized by freedom and equal rights, as envisioned by the new constitution. However, it was precisely at this pivotal moment—when the nation aimed to establish a society rooted in the rule of law and extend citizenship to large contingents previously regarded as pariahs—that the elites began to construct a discourse of difference. They did so by drawing on the teachings of the positivist school, particularly those of Lombroso and Ferri.

Raimundo Nina Rodrigues exemplifies this effort to devise mechanisms that undermined the egalitarian principles of citizenship. Outraged by the prospect that individuals of different races could be held to the same level of criminal responsibility under the law, in 1894 he made a striking proposal based on his racial studies in Brazil. He argued that the country should not have a single penal code but rather distinct codes, each tailored to different geographic regions according to the predominant ethnic groups—white, Black, and Indigenous—within them (Rodrigues 1957: 715).

On an intellectual level, the final decades of the nineteenth century in Brazil were strongly influenced by the philosophical positivism of Auguste Comte. The political elites who supported the republican regime embraced his enthusiasm for science, along with the principles of order and progress.[2] During a time of intense social transformation, these values translated into an unrelenting campaign against vagrancy, madness, begging, crime, child abandonment, strikes, and anarchism—all of which were identified as sources of urban disorder and, consequently, obstacles to national advancement.

Science, regarded as a repository of truth, provided justification for the social control measures implemented by the elites, even when its doctrines were steeped in discriminatory views about subjects at the margins of society, such as Black people, the poor, the unemployed, vagrants, prostitutes, people with mental disorders, and abandoned children. While female criminality did not attract intense scrutiny in the first two decades of the twentieth century, the situation of prostitutes garnered significant attention from jurists and law enforcement, driven more by moral concerns than by criminological reasons. In the 1920s, as crimes committed by women began to receive greater interest in legal and criminological circles, the debate shifted to who should oversee the correction of criminals and what this process should entail. This transition marked a move from strictly scientific concerns to a moral and religious approach, wherein the responsibility for rehabilitating criminals was assigned to religious congregations. The emphasis was on penitentiary "treatment" that relegated women to domestic chores and the role of motherhood.

One of the underlying issues of this period was therefore the incarceration of women. However, this will not be the focus of our analysis in this chapter, as addressing it fully would require drawing on specific references and studies that lie beyond the scope of this text. Nonetheless, it is important to highlight that criminological discourse regarding women's prisons was deeply intertwined with religious and traditional conceptions. This issue has been the subject of political conflict and state intervention, oscillating between the direct state management of prisons and the delegation of responsibility for the correction of female offenders to religious institutions. Among these was the Congregation of Our Lady of Charity of the Good Shepherd of Angers, which operated asylums worldwide for the correction of women offenders and prostitutes and, in some cases, even administered women's prisons owned by the state.

In Brazil, a consensus emerged on the need to separate women's from men's prisons and establish dedicated facilities for them. In the early 1940s, women's prisons were created in the two main urban centers—Rio de Janeiro and São Paulo—under the management of the Bom Pastor religious congregation. However, due to the country's diverse local conditions, makeshift arrangements for women's incarceration remained in place. Women continued to be housed in male facilities, while in other regions, prisons run by the Bom Pastor nuns took years to materialize. Even later, some women's prisons were established and administered directly by the state itself (Lima 1983; Artur 2011; Karpowicz 2017; Wit 2021; Borges, Salla and Wit 2022).

The social transformations of the late nineteenth century in Brazil posed new challenges for maintaining social and urban order, controlling crime, and determining appropriate forms of punishment for criminals. The Criminal Code of 1830 reflected outdated punitive ideas and practices associated with the monarchical regime (1822–89). Throughout the 1880s, criticism of the 1830 Code intensified, and the principles of Lombrosian-inspired criminology began to permeate the national legal and medical landscapes.

Alfredo Frassati, who would later become one of Italy's most significant newspaper editors and owners, noted that the first mention of the positivist school in Brazil appeared in 1888 in the newspaper *Diário de Pernambuco*, in articles by João Vieira de Araújo. João Vieira was a critic of the 1830 Code and even published a short piece in the positivist journal *Archivio di psichiatria* in 1889. He also corresponded with Lombroso.[3]

Despite João Vieira's enthusiasm for Lombroso's ideas, as well as that of other jurists of the time (Alvarez 2003), the 1890 Code replaced the 1830 Code without substantially incorporating any proposals from the Italian positivist school (Alvarez, Salla and Souza 2003). However, the perceived "failure" of Lombrosian thought in Brazilian legislation—whether in the Penal Code of 1890 or in ordinary laws until 1940—did not prevent its influence on the everyday practices of social control, particularly in policing and penal institutions (Alvarez 2002 and 2003; Salla 1999). The impacts of Lombroso's ideas were apparent in the professional profiles of those working in these agencies, including police officers and psychiatrists, as well as in the documentation they produced, such as examinations and inmate diagnoses.

This chapter provides examples of the influence of Lombrosian thought on the daily practices of two Brazilian penitentiaries—one in the state of São Paulo and the other in the state of Santa Catarina—during the early decades of the twentieth century. While his concepts were not firmly established in legal provisions, they played a key role in shaping Brazilian and Latin American criminology.[4]

To demonstrate the presence of these ideas in everyday prison life, we will primarily examine the documentation produced within these penitentiaries. Since the nineteenth century, prisons have generated a wide variety of records, including reports on prisoners' lives, daily activities, family relationships, and health, as well as photographs and body measurements. These materials were typically compiled in so-called prisoner records, which serve as vital sources for exploring the prison environment and provide an inside perspective on penitentiary life. However, despite their significance, prisoner records have been notably underutilized in research conducted in Brazil. This is not due to a lack of interest among researchers; rather, it stems primarily from the widespread loss of documentation, largely resulting from a lack of concern for its preservation on the part of the authorities. Long-term sequential records of common prisoners are therefore rare, restricting the ability to construct a comprehensive overview of prison life across different Brazilian states during specific periods.[5]

The São Paulo State Penitentiary

Throughout the nineteenth century, Brazilian penitentiaries were consistently in a state of degradation. However, by the end of the century, conditions in prisons in the state of São Paulo had deteriorated even further. In 1893, the Secretary of Justice, Siqueira Campos, addressed the dire situation in the State Capital Prison, highlighting above all its physical and operational inadequacies. He remarked: "The solutions to the case can only be two: either the development of the current building, to better adapt it to its respective purposes, or the construction of an entirely new one" (RSJSP 1893: 81). State Senator Paulo Egydio and Deputy Candido Motta, both supportive of the new penal school's ideas, became the main proponents for reforming the penitentiary system (Salla 1999; Alvarez and Salla 2018). This movement led to the proposal for the construction of the State Penitentiary of São Paolo, which began operations in 1920.

Designed to confine 1,200 inmates, the penitentiary was considered the most advanced penal institution of its time. It featured workshops, appropriately sized cells, a well-planned corridor layout, and good amenities for lighting and ventilation. For two decades, the prison was a source of pride for local leaders, symbolizing the state's progress in the area of legal punishment. On a national level, it was presented as a model establishment, demonstrating how the Penal Code of 1890, despite always being considered "imperfect," could be implemented effectively.

In the penitentiary's first decades, numerous visitors toured the facility and left glowing reviews. A brief article from 1922 by Ernesto Bertarelli,[6] a professor at the University of Pavia, recounts his visit to the prison in its early days. Published in the *Archivio di antropologia criminale*, the journal founded by Cesare Lombroso, Bertarelli's account is introduced by a note from the editors highlighting that both the São Paulo Penitentiary and the one in Buenos Aires exemplified the "transformative influence that Lombroso's doctrines have exerted on penitentiary technique and organization." In his brief report, Professor Bertarelli praised the facility's hygiene standards, the examinations conducted, and the work and educational activities available to inmates. He concluded: "the penitentiary must be highlighted as one of the most perfect human prison works and as one of the collective establishments that most honor South America" (Bertarelli 1922: 29).

A few years later, in 1926, the *Archivio* once again featured a short and favorable account of a visit to the São Paulo State Penitentiary, this time by the engineer Enrico Carrara.[7] In his article, Carrara not only pointed out the facility's numerous qualities but also praised the São Paulo elite, crediting their entrepreneurial spirit and bold initiative for the establishment's creation: "The resourcefulness, modernity, and audacious spirit of initiative inherent in the São Paulo character achieve a practical organization that rivals the most civilized European states. I want to mention an institution that, in its completeness and perfection, is unique, I believe, in the world: the penitentiary" (E. Carrara 1926: 693).

On the day of the inauguration of the prison, April 21, 1920, the ideas of the positivist school transitioned from abstract legal theory to concrete reality in the speech given by its first director, Franklin de Toledo Piza:

> From the discussion between free will and determinism, a new orientation in penalty studies was born. The positivist school, founded by Lombroso, Garofalo, Ferri, and Tarde, bases the right to punish on other foundations, looking for them in the study of the delinquent and of crime as a social phenomenon, governed by the same laws that regulate the physical world … If the objective of punishment is social defense rather than punishment, what should be targeted is not the crime but the criminal.[8]

The organization of the penitentiary's medical and psychiatric service provided the most concrete expression of the director's adherence to the teachings of the new penal school. The psychiatrist José de Moraes Mello, who worked at the penitentiary until the late 1930s, was also a supporter of Lombroso's ideas. In 1934, he published an article in the *Archivio* titled "Otto volte omicida!" (Mello 1934), which competed for the Lombroso Prize for the best contribution to criminal anthropology in 1933.

Mello was responsible for organizing the Medicine and Criminology Section, which produced key documents—including the Medicine and Surgery Service Bulletin and the Criminology Bulletin—containing detailed medical information as well as the social and criminological histories that became part of each prisoner's record. He also compiled a notebook called the "Tattoo Archive," recording observations and photographs of inmates with tattoos. With the aim of studying prisoners in even greater depth, a fourth notebook, called "Psychiatry Service," was reserved for inmates deemed to have mental illnesses.

The documents designed and completed by the penitentiary's psychiatrist reveal a great concern for gathering the most detailed information possible about the inmates' bodies, including measurements of various types and identifications of illnesses. A comprehensive survey of each prisoner's biography was also deemed crucial, covering family background, kinks, addictions, work history, emotional and psychological characteristics, educational background, religious beliefs, and other personal characteristics. The crimes committed by the prisoners remained somewhat in the background, as the documents reserved much more space for in-depth information about the prisoner's identity before and during his incarceration.

One of the most significant legacies of the influence of the positivist school on the 1940 Penal Code was the introduction of security measures allowing a certain indeterminacy of sentences based on an assessment of the criminal's "dangerousness" (Sabadell and Dimoulis 2022). Information relating to this recorded by Mello throughout the 1920s and 1930s in the documents mentioned above demonstrates how institutional practices helped shape these legal provisions. Each year, he recorded notes on a convict's "dangerousness" and "incorrigibility" and whether there had been any change in his condition or not.

The scientific approach to criminal rehabilitation required not only an in-depth understanding of a convict's physical and biological characteristics, as well as their social and familial background, but also a broad range of disciplinary interventions. At the São Paulo State Penitentiary, the psychiatrist wielded significant authority in carrying out this work. Decree no. 3,706, issued on April 29, 1924, which regulated the penitentiary's organization and operations, outlined the wide scope of the responsibilities assigned to this role:

> a) examine and observe all convicts who enter the establishment and, in particular, those who show symptoms of mental alienation, epileptics and alcoholics, and victims, in general, of all physico-psychological disorders ….
> c) intervene in all cases of suicides and attempted suicides, in criminal acts that occur in the establishment, and in incidents that disturb the disciplinary regime, investigating their causes and observing the mentality of their perpetrators;
> d) frequently visit the pavilions, schools, and workshops, and interact with the convicts, to get to know them better and carry out the duties of their position;
> e) inform the chief physician about everything relating to the treatment, moral and intellectual education, and work of convicts (São Paulo 1924).

It is worth noting that the psychiatrist's duties extended beyond treating and caring for prisoners as mere patients. His role encompassed oversight of various prison spaces, including the school and workshop, where the inmates spent their days. He was also responsible for providing guidance on the prisoners' work and moral education. The psychiatrist thus occupied a central position in organizing and upholding the disciplinary structure of the institution.

The Florianópolis Penitentiary

At the Florianópolis Penitentiary, located in the state of Santa Catarina in southern Brazil, the influence of Lombrosian thought on prison practices during the 1930s and 1940s is evident in the examination of approximately 4,200 records of common prisoners. In many respects, the practices implemented in the institution, both in the management of daily prison life and the organization of documentation, were similar to those implemented by the São Paulo State Penitentiary.

A particularly noteworthy period began in 1935, when structural and administrative reforms were introduced by the lawyer Edelvito Campelo D'Araújo, who assumed leadership of the institution that year and remained in charge until 1945. Under Araújo's direction, efforts were made to incorporate a scientific basis into the institution's practices, particularly through the production of documentation based on observations of inmates. The director oversaw the prison's first major structural overhaul in 1936, including the construction of new pavilions, the establishment of new workshops, and the creation of an Identification Office, which operated under the Medicine and Criminology Sector. At the administrative level, Araújo reformed internal regulations and initiated the hiring of new personnel (Borges 2016: 187).

The framework devised by Araújo for studying the penitentiary's inmates was rooted in theories of degeneration, born criminality, and racial inferiority—ideas central to medical and legal thought from the late nineteenth to the early twentieth centuries (Rebelo and Caponi 2007). An example of this from 1940 involved M. W., a 46-year-old widow and domestic worker. After serving nearly four years of her six-year sentence for involuntary manslaughter, she applied for parole, which was granted due to her good conduct. Rubens Ramos, Deputy Director of the Department of Medicine and Criminology, classified her as "an honest or criminaloid delinquent" who lacked the somatic and psychic markers typical of habitual offenders. Supporting his assessment, Dr. Ramos—who explicitly referenced Lombroso's classification of female offenders—pointed to the prisoner's consistent concern for her six children. This was evidenced by her letters from prison and her courtroom testimony, in which she exonerated her son of all responsibility for the attack that led to the homicide, despite his involvement.[9] It is worth noting that Lombroso viewed a lack of maternal and familial attachment as a strong indicator of innate criminality.

Between 1930 and the late 1950s, references to figures like the Italian psychiatrist, Antonio Marro,[10] a collaborator of Lombroso known for his studies on criminology and puberty, and the forensic psychiatrist Júlio de Matos,[11] a Portuguese exponent of criminal anthropology, appeared in reports and occasionally in institutional opinions included in prisoner records. Other notable European criminologists were also cited, including members of the International Standing Committee, which was founded during the First International Penitentiary Congress held in London in 1872. There are also important references to Brazilian criminologists, including Vieira de Araújo, Heitor Carrilho, Afrânio Peixoto, and Leonídio Ribeiro (the 1933 recipient of the Lombroso Prize), all of whom were sympathetic to Lombrosian thought.

Furthermore, at the Florianópolis Penitentiary, supervisors and professionals were encouraged to participate in national and international scientific events and to visit other institutions considered exemplary, such as the São Paulo and Minas Gerais Penitentiaries and the Rio de Janeiro Judiciary Asylum. These exchanges exposed them to the dominant currents in Brazilian criminology and the prison practices influenced by positivist criminology.

In 1937 and 1938, a significant rise in the number of records pertaining to prisoners can be observed, along with a notable improvement in the level of detail documented. The records began to systematically cover administrative and disciplinary routines as well as general information about prisoners, including birthplace, profession, age, education, and the crime committed. They also tracked absences, punishments, and participation in workshops and educational activities.

The Identification and Photographic Office was responsible for compiling the convicts' "Anthropological Records," a document dedicated to collecting data through anthropometric methods. These records included a wide range of details: fingerprints, mugshots, body marks (like scars and tattoos), body measurements (including head, eye, and ear size), skin and hair color, criminal background, and other physical and hereditary characteristics. Although not every field was consistently filled out, the very existence of these records underscores the institution's commitment to the data.

Although the Florianópolis Penitentiary was inaugurated in 1930, many records were backdated and completed only after 1935, the year Araújo assumed the directorship. This highlights his concern with creating individual records for each convict as well as the fact that many prisoners lacked such documentation in the institution's early years.

The analysis conducted by the Medicine and Criminology Sector informed the convicts' "biographical data," which included records on their family life and time before incarceration. An inmate's ability to work was assessed based on the tasks they performed within the prison, regardless of their prior occupations. Additionally, their ability to comply with the institution's rules was considered as a favorable factor in these evaluations.

Mixed Races

Lombroso believed that specific physical characteristics could indicate a predisposition to criminal behavior. On the other hand, regarding the mixing of different "races," Lombroso—a racist but also a Jew and a supporter of an assimilationist approach—oscillated significantly, allowing his readers to interpret the issue according to their preferences. This was also the case in the example studied here.

From the late nineteenth into the early twentieth century, jurists, doctors, and politicians regarded miscegenation as an obstacle to the advancement of the Brazilian people (Fonseca 1992). As Lilia Moritz Schwarcz observes, "existing miscegenation in Brazil was not only described but given specific adjectives, constituting a clue to explain the delay or possible unviability of the nation" (Schwarcz 2005: 28). Racial mixing was believed to result in atavism—that is, the "manifestation, in the individual, of the inheritance of the mental stage of only one of the races involved, normally the inferior" (Costa 2009: 95). To contain this mixing and the supposed degeneration, Brazilian elites promoted a "whitening" policy, encouraging the immigration of people of European descent. These ideas of racial inferiority served as ideological instruments that justified patterns of racial discrimination even after the abolition of slavery.

At the Florianópolis Penitentiary, prisoner records were used as the basis for reports seeking to "prove" that racial mixing was a major cause of criminal behavior. In 1940 the prison's director compiled a statistical report that sought to correlate crime with factors such as skin color and social conditions.

A graph produced by Araújo in the 1940 report shows that the prison population at the Florianópolis Penitentiary consisted of 288 inmates, 190 registered as white, 79 as mixed race, and 19 as Black. However, in his analysis, Araújo focused entirely on the "mulattoes" or "pardos" (i.e., mixed race inmates), ignoring both white and Black prisoners. Drawing on the theory of degeneration, he asserted that "mulattoes" were the demographic that committed the most offences, given their "predisposition to crime." He claimed that, as the product of the "morbid heredity" of characteristics from different ethnic groups, they were "generally degenerate," "averse to discipline," and immoral.

Throughout the Araújo report, statistical data were used to reinforce the dominant criminological theories of the time. The director suggested that certain crimes were more commonly committed by "pardo" or mulatto inmates but did not clarify the sources of his data or the methodology he used to extract them. According to him, "two thirds of the crimes committed by mulattoes were blood crimes, and the remainder [were crimes] against property." Furthermore, he asserted that mulattoes had the highest rates of recidivism.

In addition to this, Araújo linked the association of mulattoes with property crimes to cases of syphilis. Despite acknowledging the unreliability of his statistics due to flawed testing methods and the lack of comparative data from other prisons, he drew connections between race, crime, and syphilis to reinforce his characterization of degenerate individuals marked by atavism. His conclusions were clearly shaped by Lombrosian theories, which were widely accepted among Brazilian jurists, doctors, criminologists, and prison directors during the period.

Final Observations

The positivist criminological thought that captivated Brazilian jurists and intellectuals from the late nineteenth century into the early twentieth century led to the establishment of a series of institutional practices designed to regulate the daily lives of those considered deviant. In the newly opened Brazilian penitentiaries of the early twentieth century, the implications of this supposedly scientific perspective on crime and criminals significantly influenced the procedures and techniques that shaped everyday prison life.

In this chapter, we have primarily drawn on the records of ordinary prisoners to illustrate the impact of Lombroso's theories on daily experiences within the prison system. These unique records provide a wealth of information about inmates, including administrative and disciplinary routines. As seen in the cases from São Paulo and Santa Catarina, the type of data recorded varied widely, encompassing details such as place and date of birth, profession, education, and type of crime. Additional information included absences, punishments, and participation in workshops and educational activities. Further details could extend to body markings (such as scars and tattoos), physical measurements (including the size of the head, eyes, and ears), skin and hair color, criminal records, and information about family members. Collected by guards, directors, and doctors, these records underscore the significance attributed to external physical traits as identifiers of criminals, reflecting the influence of Cesare Lombroso's theories and the broader field of criminal anthropology in Brazilian society at the time.

The documentation provides additional insights into institutional management practices, the daily lives of prisoners, and the ways in which conflicts emerged and were handled. Medical records, in particular, trace the trajectories of individuals who might otherwise remain anonymous, revealing how institutions of social control shaped their lives.

Prisoner records, therefore, cannot be viewed in isolation from the broader operational patterns of institutions dedicated to the incarceration and correction of offenders since the early nineteenth century. These institutions confined individuals deemed violators of existing laws or societal moral standards, often through measures imposed without their awareness or consent. Whether adhering to a formal set of regulations, or acting beyond them, authorities exerted control over these individuals in ways that left lasting impacts on their lives.

Notes

1. It is worth remembering that voting, as stipulated in the first Brazilian Constitution of 1824, was restricted to individuals who could demonstrate a certain level of income (art. 92, item V).
2. A major manifestation of the influence of Comte's ideas on Brazilian elites was the incorporation of the slogan "Order and Progress" into the national flag of the Republic.
3. LP, Letter of J. Vieira to C. Lombroso, June 7, 1889.
4. The 1890 Code was the target of numerous criticisms and reform proposals, but survived until 1940, when a new Code was enacted. This new legislation introduced a security measure that permitted a degree of indeterminacy in the sentencing, contingent on the assessment of the subject's dangerousness. This was a change that many jurists saw as indicative of Lombroso's influence.
5. The Florianópolis Penitentiary archive is an exception as it contains a substantially complete series of records covering the period from 1930 to 1979. The preservation, dissemination, and research of this collection is the work of the Marginal Archives Project, created in 2011: www.arquivosmarginais.com.
6. Ernesto Bertarelli (1873–1957) graduated in medicine and surgery in Turin in 1898 and held the chair of hygiene at the University of Pavia from 1919 to 1946. https://www.treccani.it/enciclopedia/ernesto-bertarelli_(Dizionario-Biografico)/.
7. Enrico Carrara was the son of Mario Carrara, Cesare Lombroso's son-in-law and the director of the *Archivio*.
8. *Correio Paulistano*, April 22, 1920, 3.
9. IDCH 1937, record 377.
10. Author of *I caratteri dei delinquenti* (1887), cited in the 1942 Florianópolis Penitentiary Report (Arquivo Público do Estado Santa Catarina, Brazil, 23-25) and in other records.
11. The *Manual das doenças mentais* (1884) is cited in IDCH Record n. 123.

17

Lombroso's Lasting Legacy in the United States: The Criminology of Women, 1910–70

Mary Gibson

A critique of the theories of Cesare Lombroso formed an essential component of the birth of feminist criminology in the United States. In her article from 1973, which has become a classic, Dorie Klein argued that Lombrosian theory had negatively influenced subsequent American research on female delinquency. Despite their rejection of Lombroso's outdated methodology, scholars in the United States, according to Klein, "rely on those sexual ideologies based on *implicit* assumptions about the physiological and psychological nature of women that are *explicit* in Lombroso's work" (Klein 1973: 4). She cites multiple passages from *The Female Offender*, the early English translation of *La donna delinquente*, that characterize women as mentally stunted, insensitive, and passive, the last explained by the "immobility of the ovule compared with the zoosperm" (ibid.: 9).[1] Characterizing *The Female Offender* as the "foremost example of the biological explanation of crime," she explains how Lombroso used the concept of atavism to construct a gendered hierarchy in which sexual anomalies determine female behavior, whether "normal" or "criminal" (ibid.: 8).[2]

Similarly, Carol Smart, in her pioneering book of 1976 entitled *Women, Crime and Criminology: A Feminist Critique* opened with a denunciation of *The Female Offender* for its "entirely uncritical attitude towards sexual stereotypes of women and girls" (Smart 1976: XIII). Although British, Smart formed part of an early Anglo-American group of feminist criminologists and, like Klein, documented the echoes of Lombroso in subsequent American research on female delinquency.[3] Smart particularly deplored Lombroso's stigmatization of the delinquent woman as masculine, which undergirded his infamous pronouncement that, as "a double exception," the female-born criminal was "consequently a monster" (ibid.: 34–5). Likewise, "prostitution *per se* represented a major sign of atavism or degeneracy" in its replication, according to *The Female Offender*, of the behavior and morals of "savage" women (ibid.: 79). That Smart devoted an entire book to exploring the faulty logic of Lombroso and his American successors underscored the belief among the pioneers of feminist criminology that "critique is a prerequisite for the formulation of an alternative perspective" (ibid.: XV). Only by demolishing Lombrosianism could a new, nonsexist theory of female crime be born.

It seems surprising that Lombroso, an Italian whose major works had been published almost a century earlier, would even be remembered by American criminologists in the 1970s. His reputation had varied over the years, beginning with a positive reception during his lifetime, as several scholars have documented. Nicole Hahn Rafter has carefully reconstructed the paths by which Lombroso's theory of atavism and the born criminal reached the United States despite the absence of any English translation of his best-known work, *L'uomo delinquente*, before 1911. Nevertheless, Americans became acquainted with, and often converted to, criminal anthropology through several channels: two major works by European followers of Lombroso (*Anatomical Studies upon Brains of Criminals* (1881) by Moritz Benedikt and *The Criminal* (1890) by Havelock Ellis); scholarly articles in American journals; and books by "popularizers" of his theories for the general public.[4] The latter group accepted, for the most part, the notion of a distinct criminal type and repeated Lombroso's list of physical and psychological anomalies, often labeled "stigmata of crime" in English. They added, however, an American twist to criminal anthropology by emphasizing the centrality of mental weakness for the identification of criminality (Rafter 1997: chs 7–8). After 1910, psychologists became obsessed with measuring intelligence, using the French Binet-Simon tests, to identify imbecility and feeble-mindedness.[5] They also blended degeneracy theory with atavism to emphasize the dangers of bad heredity. This expansive version of Lombrosian theory led to the construction of a new category, the "defective delinquent." In certain states like New York, eugenic laws were passed to subject those labeled mentally inferior to indefinite incarceration or even sterilization.

Patrizia Guarnieri has also argued that Lombroso's theories were well received in the United States. She points out that, at the turn of the twentieth century, Americans still identified scientific advancement with European universities and were therefore open to the new field of Italian criminal anthropology (Guarnieri 2013). Although most of his work remained untranslated, Lombroso himself was commissioned to write articles for a variety of English-language magazines intended for an educated but not specialist audience.[6] More than his theory, however, Guarnieri notes that his practical proposals for preventing crime and rehabilitating criminals were particularly appealing to a young nation interested in pragmatic reforms. This admiration was returned by Lombroso, who boasted that his theories had inspired innovative American policies such as probation, and new institutions such as juvenile courts. Lombroso had to decline an invitation to lecture in the United States in 1909, the year of his death, but the long-awaited publication in 1911 of a mutilated version of *Criminal Man*, entitled *Crime: Its Causes and Remedies*, shows that his name was still in high repute.[7]

But did the popularity of Lombroso endure in the United States after his death? Did biological explanations of criminal behavior, which had captured the imagination of both professionals and the general public, remain central to the development of American criminology? The most obvious answer would be *no* because the study of crime shifted to the new and increasingly prestigious field of sociology in American universities (Triplett 2018). By the 1920s, "eugenic criminology," according to Rafter, had "lost impetus," and during the following decades, few criminologists continued to correlate criminality with inferior biological, psychological, or mental traits (Rafter 1997: 210).[8] Instead, in the 1920s the "Chicago School" began to develop a different perspective based on the spatial analysis of urban centers. According to young criminologists such as W. I. Thomas, Clifford Shaw, and Henry McKay, the social disorganization of certain neighborhoods marked by poverty, immigration, and demographic turnover explained individual offending.[9] In addition to urban mapping, members of the Chicago School interviewed delinquents to uncover their perspectives and compiled their life histories. Subsequently, in the 1930s Robert Merton developed his "strain theory," which argued that crime resulted from a mismatch between the goals prescribed by society and the means to obtain them. Such strain caused "anomie" among disadvantaged individuals, a term clearly demonstrating the influence of Emile Durkheim on American sociologists.[10] Edwin Sutherland's theory of "differential association" provided a third influential contribution to the American sociological approach by positing that all behavior, including criminality, is learned. Delinquents do not constitute a separate, dangerous class but could also be found among the wealthy, such as corporate leaders who broke financial laws and often escaped with only a fine.[11] Such innovative and influential theorists pulled American criminology away from biological and psychological explanations and toward an understanding of individual behavior as a product of interaction with the surrounding social and symbolic world.[12]

Criminology of Women

How did this "sociological turn" in American criminology during the fifty years after the death of Lombroso affect the methodology and theoretical findings of research on the female offender? This question is difficult to answer because most criminological studies focused on men during this period and have continued to do so today.[13] Yet women constituted the subject of several notable investigations into the causes of crime, several of which were authored by women. Four will be analyzed below, in chronological order, to assess the impact of Lombroso's *Female Offender* on subsequent research on female delinquency.

Mabel Ruth Fernald et al., *A Study of Women Delinquents in New York State* (1920)

Published in 1920, *A Study of Women Delinquents in New York State* reported the findings of a group project coordinated by Mabel Ruth Fernald, professor of psychology at the University of Minnesota and former director of the Laboratory of Social Hygiene in New York. Her coauthors, psychologist Mary Holmes Stevens Hayes and sociologist Almena Dawley, had also held positions at the Laboratory of Social Hygiene, a private research organization established in 1911 next to Bedford Hills Women's Reformatory. Funded by John D. Rockefeller, Jr., the laboratory at Bedford Hills formed part of his endeavor to combat prostitution by compiling data on female inmates. As a former member of the Committee of Fifteen, the early twentieth-century "vice commission" of New York City, Rockefeller was obsessed with combating the supposed white slave trade in the United States and Europe. His longtime collaborator, Katherine Bement

Davis, who was the former superintendent of Bedford Hills and the laboratory's first director, contributed an introduction to Fernald's volume.[14]

Mentioned on the first page of the book, Lombroso is offered mixed praise by Fernald:

> Lombroso introduced at least the appearance of investigation, puerile though it was for the most part … The insistence upon the fact that the understanding of the criminal should play a larger part in determining his treatment than should the facts concerning his crime, constitutes Lombroso's great achievement; an achievement which stands out even after it has become clear that the majority of the conclusions which he proffered are unsound. (Fernald, et al. 1920: 3)

Intent on improving on Lombroso's methodology, her team gathered a sample of 587 women already convicted by New York State courts. The majority were interned in different types of penal institutions, including, in addition to the Bedford Hills Reformatory, a state prison, a Magdalyn home, a county jail, and a municipal workhouse; a smaller group had received probation from Manhattan's Night Court. Five introductory chapters explain in minute detail the methodology of the study, which combined case studies with quantitative methods. Data for the case studies were recorded on two long questionnaires, one entitled "Statement of the Girl" and the other "Verified History" drawn from official sources. The answers were then compiled into a wealth of tables and graphs that purportedly measured the rates of biological, psychological, and social traits within the group.

The goal of this elaborate investigation, according to Fernald, was to turn prisons into "places for readjustment of individuals to society." To do so, "it becomes of primary importance to know of what nature this human material is" (ibid.: 4). Such a goal seemed to presume that female offenders could be rehabilitated, and in fact, part of the questionnaire concerned environmental influences such as family history, home conditions, educational achievement, and work experience. Like many of the concurrent sociological studies of male delinquency, Fernald concluded that one of the two main causes of delinquency was "a poor economic background with few advantages or opportunities, including such conditions as poor homes, very limited schooling, early age at starting work and meager industrial training" (ibid.: 525). Yet she differed with "the Socialist School" that economic factors were "the direct and immediate causes of the delinquency" rather than simply an indirect influence (ibid.: 279). The second cause was "inferior mentality" measured according to a plethora of intelligence and psychological tests, including the Binet-Simon scale, the Yerkes-Bridges Point scale, the Stanford-Binet scale, and the Woolley Series. In accordance with positivist principles, Fernald concluded that "the average mental capacity of delinquent women … is lower than that of any group of non-delinquent adults" (ibid.: 433).

Finally, the topic of sexuality recurred throughout the questionnaire and Fernald's analysis. Under the section entitled "Sex History," for example, each woman was asked about her first sexual "offense" and whether this encounter was consensual or rape; her age of entering prostitution; and the amount of her earnings. She was also submitted to a Wassermann test for syphilis and a complement fixation test for gonorrhea. In the chapter on "sex irregularities," Fernald concluded that a large majority of her sample of inmates had been sexually promiscuous or prostitutes, while only 16 percent of the sample "were not serious sex offenders" (ibid.: 410). In a tone of clear disapproval, she added that "it is appalling to contemplate the chance for infection by many of these women … who have no moral scruples about spreading the disease they have contracted" (ibid.: 411). Such words echoed the obsession of Rockefeller Jr. with the supposed blight of prostitution in American cities and its identification with female crime.

W. I. Thomas, *The Unadjusted Girl* (1923)

William Isaac Thomas was a founder of the Chicago School, which sought to take American criminology out of the hands of doctors, philanthropists, and amateurs and place it squarely into the new and vibrant field of sociology. In addition to a long teaching career at the University of Chicago, he also edited the *American Journal of Sociology* and was elected president of the American Sociological Society.[15] Thomas's most famous book, *The Polish Peasant in Europe and America* (1918–20)—written with Florian Znaniecki and published before the *Unadjusted Girl*—became a foundational text for the Chicago School. Sociological in methodology, it examined the lives of immigrants to Chicago based on oral histories, diaries, Polish-language newspapers, and other written documents from the local community. The authors concluded that immigrant neighborhoods were prone to disorganization and crime because of the dissolution of traditional family and community ties that had regulated behavior in European villages.

Yet in an earlier book, *Sex and Society*, Thomas had employed a biological approach to gender that emphasized the "organic differences in the sexes" and frequently cited Lombroso and his positivist colleagues (Thomas 1907: 3). Like Lombroso, he characterized the male as active, or in his words "katabolic," and the female as passive or "anabolic," with the result that "woman stands nearer to the plant process" than the male animal always in movement (ibid.: 3–4). Echoing the Lombrosian assertion of women's inability to achieve a general level of civic responsibility, Thomas concluded that

> Morality, in the most general sense, represents the code under which activities are best carried on, and is worked out in the school of experience. It is pre-eminently an adult and a male system, and men are intelligent enough to recognize that neither women nor children have passed through this school. (ibid.: 234)

This comparison of women to children permeates a book marked by a long discussion of physical and psychological research on gender carried out by other evolutionists such as Darwin himself, Havelock Ellis, Guglielmo Ferrero, Francis Galton, Richard von Krafft-Ebing, Enrico Morselli, and Herbert Spencer.

In *The Unadjusted Girl*—written fifteen years later and after the *The Polish Peasant*—Thomas adopts a less biological approach than in *Sex and Society* and adapts his newer social organization theory to analyze female psychology. In place of the Darwinian perspective, the book identifies four wishes that are innate to all human beings: the desire for new experience, security, response, and recognition. Individuals pursue these wishes within their own "definition of the situation," which may differ from norms set by groups such as the family, school, church, and larger community. With the rapid changes typical of the early twentieth century, marked by industrialization, urbanization, and migration, individuals were increasingly likely to adopt deviant or even criminal means to fulfill their wishes.

Such behavior was particularly dangerous in girls who, like boys, craved excitement and recognition. Thus, according to Thomas, female delinquency typically stemmed from "an impulse to get amusement, adventure, pretty clothes, favorable notice, distinction, freedom in the large world which presents so many allurements and comparisons" (Thomas 1923: 109). His 3,000 cases led him to conclude that, in the case of girls, "their sex is used as a condition of the realization of other wishes. It is their capital" (ibid.). The solution was for the family, and other community organizations, to teach them that virtue and purity have "an almost magical value" for girls and that only marriage will prevent their "demoralization" (ibid.: 98). In the absence of such groups, governmental departments and private committees must be organized "to control the behavior of girls who were either wild already or went wild" by teaching them to regulate and sublimate their desires (ibid.: 200). Despite the more sophisticated analysis of gender compared to *Sex and Society*, Thomas nevertheless echoed his earlier study by identifying women's nature, and therefore their deviancy, as rooted in their biological sexuality. Rather than questioning the rigidity and narrowness of female gender norms, he prescribed that girls adjust to them.

Sheldon and Eleanor Glueck, *Five Hundred Delinquent Women* (1934)

Sheldon and Eleanor Glueck formed a criminological team that published a series of studies on adult and juvenile crime such as *Five Hundred Criminal Careers* (1930) and *One Thousand Juvenile Delinquents* (1934). As is clear from these titles, the couple compiled large databases of inmates in penal institutions and, in some cases, followed up on their lives after release.[16] The most famous of these diachronic studies, *Unraveling Juvenile Delinquency* (1950), claimed that potential delinquents can be identified by the age of six years old using their "Social Prediction Tables."[17] Both Gluecks were employed by Harvard Law School, although Eleanor, as a woman, was barred from holding a teaching post. Remaining a research assistant while Sheldon advanced to the rank of distinguished professor, she has nevertheless recently gained the reputation of "an unsung pioneer in criminology" (Laub and Smith 1995).

Only one of the Gluecks's books, *Five Hundred Delinquent Women*, focused on gender. Following the pattern of their other large, statistical studies, multitudinous tables trace the lives of five hundred inmates of the Massachusetts Reformatory for Women from their incarceration through the period of parole and finally into the early years after release. In their introduction, the Gluecks praise "the Italian criminalist Lombroso, who was the first to make a systematic study of prisoners from the anthropologic point of view," although they note his "questionable scientific research" (Glueck and Glueck 1934a: 5). While lauding their own more modern methodology, they nevertheless echo Lombroso's language when pronouncing their research subjects to be "*on the whole a sorry lot*" marked by "feeble-mindedness, psychopathic personality, and ... emotional instability" (ibid.: 299). Interrogating each woman about her age of menstruation, first sexual experience, illegitimate pregnancies, and entrance into prostitution, the Gluecks also replicated the positivist obsession with female sexuality, which led them to conclude that "*Illicit sexual indulgence was the chief form of their adolescent and early-adult misbehaviour*" (ibid.: 300).[18] Similar questions about sexual conduct were absent from their studies of men and boys.

Known for their eclectic theories, the Gluecks were more attentive than Lombroso to economic and social factors that encouraged innate deviancy to become manifest. For example, the questionnaires asked about education, employment, and, most extensively, family history in addition to biological, psychological, and mental deficiencies. Yet, they denied that "even the most ardent exponent of economic determinism" could offer proof that poverty caused crime. Consequently "No one can as yet say with precision which of the handicaps of mental defect, psychopathy, neuroticism, and poor physical health found among our women and their families are innate, and how many or which are acquired" (ibid.: 309). Thus, while advocating for government assistance for poor women and their families, they also embraced a eugenic solution for the majority of their subjects, who "may truly be regarded as irresponsible members of society, requiring, in many cases, continuous control if not lifelong quarantine" to prevent reproduction (ibid.). Such words echoed Lombroso's recommendation of life sentences for "born" criminals, whose biological and psychological anomalies signaled their dangerousness and inability to reform.[19]

Otto Pollak, *The Criminality of Women* (1950)

Despite the late date of his book, Otto Pollak cites Lombroso more often than the three earlier authors and repeats many of his specific arguments. A sociologist at the University of Pennsylvania, he nevertheless devotes a large part of his book, *The Criminality of Women*, to biological rather than environmental factors as the cause of female deviance. Overall, he argues "that female crime is perhaps the outstanding area of undiscovered, or at least unprosecuted, crime in our culture and that its actual amount as well as its relation to male criminality has been greatly underrated" (Pollak 1950: 154). Pollak supports this argument in several ways, first by pointing to the supposed protective attitude of male police officers, judges, juries, and even victims of crime toward women. According to this "chivalry" thesis, official crime statistics are unreliable because they severely underreport many types of illegal female behavior.

While the chivalry thesis appears cultural in nature, Pollak's other major arguments reprise Lombrosian conceptions of female biology. First, women are instinctively deceitful because they can fake sexual orgasms, unlike men who require erections, and must hide their periods of menstruation. Inherently dishonest, women favor poison to kill their victims within the secrecy of their family homes and falsely accuse men of sexual offenses against them. Other hidden female crimes include instigation to robbery and burglary, blackmail, fraud, shoplifting, abortion, baby farming, and infanticide.

Secondly, Pollak asserts that "it cannot be questioned" that "prostitution is a specifically feminine form of behavior" (ibid.: 90). He approvingly cites Lombroso's opinion that gender differences in crime rates would disappear if prostitution were included, particularly because it involves two offenses: that of soliciting and that of illicit sex. In the case of men, "resorting to a house of ill fame for an isolated act of intercourse does not constitute open and gross lewdness" (ibid.: 55). Although Pollak does not employ Lombroso's trope of atavism, he perpetuates a double standard of morality that labels women as dangerous because of their innate tendency toward sexual deviance.

While ignoring social and economic factors, Pollak concedes some importance to culture and particularly to women's role within the family, which offers them convenient opportunities for murder as they prepare food and nurse the sick. Department stores mesmerize female shoppers with their displays of merchandise, while domestic service offers a convenient setting for petty theft. Yet Pollak prioritizes women's inborn characteristics by concluding that "the criminality of women reflects their biological nature in a given cultural setting" (ibid.: 161). And as in the case of Lombroso, this biological nature was, in women, sexual.

Conclusion

After an analysis of these major works, what can we conclude about the legacy of Lombroso on American theories of female crime? Did researchers in the United States locate a common etiology of crime for both men and women or were their conclusions gendered? In no case was Lombroso's theory accepted in its entirety, a fact that seems to support the first hypothesis. While each author mentioned and sometimes praised certain aspects of Lombrosian criminal anthropology, none subscribed to his theory of atavism or to his sloppy statistical approach. Fernald and the Gluecks, for example, were particularly proud of their extensive tables, taking care to explain their painstaking methodology in comparison to that of Lombroso. All the authors agree that sociological or cultural factors—including a corrupt family environment, poverty, or low levels of education—contribute to delinquency. Women's roles within the family and society, rather than simply female physiology, were recognized as shaping the behavior of not only "normal" but also "deviant" women.

However, Lombroso continued to cast a shadow over these studies in two ways. First, these authors sexualize the female subjects of their research in a manner that is absent in books about male criminology from the same period. These authors continue to epitomize the criminal woman as a prostitute, even though several admit that American prohibitionist laws, rather than innate depravity, account for the large number of prostitutes in their samples. Yet, to them, any hint of "sexual corruption" in young girls forbodes a life of crime and therefore justifies the routine vaginal examinations inflicted on them after arrest, and venereal disease itself constitutes evidence of delinquency. The female subjects of their studies are relentlessly questioned about the age of their first menstruation, of their initiation into sexual intercourse, of their pregnancies, and of menopause. Any sexual activity outside of marriage is labeled as illicit, a sign of demoralization, feeble-mindedness, or psychopathology. In short, despite a partial shift toward a sociological analysis during the mid-twentieth century, sexuality was still emphasized as the key to female behavior.

These criminologists imitate Lombroso in another way: by ignoring their own more subtle analyses of individual female offenders when making final grand theoretical pronouncements. Lombroso himself of course did not ignore sociological factors of crime and often offered sympathetic and complex readings of specific cases of, for example, women accused of infanticide and abortion or women who killed their abusive husbands. However, like Lombroso, American criminologists could not resist the temptation to amplify traditional stereotypes of women in lurid and demeaning language. For Thomas, society had "to control the behavior of girls who were either wild already or went wild" (Thomas 1923: 160); for the Gluecks, female reformatories were filled with a "swarm of defective diseased, antisocial misfits" (Glueck and Glueck 1934a: 303); for Pollak, women offenders were "usually ... women suffering from hysteria" (Pollak 1950: 25). Although these statements were partially contradicted by their more nuanced statistics and case studies, these authors continued to perpetuate an image of female criminals as weak-willed, mentally deficient, overly emotional, and even hysterical. Linked in popular mentality with women's biology, these labels reinforced, rather than complicated, widespread beliefs about the dualism between men and women.

Finally, American criminologists shared with Lombroso—and positivist theories more generally—the notion that the individual rather than society was at fault. As clearly expressed in the title of Thomas's book, *The Unadjusted Girl*, the solution of all the American authors discussed above was to realign women to their proper social roles of sexual purity before marriage and maternity afterwards. Even sociological arguments at their most sympathetic located the problem of deviancy in the individual rather than in the legal norms and the larger social structure that denied equality for women in private and public life. When Dorie Klein and Carole Smart criticized the American successors of Lombroso, they were speaking during a wider shift in criminology—which included theories of male delinquency—from blaming the individual to examining the power of police and the courts to label certain groups as deviant and submit them to unjust strategies of social control. This profound rupture in the criminological tradition in the 1970s constituted an important context for the vehement attacks by feminists on Lombroso and the perception that his gendered theory had to be torn down before they could envision new criminological approaches to researching women. In conclusion, the legacy of Lombroso in the United States was complex and gendered: weak with regard to men (or more specifically white men), it was more lasting in theories of the female offender, who remained sexualized and outside the mainstream of American criminology for a half century after his death.[20]

Notes

1. Quotes from Klein and other Anglo-American criminologists come from the *The Female Offender*, the original 1895 English translation of *La donna delinquente, la prostituta, e la donna normale* by Lombroso and his assistant, Guglielmo Ferrero. For an updated translation, see Lombroso and Ferrero (2004).
2. While Klein generally interprets Lombroso correctly, she erroneously maintains that Lombroso favored sterilization of women as a punishment for crime (14).
3. A third member of this group, Frances Heidensohn, mentioned Lombroso as early as 1968 in her article, "The Deviance of Women: A Critique and Enquiry," *The British Journal of Sociology*, 19 (2). In her subsequent book, *Women and Crime* (1985), New York: New York University Press, she devoted a chapter to criticizing *The Female Offender* and American criminologists who had drawn on this text (110–24).
4. For a careful reconstruction of the work of American "popularizers" of Lombroso, see Rafter (2006).
5. For an extended discussion of the different forms of mental testing used to measure feeble-mindedness, see Fink (1938).
6. These articles have been collected in Horton and Rich (2004). Only one of these articles concerned gender: 'The Physical Insensibility of Woman' (1892), *Fortnightly Review*, (57): 354–7.
7. In penal law, the positivist recommendation to individualize punishment was popular in the United States and took the form, throughout this period, of experimenting with indeterminate sentencing. For debates between American and European jurists over legal positivism, see Pifferi (2013).
8. These exceptions included Ernest A. Hooten and William H. Sheldon.
9. The Chicago School was named after the University of Chicago, which fostered the growth of sociological criminology. For an overview, see Hardyns and Pauwels (2018). Notable works of the Chicago School include W. I. Thomas and F. Znaniecki, *The Polish Peasant in Europe and America: A classical work in immigration history* (1920); C. R. Shaw, F. M. Zorbaugh, H. D. McKay, L. S. Cotrell, *Delinquency areas: A Study of the Geographic Distribution of School Truants, Juvenile Delinquents, and Adult Offenders in Chicago* (1929); and C. Shaw, *The Jack-Roller* (1930).
10. For Merton's classic article formulating his theory, see R. K. Merton (1938), "Social Structure and Anomie," *American Sociological Review*, 3: 672–82.
11. Sutherland first elaborated his theory of differential association in the third edition of his influential textbook, *Principles of Criminology* (3rd ed., 1939). *White Collar Crime* was published in 1949.
12. Jonathan Simon, argues for an even longer impact of Lombroso on United States criminal justice policy. His search of the large database HeinOnline for the years 1891–1990 found more citations to Lombroso than to other prominent criminologists, with the exception of Sheldon Glueck (and only during the 1903s and 1940s). Simon also introduces the useful concept of "populist positivism" to explain the widespread American belief that science can identify monstrous criminal types—such as "natural born killers," "super predator youth" and "drug kingpins"—who need to be incarcerated for life or executed. See Simon (2006).
13. For an analysis of continued gender bias in criminological research, see Chesney-Lind and Chagnon (2016).

14. On Davis and the Rockefeller Foundation, see Bullough (1988) and Fitzpatrick (1990, Chapter 5).
15. Now the American Sociological Association.
16. S. Glueck and E. T. Glueck, *Five Hundred Criminal Careers* (New York: A. Knopf, 1930); S. Glueck and E. T. Glueck, *One Thousand Juvenile Delinquents* (Cambridge, MA: Harvard University Press, 1934).
17. S. Glueck and E. T. Glueck, *Unraveling Juvenile Delinquency* (New York: Commonwealth Fund, 1950),
18. The italics are in the original.
19. The Glueck's multifactor approach incited a strong reproach from Sutherland, who in the same years was committed to establishing criminology as a purely sociological inquiry. On the "Sutherland-Glueck debates," see the essay by J. M. Eassey and M. D. Krohn in P. Knepper and A. Johansen, *The Oxford Handbook of the History of Crime and Criminal Justice* (Oxford: Oxford University Press, 2016), 161–2, .
20. An analysis of criminological studies of African American men and women during the same period would likely come to a similar conclusion by finding that the essentialism of race, that is biological determinism, overshadowed sociological explanations for Black crime.

18

Criminal Somatotypes and Ambivalent Lombrosianism in the United States, *c.* 1940–60

John Shepherd

Introduction

Four decades after the death of Cesare Lombroso, a small but noteworthy group of US criminologists hoped to renew their field's interest in the criminal body, through a new classification of "somatotypes." Psychologist William Sheldon (1898–1977), published his *Varieties of Delinquent Youth* in 1949, where he reported that delinquents were predominantly "mesomorphic," characterized by bone, muscle, and connective tissue, while tending "towards massive strength and muscular development." Moreover, in keeping with his "constitutional psychiatry," these criminal mesomorphs were thought to exhibit particular character traits, including "assertiveness" and "love of physical adventure," but also "love of dominating, lust for power," "psychological callousness," and "Spartan indifference to pain" (1949: 14–28, 726–46). Incorporating William Sheldon's somatotypes in their own larger comparison of 500 delinquent and 500 nondelinquent youth, Harvard criminologists Sheldon (1896–1980) and Eleanor (1898–1972) Glueck published *Unraveling Juvenile Delinquency* in 1950, where they also identified a pattern of delinquent mesomorphy and speculated on the increased physical energy of these restless youth (1950: 183–97).

But could this somatotyping be considered "Lombrosian"? On this point, these criminologists disagreed. In passages discussing Lombroso, William Sheldon positioned his somatotypology as a direct successor to earlier biocriminology, his own advance providing "a further sharpening of the tools of constitutional description" (1949: 759). Conversely, the Gluecks attempted to renounce any such association. In setting out their chapter on criminal constitution there was, they claimed, "no implication in this of any Lombrosian hypothesis of a born criminal type. Nor is there any implication of the relative importance, in the total system of causal forces of the bodily constitution as opposed to either the psychiatric-psychologic or the socio-cultural forces" (Glueck and Glueck 1950: 183). The Gluecks had included somatotyping as one element of an eclectic, multifactor study but, as will be seen, subsequently tried (and failed) to purge their work of its embarrassing Lombrosian connotations.

This chapter attempts to account for varying appeals to and resistance against Lombroso's legacy among US researchers who subsequently studied the criminal body, focusing in particular on the above example of somatotype classification and the figure of the mesomorphic criminal. I explore these ambiguous attitudes through the lens of what I term "ambivalent Lombrosianism." Alongside increasing criticism of earlier criminal anthropology from competing criminological traditions in psychiatry and sociology, those continuing in biocriminology also held ambiguous positive and negative attitudes toward Lombroso. This ambivalence saw him alternately placed as a founding figure and derided as outdated, praised for his empirical outlook and criticized for his unscientific methods, alongside varying moves to invoke, renounce, or obscure his legacy. This perspective allows for a more precise understanding of Lombroso's ongoing influence in the United States as well as the limits of that influence. Examining these instances of ambivalence reveals the changed disciplinary landscape of mid-century criminology and new pressures to qualify or suppress Lombrosian theory, but also illustrates how tropes and suspicions of embodied criminality could still persist.

This ambivalence also points to the difficulty of neatly demarcating the boundaries of "Lombrosianism," sometimes referring to specific atavistic, determinist, or hereditarian views of crime, sometimes referring to a wider range of positivist, medical approaches to the supposedly abnormal offender. Indeed, other historians have frequently discussed the "imprecision," "elasticity," and "heterogeneity" of criminal anthropology in its shifting classification of various offenders across successive editions of *L'uomo delinquente* and in its reception and modification by international audiences (Lombroso 2006; Rafter 1997: 110–32; Wetzell 2000: 39–71; Gibson 2002: 18–38, 43–4, 247–50; Horn 2003: 1–27; Becker and Wetzell 2006). Such reinventions and recontextualizations of Lombroso have continued long after his death in both criminology and history. As Silvano Montaldo argues, "the continuous oscillations between criminological theories often end up finding in this character a symbol on which to clash and, in the end, these tensions are the result of a tendency to project the ideas of the present onto the past" (2018b: 53). Following Montaldo, I will be exploring the Lombrosian "myths" articulated by competing criminological disciplines along with mid-century biocriminology's attempts to renew, qualify, or escape these myths.

From this analysis, I draw three conclusions: Firstly, within a field increasingly pervaded by sociological methods and models, those studying "the criminal" increasingly qualified and critiqued Lombroso as a foil from which to launch their own, more legitimate, somatic research. Despite these efforts, critics ultimately saw somatotyping as part of a broad Lombrosian tradition. Secondly, the practice of somatotyping reveals how different juvenile bodies were alternately exposed to or guarded against criminological scrutiny, informed by varying judgments of innocence or incorrigibility. Thirdly, and in connection with the prior point, the eventual figure of the mesomorphic criminal reflected ambivalent attitudes toward youth, re-articulating earlier Lombrosian tropes of embodied atavistic threat, while also modifying these tropes with ambiguous notions of American masculinity and its heroic or destructive potential. I begin by briefly outlining the ambivalent reception and memorialization of Lombroso in the United States in the decades following his death. Then, using their archival research materials, I examine the Gluecks' use of somatotyping and the controversy it provoked before evaluating the Lombrosian aspects of this work in comparison with William Sheldon's own somatotype study. Finally, I turn to the reception of somatotyping by sociologist critics and the eventual placement of the Gluecks' eclectic research program within a broadly defined "Lombrosian" tradition.

An Ambiguous Legacy

As Rafter notes, the 1910s and subsequent interwar period saw the steady decline of criminal anthropology in the United States in favor of alternative eugenic, dynamic, and environmental viewpoints. Earlier US proponents from diverse professional backgrounds in medicine, penology, charity, and other social work had been "neophyte criminologists, amateurs who became overnight specialists in the field" (Rafter 2006: 170). Conversely, in the years following Lombroso's death, psychologists, psychiatrists, and eugenicists turned to intelligence testing and psychopathy, whereby, in Rafter's words, "the somatic territory of the born-criminal idea steadily shrank" (1997: 167–8). With the creation of the interdisciplinary American Institute of Criminal Law and Criminology (AICLC) in 1909, contributing researchers and practitioners frequently regarded Lombroso with ambivalence and implicitly contrasted his flawed methods with the professionalization of American criminology. Writing in 1911 in the AICLC's journal, John Henry Wigmore's "Memorial to Lombroso" thus summarized that "many of his specific conclusions have since been doubted or disproved but his beneficent influence as the father of the modern methods and spirit has been universally conceded" (1911: 491).

This sentiment was also reflected in the AICLC's republication of *Crime It's Causes and Remedies*, where Maurice Parmelee introduced Lombroso as "somewhat ignorant of biology, and especially the theory of heredity" (ibid.: xxxi). Nevertheless, after critiquing his confused notions of atavism and criminal heredity, Parmelee still referred to Lombroso as "the great pioneer" in applying "the positive, inductive methods of modern science to the problem of crime" (ibid.: xxxii). In a 1912 review of Lombroso's works, sociologist and associate editor Charles Ellwood similarly derided his overextension of the "organic factor" and of epilepsy in particular, while conversely praising him as an empiricist whose call to study criminal man "will remain forever a monument to his name" (1912: 716–23). Criticism of criminal anthropology and its organic theories thus mingled with more generic appeals to Lombroso's modern, scientific spirit, which could be fulfilled by the AICLC.

Even so, while contributors continued to discuss "mental defect," sterilization, and other eugenic topics, critics from psychiatry and sociology increasingly contrasted their new efforts with outdated criminal anthropology. Psychiatrist and child guidance pioneer William Healy, preparing to start work in Chicago's Juvenile Psychopathic Institute in 1908, wrote to a colleague of his ambition to produce "a work that may be as classical as that of Lombroso, that may be much more scientifically founded and a thousand times more practically beneficial."[1] Indeed, *The Individual Delinquent*, published by Healy in 1915, became a foundational text for interwar "mental hygiene" and child guidance movements in their attempts to treat and rehabilitate "maladjusted" youth (Grob 1983: 144–78; Horn 1989; Jones 1999: 38–61). Here he contrasted his own individualized approach with crude Lombrosian classification: "any classification according to theories of epileptoidism or atavism or any other biological causation would end in the mere giving of a name; whereas a complete survey of the facts leads to the realisation of a many-sided etiology" (Healy 1915: 18). Other reevaluations of Lombroso's legacy would come from Chicago School sociologists, mapping crime across the metropolis to present zonal and sociocultural explanations of offending (Smith 2023: 63–105). Writing in 1937 in the *American Journal of Sociology*, Alfred Lindesmith and Yale Levin thus described "The Lombrosian Myth in Criminology," whereby they denied Lombroso's founding status and traced an alternative genealogy through nineteenth-century sociology back to Adolphe Quetelet's criminal statistics. Notably they also implicated psychiatry by connecting the "Lombrosian myth" to " 'a seizure of power,' so to speak, by the medical profession" (Lindesmith and Levin 1937: 669). Lombroso's legacy was thus invoked to promote or deride alternative disciplinary trajectories in US criminology. Meanwhile, those continuing biological and anthropological projects viewed themselves as increasingly embattled. In his 1939 *Crime and the Man*, Harvard physical anthropologist Earnest A. Hooton, perhaps the most outspoken US neo-Lombrosian of this period, thus introduced his field as "an obvious ugly duckling… greeted by the lords of the criminological dung hill with cries of "Quack! Quack! Quack!"" (1939: 3).

Hooton went on to present crime statistics, "mosaic" depictions of criminal physiognomy across different US states, and his eugenic proposals for crime prevention. However, he offered regular criticisms of Lombroso to justify these new biocriminological efforts. Discussing his motivations for the study, Hooton described "dissatisfaction with the futile and almost childish attempts of Lombroso to establish a tenable hypothesis by essentially unscientific methods," but also "the sanctimonious statistical deviousness" of his critics (ibid.: 371). Elsewhere, he outlined Lombroso's "faulty" and "partisan" approach, including an inadequate sample size, inappropriate comparisons across ethnic and racial groups, and ignorance of later statistical methods (ibid.: 14). His reputation was further tarnished by "the fascist prostitution of anthropology to political and economic oppression" (ibid.: 3). Nevertheless, these scientific and political sins left the way open for Hooton and others to produce new, more "legitimate" studies. Thus, the central thesis of offenders' distinct physical and mental abnormality "was not proved by Lombroso and the criminal anthropologists, but it has never been refuted" (ibid.: 15). These two drives, to surpass Lombroso and renew biological investigations, would also be reflected in the somatotyping subsequently adopted by the Gluecks' study.

Constitution and Controversy in the Study by Sheldon and Eleanor Glueck

After receiving their doctorates in social ethics and education from Harvard in 1924 and 1925, Sheldon and Eleanor Glueck undertook a lifelong collaboration in criminological research. Focusing on multifactor comparisons across large samples of offenders, their works throughout the 1930s included *Five Hundred Criminal*

Careers (1930), *Five Hundred Delinquent Women* (1934a), and *One Thousand Juvenile Delinquents* (1934b). By 1938, Eleanor described their next study as "an eclectic approach to an analysis of crime causation."[2] This study, begun in 1939 and eventually published in 1950 as *Unraveling Juvenile Delinquency*, involved a comparison of 500 matched pairs of delinquent and nondelinquent boys aged between eleven and sixteen, producing correlated factors that would form the basis of the Gluecks' new "prediction tables" (Shepherd 2024: 146–275). As Mary Gibson notes elsewhere in this volume, the Gluecks were familiar with Lombroso and had previously reiterated his claims about female offenders. However, constitution remained one part of this new "eclectic study." With eight years of funding from the Commonwealth Foundation, the Gluecks hired ten social investigators, six psychometric testers, one psychiatrist-physician, two Rorschach test analysts, two statisticians, two physical anthropologists, and a secretarial staff of eight women, accumulating, codifying, and tabulating data on 402 socio-cultural, somatic, intellectual, and emotional-temperamental factors (1950: ix, 15, 73).

The Gluecks' methodology centered on matching 500 delinquents, selected from Massachusetts Lyman School for Boys and Shirley Industrial School ("accepted as serious delinquents solely on the basis of their commitment"), with 500 "controls" selected from Boston's public schools.[3] These boys were matched in pairs by age, IQ, "race," and residence in "underprivileged neighbourhoods" to establish "why it is that even in regions of most adverse social conditions, most children do not commit legally prohibited acts" (Glueck and Glueck 1950: 14–15). "Race" here was used interchangeably with ethnicity or nationality, and crucially, the Gluecks specified that cases "must not be negroes," ending up with boys predominantly from immigrant, especially Italian and Irish, backgrounds.[4] Frustratingly, this decision was never explicitly discussed in their research materials but may have indicated desires for a "normal" sample, following contemporary assumptions that African American crime reflected a distinctively unusual social and demographic trajectory following the trauma of slavery (Muhammad 2010). Hooton had similarly provided statistics, physiognomic portraits, and even racist caricatures of "negro and negroid criminals," while conversely noting "the criminological ambiguities which seem assignable to the rigid social and economic strait-jacket in which the negro is confined" (1939: 386, 290–341). In fact, the Gluecks consulted Hooton on their own "racial" matching, stressing their desire "to avoid the complications and implications of the relationship of crime to nationality."[5] Turning to the Gluecks' interest in constitution, Hooton also referred them to William Sheldon, who succeeded in incorporating his own somatotype classification into their growing study.

Alongside the Gluecks' criminological projects, William Sheldon promoted his "constitutional psychiatry" through collaborations with Hooton in photographing Harvard students in a study of "normal" American bodies (Creadick 2010: 42–65). A 1940 article in *Time Magazine* described how, while completing his Ph.D. in psychology, William Sheldon had also collected over 4,000 nude photographs for measurement, becoming convinced of the whole body's role in determining personality (Judging Mind by Body 1940). Dissatisfied with the complex physique types of German psychiatrist Ernst Kretschmer, he instead proposed a simplified seven-point scale to rate each of three structural components (ibid.: 53; Gibson 2002: 217–23): "endomorphy," referring to "the soft fatty element"; "mesomorphy," referring to "the hard, strong, muscular element"; and "ectomorphy," referring to the "relative predominance of the skin" in thin, lanky bodies.[6] He also listed exhaustive character traits for each of these somatotypes in materials provided to the Gluecks. Endomorphs were thus "viscerectonic," noted for relaxation, "manifest warmth of fellowship," tolerance and "love of physical comfort." Meanwhile the "somatotonic" mesomorphs were associated with energy, "love of adventure and physical danger" and "natural aggression" as well as "natural leadership." Finally, ectomorphs' "cerebrotonia" was characterized by tenseness, restraint, "the hyperattentional trait," and "sociophobia."[7]

In his standardization, measurement, rating, and accumulation of physique photographs, William Sheldon joined a longer history of appeals to photography's combined experimental, "museological" (archival), and teaching functions (Didi-Hubermann 2003: 29–66; Maehle 1993). He himself later stressed the procedure's convenience, objectivity, and persistence, claiming that "when [the photographer] snaps the camera it is as if he were to take—and to certify—a potentially infinite series of bodily measurements" (Sheldon 1949: 30). Having discarded endocrinological tests, pneumographs, and electroencephalograms as too technical and vague in their implications, the Gluecks favored William Sheldon's physique photographs for their apparent convenience, consistency, and comparability with their overall dataset.[8] Yet the circumstances of photographic procedure also implicitly demarcated the delinquent from the nondelinquent. Historians such as Allan Sekula and Georges Didi-Hubermann critically note the role of photography and archival practices in constructing such typologies, "crystalizing" the case into "a tableau in which the type was condensed in a unique image, or in an unequivocal series of images" (Didi-Hubermann 2003: 48; Sekula 1986). Most saliently, in the Glueck study, photography echoed the by now well-known procedures of criminal arrest and identification (Finn 2009: 1–30). In turn, the exposure and photographic capture of innocent non-delinquents roused strong protests in defense of children's modesty.

Over the summer of 1940, plans to photograph and classify nondelinquent cases in Boston's public schools briefly threatened the entire study. In May the Gluecks' negotiations with Superintendent Arthur Gould to secure his and parents' permissions were disrupted by a *Boston Post* article: "Can't Photo Children in Nude Poses, School Board Denies Professor Glueck's Request." The Gluecks, it was alleged, had made scandalous proposals to pose and photograph mixed groups of boys and girls together in classrooms, arguing that "such exposure in this 'modern world' could no longer be considered immodest." Sponsors of the Massachusetts Child Council, who were believed to be backing the study, were also listed and implicated in the smear ("Can't Photo Children in Nude Poses" 1940b). The Gluecks rejected this "outrageous news story" as a "vicious design," but Superintendent Gould still had serious reservations.[9] In late July, he wrote to Eleanor, that he "would not allow [himself] to be associated in any way with this type of procedure" and, moreover, doubted the criminological importance of the photographs: "their use in the study of the problem of delinquents is not apparent and the danger of spoiling an otherwise worthwhile study is considerable."[10] Having risked a breach with Gould and the public schools, somatotyping was eventually salvaged by a compromise in September. It was agreed that, following appropriate parental permissions, nondelinquent boys in the public schools could be photographed wearing trunks, despite William Sheldon's protests that "much of scientific value would be lost by this procedure."[11]

Even following the schools' cautious approval, the revealing photographs still caused problems among boys who were "particularly sensitive about appearing in shorts in the presence of other boys."[12] Arrangements were made for private rooms, and scheduling adjustments ensured the separate photography of any boys with physical disabilities or abnormalities to avoid embarrassment.[13] After one instance of agitation where a group of boys refused to undress, it was deemed advisable to take nondelinquent cases individually. Conversely, to overcome the pupils' objections, the physical examination and photographing were presented as an attempt "to find any handicaps which may interfere with their ambitions," particularly stressing "the matter of muscular development and growth" with which boys were thought to be most concerned.[14]

The controversy that surrounded somatotype photographs of nondelinquent cases in the public schools is especially notable given that there was no similar outcry on behalf of the delinquent sample. Attempts to persuade nondelinquents throughout the study contrasted with the routine examination of institutional cases who, according to one memorandum, "considered us as somehow vaguely connected with the official administration and… were not too conscious of having rights in the matter." Inmates reportedly described the Gluecks' research staff as "bug doctors" and joked that "they were going to be 'bugged' (their sanity was going to be tested)."[15] Returning to somatotyping procedures specifically, delinquents at Lyman were examined from late 1939 (before the aforementioned compromise on trunks was reached) apparently without incident. Another memorandum described how Lyman cases were taken in groups of twelve to the hospital basement, where each boy "fully undressed" for their medical examination and physique photograph.[16] Such accounts are given added salience by the subsequent exposure of conditions and abuses in these institutions years after the Gluecks' study. Institutional reformer Jerome G. Miller thus later recalled how, as Massachusetts's new Commissioner of Youth Services, he visited Shirley in 1969 where he made the haunting discovery of a sixteen-year-old in solitary confinement, "nude in the darkness of his own tomb" (Miller 1991: 65).

Somatotype photographs taken for the Gluecks' study indicated how different boys and their bodies could be guarded against or exposed to the gaze of criminologists. The resistance, negotiation, and placation of skeptical school officials, parents, and pupils evidently did not extend to "serious" delinquents isolated in the disciplinary regime of the training schools. The possibilities of somatic research were thus mediated not only by their theoretical status and acceptance but also by situated impressions of juvenile innocence or criminality. In turn, these photographs would also prompt ambivalent interpretations of the mesomorphy they purportedly revealed and its future promise or peril.

Searching for Stigmata?

Along with the above controversy, somatotyping would also prove contentious among the Gluecks' research staff. William Sheldon had briefly raised the issue that his own 4,000 cases only established eighteen-year-old norms and that "the reliability of the somatotypes on our boys cannot be determined without working out norms for that age" (S. Glueck 1939). However, following his early departure from the study, photographic work fell to psychiatrist Bryant E. Moulton, who wrote to the Gluecks in 1945, feeling he "should go on record regarding this part of the work." He noted the difficulty of establishing a "personality picture" from the photographs and reiterated William Sheldon's own admission that, without a juvenile series and follow-up, there was no proof for the permanence of somatotypes. Moulton thus suggested that "if the somatotype is shifting during adolescence its significance at any one time is not so great."[17] Around this time, the Gluecks transferred responsibility for rating the photographs to a colleague of Hooton and William Sheldon, physical anthropologist Carl Seltzer, warning him that Moulton was "still acting as if he were directing this portion of the work" and seemed to "need considerable ego satisfaction."[18]

In the process of rating, measurement, and analysis somatotype photographs raised Lombrosian implications; however, the Gluecks evidently shifted between caution and curiosity. One memorandum from 1940 referred to Lombroso as a fraud who "modified his evidence in support of his conclusions" but nevertheless suggested physiognomic correlates of criminality to be considered in the study.[19] Briefing Seltzer at the beginning of 1945, Sheldon Glueck explicitly raised the "possibility of obtaining reliable data in line with Lombrosianism" from the physique photographs. This might include cephalic indices as well as large jaws, "handle ears," chins "flat as in apes," and "excessive hairiness in general," also referring to Hooton for other data on Lombrosianism. Directly invoking the "atavistic" criminal type, Sheldon Glueck here wrote that "what we are largely after in our study is evidence, one way or the other, of a rough picture of quasi-simean or primitive man."[20] Evidently, however, in their search for stigmata "one way or the other," the Gluecks ultimately settled on skepticism and, by 1950, resisted any "Lombrosian hypothesis" in *Unraveling*.

Based on Seltzer's ratings, the Gluecks concluded that mesomorphy was the dominant structural component in 60.1 percent of the delinquents, compared to 30.7 percent of the nondelinquents. Conversely, 39.6 percent of the nondelinquents were judged ectomorphic. The somatotype was, however, of limited use in the Gluecks' overarching project of predicting delinquency. Having presented hundreds of comparative tables, *Unraveling* organized some more highly correlated social, psychiatric, and Rorschach factors into prediction tables with which to score the percentage likelihood of future delinquency in six-year-old school entrants. But, citing the fact that the supposed immutability of somatotypes was still unproven, the Gluecks chose to omit them and did not create a comparable somatotype prediction table (1950: 257–71). Here and in later works, constitution was factorized and considered "a field of inquiry that may yield relevant insights and afford bases for intercorrelation with other fields." Meanwhile, they further attempted to distance themselves from "dogmatic generalizations regarding the exact participation of heredity and environment" and contrasted their work and William Sheldon's statements with those of the Italian neo-Lombrosians DiTullio and Ottolenghi on "defective or degenerate heredity" (ibid.: 183–4).

In fact, William Sheldon was far more sympathetic to Lombroso and drew direct connections between his study of constitution and earlier efforts to describe criminal physiognomy. In his *Varieties of Delinquent Youth*, published a year before *Unraveling*, he presented his conclusions on 200 boys studied at the Hayden Goodwill Inn, located in Boston, and also pointed to a majority of mesomorphic cases. William Sheldon now discussed Lombroso at length in relation to his own "*t* component," an attempt to numerically rate "thoroughbredness" in appearances pleasing or displeasing to a "person of average aesthetic perception" (1949: 20–3). Like Hooton, he framed this contribution by criticizing Lombroso's "poorly objectified insights," which had "provided two generations of academic social scientists with a sort of push-over whipping boy." According to William Sheldon, however, his contemporaries' "ego-inflative lectures" describing "what a half-wit Cesare Lombroso had been" simply obscured the ongoing significance of a common project to name the physical features of criminality (ibid.: 757). "At the HGI, and in various penitentiaries," he concluded, "I too have probably seen the same thing that Lombroso and Hooton saw, and I have felt the same frustration because of profound inadequacy both in descriptive vocabulary and in available statistification procedure to reflect and set down for educational purposes what was manifestly there" (ibid.: 159).

While William Sheldon ambivalently described the hopes and shortcomings of his and Lombroso's constitutional vocabulary, the Gluecks ambivalently intercorrelated their somatotype data with myriad other factors while avoiding Lombroso altogether. Their 1956 *Physique and Delinquency* was dedicated to the memory of Hooton but also began by reiterating, "the present work is not animated by any notion of respectful reawakening of the somnolent Lombrosian theory that '*the* criminal' is a distinct species of "atavistic" or of degenerative nature" (Glueck and Glueck 1956: 2). Having set out a wide range of social and mental factors as a "common ground" of delinquency, statistically unrelated to physique, they then set apart the distinctive traits and needs of each somatotype. Mesomorphic delinquents were thus more destructive and sadistic but could be further endangered by emotional instability and conflicts thought "uncharacteristic" of their physique. Meanwhile, the smaller proportion of ectomorphic delinquents were considered especially sensitive to appropriate or inappropriate maternal supervision and affection (ibid.: 217–27, 235–42). More importantly, the "delinquency potential" of a given somatotype was only useful insofar as it nuanced the Gluecks' existing prediction tables (E. T. Glueck 1958). In both explanation and prediction, physique was thus factorized, in line with the Gluecks' insistence on crime causation as a "*totality* of conditions necessary to bring about the delinquency result" (S. Glueck 1960: 297).

The Gluecks' stated disavowal of Lombroso, however, must still be compared with the Lombrosianism implied by their descriptions of criminal somatotypes, especially the tropes of criminality that resurfaced in the criminal mesomorph. As stated above, William Sheldon connected mesomorphy to "somatotonic" traits of aggression, callousness, and even resistance to pain, all evoking the supposed characteristics of the earlier atavistic, born criminal. The Gluecks qualified but also subtly rearticulated these tropes when describing the increased energy of mesomorphs, their parents' accounts of unexplained restlessness and aggression, and their "adventures" into unsupervised street life and crime. Concluding on the "dynamic pattern of delinquency," they thus summarized how:

> In the exciting, stimulating, but little-controlled and culturally inconsistent environment of the underprivileged area, such boys readily give expression to their untamed impulses and their self-centred desires by means of various forms of delinquent behaviour. Their tendencies toward uninhibited energy-expression are deeply anchored in soma and psyche and in the malformations of character during the first few years of life. (Glueck and Glueck 1950: 282)

While the Gluecks gestured at "untamed impulses," William Sheldon was characteristically overt in depicting mesomorphic delinquents as brutal and atavistic. Ending his own series of 200 cases with those of "primary" or "residual" criminality (unmodified by mental "insufficiency" or instability), he regularly compared these boys to prowling tomcats and summarized their fighting ability. One appeared to know " 'by instinct' who are the easy ones from whom he can get what he wants" (Sheldon 1949: 690). Another was noted for "strength and a mastiff-like menace in the face and throughout the body," apparently "[looking] upon life through the eyes of a predator" (ibid.: 716–17). Unlike the Gluecks, William Sheldon included African American adolescents and described one youth "from the heavier West Coast Negro stock" who reportedly moved with "tiger-like suppleness." Alongside his "almost extreme mesomorphy," "predatory" delinquencies, and "thirst for violent altercation," this case was explicitly characterized as a racial and reproductive threat: "He has three passions—for gambling, for white girls, and for suppressing the 'arrogant white race' " (ibid.: 698–9). Moreover, his "resolute" resistance to reform was taken as a sign of future criminality. Conversely, William Sheldon noted his confidence and leadership among other delinquents and called him "something of a hero in his circle, as fighting mesomorphs usually are" (ibid.: 700).

Indeed, the brutality of mesomorphy was also modified by another form of ambivalence toward conflicting tendencies perceived in American masculinity. This was reflected in contemporary psychiatry's depictions of "normal" adolescent delinquency, even characterizing male delinquents as "necessary rebels" exemplifying and renewing American individualism following the Second World War (Mackert 2014). Meanwhile, William Sheldon regularly described mesomorphic predation alongside accounts of athletic, social, and even political prowess. Clustered around mesomorphy, his delinquent cases were therefore also associated with "energetic vitality and freedom from inhibition, two cardinal factors in success at most of the things men undertake" (Sheldon 1949: 745). William Sheldon similarly regarded the Gluecks' 500 delinquents as a "varsity of young criminals" showing "an energy and lusty enterprise equal to that which the 500 best young football players in Massachusetts bring to bear on their football objective" (1957: 125–6). Such comparisons reappeared following long digressions on the "delinquency" of recent war, overpopulation, and "irresponsible reproduction," through which William Sheldon contextualized and reflected on his cases:

> Probably the majority of them would have failed to play the game in any society, and by the criteria of almost all cultures would have fallen short of reasonable expectations. But among them are a few who seem to have been delinquent to their society not through manifest shortcomings but because of the presence of qualities which in a "right" society (right for them) might have made them heroes, along with Roosevelt, Babe Ruth and Hitler. (Sheldon 1949: 863)

These wildly disparate examples were, for William Sheldon, all visible in the mesomorphic, delinquent body, encapsulating the potential for predation and war as well as success and "heroism."

The Gluecks as Lombrosians

The Gluecks continuously qualified their constitutional results within larger causal complexes while William Sheldon avidly placed constitution at the root of recent and future conflict, catastrophe, and "degeneration of the human organism." Their subsequent reception as Lombrosians was, in any case, shaped by the disciplinary contestation of mid-century criminology. As Laub and Sampson argue, the Gluecks in particular found themselves increasingly marginalized by the consolidation of sociological criminology around the legacy of Edwin Sutherland, his *Principles of Criminology*, and its eventual theory of "differential association." Articulating an overall explanatory framework of delinquent enculturation through association, Sutherland conversely targeted the Gluecks with increasing criticism, "aimed largely at extinguishing their interdisciplinary model so that sociology could establish proprietary rights to criminology" (Laub and Sampson 1991: 1404). Indeed, the especially negative reception of *Unraveling* among sociologists led Sheldon Glueck to eventually characterize its detractors as "fire-breathing chevaliers eager to do battle for that purest queen of the exact sciences, sociology" (S. Glueck 1960: 284). Resistance to somatotyping specifically was meanwhile explained by William Sheldon as a result of the dominance of social science by "a sort of lunatic fringe" (1957: 125).

Much like Hooton before them, The Gluecks and William Sheldon portrayed themselves as embattled "heretics" against sociology. Conversely, sociologists immediately connected their somatotyping to a longer Lombrosian heritage. Following Sutherland's death in 1950, the *American Sociological Review* published "a critique of [William] Sheldon's Varieties of Delinquent Youth" as "probably the last paper that Dr. Sutherland wrote" (Sutherland 1951: 10). Here Sutherland steadily dismantled William Sheldon's subjective scores, meaningless classifications, and eugenic proposals before concluding on the obvious "futility" of the study: "Sheldon is added to the list of Lombroso, Kretschmer, Hooton, and other failures who attempted to demonstrate a physical difference between criminals and non-criminals. Analogous efforts to differentiate criminals from non-criminals as to generic traits of personality have been equally futile" (ibid.: 13). Sutherland identified William Sheldon's somatotyping as a successor to Lombroso's criminal anthropology but, like Lindesmith and Levin, also extended this tradition to broader psychiatric investigations of criminal personality.

Following the Gluecks' publication of *Physique and Delinquency*, critics similarly placed them in an expansive "Lombrosian tradition." Among the negative reviews, sociologist Frank E. Hartung noted a continuing skepticism toward the Gluecks' claims while, in a separate article critiquing sociological methods, he introduced the Gluecks as a foil for his own discipline (Hartung 1958a; 1958b). The critical response to *Unraveling*, according to Hartung, had seen unusual unity among sociologists who rejected the Gluecks methods of sampling, their use of dubious Rorschach testing and somatotyping, and their evident theoretical bias for personal developmental and temperamental factors. Most notably, Hartung presented the Gluecks' study of individuals in contrast to sociology's situational approach and now traced the former back to Lombroso, along with any other psychiatric and pathological conceptions:

> the study of the individual criminal in the fashion popularized by Lombroso has resulted in a succession of conceptions of the criminal as being pathological, as follows:
>
> Psychiatric: neurologically pathological
> Psychiatric: psychopathic
> Psychological: mentally deficient
> Psychological: abnormal personality
> Psychoanalytic: sexually repressed
> Racialistic: inferior race or nationality
> None of these instinctivist, pathological concepts has endured the test of empirical and logical analysis. (ibid.: 711)

The Gluecks had hoped to distance their work from Lombrosianism, which they understood narrowly as a dogma of the atavistic, born criminal. Conversely, their critics regarded them as Lombrosians in a broad sense, continuing a tradition of positivist inquiry into the individual criminal, abnormal or pathological either in body or mind. The Gluecks' place in this succession would be repeated in subsequent decades with the somatotype looming ever larger in the memory of their work. As Laub and Sampson note, the Gluecks would eventually make one sole appearance in Larry Siegel's influential 1983 textbook, *Criminology*, noted for their use of William Sheldon's somatotypes in a section on biocriminology which, naturally, began with Lombroso (Laub and Sampson 1991: 1434; Siegel 1983: 12–30). Having attempted to salvage somatotyping from such connotations as part of an eclectic research program, the Gluecks instead found themselves placed at the end of a defunct biocriminological trajectory alongside Hooton, William Sheldon, and other Lombrosians.

On one hand, the Gluecks' reception as Lombrosians is understandable, especially when considering the familiar tropes of mesomorphy discussed above. Despite other factors and qualifications, the Gluecks still presented a physically distinct, constitutionally abnormal, form of "untamed" criminal, which may lead us to look askance at their stated rejection of Lombroso. Indeed, Kevin Walby and Nicholas

Carrier instead argue that "from Lombroso to the Gluecks, claims about physique, delinquency, as well as the rationale for and means of punishing the criminal body, remain similar, but terms change" so as to remain "palatable" (Walby and Carrier 2010: 273–4). On the other hand, however, by repeating this succession from Lombroso to the Gluecks we risk distorting the former's influence and re-creating an all-too-neat dichotomy between positivist "Lombrosians" and situationist sociologists. Moreover, we risk obscuring the role played by those sociologists in formulating this eclectic "Lombrosian" tradition as a foil to the consolidation of their own discipline.

Recapturing the ambivalence of these biocriminologists reveals their own motivations separate from Lombroso's influence. The Gluecks' interest in somatotyping, placed alongside myriad other factors and social prediction tables, was evidently not motivated by any specifically "Lombrosian" allegiance and whether, from scientific prudence or embarrassment, they were ready to discard him. Opposite the Gluecks, more enthusiastic figures like Hooton and William Sheldon were also ready to belittle Lombroso in promoting their own hopes for a renewed biocriminology. Apart from "Lombrosianism," however, the case of somatotyping also points to broader ambivalence toward the criminal body itself. Criminal mesomorphy suggested ambiguous potential in the masculine bodies it purportedly classified, mixing the danger of crime with physical and social prowess. Meanwhile, varying notions of innocence and incorrigibility left "real" delinquents, sequestered in custodial institutions, open to photographic capture while others were more protected. In turn, the Gluecks' study, and its focus on white boys in particular, must be viewed and compared with other chapters detailing highly racialized and gendered characterizations of embodied criminality as well as broader histories of crime prevention in which the sympathetic correction of white youth frequently contrasts with the fearful and forceful removal of children of color (Chávez-García 2012: 47–70; Di Castri 2023). In this way, criminal somatotypes illustrate how, with or without Lombroso, different bodies have been variously construed as pathological or predatory.

Notes

1. Ethel Sturges Dummer Papers (1689–1962), A-127, Folder 578, Cambridge, MA, Schlesinger Library, Radcliffe Institute (ESDP), Letter of W. Healy to Julia Lathrop, April 4, 1908.
2. ETSGP, Box 31, Folder 1, Letter of E. T. Glueck to Elizabeth Hincks, February 14, 1938.
3. ETSGP, Box 31, Folder 3, "Case Selection," June, 1946.
4. ETSGP, Box 31, Folder 3, "Rules for Selection of List of Delinquent Boys to be considered in Study," September, 1940.
5. ETSGP, Box 31, Folder 4, Letter of E. T. Glueck to Earnest Hooton, November 1, 1939.
6. ETSGP, Box 32, Folder 2, "Definitions," (n.d.).
7. ETSGP, Box 32, Folder 2, [W. H. Sheldon], *Psychology 238 (1940–1941) Harvard University – Description of Traits Defining the Primary Components of Temperament*, 1940–1.
8. ETSGP, Box 32, Folder 3, "Memorandum," November 17, 1939.

9. ETSGP, Box 34, Folder 1, Letter of E. T. Glueck to Herbert Parsons, July 18, 1940.
10. ETSGP, Box 34, Folder 1, Letter of A. Gould to Eleanor Glueck, July 26, 1940.
11. ETSGP, Box 34, Folder 1, Letter of E. T. Glueck to Arthur Gould, September 30, 1940.
12. ETSGP, Box 31, Folder 2, G. F. M[cGrath], "Winning and Maintaining the Cooperation of the Boys," April 1, 1948.
13. ETSGP Box 31, Folder 2, G. F. M[cGrath], "Maintaining the Interest of the Non-Delinquent Boys," April 9, 1948.
14. ETSGP, Box 33, Folder 3, "Procedures in Psychiatric Examination," May 27, 1943.
15. ETSGP, Box 31, Folder 2, G. F. M[cGrath], "Winning and Maintaining the Cooperation of the Boys," April 1, 1948.
16. ETSGP, Box 31, Folder 2, G. F. M[cGrath], "Memorandum to Mrs. Glueck from G.F.M. Re. Procedures Employed in Arranging for the Study of Delinquents and Non-Delinquents," April 1, 1948.
17. ETSGP, Box 32, Folder 2, B. E. M[oulton], "Recommendations Regarding Somatotyping," February 6, 1945.
18. ETSGP, Box 32, Folder 2, Letter of E. T. Glueck to Carl Seltzer, February 16, 1945.
19. ETSGP, Box 32, Folder 2, "Memorandum," January 25, 1940.
20. ETSGP, Box 32, Folder 2, Letter of S. Glueck to Carl Seltzer, January 17, 1945.

19

The Problematic Gravitation of Cesare Lombroso in the Work of José Ingenieros and in the Journal *Archives of Psychiatry and Criminology*

Alejandra Mailhe

Several authors (Geli 1992, Caimari 2009, and Sozzo 2017, among others) emphasize the swift and active reception of Lombroso's *L'uomo delinquente* (1876) in Argentina. This work, read in either Italian or translations into French or Spanish, circulated during a period of "alluvial" immigration to the country, prompting the elite to urgently map out the underworld of the popular classes and the "bad life" (*mala vida*), viewing them as dangerous spaces in need of control.

In Argentina's academic environment, Lombroso's theory of the "born criminal" arrived alongside critiques from both the Italian school (e.g., from Ferri and Garofalo) and the more strongly anti-Lombrosian French school. Due to a certain asynchrony, and the greater freedom afforded by Latin America's peripheral context—along with the emerging nature of intellectual fields in this area—Lombroso's hypotheses were relativized, especially those concerning morphological determinations, with Argentinian criminologists tending to favor multicausal explanations of crime.

This chapter focuses on the critical reception of Cesare Lombroso's work in turn-of-the-century Argentina, particularly as reflected in the journal *Archivos de psiquiatría y criminología*,[1] and in several texts by the psychiatrist, criminologist, and essayist José Ingenieros. The director of the journal, Ingenieros, played a pivotal role in modernizing these disciplines in Argentina and across South America.

This work examines a broad range of sources by Ingenieros and other authors associated with the *Archivos*, analyzing the various rhetorical strategies through which this intellectual circle distanced itself from criminal anthropology. These strategies, ranging from theoretical discussion to a parodic critique of Lombroso himself—a kind of symbolic patricide—reveal how Argentine criminology and psychiatry were consolidated through an open confrontation with Lombroso's ideas. This opposition not only challenged his international prestige but also aimed to reorient these disciplines across Latin America, steering them away from biological determinism.

Archivos's Symbolic Patricide

The *Archivos* played a crucial role in the consolidation of psychiatry and criminology in Argentina and Latin America. Building on the foundation laid by *Criminalogía moderna* (Modern Criminology), a journal directed by the anarchist lawyer Pietro Gori, *Archivos* represented a significant step forward for these disciplines.[2] It facilitated the creation of an influential Latin American network of authors and ideas centered in Buenos Aires. Directed by Ingenieros from 1902 onward,[3] *Archivos*, which was published bimonthly from 1907, functioned as the official organ of the Institute of Criminology, located in the National Penitentiary of Buenos Aires. Notably, the journal was printed by inmates who were also among its subjects of study. The journal's longevity—more than a decade—and the participation of numerous prominent Latin American and European authors made *Archivos* a distinguished platform for exploring certain aspects of the history of ideas linked to Argentine and Latin American positivism, which was hegemonic at the beginning of the century.

The theoretical stances of some works and the journal's emphasis on psychological theories—favoring them over the dominant biological determinism of Lombroso's theses—demonstrate *Archivos*'s effort to establish a new research agenda and to position itself within the various conflicting theoretical models. Through sustained critical engagement, it reinforced Buenos Aires's position as a central hub of knowledge production on a continental scale, capable of integrating other Latin American intellectual centers, which were thus symbolically relegated to the periphery.

The journal's title signaled its intention to follow the model of *Archivio di psichiatria*, founded by Lombroso in Turin in 1880. The deliberate strategy of affiliating with such a prestigious international publication is clear, although the Argentine publication always maintained a critical distance from the Lombrosian criminological model. This differentiation was evident in the journal's greater emphasis on psychological and social factors in explaining the origins of crime and mental illness. It pointed to familial pathological tendencies, which contributors regarded as indicators of a possible hereditary predisposition to pathology. This view encompassed the influence of the family and social environment in early childhood and adolescence as well as social and moral behaviors—including aspects of sexual life—within a broader space of social interaction.

Even in its analysis of specific cases, the journal attributed significant importance to traumatic experiences, proposing that psychological trauma could trigger mental disturbances. For instance, in "Fetichista con hermafrodismo psíquico activo" (Fetishist with Active Psychic Hermaphroditism; Ingenieros 1902a), Ingenieros examined the case of a cultured, bohemian young man from the middle class, who had a habit of masturbating by rubbing against the clothing of passersby in public spaces. Ingenieros dismissed the notion of morphological degeneration in this case (although he briefly mentioned finding some evidence of it),[4] instead focusing on investigating the roots of the young man's sexual fixation, tracing it back to a decisive sexual experience in his childhood or early adolescence. In doing so, Ingenieros implicitly established a framework that went beyond Lombroso's model, one which drew parallels to the later work of Jean-Martin Charcot and even anticipated Freud.[5]

Similarly, Francisco de Veyga's series of articles on "invertidos" (an archaic term for homosexuals and transsexuals) in Buenos Aires also emphasized the psychological origin of pathologies, generally rejecting biological determinism. Even in the only case where de Veyga identified a "congenital inversion" (de Veyga 1902), the tension between biological determinism and biographical experience was not resolved in favor of the former. In addition to acknowledging the psyche's role as a determinant of homosexual pleasure, he highlighted the significance of childhood trauma as the genesis of this "pathology."[6]

This relative distance from biological determinism—whether racial, anatomical-pathological, physiological, or hereditary—was significantly influenced by critiques of Lombroso's theory of the "born criminal." From its first article, "Valor de la psicopatología en la antropología criminal" (The Value of Psychopathology in Criminal Anthropology; 1902c), the journal emphasized psychopathology, with Ingenieros limiting the emphasis on morphological determinants and even proposing a refoundation of the *nuova Scuola* as a "psychopathological school." Furthermore, as we shall see, several explicit remarks by Ingenieros in *Archivos* regarding Lombroso's work confirm the former's greater inclination toward psychology.

The perspective of the journal's director contrasted with the more deferential view of Lombroso held by other Latin American authors who published in *Archivos*. For instance, aligning with the dominant racialist views in Brazilian criminology (perceptible in the work of forensic doctor Raimundo Nina Rodrigues), criminal lawyer Evaristo De Morães published "La teoría lombrosiana del delincuente" (De Morães 1902: 321–33), generally adhering to the Italian master's theory, though with some mild reservations.

This piece elicited a forceful response in "Las teorías de Lombroso ante la crítica" (Lombroso's Theories in the Face of Criticism), where Ingenieros noted that, despite his erudition, the Brazilian author "does not seem to have a clear idea of the Lombrosian doctrine as a whole … He dwells on disputing facts that no one disputes anymore; he refutes doctrines that no one professes anymore … Let us say … that we are not supporters of Lombroso's doctrines taken *strictu sensu*, as De Morães considers them" (Ingenieros 1902b: 334–6). Recalling that this critical distance from the Italian school had been a hallmark of the journal since its inaugural article, Ingenieros went so far as to suggest that De Morães displayed a certain intellectual limitation, accusing him of formulating "myopic criticisms [typical] *of those who do not know how to synthesize* … immersed in the onanistic enjoyment of martyring their brains in search of minute contradictions" (ibid.: 335; italics in the original).

Ingenieros also underlined a paradoxical aspect of Lombroso's reception:

> [Lombroso] has cited as his supporters people who claim not to be so. But the reason is simple: those cited have gathered facts that confirm the ideas of the quoter, and although they claim not to be supporters of Lombroso's ideas, they are in fact so because of their writings. Such is the case, among Argentines, of [José María] Ramos Mejía: Lombroso cites at every turn, in *L'uomo di genio* [1888], his book *La neurosis de los hombres célebres en la historia argentina*, and the

> truth is that Ramos Mejía … has contributed to giving him vigor with his book. (ibid.: 337)

Indeed, in his 1878 essay, Ramos Mejía demonstrated that he had an understanding of psychiatry and anthropology similar to that of Lombroso, although he did not reference Lombroso's studies on genius and madness. He combined the analysis of biographical experiences with the study of skull and facial morphology, seeking evidence of neuroses on both fronts in his examination of the "famous" figures of Argentine leadership.

The paradox noted by Ingenieros reappeared in numerous instances where Lombroso himself made an overly optimistic assessment of the critical reception of his work. For example, in the *Archivio di psichiatria*, alongside a review by Aly Belfàdel of Ingenieros's first article in *Archivos*, two lines were published in which Lombroso praised the courage with which "this strong thinker" defended the "nuova Scuola" against the attacks of French critics, rather comically referencing the inaugural text in which Ingenieros took such a critical stance toward him!

Furthermore, in the prologue to *I criminali nati* (Born Criminals; 1890)—the Italian translation of Luis Maria Drago's *Los hombres de presa* (1888) (The Men of Prey)—Lombroso boasted of the spectacular impact of his *scuola* on Spanish and Portuguese America. He downplayed Drago's criticism of his hypotheses, insisting that the work exemplified "how the acceptance of the new ideas did not harm the originality of research, nor the perfect independence of judgment, for while many are the confirmations of our theories, the criticisms of them are not few" (Lombroso 1890a: XXXV). In this way, Drago's criticisms were reframed as evidence of a broader alignment with Lombroso's theory, thereby neutralizing any challenges by presenting them as part of theory's expanding influence.[7]

Reinforcing his unease with the biological determinism of Brazilian authors, in 1902 Ingenieros published a highly critical review of Nina Rodrigues's *La folie des foules* (The Madness of Crowds) in *Archivos*.[8] He accused Nina Rodrigues of misrepresenting Scipio Sighele's work by overemphasizing the principle of association among the alienated, exaggerating the pathological state of the crowd.[9] According to Ingenieros, delirious crowds could not simply result from the association of alienated individuals; rather, they were the product of mere suggestion, with one alienated person acting upon a crowd of predisposed individuals.

Nina Rodrigues defended himself against this accusation in a public letter published in *Archivos* later that same year, titled "À propos du mémoire: 'La folie des foules'"(About the Memoir: 'The Madness of Crowds'; Nina Rodrigues 1902: 290–3). In this letter, he took a conciliatory stance, seeking to reconcile his views with those of both Sighele and Ingenieros. He cited them to demonstrate his own recognition of the influence that the alienated could exert on neuropaths or degenerates, thus acknowledging the potential for their association.[10] Ingenieros, however, responded harshly in a brief yet forceful note emphasizing their points of disagreement. He even invoked the French language as a tool in their intellectual sparring, boasting of his command of the prestigious language to assert his superiority over his opponent (Ingenieros 1902e: 293–5).

Following this dispute, Brazilian authors became less involved in the journal, likely due to the tensions between these two figures. This suggests that Ingenieros's strong leadership curtailed collaborations that aligned more closely with Lombroso and biological determinism in general.

Despite such sharp criticism, the symbolic prestige of the author of *L'uomo delinquente* was evident in the tribute paid to him by the journal in 1906, during the Sixth International Congress of Criminal Anthropology in Turin—an event that coincided with celebrations marking the retiring master's jubilee. *Archivos* published a dossier on Lombroso, featuring extensive articles by Francisco de Veyga, Cuban lawyer José Antonio González Lanuza (a professor of Criminal Law at the University of Havana), Italian immigrant Emilio Zuccarini (a journalist based in Buenos Aires), and Lombroso himself—his only contribution to *Archivos*.

The dossier was preceded by a full-page portrait of the Turin professor—an unusual move given the journal's typically austere approach to publishing images. Notably, it did not include any contribution from Ingenieros, which—considering his strong leadership in the journal—suggests a certain ambivalence: while he was willing to allow space for a suitable tribute, he did not want to add his own voice to it.

In the dossier, de Veyga celebrated both the recognition of the Italian master at the anthropology congress in Turin—seen as a key moment for his well-deserved, albeit delayed, consecration in old age—and the publication of several volumes dedicated to his work and life. These ranged from a book compiling writings by his disciples and admirers (including Morselli, Sergi, Ferri, Loria, and Sighele) to a biography published by his daughters. In his review of Lombroso's ideas, de Veyga hesitantly noted the professor's somewhat careless writing, almost as an afterthought. However, beyond this minor criticism—and despite his own analyses, which diverged significantly from biological determinism—de Veyga offered some praise, even uncritically accepting the definition of the "born delinquent" as a living reflection "of the millenary past of the species" (de Veyga 1906b: 263). His exaltation reached its peak in his proclamation that Lombroso's work was "holy" due to his "Christian" intention of moving society beyond confinement as punishment toward the idea of the "asylum of reform or pious custody" (ibid.: 271).

The dossier concluded with the article "Mi museo criminal" (My Criminal Museum), in which Lombroso offered his scientific autobiography (1906c). He recounted his beginnings as a military physician and his subsequent obsession with collecting skulls and brains from a diverse array of subjects, including the mentally ill, epileptics, criminals, so-called savages, and even individuals deemed normal. The collection was part of his relentless search for traces of pathology in the morphological features shared by "inferior peoples." Adopting the retrospective tone characteristic of the later stages of his career, Lombroso sought to defend the theses questioned by Ingenieros. He reflected on how his collection of skulls, skeletons, and masks—acquired through various means—had allowed him to realize his ambition of founding a "criminal museum." The museum was not limited to anatomical specimens; it also included daggers and "works of art"—such as sculptures and paintings—created by criminals and madmen, as well as instruments of detention and torture, which he believed illustrated a pattern of repressive cruelty that society was, at last, beginning to overcome.

In 1909, after Lombroso's death, *Archivos* published a brief, unsigned obituary—preceded by the same full-page portrait that had appeared in the 1906 dossier—in the form of a review of a lecture recently given by Ingenieros in his role as professor of experimental psychology. The piece, most likely written by Ingenieros himself, served as the journal's only tribute to the Turinese professor and clearly marked the culmination of the distancing strategy that Ingenieros had initiated in the earlier dossier. While in 1906 the director of *Archivos* had chosen to remain silent so as not to undermine the laudatory objective of the tribute, this text took refuge in the use of the third person, thereby de-emphasizing his role in the journal's editorial group. Slightly tempering the virulence of his earlier interventions, the note stated that Lombroso's theory, "already corrected and expanded by his continuators, is destined to endure in science." However, it also remarked that the master from Turin had produced work "without stopping to pay much attention to the accuracy of his own innovations" ([Ingenieros] 1909: 515). While the audacity of Lombroso's hypotheses was acknowledged as characteristic of a "man of genius," the note also asserted that "his passion for his own doctrines was obsessive, preventing him from exercising the most elementary self-criticism … That is why he incurred many ingenuities and contradictions … He was, therefore, a truly brilliant man, lacking the harmonious and balanced qualities of talent" (ibid.: 516).

Beyond Ingenieros's explicit positions—ranging from nuanced criticism within this final homage to his harshest attacks elsewhere—the journal's increasing distance from Lombroso can also be discerned indirectly in its measured and nonmimetic use of photography. Unlike local publications more closely aligned with Lombroso's approach, such as *Criminalogía moderna* (Modern Criminology), which placed great faith in the supposed truth of the image, *Archivos* used photography to underscore the risks of such a supposedly naïve interpretation. This shift aligned with Ingenieros's social theory, which subtly countered Lombrosianism by highlighting the problem of simulation, particularly the "baroque" theatricality it generated. This perspective emerged precisely when, from a technical point of view, fingerprinting became the dominant method of identification, displacing "thieves' galleries" and Bertillonage, which were more limited techniques.

In parallel to its greater adherence to Lombroso's theses, *Criminalogía moderna* continued to rely on the mimetic illusion of the image and the literal interpretation of faces and bodies as valid criminological indexes, aspiring to read them as "transparent" textualities. In contrast, *Archivos* undertook a sort of anti-mimetic turn, in line with Ingenieros's emphasis on the "social simulator." For instance, the portraits edited by Juan Vucetich accompanying the article "Delirio sistematizado religioso" (Religious Systemized Delirium; Vucetich 1902: 164–71) presented starkly different images of the same individual—the murderer Cavellone—before and after his internment at Melchor Romero. The transformation illustrated how the effects of confinement rendered identification of the subject impossible, as Cavellone metamorphosed from a messianic prophet to an inmate of a hospice.

Even more prolific in its anti-mimetic approach was the gallery of Buenos Aires "invertidos" (inverted people) studied by de Veyga. The photographs captured the extreme identity transformations achieved through gender simulation, facilitated by both bodily interventions and modifications to the images themselves. This photographic gallery, featuring trans women posing in the attire of bourgeois ladies, implicitly underscored the precarious equivocality of images in defining identity, revealing their fragility as criminological documents. This skepticism toward the transparency of images paralleled the critical distance from Lombrosian determinism: in both cases, the assumed relationship between appearance and essence was called into question.

The Trip to Europe and the Dethronement of the Father

In 1905, Ingenieros was sent by the Argentine government to participate in the Fifth International Congress of Psychology in Rome and to study European penitentiary systems. At the same time, the director of the newspaper *La Nación* hired him as a correspondent to report on his European journey. Several chronicles that Ingenieros wrote about this trip are crucial for understanding his perception of Lombroso and reinforce his self-legitimization as a scientist through his persistent opposition to the master from Turin.

Ingenieros's attack on Lombroso was particularly sharp in the chronicle "Lombroso y los hombres pobres" (Lombroso and the Poor Men; 1906 [1905]).[11] The director of *Archivos*—who presided over the fourth section of the Rome congress alongside Ferri, Sommer, and Lombroso himself (a section dedicated to presenting works on the Italian criminological school)—began by declaring that while Lombroso had been a brilliant man, he was not intelligent. Ingenieros claimed that Lombroso's "brain [is] always nebulous … like a perpetual night of tempest … Lombroso [has] that mental peculiarity: genius sparks and absolute lack of talent" (Ingenieros 1906: 45). Moreover, he remarked, "he [does] not think, he guess[es]; he play[s] blind man's buffoonery with scientific ideas." While he had "some truly brilliant intuitions" (ibid.: 45), these were only valuable because they had been developed by others; on their own, they lacked merit:

> Lombroso could not have created a solid body of doctrine or started a systemic school [because] he lacks the two fundamental attitudes of intelligence: the critical spirit that allows analysis, and the generalizing spirit that makes synthesis possible. These two paths … were never opened in the dense undergrowth of his cerebration. (ibid.: 46)

In this context, Ingenieros implicitly applied the category of "mesological" simulator to Lombroso, a concept he had introduced in his essay *La simulación en la lucha por la vida* (Simulation in the Struggle for Life; Ingenieros 1996a). He identified Lombroso with what he would later describe in *El hombre mediocre* (The Mediocre Man; Ingenieros 1996b): a figure of moral and intellectual mediocrity.

In "Lombroso y los hombres pobres," Ingenieros delivered a second blow to the master from Turin by asserting that "Lombroso's *school* constitutes an interesting phenomenon of collective psychology … No one believes in him without reservations … but everyone calls him Master … he is a symbol; he is the standard of a new scientific current [in which the disciples form] an assembly of unbelieving priests, a council of idolaters who worship him out of habit, but without faith" (Ingenieros 1906: 46; italics in the original). Ingenieros ironically observed that, by the end of the congress, the attendees were eager "to say that they had argued with Lombroso," even though it had been a long and insubstantial debate, "as if the contact with the mature celebrity could infect the germ of the desired glory to come" (ibid.: 49). These passages suggest, according to Ingenieros's own theoretical framework, that Lombroso's hollow prestige was sustained through the simulation of his disciples, who derived symbolic benefit from him in their struggle for intellectual survival.

In the same chronicle, Ingenieros pointed out that Lombroso was absent on the day he was supposed to preside over the debate, appearing instead when Ingenieros was meant to take the lead. He framed this situation as a pivotal moment for gauging the balance of power. In narrating Lombroso's "triumphal entry," the director of *Archivos* offered a provocative Lombrosian analysis of Lombroso's own physiognomy:

> A short, rather thick, seventyish-looking little man entered the classroom, with a bushy whitish-yellow mustache and a small goatee of the same color; a misshapen head, a physiognomy like many others, bulging eyes, a nose adorned with glasses, a thick, loose neck, a bag-like body, short legs and slow movements … He speaks with a slight dialectal accent … His naive and satisfied face seems to have a smile for each of those present, for in each one he sees a disciple or an admirer. (ibid.: 48)

Furthermore, Ingenieros subtly undermined Lombroso by presenting him as "the precursor of modern criminology," eliciting an astonished look from Ferri, who asked him "in a low voice and with a kindly smile: 'do you think him only a precursor?'" Ferri seemed to expect Ingenieros to correct himself by referring to Lombroso as the "master," but this did not occur.

Not satisfied with this disavowal, the director of *Archivos* made a point of emphasizing his disagreements with the Turin professor during every presentation at the congress, including his own. In his talk, Ingenieros argued that psychological traits were more significant than physical ones in the study of criminals. He also insisted, as he did in other texts, on warning that in every session at the congress Lombroso naively underestimated the criticisms of the speakers, instead choosing to enthusiastically—or stubbornly—expound the full validity of his own ideas.

Given that the chronicle was aimed at the broad readership of *La Nación* in Argentina, it is evident that Ingenieros was engaging in a form of symbolic patricide, particularly effective for his own self-legitimization. He staged the dethronement of the father figure within his own intellectual field, first for the readers of *La Nación* in the year of the congress, and later for the potentially larger audience of the book published in Spain in 1906.

In addition, Ingenieros introduced a new classification of criminals at the congress, based on the study of psychopathological characteristics, directly challenging Ferri's model. This move prompted Ferri to question him in return.[12] By asserting his own theoretical framework, the director of *Archivos* once again undermined the authority of the "nuova Scuola," positioning himself as an intellectual equal to the "center."[13] This stance directly contradicted Lombroso's view of South American intellectuals as mere repeaters of theoretical models originating from Europe.

Ingenieros even suggested that Lombroso's presence might hinder the renewal of his own school, ironically wondering whether it would be necessary to wait for Lombroso's disappearance "so as not to embitter his old age with these heterodoxies, imposed by the new scientific advances" (ibid.: 51).

Shortly afterward, in *Criminología*, a compilation of works produced between 1900 and 1911, Ingenieros asserted his role as the first person to study psychological anomalies as a means of classifying criminals, thereby defending his theoretical contribution within an "equitable" international context. He also continued to question the study of morphological anomalies, criticizing "the noisy discoveries that have spread the fame of the psychiatrist from Turin throughout the world" (Ingenieros 2012: 113). Ingenieros even celebrated the fact that "Professor M. L. Patrizi, Lombroso's successor in the chair of criminal anthropology in Turin, inaugurated his courses … with a lecture on 'La fase psicologica dell'antropologia criminale' [The Psychological Phase of Criminal Anthropology] *in accordance with the doctrine sustained in all our* [my] *previous writings on the subject*" (ibid.: 121; my italics).

Beyond—or alongside—his theoretical differences with Lombroso regarding the biological determinism of crime, it is important to note that Ingenieros sometimes exhibited extreme racialist views, which conflicted with his own emphasis on psychological and environmental motivations for crime. A paradigmatic example appears in his chronicle "Las razas inferiores" (The inferior races; Ingenieros 1919), written during his stop in Cape Verdeen en route to the 1905 congress in Rome. In this piece, the island symbolized a hell that the traveler must descend into before continuing his journey to the cradle of Western civilization.

As a supposed witness to the primitive savagery of Black people, Ingenieros declared that "men of inferior races should not be politically and juridically our equals … they should not be considered 'persons'" (ibid.: 164). This judgment revealed a disturbing convergence with the ideas of Nina Rodrigues, the author he had recently dethroned in *Archivos*, yet who, in *As raças humanas e a responsabilidade penal no Brasil* (Human Races and Penal Responsibility in Brazil; Nina Rodrigues 1894), similarly defended the intellectual, moral, and juridical asymmetry between white and Black people. Rejecting any "sentimentalism," Ingenieros further asserted that "whatever is done in favor of the lower races is unscientific; at most, they could be protected so that they may become pleasantly extinct" (Ingenieros 1919: 165). A similar idea appeared in "Lombroso y los hombres pobres," where he agreed with Niceforo that the lower classes constituted a "backward race" (Ingenieros 1906: 54), possessing beliefs and customs akin to those of "primitive peoples." However, in this instance Ingenieros acknowledged that economic conditions, rather than biological determinations, played a decisive role in shaping these social differences.

A Final Blow to Lombroso

Another aspect of the confrontation between Ingenieros and Lombroso concerns their differing views on Spiritism. Lombroso, initially skeptical, became convinced of the "truth" of this practice after conducting a study of Spiritists, highlighting the case of medium Eusapia Palladino.[14] In contrast, Ingenieros strongly discredited esoteric phenomena in several of his writings, despite being willing to carry out some experiments, which he ultimately deemed unsuccessful. For example, during his 1905 trip, he carried out an experiment on the "transmission of thought." The failure of these experiments only deepened his suspicion of supernatural phenomena. In his chronicle "La transmisión del pensamiento" (The Transmission of Thought), he stated: "telepathy, mediumship, apparitions of ghosts, prophetic dreams, etc.—we have found nothing that stands up to severe scientific criticism" (Ingenieros 2009b: 291).

This fight against esotericism highlights another facet of Ingenieros's attack on Lombroso and other prominent scientists (such as Charles Richet, a professor of Physiology in France) for their adherence to Spiritism. In "Últimas notas de un congreso" (Last Notes on a Congress) (Ingenieros 2009a: 60), Ingenieros openly criticized these colleagues, portraying the medium as a simple person under suggestion and associating Spiritism with a primitive stage in the interpretation of natural phenomena. Ingenieros even identified himself as a "fumist" simulator (the "superior" model in *La simulación en la lucha por la vida*) when recounting a deception he perpetrated against Camille Flammarion: he sent Flammarion two fabricated accounts of "really extraordinary … apparitions of the deceased," which convinced the "inveterate spiritist" to the point that he included them in *Lo desconocido y los problemas psíquicos* (Unknown and Psychic Problems; Ingenieros 2009b: 60).

Ingenieros maintained that the interest in Spiritism exhibited by some scientific minds, including Lombroso and Richet, was a symptom of the mental decay of old age. For instance, in the chronicle "Siluetas" (Silhouettes; 1906; Ingenieros 2009c), he attacked Richet without hesitation, bluntly diagnosing him as "hopelessly ill with senile mysticism … It is saddening to talk to him about spiritism, mediumship, and ghosts; he talks like an old woman from the countryside, and it is miraculous that he does not cross himself" (Ingenieros 2009c: 197). Ingenieros mockingly recalled a famous séance held in Algeria, where Richet supposedly verified the materialization of a spirit, even managing to capture the phenomenon in a photograph. Ingenieros analyzed every detail of this "materialization" and dismissed it as crude staging.[15]

The discrediting of Lombroso due to his esoteric interests extended to the Argentine intellectual and psychiatrist Aníbal Ponce, a disciple of Ingenieros. In his chronicle "Un cónclave de metapsíquicos" (A Conclave of Metapsychics, a title referencing Ingenieros's "Un cónclave de psicólogos"), Ponce reflected on esotericism in science, drawing on a 1930 congress of "psychic sciences" and revisiting classic examples, including Lombroso and Richet. Taking up his mentor's aggressive stance, Ponce stated that "the most brilliant man of science can be a perfect fool outside of it" (Ponce 1946: 304).

In addition to recalling Richet's experience in Algeria, Ponce narrated a similarly disqualifying anecdote about Lombroso. The famous Belgian magician and mentalist Jean Lambert Pickman publicly confessed to having deceived Lombroso, who had become obsessed with studying his paranormal powers.[16] Ponce described how Pickman, "with the perverse pleasure of the ignoramus who indulges in the luxury of mocking a wise man, but also with the glee of the clever man who takes pleasure in deceiving a fool" (ibid.: 304), grew tired of being studied as a "case" by Lombroso. Thus, "between pleismographs and smoked drums," Pickman proposed to test his "psychic fluid" directly on Lombroso. After positioning himself behind him and taking him by the jacket, he pushed Lombroso, leaving him "enchanted" by the "paranormal" manifestation.[17] Ponce concluded his desacralization by imagining a conference of sages like Richet and Lombroso recounting their esoteric experiences, portraying it as a "grotesque" spectacle that would "repay the routine of living for a long time" (ibid.: 305).

Brief Concluding Remarks

Lombroso's theses, which emphasized biological determinism as an irreversible fatality, contradict the necessity of integrating European immigration into Argentina with traditional cultural substrates—a vital element of national consolidation. The reformism prevalent in *Archivos* served to counter this determinism, instead highlighting psychological and social variables as the primary causes of crime and mental pathology.

Ingenieros's control over the journal is evident not only in his explicit critiques of Lombroso's readings but also in other aspects. This includes the fierce controversies he engaged in with Latin American authors who were more respectful of Lombroso, as well as more subtle approaches, such as the journal's cautious and nonmimetic use of photography. *Archivos* underscored the risks of naive interpretations of photography, aligning with Ingenieros's social theory. In contrast to Lombrosianism, he focused on the issues of individual and collective simulation "in the struggle for life," drawing attention to the baroque theatricality it produced.

At a pivotal moment in the consolidation of disciplines like criminology and psychiatry, the reception of Lombroso became a key measure of the balance of power between local intellectuals and those of the "center." Ingenieros viewed himself as Lombroso's equal and embraced confrontation in his efforts to establish criminology at the expense of criminal anthropology. His interventions ranged from his academic questioning of Lombroso, which maintained a level of scholarly formality, to engaging in a form of parodic desacralization. This included not only applying Lombrosian analysis to Lombroso's own physiognomy but also ridiculing his esoteric beliefs. Ultimately, the critical reception of Lombroso served as a valuable tool for Ingenieros to consolidate his own scientific authority and to champion the "civilizing" potential of Argentina.

Notes

1. Hereafter referred to as *Archivos.*
2. *Criminalogía moderna* was one of the first criminology journals in Buenos Aires. With the involvement of important figures from the local elite, including Ingenieros himself, the journal maintained a moderate distance from Lombroso. Under the

influence of Ferri and Garofalo, it shifted its focus toward explanations of crime rooted in social causes.

3. The central role of Ingenieros as the director of *Archivos* is evident in his efforts to shape the entire agenda of criminological and psychiatric positivism across South America. Between 1902 and 1913, he published ninety signed articles, in addition to numerous unsigned notes in other sections of the journal. He also contributed to all the texts published in the journal, including those authored by others (Bagú 1953: 76).
4. He stated, in a succinct and formal manner: "The examination of this patient reveals some degenerative morphological characters, which are unnecessary to detail" (Ingenieros 1902a: 618).
5. On the development of Jean-Martin Charcot's theory—including its later stage, which considers that hysteria may not solely depend on a physical wound but rather on some kind of traumatic experience—see Gauchet and Swain (2002). Ingenieros actively engages with the theories associated with the French school of La Salpêtrière (the hospital where Chalcot worked and taught), while acknowledging the shift in the central role that hysterics had played in France during the 1890s. He also reflected on the dogmatic tendencies of Charcot's work as perpetuated by his later disciples and even critiqued the amplifications applied to the concept of "suggestion" from the "School of Nancy's" point of view (e.g., in "Interpretación científica del hipnotismo y la sugestión" (Scientific Interpretation of Hypnotism and Suggestion; Ingenieros 1903a: 355–65).
6. The patient's account suggested a history of abuse by a teacher during childhood. De Veyga further posited that "it is possible that if the initial sexual sensations had been elicited by female individuals, the psycho-sexual images would have been formed normally, either superimposing or overshadowing the congenital tendencies. There is no doubt that the education of sexual functions ... plays a significant role in determining whether inversion occurs in congenitally predisposed subjects" (de Veyga 1902: 47–8).
7. Alongside this strategy, which inflated his own success and downplayed opposition, Lombroso presented a hierarchical and unidirectional view of theoretical production. He characterized Italy as a conservative nation, but one with innovative thinkers whose theories were interpreted by innovative peoples—such as those in South America—who were, however, deemed conservative thinkers incapable of developing their own ideas. Thus, Lombroso argued that while his school faced resistance in Europe, it found considerable support in the New World (Lombroso 1890a: XXXIX).
8. This article by Nina Rodrigues, which explores crowd psychology in the context of the millenarian movement of Canudos, was first published in the *Annales médico-psychologiques* (Medical Psychological Annals; Paris, 1901) and subsequently criticized by Ingenieros in the *Archivos* (1902d: 188–9).
9. Scipio Sighele was an Italian psychologist, sociologist, and criminologist, a pioneer in the psychology of the masses. His work was influenced by Lombroso and also entered into dialogue with Gabriel Tarde, besides having an impact on the work of Gustave Le Bon. See, for example, *La folla delinquente* (The Criminal Crowd; 1891).
10. Nina Rodrigues insisted that this capacity should not be underestimated, as demonstrated by collective rebellions in mental asylums, where the alienated could associate, albeit with certain limitations and as an exception.
11. A first version of this chronicle was written while Ingenieros attended the congress in Rome and was published by *La Nación* in Buenos Aires in June 1905. It is worth noting that Ingenieros was representing the Argentine government as physician while also serving as a traveling correspondent for the prestigious Buenos Aires newspaper. A second edition—which includes differences resulting from reordering as well as the

types of additions and deletions that Ingenieros himself carried out on many of the texts he reedited—corresponds to the book *Italia en la ciencia, en la vida y en el arte* (Italy in Science, in Life and in Arts; edited in Valencia in 1906), which is the version that is cited here. In this edition, "Lombroso y los hombres pobres" (Lombroso and the Poor Men) appears alongside three other chronicles about the same congress. Bearing in mind the dates of the edition, it does not seem that Ingenieros waited for Lombroso's death to question his authority, even though the fact that the chronicles on the congress were first published in a Buenos Aires newspaper—and not in Europe—may have softened the initial impact of such an attack.

12. Ingenieros did not delve deeply into the classification he proposed, which is understandable if one takes into consideration the massive readership of *La Nación,* to whom the chronicle was initially targeted. However, he noted that the following day, the newspaper *Avanti,* directed by Ferri himself, acknowledged that Ingenieros "revealed in the controversy the vast psychological, psychopathological, sociological, and legal preparation that served as the basis for his new classification" (Ingenieros 1906: 51). The *Avanti* article added that the discussions "announce the imminence of a new orientation in the study of criminals, completing the ideas of the Italian Positive School itself ....The study of anthropological anomalies in criminals is bound to pave the way for the study of their psychological abnormalities" (ibid.: 51).
13. Not coincidentally, in "Un cónclave de psicólogos" (A Conclave of Psychologists), Ingenieros defined the conference as an ideal space for universal fraternization, emphasizing the transcendent nature of scientific knowledge. The conflicts he recorded did not pertain to the center/periphery dichotomy but rather to the tension between spiritualist psychology (which he considered in retreat) and experimental psychology" (Ingenieros 1919: 151–2).
14. His interest in these issues would materialize, for example, in the publication of the book *Ricerche sui fenomeni ipnotici e spiritici* (Research on Hypnotic and Spiritual Phenomena; Lombroso 1909b).
15. The episode was also addressed in *Archivos* by the Parisian scientist Paul Valentin in "Fantasmas y espíritus materializados" (Ghosts and Materialized Spirits; Valentin 1906: 40–4), which analyzed the same séance.
16. In addition, Lombroso became obsessed with the study of the Italian medium Eusapia Palladino, also taken up by Ingenieros in order to discredit Lombroso. in order to discredit Lombroso (Ingenieros 2009b: 59–60).
17. In the Lombroso Museum there is a letter from Pickman (in which he identified himself as "Liseur de pensées" [Mind reader]) inviting Lombroso (and Professor Giovanni Lava) to study him at the hotel where he was staying, on March 18, 1890. https://lombrosoproject.unito.it/en/correspondence-detail/?id=3218

References

"A Project of a System of Statistic Applicable to the Study of Mental Disease, Approved by the International Congress of Alienist of 1867" (1869–70), *The American Journal of Insanity*, 26: 49–52.

"A Psychic Suggestion" (1894a), *The Helena Independent*, 35 (41), March 30: 3.

"A Psychic Suggestion" (1894b), *Lincoln County Leader*, 2 (9), May 3: 3.

"A Roman Séance" (1894), *The Morning News*, September 12: 5.

"A Study of Criminal Types" (1886a), *The McCook Tribune*, 5 (12), August 19: 6.

"A Study of Criminal Types" (1886b), *New Ulm Weekly Review*, 9 (34), August 25: 7.

"A Theory of Criminality" (1886), *Public Opinion*, 1, July 10: 254–5.

"A Woman's Heart" (1892), *The Seattle Post – Intelligencer*, 22 (90), August 14: 4.

Abascal, H. (1930), "La obra cientifica de Israel Castellanos," *Revista Bimestre Cubana*, 16: 199–209.

Actes du premier congrès international d'anthropologie criminelle. Biologie et sociologie (Rome, novembre 1885) (1886–7), Turin: Bocca.

Aguirre, C. (1996), "The Lima Penitentiary and the Modernization of Criminal Justice in Nineteenth-Century Peru," in R. D. Salvatore and C. Aguirre (eds.), *The Birth of the Penitentiary in Latin America: Essays on Criminology, Prison Reform, and Social Control, 1830–1940*, 44–77, Austin: University of Texas Press.

Aguirre, C. (1998), "Crime, Race, and Morals: The Development of Criminology in Peru 1890–1930," *Crime, History & Societies*, 2 (2): 73–90.

Aguirre, C. (2004), "'Los irrecusables datos de la estadística del crimen': la construcción social del delito en la Lima de mediados del siglo XIX," in C. McEvoy (ed.), *La experiencia burguesa en el Perú (1840–1940)*, 309–29, Frankfurt: Vervuert/Iberoamericana.

Aguirre, C. (2005), *The Criminals of Lima and Their Worlds. The Prison Experience, 1850–1935*, Durham, NC: Duke University Press.

Albornoz, M. (2014), "Pietro Gori en la Argentina (1898–1902): anarquismo y cultura," in P. Bruno (ed.), *Visitas culturales a la Argentina, 1898–1936*, 23–49, Buenos Aires: Biblos.

Albornoz, M. (2021), *Cuando el anarquismo causaba sensación. La sociedad argentina entre el miedo y la fascinación por los ideales libertarios*, Buenos Aires: Siglo XXI.

Albrecht, P. (1884), "Sur la fossette vermienne du crâne des mammifères," *Bulletin de la Société Royale Belge d'Anthropologie*, 2: 138–57.

Albuquerque, W. (2009), *O jogo da dissimulação. Abolição, raça e cidadania no Brasil*, São Paulo: Companhia da Letras.

Alvarez, M. C. (2002), "A Criminologia no Brasil ou como tratar desigualmente os desiguais," *Dados Revista de Ciências Sociais*, 45 (4): 677–704.

Alvarez, M. C. (2003), *Bacharéis, Criminologistas e Juristas: Saber jurídico e Nova Escola Penal no Brasil*, São Paulo: IBCCRIM.

Alvarez, M. C., and F. Salla (2018), "Os novos contornos do bacharelismo liberal: uma análise da trajetória de Candido Motta (1870–1942)," *Política & Sociedade*, 17 (39): 86–120.

Alvarez, M. C., F. Salla and L. A. F. Souza (2003), "A Sociedade e a Lei: o Código Penal de 1890 e as novas tendências penais na Primeira República," *Justiça & História*, 3 (6): 97–130.

Amador, J. (2016), "Caught between Crime and Disease: Chinese Exclusion and Immigration Restrictions in Early Twentieth-Century Cuba," in Z. M. Rivas and D. Lee-Di-Stefano (eds.), *Imagining Asia in the Americas*, 85–103, New Brunswick: Rutgers University Press.

America & Lewis Hine: Photographs 1904–1940 (1977), New York: Aperture.

"American Prison Systems" (1892), *The Evening World*, April 23: 2.

Andrée, R. (1881), *Zur Volkskunde der Juden. Mit einer Karte über die Verbreitung der Juden in Mitteleuropa*, Bielefeld: Velhagen & Klasnig.

Ansolabehere, P. (2012), *Literatura y anarquismo en Argentina (1879–1910)*, Rosario: Beatriz Viterbo.

"Antropologia contro antropologia" (1886), *Rivista penale di dottrina, legislazione e giurisprudenza*, 23: 244–8.

Arnedo Gómez, M. (2022), "Fernando Ortiz's Transculturation: Applied Anthropology, Acculturaction, and Mestizaje," *The Journal of Caribbean Anthropology*, 27 (1–2): 123–45.

Arnold, A. B. (1893), "Notes on Vital Statistics in Relation to the Jews," *The Reform Advocate*, October 28: 174.

Artières, P. (2013), *Clinique de l'écriture: une histoire du regard médical sur l'écriture*, Paris: La Découverte.

Artom, P. (1900), "Les Tatuages. Studio psicologico e medico-legale sui delinquenti e militari dello Stato del Messico," *APS*, 21 (2): 512–15.

Artur, A. T. (2011), *As origens do Presídio de Mulheres do estado de São Paulo*, São Paulo: Universidade de São Paulo.

"As to that English Screed on American Reformatories" (1892), *The Prison Mirror*: 5 (45), June 16: 1.

"Attraverso la stampa. Stampa inglese. Il Genio, la pazzia e la delinquenza fra gli Ebrei" (1908), *Il Corriere Israelitico*, October 31: 173–5.

Bagú, S. (1953), *Vida ejemplar de José Ingenieros*, Buenos Aires: El Ateneo.

Balibar, E. (2008), "Racism Revisited: Sources, Relevance, and Aporias of a Modern Concept," *PMLA*, 123 (5): 1630–9.

Bambarén, C. A. (1930), *Casos de Clínica Criminológica*, Lima: Sanmarti y Cía Impresores.

Barnes, H. (2013), "The Struggle of Races and Social Groups as a Factor in the Development of Political and Social Institutions: An Exposition and Critique of the Sociological System of Ludwig Gumplowicz," *The Journal of Race Development*, 9 (4): 394–419.

Barrios, M. C. (1891), "Discurso pronunciado por el catedrático de la Facultad de Medicina, Dr. Manuel C. Barrios, en la ceremonia de apertura del año escolar de 1891," *La Gaceta Judicial*, Lima, March 31–April 1.

Barros Sazo, V. (2009), "*Enferma de crimen … La mujer criminal en el discurso médico-científico. Valparaíso-Santiago, 1890–1950*," Bachelor's diss., Departamento de Ciencias Históricas, Universidad de Chile, Santiago.

Barros Mendez, L. (1890a), "La nueva escuela penal italiana," *El Diario Judicial*, Lima, December 4–6.

Barros Méndez, L. (1890b), "La nueva escuela penal italiana," *Revista Forense Chilena*, 6: 241–50.
Barsotti, E. M. (2021), *At the Roots of Italian Identity: "Race" and "Nation" in the Italian Risorgimento, 1796–1870*, London: Routledge.
Bass, P. (2019) "Cesare Lombroso and the Anarchists," *Journal of the Study of Radicalism*, 13 (1): 19–42.
Beard, G. M. (1881), *American Nervousness: Its Causes and Consequences, a supplement to nervous exhaustion (neurasthenia)*, New York: G. P. Putnam's Sons.
Beca, M. (1898), *Antropolojía i antropometría criminal. Estado de la cuestión. Estudio presentado al V Congreso Científico Jeneral Chileno de 1898*, Santiago: Imprenta Cervantes.
Becker, P., and R. F. Wetzell, eds. (2006), *Criminals and Their Scientists: The History of Criminology in International Perspective*, Cambridge: Cambridge University Press.
Beirne, P. (1993), *Inventing Criminology*, Albany: State University of New York Press.
Ben Plotkin, M. (2021), *José Ingenieros: El hombre que lo quería todo*, Buenos Aires: Edhasa.
Benedikt, M. (1881), *Anatomical Studies upon Brains of Criminals*, New York: W. Wood.
Benítez-Rojo, A. (2001), *The Repeating Island. The Caribbean and the Postmodern Perspective*, Durham: Duke University Press.
Benton-Cohen, K. (2018), *Inventing the Immigration Problem*, Cambridge, MA: Harvard University Press.
Bertarelli, E. (1922), "La "penitenciaria" di San Paulo (Brasile)," *AAC*, 42: 26–30.
Bertonio, L. (1612), *Vocabulario de la Lengua Aymara*, Compañia de Iesus Iuli Pueblo, Pueblo: Francisco del Canto.
Bingham, T. A. (1908a), "Foreign Criminals in New York," *North American Review*, September: 383–94.
[Bingham, T. A.] (1908b), "The Editor's Diary: Jewish Criminality in New York," *North American Review*, October: 639–40.
Bivar, C., R. Campos, F. Pereira and S. de Matos, eds. (2017), *A nova escola de antropologia do Recife: ideias, personagens e instituições*, Recife: Editora UFPE.
Blanckaert, C. (1987), "Les vicissitudes de l'angle facial' et les débuts de la craniométrie (1765–1875)," *Revue de synthèse*, 4 (3–4): 417–53.
Blanckaert, C. (2009), *De la Race á l'Évolution. Paul Broca et l'anthropologie française (1850–1900)*, Paris: L'Hartmattan.
Blumenthal S. L. (2022), "Positivism's Humbugs: Criminology and Its Cranks in Progressive America," in M. Pifferi (ed.), *The Limits of Criminological Positivism: The Movement for Criminal Law Reform in the West, 1870–1940*, 196–230, London: Routledge.
Boas, F. (1911), *Changes in Bodily Form of Descendants of Immigrants*, 38, *Reports*, U.S. Immigration Commission, Washington, DC: Government Printing Office.
Boas, F. (1917), "'Inventing a Great Race,' a Review of *The Passing of the Great Race* by Madison Grant," *The New Republic*, 9, January 13: 305–8.
"Bonfigli on Moral Insanity" (1879–80), *The American Journal of Insanity*, 36: 476–96.
"Book Reviews. The Criminal. By Havelock Ellis. London, Walter Scott; New York, Scribner & Weford" (1890), *Science*, 15 (385), June 20: 376–7.
Borges, V. (2016), "Abandonados e pervertidos, ou em perigo de o ser: Biopoder e práticas de normalização dos menores enviados à Penitenciária de Florianópolis (SC, década de 1930)," *Trashumante: Revista Americana de Historia Social*, 8: 176–99.

Borges, V., F. Salla and C. Wit (2022), "'So That in the Practice of Good Manners, She Will Find a Dignified and Happy Life': Institutional Practices towards Incarcerated Women (Brazil, 1930s)," in A. P. Barbosa-Fohrmann and S. Caponi (eds.), *Latin American Interdisciplinary Perspectives on Bioethics and Disabilities*, The International Library of Bioethics, vol. 102, 139–51, Cham: Springer.

Bosc, O. (2003), "De la *folla delinquente* à la *folla cultura*: Scipio Sighele et Pasquale Rossi prophètes italiens de la modernité au tournant du siècle," *Laboratoire italien*, 4, 37–56.

Bovo, E. (2021), *Pensée de la foule, pensée de l'inconscient. Généalogie de la psychologie de la foule (1875–1895)*, Besançon: Presses Universitaires de Franche Comté.

Bovo, E. (2024), "The 'Psychiatric-Zoological Theory' of the Phenomena of Political Action," in S. Montaldo and C. Cilli (eds.), *The Lombroso Museum*, 95–100, Turin: Hapax.

Brangier, V. (2008), *La fragilidad de la simbiosis médico-judicial y la producción de una antropología criminal. Juzgados del Crimen de Santiago, 1874–1906,* Master's diss., Universidad de Chile, Santiago.

Brinton, D. (1890), *Races and Peoples. Lectures on the Science of Ethnography*, New York: Hodges.

Bronfman, A. (2004), *Measures of Equality: Social Science, Citizenship, and Race in Cuba, 1902–1940*, Chapel Hill: University of North Carolina Press.

Bronfman, A. (2007a), "Mismeasured Women: Gender and Social Science on the Eve of Female Suffrage in Cuba, in Gender, Sexuality and Power in Latin America since Independence," in W. E. French and K. E. Bliss (eds.), *Gender, Sexuality and Power in Latin America since Independence*, 71–86, Lanham, MD: Rowman & Littlefield.

Bronfman, A. (2007b), "The Allure of Technology: Photographs, Statistics and the Elusive Female Criminal in 1930s Cuba," *Gender & History*, 19 (1): 60–77. https://doi.org/10.1111/j.1468-0424.2007.00464.x.

Brusa, E. (1886), El Tercer Congreso Internacional Penitenciario y el Antropológico-Criminal," *Revista Jurídica*, 3: 1061–74, 1261–72.

Buffington, R. (2001), *Criminales y ciudadanos en el México moderno*, Mexico City: Siglo XXI Editores.

Bullough, V. L. (1988), "Katherine Bement Davis, Sex Research, and the Rockefeller Foundation," *Bulletin of the History of Medicine*, 62 (1): 74–89.

Bustos, J. (1983), "Estado y control: la ideología del control y el control de la ideología," in Roberto Bergalli; Juan Bustos Ramírez; Carlos Gonzàlez Z.; Teresa Miralles; Ángel de Sola; Carles Viladas (eds.), *El pensamiento criminológico, vol. II. Estado y control,* Bogotá: Temis.

Caimari, L. (2004), *Apenas un delincuente: Crimen, castigo y cultura em la Argentina, 1880–1955*, Buenos Aires: Siglo XXI.

Caimari, L., ed. (2007), *La ley de los profanos. Delito, justicia y cultura en Buenos Aires (1870–1940)*, Buenos Aires: Universidad de San Andrés-F.C.E.

Caimari, L. (2009), "L' America Latina," in S. Montaldo and P. Tappero (eds.), *Cesare Lombroso cento anni dopo*, 193–201, Turin: UTET.

Cajías, H. (1997 [1955]), *Criminología*, La Paz: Editorial Juventud.

Campos, R. (2021), *La sombra de la sospecha. Peligrosidad, psiquiatría y derecho en España (siglos XIX y XX)*, Madrid: Los Libros de la Catarata.

"Can't Photo Children in Nude Poses: School Board Denies Professor Glueck's Request" (1940), *Boston Post*, June 21: 10.

Canestrini, G. (1877), *La teoria dell'evoluzione esposta ne' suoi fondamenti come introduzione all'opera di Darwin e de' suoi seguaci*, Turin: UTET.

Capozzi, F. (2022), “Mario Carrara, l’erede di Lombroso che non giurò fedeltà al fascismo,” *Rivista di Storia dell’Università di Torino*, 10: 35–51.

Carnevali, R. (2008), “La ciencia penal italiana y su influencia en Chile,” *Política Criminal*, 6: 1–19.

Carpena, F. (1909), *Antropología criminal*, Madrid: Fernando Fe.

Carranza, L. (1888), “Consideraciones generales sobre los departamentos del Centro,” in *Colección de artículos publicados por Luis Carranza, médico*, II series, *Estudios geográficos y estadísticos de algunos departamentos centrales del Perú*, 47–84, Lima: Imprenta del “Comercio.”

Carranza, L. (1892), “Condiciones físicas e intelectuales del indio,” *Boletín de la Sociedad Geográfica de Lima*, 2 (1): 28–39.

Carrara, E. (1926), “La penitenciaria di San Paulo,” *AAC*, 46: 693–4.

Carrara, M. (1895), “Riformatorio di Elmira,” *APS*, 16: 487–9.

Carrara, M. (1913), “Un Museo per la criminalità infantile,” *AAC*, 34: 697–703.

Carrara, M. (1915), “Castellanos, A través de criminología,” *AAC*, 36: 576–7.

Carrara, M. (1918), “Castellanos, La brujería y el ñañiguismo,” *AAC*, 39: 291–2.

Carrara, M. (1929), “Castellanos, La delincuencia femenina en Cuba,” *AAC*, 49: 559–62.

Carvalho, E. (1913a), *O Professor R. A. Reiss no Brasil*, Rio de Janeiro: Biblioteca do Boletim Policial.

Carvalho, E. (1913b), “A literatura das prisões I: Os poetas,” *A Illustração Brasileira*, 107: 369.

Carvalho, E. (1913c), “A literatura das prisões III: Os prosadores,” *A Illustração Brasileira*, 109: 406.

Carvalho, E. (1913d), “A literatura das prisões IV: O que leem os criminosos,” *A Illustração Brasileira*, 110: 422.

Carvalho, E. (1913e), “Cinematographo e criminalidade: A propósito do crime da rua Fluminense,” *O Imparcial*, 267: 6.

Carvalho, E. (1913f), “Contra os filmes sensacionais,” *O Imparcial*, 268: 11.

Castellanos, I. (1914a), “Anomalía atávica en el occipital de un criminal Cubano,” *Vida Nueva*, 6: 222–5.

Castellanos, I. (1914b), *A través de criminología: Atlas*, Havana: Editorial Salas.

Castellanos, I. (1914c), “Contribución al estudio de las bocas simiescas,” *Gaceta Medica del Sur*, 32: 3–4.

Castellanos, I. (1914d) “La briba hampona,” *Revista Bimestre Cubana*, 9 (2–4): 94–104, 183–98, 253–66.

Castellanos, I. (1914e), *La mandíbula del criminal*, Havana: Imprenta Moderna.

Castellanos, I. (1914f), “Los chinos en Cuba: Su criminalidad,” *Gaceta Medica del Sur*, 33: 73–9, 102–5.

Castellanos, I. (1917a), “Confidencias de Israel Castellanos,” *Archivos Hispano-Americanos de Ciencias Médicas*, 2: 307–16.

Castellanos, I. (1917b), “Contributo allo studio craniometrico dei negri delinquenti,” *AAC*, 38 (1): 118–23.

Castellanos, I. (1929a), *La delincuencia femenina en Cuba: Estadísticas judiciales, penitenciarias y clínicas. Graficas criminológicas*, Havana: Imprenta Ojeda.

Castellanos, I. (1929b), *La delincuencia femenina en Cuba: Índices filiativos y álbum identoscópico*, Havana: Imprenta Ojeda.

Castellanos, I. (1936 [1916]), “La brujería y el ñañiguismo desde el punto de vista médico-legal,” *Revista de Tecnica Policial y Penitenciaria*, 4: 83–186.

Castellanos, I. (1937a), "Lopera di Mario Carrara," *AAC*, special issue in memoriam of Mario Carrara: 377–9.
Castellanos, I. (1937b), *Medicina legal y criminología afro-cubanas*, Havana: Molina y Cia.
"Castellanos, La delincuencia femenina en Cuba" (1934), *La Giustizia Penale*, 15: 110–11.
Castellucci, A. (2023), "Depois do incêndio. Classe, nação, racismo e antirracismo na reconstrução da Faculdade de Medicina da Bahia (1905–1908)," *História*, 42 (e2023028): 1–31.
Cavalli Sforza, L., and D. Padoan (2013), *Razzismo e noismo. La declinazione del noi e l´esclusione dell´altro*, Turin: Einaudi.
Cenno Storico sulla Regia Università di Pavia (1873). "Clinica delle Malattie Mentali," 111–16, Pavia: Stabilimento Tipografico-Librario Successori Bizzoni.
Censo general de la República del Perú formado en 1876 (1878), vol. VII, *Apéndice*, Lima: Imprenta del Teatro.
Cerro, G. (2017), "Giuseppe Sergi: The Portrait of a Positivist Scientist," *Journal of Anthropological Sciences*, 95: 109–36.
Chambers, C. A. (1971) *Paul U. Kellogg and the Survey: Voices for Social Welfare and Social Justice*, Minneapolis: University of Minnesota Press.
Chaves, F. G. (1898), "Evoluciones del régimen penitenciario," *Anales Universitarios del Perú*, 23: 75–106.
Chávez-García, M. (2012), *States of Delinquency: Race, Science and the Making of California's Juvenile Justice System*, Berkeley: University of California Press.
Cházaro, L., and C. Rodríguez de Romo (2006), *A 2774 metros de altitude. La fisiología de la respiración de Daniel Vergara Lope Escobar (1865–1938)*, Mexico City: CONACYT/ Instituto de Investigaciones Filosóficas, UNAM/Fractal.
Chervin, A. (1908), *Anthropologie bolivienne*, Paris: Imprimerie nationale, Librairie H. Le Soudier.
Chesney-Lind, M., and N. Chagnon (2016), "Criminology, Gender, and Race: A Case Study of Privilege in the Academy," *Feminist Criminology*, 11 (4): 311–33.
Chiarugi, G. (1885), "Delle omologie e dei rapporti reciproci della fossetta occipitale media e del lobo mediano del cervelletto nell'uomo e negli altri mammiferi," *Atti della Regia Accademia dei fisiocratici 1880–85*: 325–45.
Chirveches, A. (1998 [1909]), *La candidatura de Rojas*, La Paz: Juventud.
Cilli, C., and S. Montaldo (2024), "The documentary heritage, the donations, the restorations, and the Lombroso Project," in S. Montaldo and C. Cilli (eds.), *The Lombroso Museum*, 29–36. Turin: Hapax.
"Clasificación de los delincuentes" (1957), *Revista de los Carabineros de Chile*, 61: 15.
Clifford, J. (1988), *The Predicament of Culture: Twentieth-Century Ethnography, Literature, and Art*, Cambridge, MA: Harvard University Press.
"Codigo (El) Maúrtua y la Sociedad General de Prisiones de París" (1919), *Revista de la Facultad de Derecho y Ciencias Políticas, Universidad Mayor de San Marcos*, II (2): 62–96.
Comisión de Investigaciones Históricas de la Revolución Mexicana (CIHRM) (1966), *Documentos Históricos de la Revolución Mexicana. Tomo X. Actividades políticas y revolucionarias de los hermanos Flores Magón*, Mexico City: Secretaría de Relaciones Exteriores.
Comunicazioni (1884), *Archivio per l'Antropologia e la Etnologia*, 14 (1): 390–1.
"Congreso Penitenciario. Antropología Criminal" (1886), *Revista Jurídica*, III: 1028–36.
"Congreso y Exposición de Antropología Criminal" (1885), *Revista Médico Quirúrgica*, 22: 226.

Cornejo, M. H. (1900), "Principios generales de la sociología. Discurso académico de apertura del año universitario de 1899," *Anales de la Universidad Mayor de San Marcos de Lima*, 27: 1–39.

Coronil, F. (2019), *The Fernando Coronil Reader*, Julie Skurski, Gary Wilder, Laurent Dubois, Eiss, Paul, Edward Murphy, Mariana Coronil, David Pedersen, Durham, NC: Duke University Press.

Correa, M. (1998), *As Ilusões da Liberdade. A escola Nina Rodrigues e a antropologia no Brasil*, Braganca Paulista: EDUSF.

Costa, R. G. (2009), "Mestiçagem, racialização e gênero," *Sociologias*, 21: 94–120.

Creadick, A. G. (2010), *Perfectly Average: The Pursuit of Normality in Postwar America*, Boston, MA: University of Massachusetts Press.

Creazzo, G. (2007), *El positivismo criminológico italiano en la Argentina*, Buenos Aires: Ediar.

"Crime and Criminals, from a Physiological Point of View" (1879), *The Burlington Weekly Free Press*, August 8: 2.

"Crime in Two Countries" (1892), *The Prison Mirror*, 5 (42), May 26: 1.

"Criminal Women" (1893), *Iowa County Democrat*, 28 (18), December 8: 2.

"Criminology" (1893), *The Sun*, March 26: 2.

Crow J. (2022), *Itinerant ideas: Race, Indigeneity and Cross-Border Intellectual Encounters in Latin America (1900–1950)*, Cham: Palgrave Macmillan.

Cruz Barrera, N. (1999), *Las ciencias del hombre en el México decimonónico. La expansión del confinamiento*, Puebla: Benemérita Universidad Autónoma de Puebla.

Cryle, P., and E. Stephens (2017), *Normality: A Critical Genealogy*, Chicago: University of Chicago Press.

Cunha, E. (2018), *Editar a revolta: edição e circulação de impressos anarquistas em Buenos Aires (1890–1905)*, São Paulo: Universidade de São Paulo.

Cunha, O. G. da (2020), *The Things of Others: Ethnographies, Histories, and Other Artefacts*, Leiden-Boston: Brill.

Curran, M. (2001), *História do Brasil em cordel*, São Paulo: Edusp.

"Curious Condensations" (1891), *Pittsburgh Dispatch*, 36, June 4: 4.

D'Agostino, P. (2002), "Criminals and the 'Cursed Race': Italian Anthropology in American Racial Thought, 1861–1924," *Comparative Studies in Society and History*, 44 (2): 319–43.

D'Agostino, E. (2020–1), "Razzismo, mito ariano e risposte ebraiche fra Italia e Francia, 1867–1873," *Beccaria*, 6: 311–37.

D'Antonio, E. (2024), "Social medicine and pellagrology," in S. Montaldo and C. Cilli (eds.), *The Lombroso Museum*, 41–6. Turin: Hapax.

D'Orbigny, A. (1839), *L'Homme Américaine consideré sous ses rapport phisiologique et moraux*, vol. I, Paris: Pitois-Levrault et fils.

Darwin, C. (1859), *On the Origin of Species*, 2 vols., London: John Murray.

Darwin, C. (1864), *Sull'Origine delle specie*, trans. G. Canestrini and L. Salimbeni, 2 vols., Modena: Zanichelli.

Darwin, C. (1868), *Variation of animals and Plants under Domestication*, 2 vols., London: John Murray.

Darwin, C. (1871), *The Descent of Man and Selection in Relation to Sex*, 2 vols., London: John Murray.

"Das Weib als Werbrecher" (1893), *Vorwärts!*, 41, October 15: 4.

"Das Weib als Werbrecher" (1895), *Wisconsin Vorwärts!*, 14 (112), May 13: 2.

"Das Wesen des Antisemitismus. A Notable New Book" (1901), *Jewish Comment*, September 20: 8–9.
Daston, L., and P. Galison (2010), *Objectivity*, New York: Zone Books.
De Cristofaro, E. (2023), "La mafia negli studi lombrosiani," in F. P. de Ceglia, E. De Cristofaro, and S. Montaldo (eds.), *Lombroso e il Sud*, 177–202, Rome: Donzelli.
De Morães, E. (1902), "La teoría lombrosiana del delincuente," *APC*, 1: 321–3.
De Sousa Bandeira Filho, A. H. (1881), "A questão penitenciaria no Brazil," *O Direito. Revista mensal de legislação, doutrina e jurisprudencia*, 9 (25): 5–43, 161–201.
De Varigny, H. (1881), "Cerebral Localization: Or, the New Phrenology," *Popular Science Monthly*, 18, March 18: 599–610.
De Veyga, F. (1897), "Anarquismo y anarquistas. Estudio de antropología criminal," *Anales del Departamento Nacional de Higiene*, 20: 437–55.
De Veyga, F. (1902), "La inversión sexual congénita", *APC*, 1: 44–8.
De Veyga, F. (1906a), "Delito político. El anarquista Planas y Virella," *APS*, 5: 513–48.
De Veyga, F. (1906b), "El espíritu y el alcance de la obra de Lombroso," *APC*, 5: 259–72.
Debierre, C. M. (1895). *Le crâne des criminales*. Paris: Maloine.
Debuyst, C. (1998), "L'École Française dite « du Milieu Social »," in A. Pires, F. Digneffe and C. Debuyst (eds.), *Histoire des Savoirs sur le Crime et la Peine*, vol. II, 301–56, Brussels: De Boeck Université.
Decker, R. J. (2014), "Citizen and his Duties: The Immigration Restriction League as a Progressive Movement," *Immigrants and Minorities*, 32 (3): 162–82.
Del Olmo, R. (1981), *América Latina y su Criminología*, Mexico City: Siglo XXI.
Del Olmo, R. (1992), *Criminología Argentina*, Buenos Aires: Depalma.
Del Río, R. (1916), *El problema penal*, Santiago: Imprenta Universitaria.
Del Vivo, C., ed. (2014), *Helen Zimmern. Corriere di Londra (1884–1910)*, Milan: Fondazione Corriere della Sera.
Dellepiane, A. (1892), *Las Causas del Delito*, Buenos Aires: Imprenta de Pablo Coni.
"Der Champion Verbrecher" (1895), *Illinois Staats-zeitung*, 49 (29), July 29: 4.
Di Castri, T. (2023), "The Settler Colonial Roots and Neoliberal Afterlife of Problem Behavior Theory," *Journal of the History of the Behavioral Sciences*, 59 (2): 107–28.
Di Natale, S. (2023). *Una donna nell'ombra: Le memorie di Gina Lombroso*, Florence: Edizioni Clichy.
Dias, A. (2010), *Dramas de sangue na cidade: psiquiatria, loucura e assassinato no Rio de Janeiro (1901–1921)*, Rio de Janeiro: Fiocruz.
Díaz Romero, B. (1910), "El genio y su determinismo psico-patológico," in *Páginas dispersas (Miscelánea científica)*, 110–37, La Paz: Litografía e Imprenta la Universal.
Díaz-Quiñones, A. (1997), "Fernando Ortiz y Allan Kardec: Transmigración y Transculturación," *Latin American Literary Review*, July–December: 69–85.
Dictionary of Races or Peoples (1911), in *Reports*, U.S. Immigration Commission, Washington, DC: Government Printing Office.
Didi-Hubermann, G. (2003), *Invention of Hysteria: Charcot and the Photographic Iconography of the Salpêtrière*, trans. Alisa Hartz, Cambridge, MA: MIT Press.
"Die Wissenschaft im Dienste der Polizei" (1881), *Illinois Staats-zeitung*, 31, August 2: 5.
Digneffe, F. (1998), "L'École Positiviste et le Mouvement de la Défense Sociale," in A. Pires, F. Digneffe, and C. Debuyst (eds.), *Histoire des Savoirs sur le Crime et la Peine*, vol. II, 233–300, Brussels: De Boeck Université.
Dinnerstein, L. (1994), *Anti-Semitism in America*, New York: Oxford University Press.
"Dissecting Female Theories" (1892), *St. Landry Democrat*, 15 (42), October 29: 3.
Do Rio, J. (1906), *As religiões do Rio*, Rio de Janeiro: Garnier.

Dolza, D. (1990), *Essere figlie di Lombroso: Due donne intellettuali tra '800 e '900*, Milan: Franco Angeli.
Drago, L. M. (1888), *Los hombres de presa*, Buenos Aires: Félix Lajouane.
Drago, L. M. (1890), *I criminali nati*, Turin: Bocca.
Drago, L. M. (1921 [1888]), *Los hombres de presa*, Buenos Aires: La Cultura Argentina.
Dreier, M. E. (1908), "Letter from Mary Dreier to Dr Stella," Guglielmo Ferrero papers, 1871–1944, 1981, bulk 1890–1942, Series I: Correspondence Box 19, Letters of Dreier, Mary E. Rare Book & Manuscript Library Butler Library, Columbia University, New York.
Dubois, F. (1894), *Le péril anarchiste*, Paris: Flammarion
Dugdale, R. L. (1877), *"The Jukes": A Study of Crime, Pauperism, Disease and Heredity*, New York: G. P. Putnam's Sons.
E. B. E. (1879), "Estudio antropológico sobre los asesinos, disertación del Sr. Montalvo en el Ateneo de la Habana," *Revista de Cuba*, 6: 165–70.
"Echoes from Europe: Lombroso!" (1908), *Emanu-El*, October 30: 4.
Eco-Aguirre, E. (1898), "Conferencia de Derecho Penal dada en la Facultad de Jurisprudencia; siendo el sustentante el alumno don Enrique Eco-Aguirre y replicantes los alumnos don Mariano Sosa y don Samuel Sayán y Palacios," *El Derecho*, September, 1st and 2nd fortnights.
Edwards, E. (2009), "Evolving Images: Photography, Race and Popular Darwinism," in D. Donald and J. Munro (eds.), *Endless Forms: Charles Darwin, Natural Science and the Visual Arts*, 166–93, Cambridge: Yale University Press.
Edwards, E. (2012), *The Camera as Historian: Amateur Photographers and Historical Imagination, 1885–1918*, Durham, NC: Duke University Press.
Efron, J. M. (1994), *Defenders of the Race: Jewish Doctors and Race Science in Fin-de-Siècle Europe*, New Haven, CT: Yale University Press.
"Eine neue Verbrecher-Theorie" (1886), *Der Deutsche Correspondent*, 134, June 5: 3.
"El cura de Olavarría Castro Rodríguez sentenciado a la horca" (1888), *El Imparcial*, November 13: 2.
"El lauro de Israel Castellanos" (1930), *Revista de Medicina Legal de Cuba*, 9: 480.
Ellis, H. (1890), *The Criminal*, New York: Scribner & Welford.
Ellis, H. (1891), "Preface," in A. Winter (ed.), *The New York State Reformatory in Elmira*, III–VIII, London: Swan Sonnenschein & Co.
Ellwood, C. A. (1912), "Lombroso's Theory of Crime," *Journal of the American Institute of Criminal Law and Criminology*, 2 (5): 716–23.
Encinas, J. A. (1919), "Causas de la criminalidad indígena en el Perú," *Revista Universitaria*, 14 (2): 192–268.
Encinas, J. A. (1932), *Un ensayo de Escuela Nueva en el Perú*, Lima: Imp. Minerva.
Escobar, R. (1900), "Disertación sobre la ciencia penal. Especialmente sobre las teorías de Lombroso," *Revista Forense Chilena*, 14: 723–30.
"Estudios de Antropología Criminal" (1885), *Revista Médico Quirúrgica*, 22: 226.
[Evidently] (1908), *The Hebrew Standard*, October 23: 8.
Fabian, J. (2002), *Time and the Other*, New York: Columbia University Press.
Fausto, B. (2001), *Crime e cotidiano. A criminalidade em São Paulo (1880–1924)*, São Paulo: Editora da Universidade.
"Female Criminals" (1895), *The Omaha Daily Bee*, November 16: 10.
"Female Offender" (1895), *Eagle River Democrat*, 3 (11), June 24: 7.
Fernald, M. R., M. H. S. Hayes, and A. Dawley (1920), *A Study of Women Delinquents in New York State*, New York: The Century Co.

Fernández, C. (2009), *Las crónicas de Ingenieros en La Nación de Buenos Aires*, Mar del Plata: UNMdelP.

Fernández, M. (2003), *Prisión común, imaginario social e identidad. Chile, 1870–1920*, Santiago: DIBAM-Editorial Andrés Bello.

Fernández, M. (2008), "Las puntas de un mismo lazo. Discurso y representación social del bebedor inmoderado en Chile, 1870–1930," in *Alcohol y trabajo. El alcohol y la formación de las identidades laborales. Chile, siglos XIX y XX*, 91–119, Osorno: Editorial Universidad de Los Lagos.

Ferrero, G. (1908), "Theodore Roosevelt: A Characterization by Guglielmo Ferrero," trans. R. T. House, *Paris weekly*.

Ferrero, G. (1914), *Ancient Rome and Modern America*, New York: G. P. Putnam's Sons.

Ferrero, G., and D. Litt (1909), *Characters and Events of Roman History: From Caesar to Nero*, New York: G.P. Putnam's Sons.

Ferri, E. (1889), "Luis M. Drago, Los hombres de presa," *APS*, 10: 102–3.

Ferri, E. (1896), *I delinquenti nell'arte*, Genova: Libreria Editrice Ligure.

Ferri, E. (1899), *Los Delincuentes en el Arte*, Madrid: Librería Suárez.

Fink A. E. (1938), *Causes of Crime: Biological Theories in the United States, 1800–1915*, New York: A. S. Barnes.

Finn, J. (2009), *Capturing the Criminal Image: From Mug Shot to Surveillance Society*, Minneapolis: University of Minnesota Press.

Fishberg, M. (1901), "The Comparative Pathology of the Jews," *New York Medical Journal*, March 30: 537–43; April 6: 576–82.

Fishberg, M. (1906), "North African Jews," in B. Laufer and H. A. Andrews (eds.), *Boas Anniversary Volume. Anthropological Papers. Written in Honor of Franz Boas*, 55–63, New York: Stechert & Co.

Fishberg, M. (1911), *The Jews: A Study of Race and Environment*, London:Walter Scott.

Fitzpatrick, E. (1990), *Endless Crusade: Women Social Scientists and Progressive Reform*, New York: Oxford University Press.

Fletcher, R. (1883), "Tattooing among Civilized People," *Transactions of the Anthropological Society of Washington*, 2: 40–68.

Foà, P. (1874), "Osservazioni cliniche e anatomiche raccolte nel manicomio di Pavia," *Il Morgagni*, 16 (7): 481–505.

Fonseca, A. M. da. (1992), *Das raças à família: um debate sobre a construção da nação*, MA diss., Universidade Estadual de Campinas, Campinas.

Forbes, D. (1870), "On the Aymara Indians of Bolivia and Peru," *Journal of the Ethnological Society of London*, 2 (3): 193–305.

Forgacs, D. (2003), "Building the Body of the Nation: Lombroso's *L'antisemitismo* and Fin-de-Siècle Italy," *Jewish Culture and History*, 6 (1): 96–110.

Forgione, F. (2018), *Il potere dell'evoluzione. Il dibattito sulla variabilità delle specie nella Torino dell'Ottocento*, Milan: Franco Angeli.

Forno, M. (2010), "Scienziati e mass-media: Lombroso e gli studiosi positivisti nella stampa tra Otto e Novecento," in S. Montaldo (ed.), *Cesare Lombroso. Gli Scienziati e la Nuova Italia*, 207–32, Bologna: il Mulino.

Fraga, W. (2014), *Encruzilhadas da liberdade: Histórias de escravos e libertos na Bahia (1870–1910)*, São Paulo: Capa Comum.

Freedman, R. (1994). *Kids at Work: Lewis Hine and the Crusade against Child Labor*, New York: Clarion Press.

Freire, O. (1907), "Etiologia das formas concretas de religiosidade no Norte do Brasil. Introdução a um estudo psycho-social criminal," Ph.D. diss. thesis, Escola de Medicina da Bahia, Bahia.

Frezza, D. (2007), *The Leader and the Crowd: Democracy in American Public Discourse*, Athens: University of Georgia Press.

Frigessi, D. (2003), *Cesare Lombroso*, Turin: Einaudi.

Fuentes Castro, P. (1892a), "Manuel Peña y Chacaliaza," *El Diario Judicial*, 2 (500), February 18.

Fuentes Castro, P. (1892b), "Dolores Gamboa," *El Diario Judicial*, 3 (514): April 1.

Fuentes Castro, P. (1892c), "Pedro Laredo," *El Diario Judicial*, 3 (537): May 2.

Gaceta Judicial (1911), 858, December 31: 11–12.

Galeano, D. (2016), "Memorias de un ratón de hotel: delito, prensa y literatura en Brasil, 1890–1912," *Claves. Revista de Historia*, 2 (3): 99–132.

Galeano, D. and M. Rodrigues (2017), "Uma história da história natural dos malfeitores," in E. Carvalho, *Escritos policiais*, 15–27, Rio de Janeiro: Contracapa.

Galera Gomez, A. (1991), *Ciencia y delincuencia: El determinismo antropológico en la España del s. XIX*, Sevilla: Consejo Superior de Investigaciones Científicas.

Galloni, M. (2015), "Gli strumenti scientifici di Cesare Lombroso," in S. Montaldo and P. Tappeto (eds.), *Il Museo di Antropologia criminale "Cesare Lombroso,"* 153–67, Turin: UTET.

Galton, F. (1878), "Composite Portraits Made by Combining Those of Many Different Persons into a Single Figure," *Nature*, 18: 97–100.

Gambara, L. (1906), *Curso de Derecho penal positivo*, Santiago: Hermanos Ponce Editores.

García Granados, R. (1911), "Raza, clima y relaciones internacionales," *Boletín de la Sociedad Indianista Mexicana*, 1: 81–2.

García Murcia, M. (2013), "Profesionalización de la antropología en México: La investigación, las instituciones y la enseñanza (1887–1942)," Ph.D. diss., Universidad Nacional Autónoma de México, Mexico City.

García Rojas, G. (2021), "Nación, lengua y raza. La configuración del 'problema indígena' en México en el siglo XIX," *Cuicuilco. Revista de ciencias antropológicas*, 28 (82): 169–90.

García, E. (1910), "Antropología criminal i derecho penal," *Revista Contemporánea*, 1: 31–45.

García, H. (2016), "Dando y dando objetos preciosos: Huesos por jarrones. Intercambios desiguales entre Francia y México, siglo XIX," in G. Mateos and E. Suárez-Díaz (eds.), *Aproximaciones a lo local y lo global: América Latina en la historia de la ciencia contemporánea*, 33–53, Mexico City: Centro de Estudios Filosóficos, Políticos y Sociales Vicente Lombardo Toledano.

Gauchet, M., and G. Swain (2002), *El verdadero Charcot*, Buenos Aires: Nueva Visión.

Geli, P. (1992), "Los anarquistas en el gabinete antropométrico," *Entrepasados*, 1 (2): 7–24.

"Genius and Insanity. Are All Men of Genius Mad?" (1891), *New York Daily Tribune*, 51, no. 16 (464), December 13: 18.

"Genius and Insanity" (1892a), *The Sun*, 59 (188), March 6: 14.

"Genius and Insanity" (1892b), *The Pittsburgh Dispatch*, 47, March 21: 4.

"Geniusz i talent u kobiet" (1893), *Dziennik Chicagoski*, 228, September 30: 6.

Gibson, M. (2002), *Born to Crime: Cesare Lombroso and the Origins of Biological Criminology*, Westport, CT: Praeger.

Gilardi, A. (1978). *Wanted!: Storia, tecnica ed estetica della fotografia criminale, segnaletica e giudiziaria*, 182, Milan: Mazzotta.
Gilimón E. (1902), "Las teorías lombrosianas," *La Protesta Humana*, Buenos Aires, March 15.
Gilman, S. (1991), *The Jew's Body*, New York: Routledge.
Girón, A. (2002), "Los anarquistas españoles y la criminología de Cesare Lombroso (1890–1914)," *Frenia*, 2 (2): 81–108.
Glueck, E. T. (1958), "Body Build in the Prediction of Delinquency," *Journal of Criminal Law, Criminology and Police Science*, 48 (6): 577–9.
Glueck, S. (1960), "Ten Years of "Unraveling Juvenile Delinquency": An Examination of Criticisms," *Journal of Criminal Law, Criminology and Police Science*, 51 (3): 283–308.
Glueck, S., and E. T. Glueck (1930), *Five Hundred Criminal Careers*, New York: Knopf.
Glueck, S., and E. T. Glueck (1934a), *Five Hundred Delinquent Women*, New York: Knopf.
Glueck, S., and E. T. Glueck (1934b), *One Thousand Juvenile Delinquents: Their Treatment in Court and Clinic*, Cambridge, MA: Harvard University Press.
Glueck, S., and E. T. Glueck (1950), *Unraveling Juvenile Delinquency*, New York: Commonwealth Fund.
Glueck, S., and E. T. Glueck (1956), *Physique and Delinquency*, New York: Harper & Brothers Publishers.
Goicovic, I. (2005), *Entre el dolor y la ira. La venganza de Antonio Ramón Ramón. Chile, 1914*, Osorno: Editorial Universidad de Los Lagos.
Goldstein, E. L. (2006), *The Price of Whiteness: Jews, Race, and American Identity*, Princeton, NJ: Princeton University Press.
Gonçalves, J. F. (2014), "'The Ajiaco in Cuba and beyond', preface to 'The human factors of Cubanidad by Fernando Ortiz'," *H: Journal of Ethnographic Theory*, 4 (3): 445–54.
Govoni, P. (2002), *Un pubblico per la scienza. La divulgazione scientifica nell'Italia in formazione*, Rome: Carocci.
Graña, L. (1899), "Factores sociales de la delincuencia en el Perú," Bachelor's thesis, Faculty of Law, *El Derecho,* October 1st and 2nd fortnights: 727–736.
Granja, J. (2009), "Contar y clasificar a la infancia. Las categorías de la escolarización en las escuelas primarias de la Ciudad de México, 1870–1930," *Revista mexicana de investigación educativa*, 14 (2): 217–54.
Grant, M. (1916), *The Passing of the Great Race. Or the Racial Basis of European History*, New York: Charles Scribner's Sons.
Green, J. R. (2006). *Death in the Haymarket: A Story of Chicago, the First Labor Movement, and the Bombing that Divided Gilded Age America*, New York: Pantheon Books.
Grob, G. N. (1983), *Mental Illness and American Society, 1875–1940*, Princeton, NJ: Princeton University Press.
Guarnieri, P. (2006), "Un piccolo essere perverso. Il bambino nella cultura scientifica italiana tra Otto e Novecento," *Contemporanea*, 9 (2): 253–84.
Guarnieri, P. (2013), "Caesar or Cesare? American and Italian images of Lombroso," in P. Knepper and P. J. Ystehede (eds.), *The Cesare Lombroso Handbook*, 113–30, London: Routledge.
Guglielmo, J., and S. Salerno, eds. (2003), *Are Italians White? How Race is Made in America*. New York: Routledge.
Guinassi y Morán, M. (1894), "El tipo criminal," *El Diario Judicial*, 6 (1303–7), June 4–7.
Halitvack (1908), "The Deputation to Commissioner Bingham: An Impression," *The Hebrew Standard*, October 23: 11.
Hamon, A. (1898) *Psicología del socialista anarquista*, Buenos Aires: Imprenta Elzeviriana.

Hamy, E. (1872) "Sur le crâne d'un monstre exencéphalien par M. Girard', *Bulletins de la Société d'anthropologie de Paris (Seance du 4 julliet)*: 648–9.

Harambour, A. (2004), "Jesto y palabra, idea y acción: La historia de Efraín Plaza Olmedo," in Colectivo Oficios Varios, *Arriba quemando el sol. Estudios de historia social chilena: Experiencias populares de trabajo, revuelta y autonomía (1830–1940)*, 137–93, Santiago: LOM Ediciones.

Hardyns, W., and L. J. R. Pauwels (2018), "The Chicago School and Criminology," in R. A. Triplett (ed.), *The Handbook of the History and Philosophy of Criminology*, 123–39, Hoboken: Wiley.

Harrowitz, N. A. (1994), *Anti-Semitism, Misoginy & the Logic of Cultural Difference. Cesare Lombroso and Matilde Serao*, Lincoln: University of Nebraska Press.

Hart, M. B. (1999), "Racial Science, Social Science, and the Politics of Jewish Assimilation," *Isis*, 90 (2): 268–97.

Hart, M. B. (2000), *Social Science and the Politics of Modern Jewish Identity*, Stanford, CA: Stanford University Press.

Hartung, F. E. (1958a), "A Critique of the Sociological Approach to Crime and Correction," *Law and Contemporary Problems*, 23 (4), 703–34.

Hartung, F. E. (1958b), "Book Review: Physique and Delinquency," *Journal of Criminal Law, Criminology and Police Science*, 48 (6): 638–9.

"Hayward a Degenerate" (1895), *The Evening Bulletin*, 15 (17), December 12: 1.

Healy, W. (1915), *The Individual Delinquent: A Text-Book of Diagnosis and Prognosis for All Concerned in Understanding Offenders*, Boston: Little, Brown and Co.

Heaney, C. (2023), *Empires of the Dead: Incas Mummies and the Peruvian Ancestors of American Anthropology*, New York: Oxford University Press.

Helg, A. (1995), *Our Rightful Share: The Afro-Cuban Struggle for Equality, 1866–1912*, Chapel Hill: University of North Carolina Press.

Hermansen, R. (1911), "De la Escuela Clásica a la Escuela Criminal," *Revista Contemporánea*, 3: 195–208.

Herrera, A. L., and R. E. Cicero (1895), *Catálogo de la colección de Antropología del Museo Nacional*, Mexico City: Imprenta del Museo Nacional.

Hesse, R. (1912), *Les criminels peints par eux-mêmes*, Paris: Bernard Grasset.

Higham, J. (1955), *Strangers in the Land: Patterns of American Nativism, 1865–1925*, New Brunswick: Rutgers University Press.

Hine, L. W. (1910), "Roving Children," *The Survey: Social, Charitable, Civic: A Journal of Constructive Philanthropy*, 23: 480–1.

Hine, L. (2022), "Social Photography: How the Camera May Help in the Social Uplift," in *Documentary Genealogies: Photography 1848–1917*, 237–41, Madrid: Museo Reina Sofia.

"Holmes's Many Crimes" (1895), *The Sun*, August 4: 4.

Hooton, E. A. (1939), *Crime and the Man*, Cambridge, MA: Harvard University Press.

Horn, D. (2003), *The Criminal Body: Lombroso and the Anatomy of Deviance*, New York: Routledge.

Horn, M. (1989), *Before It's Too Late: The Child Guidance Movement in the United States, 1922–1945*, Philadelphia, Temple University Press.

Horton, D. M. and K. E. Rich, eds. (2004), *The Criminal Anthropological Articles of Cesare Lombroso Published in English Language Periodical Literature During the Late 19th and Early 20th Centuries*, Lewiston: The Edwin Mellen Press.

"How We Endure Pain" (1892), *The Salt Lake Herald*, 23 (19), June 26: 13.

Howe, S. (1998), *Afrocentrism: Mythical Pasts and Imagined Homes*, London: Verso.

Huertas, L. E. (2016), "Race, Identity, and Crime in Peru, 1890s–1930s," in L. E. Huertas, B. Lucero, and G. J. Swedberg (eds.), *Voices of Crime: Constructing and Contesting Social Control in Modern Latin America*, 51–73, Tucson: University of Arizona Press.
Huertas, R. (1991), *El delincuente y su patología. Medicina, crimen y sociedad en el positivismo argentino*, Madrid: CSIC.
Hughes, W. (2015), *That Devil's Trick: Hypnotism and the Victorian Popular Imagination*, Manchester: Manchester University Press.
Hurtado Pozo, J. (1979), *La ley "importada." Recepción del derecho penal en el Perú*, Lima: Cedys.
"Informe al Cancelario" (1893), *El Comercio*, February 11.
Ingenieros, J. (1898), "Psicología colectiva. Un libro de A. Hamon," *El Mercurio de América*, July.
Ingenieros, J. (1899), "El delito como vínculo entre la ciencia y el arte," *La Revista*, 7: 193–7.
Ingenieros, J. (1902a), "Fetichista con hermafrodismo psíquico activo," *APC*, 1: 616–21.
Ingenieros, J. (1902b), "Las teorías de Lombroso ante la crítica," *APC*, 1: 334–8.
Ingenieros, J. (1902c), "Valor de la psicopatología en la antropología criminal," *APC*, 1: 1–11.
Ingenieros, J. (1902d), "La folie des foules," *APC*, 1: 188–9.
Ingenieros, J. (1902e), "Deux mots de reponse," *APC*, 1: 293–5.
Ingenieros, J. (1903a), "Interpretación científica del hipnotismo y la sugestión," *APC*, 2: 355–65.
Ingenieros, J. (1903b), "La psicopatología en el arte," *APC*, 2: 27–41.
Ingenieros, J. (1906), "Lombroso y los hombres pobres," *Italia en la ciencia, en la vida y en el arte*, Valencia: Sempere.
Ingenieros, J. (1907), "La vanidad criminal," *Archivos de Pedagogía y Ciencias Afines*, 2 (4): 14–23.
[Ingenieros, J.] (1909), "Homenaje a César Lombroso," *APC*, 8: 515–16.
Ingenieros, J. (1919), *Crónicas de viaje*, Buenos Aires: Rosso.
Ingenieros, J. (1996a [1903]), *La simulación en la lucha por la vida*, Buenos Aires: Losada.
Ingenieros, J. (1996b [1913]), *El hombre mediocre*, Buenos Aires: Losada.
Ingenieros, J. (2009a [1905]), "Últimas notas de un congreso," in C. Fernández (ed.), *Las crónicas de Ingenieros en La Nación de Buenos Aires*, 53–61, Mar del Plata: Editorial Martín.
Ingenieros, J. (2009b [1906]). "La transmisión del pensamiento," in C. Fernández (ed.), *Las crónicas de Ingenieros en La Nación de Buenos Aires*, 291–6, Mar del Plata: Editorial Martín.
Ingenieros, J. (2009c [1906]), "Siluetas," in C. Fernandez (ed.), *Las crónicas de Ingenieros en La Nación de Buenos Aires*, 196–7, Mar del Plata: Editorial Martín.
Ingenieros, J. (2012 [1913]), *Criminología*, Córdoba: Buena Vista.
"Insanity and Crime" (1886a), *Charlotte Messenger*, 3 (14), August 14: 4.
"Insanity and Crime" (1886b), *News and Citizen*, 14 (22), August 19: 1.
"Insanity and Crime" (1886c), *The Kimball Graphic*, 240, November 12: 1.
"Insanity and Crime" (1886d), *Wessington Springs Herald*, 192, November 26: 6.
"Insanity and Crime" (1889), *The Midland Journal*, 26, March 18: 3.
"Insanity and Genius" (1892a), *The Omaha Daily Bee*, XXI (207), January 10: 11.
"Insanity and Genius" (1892b), *The St. Johns Herald*, VIII (13), January 14: 1.
"Insanity and Genius" (1892c), *Freeland Tribune*, 4 (32), January 28: 3.
"Is a Study in Crime" (1895), *The Philipsburg Mail*, 9 (43), November 21: 6.

J. B. (1891–92), "Genius and Insanity," *The American Journal of Insanity*, 48: 529–31.
J[ellinek, A.] (1893), "Cesare Lombroso und der Antisemitismus," *Die Neuzeit*, June 23: 243–4.
Jacobson, M. F. (1998), *Whiteness of a Different Color: European Immigrants and the Alchemy of Race*, Cambridge, MA: Harvard University Press.
Jastrow, J. (1886), "A Theory of Criminality," *Science*, 8: 20–2.
Jensen, R. B. (2014), *The Battle against Anarchist Terrorism. An International History, 1878–1934*, Cambridge: Cambridge University Press.
Jiménez de Asúa, L. (1926), *El Derecho Penal en la República del Perú*, Valladolid: Universidad de Valladolid.
Jiménez, P. (1898), "La Sociedad y el Delito," Ph.D. diss., *Anales Universitarios del Perú*, 23: 107–354.
Jones, K. W. (1999), *Taming the Troublesome Child: American Families, Child Guidance, and the Limits of Psychiatric Authority*, Cambridge, MA: Harvard University Press.
Jourdanet, D. (1861), *Les altitudes de l'Amérique tropicale Comparée aux Niveaux des Mers au Point de Vue de la Constitution Médicale*, Paris: J.B. Baillière et Fils.
"Judging Mind by Body" (1940), *Time*, July 15: 53–4.
Kalifa, D. (1995), *L'encre et le sang: Récits de crimes et société à la Belle Epoque*, Paris: Fayard.
Kalifa, D. (2005), *Crime et culture au XIXe siècle*, Paris: Perrin.
Karpenko, L., and S. Claggett, eds. (2017), *Strange Science: Investigating the Limits of Knowledge in the Victorian Age*, Ann Arbor: University of Michigan Press.
Karpowicz, D. S. (2017), *Do convento ao cárcere: Do caleidoscópio institucional da Congregação Bom Pastor D'Angers à Penitenciária Feminina Madre Pelletier (1936–1981)*, Porto Alegre: Pontifícia Universidade Católica do Rio Grande do Sul.
Kemner J. (2012), "¿Eran ciudadanos los afrodescendientes libres en las sociedades esclavistas? Cuba, Brasil y Estados Unidos en el siglo XIX," *Revista Ecuatoriana de Historia*, 35: 9–36.
King, C. (2019), *Gods of the Upper Air: How a Circle of Renegade Anthropologists Reinvented Race, Sex and Gender in the Twentieth Century*, New York: Doubleday.
Klein, D. (1973), "The Etiology of Female Crime: A Review of the Literature," *Issues in Criminology*, 8 (2): 3–30.
Klimpel, F. (1962), *La mujer chilena (El aporte femenino al progreso de Chile) 1910–1960*, Santiago: Editorial Andrés Bello.
Knepper, P. (2010), *The Invention of International Crime: A Global Issue in the Making, 1881–1914*, Basingstoke: Palgrave McMillan.
Knepper, P. (2018a) "Clocks and Crime: Conceptions of Time in the Writings of Cesare Lombroso," *Crime, History & Societies*, 22 (2): 9–29.
Knepper, P. (2018b), "Laughing at Lombroso: Positivism and Criminal Anthropology in Historical Perspective," in R. A. Triplett (ed.), *The Handbook of the History and Philosophy of Criminology*, 51–67, New Jersey: Wiley.
Kraut, A. (1994), *Silent Travelers: Germs, Genes and the "Immigrant Menace,"* New York: Basic Books.
"La entrevista Creelman" (1916), *Revista Mexicana*, June 25: 42.
"La moral en la instrucción" (1893a), *El Comercio*, February 11: 2.
"La moral en la instrucción" (1893b), *El Imparcial*, March 11: 2.
"La muerte de un sabio" (1897), *El Imparcial*, March 24: 2.
Landa, G. (1940), "El delincuente desde el punto de vista social," *Revista de la Policía Boliviana*, La Paz, 3 (10): 29–30.

"Latest News from Europe" (1892), *The Sun*, 59 (342), August 7: 1.
Latour, B. (1995), "¿Tienen historia los objetos? El encuentro de Pasteur y de Whitehead en un baño de ácido láctico," *Isegoría*, 12: 92–109.
Laub, J. H. and R. J. Sampson (1991), "The Sutherland-Glueck Debate: On the Sociology of Criminological Knowledge," *American Journal of Sociology*, 96 (6): 1402–40.
Laub, J. H., and J. S. Smith. (1995), "Eleanor Touroff Glueck: An Unsung Pioneer in Criminology," *Women and Criminal Justice*, 6 (2): 1–22.
Laurent, E. (1908), *Le criminel aux points de vue anthropologique, psychologique et social*, Paris: Vigot.
Le Riverend, J. (1995) "Ortiz, Fernando," in N. Osorio (ed.), *Diccionario Enciclopédico de las Letras de América Latina*, Caracas: Biblioteca Ayacucho.
Leal, A. (1895), *Prisão preventiva*, Salvador: Imprensa Economica.
Leal, A. (1896), *Germens do crime*, Salvador: Livraria Magalhaes.
Leal, A. (1898a), *A religião dos condenados da Bahia*, Amargosa: Notre Dame.
Leal, A. (1898b), *Regímen penitenciário na Bahia*, Salvador: Diário da Bahia.
Leal, A. (1899), "La religion chez les condamnes a Bahia," *Archives de Anthropologie Criminelle*, 14 (84): 605–31.
Leal, A. (1902), *Estudos de sociologia e psicologia criminal*, Salvador: Reis.
Leal, A. (2014 [1915]), *História constitucional do Brasil*, Brasília: Edições do Senado Federal.
Leal, C. (2006), "Pensiero e Dinamite. Anarquismo e Repressão em São Paulo nos anos 1890," Ph.D. diss. thesis, Universidade Estadual de Campinas, Campinas.
Leal, H. (1968), *Aurelino Leal. Sua vida, sua época, sua obra*, Rio de Janeiro: Agir Editora.
Lejeune, P. (1986), "Crime et testament. Les autobiographies de criminels au XIXe siècle," *Cahiers de sémiotique textuelle*, 8-9: 73–98.
León, M. (2015), *Construyendo un sujeto criminal. Criminología, criminalidad y sociedad en Chile. Siglos XIX y XX*, Santiago: Editorial Universitaria-Centro de Investigaciones Diego Barros Arana.
León, N. (1919a), "Historia de la Antropología física en México," *American Journal of Physical Anthropology*, 2 (3): 229–64.
León, N. (1919b), *La capacidad craneana de algunas tribus indígenas de la República Mexicana*, Mexico City: Congreso Internacional de Americanistas.
León, N. (1922), *Catálogo del Departamento de Antropología Física*, Mexico City: Imprenta del Museo Nacional.
Leonardi, N. (2015), "Il metodo lombrosiano e le fotografie come oggetti sociali," in S. Montaldo (ed.), *Il Museo di Antropologia criminale Cesare Lombroso dell'Università di Torino*, 36–51, Turin: Silvana.
Leonardi, N. and N. Pugliese (2024), "The Human Face in Photographs and Drawings," in S. Montaldo and C. Cilli (eds.), *The Lombroso Museum*, 138–43, Turin: Hapax.
Leroy-Beaulieu, A. (1893), *Israël chez les nations. Les Juifs et l'antisémitisme*, Paris: Calmann-Lévy.
Leschiutta, P. (1996), *Palimsesti del carcere. Cesare Lombroso e le scritture proibite*, Naples: Liguori.
Levaggi, A. (2006), "Impacto que produjo en la ciencia penal argentina la presencia de Enrico Ferri," in *El Derecho en Red*, 757–65, Madrid: Dykinson.
Lewis, H. S. (2001), "The Passion of Franz Boas," *American Anthropologist*, 103 (2): 447–67.
"Librería de José M. Farfán" (1895), *El Imparcial*, November 29: 1.
"Life in London" (1895), *The Perrysburg Journal*, December 7.

"Lillian Wald Dies: Friend of the Poor" (1940), NYT, September 2.
Lima, E. M. (1983), *Origens da Prisão Feminina no Rio de Janeiro: O período das freiras (1942–1955)*, Rio de Janeiro: OAB.
Lindesmith, A. and Y. Levin (1937), "The Lombrosian Myth in Criminology," *American Journal of Sociology*, 42 (5): 653–71.
"Literary Notes. New Books" (1893), *The Reform Advocate*, August 19: 12.
Livingstone, D. (2003), *Putting science in its place. Geographies of Scientific Knowledge*, Chigaco: University of Chicago Press.
Locard, E. (1929), "Castellanos, La delincuencia femenina en Cuba," *Revue Internationale de Criminalistique*, 1: 410–11.
"Lombroso on Nordau" (1895), *The Anaconda Standard*, October 13: 2.
"Lombroso" (1895), *Waterbury Evening Democrat*, December 9.
"Lombroso's "Woman"" (1895), *The Anaconda Standard*, 6 (292), June 22: 2.
"Lombroso's Theory" (1893a), *The Wichita Daily Eagle*, November 1: 5.
"Lombroso's Theory" (1893b), *Griggs Courier*, November 3.
Lombroso, C. (1867), "Sulla mortalità degli Ebrei di Verona nel decennio 1855–1864," in C. Lombroso, *Studi statistico-igienici sull'Italia*, 33–49, Bologna: Fava e Garagnani.
Lombroso, C. (1871a), "Esistenza di una fossa occipitale mediana nel cranio di un delinquente," *Rendiconti del Reale Istituto Lombardo di Scienze e Lettere*, 4 (1): 37–41.
Lombroso, C. (1871b), "Esistenza di una fossa occipitale mediana nel cranio di un criminale," *Archivio per l'Antropologia e la Etnologia*, 1 (1): 65–7.
Lombroso, C. (1871c), *L'uomo bianco e l'uomo di colore*, Padua: Sacchetto.
Lombroso, C. (1872), "Della fossetta occipitale mediana nel cranio di un criminale," *Rendiconti. Reale Istituto lombardo di scienze e lettere*, 2 (5): 1058–65.
Lombroso, C. (1874a), "Antropometria di 832 delinquenti italiani," *Rendiconti del Reale Istituto Lombardo di Scienze e Lettere*, 2 (7): 20–32.
Lombroso, C. (1874b), "Antropometria e fisionomia dei delinquenti italiani," *Rendiconti del Reale Istituto Lombardo di Scienze e Lettere*, 2 (7): 93–108.
Lombroso, C. (1876), *L'uomo delinquente studiato in rapporto alla antropologia, alla medicina legale e alle discipline carcerarie*, Milan: Hoepli.
Lombroso, C. (1878), *Pensiero e Meteore. Studii di un alienista*. Milan: Fratelli Dumolard.
Lombroso, C. (1882), *Genio e follia in rapporto alla medicina legale, alla critica ed alla storia*, Turin: Bocca.
Lombroso, C. (1883a), "Fossa occipitale mediana nelle razze umane e nei criminali," *APS*, 4 (1–2): 505–7.
Lombroso, C. (1883b), "La fossette aymarienne chez les criminels et dans la race humaine," *Bulletin de la Société d'Anthropologie de Paris*, 6: 409–410.
Lombroso, C. (1884), *L'uomo delinquente*, 3rd edn, Turin: Bocca.
Lombroso, C. (1885), "G. Chiarugi, Delle omologie dei rapporti reciproci della fossetta occipitale media e del lobo mediano del cervelletto nell'uomo e negli altri mammiferi," book review, *APS*, 6 (1–2): 535–6.
Lombroso, C. (1886), "Du délit politique au point de vue de l'anthropologie criminelle," *La Nouvelle Revue*, 40: 71–87.
Lombroso, C. (1887a), *Genie und Irrsinn in ihren Beziehungen zum Gesetz, zur Kritik und zur Geschichte*, Leipzig: Reclam.
Lombroso, C. (1887b), "La detenzione a tempo indeterminato ed il riformatorio di Elmira," *APS*, 8: 547–8.

Lombroso, C. (1887c), *L'homme criminel. Étude anthropologique et médico-légale*, Paris: Ancienne Libraire Germer Bailliére.
Lombroso, C. (1888a), *L'uomo di genio in rapporto alla psichiatria, alla storia ed all'estetica*, Turin: Bocca.
Lombroso, C. (1888b), *Palimsesti del carcere. Raccolta unicamente destinata agli uomini di scienza*, Turin: Fratelli Bocca.
Lombroso, C. (1889), *L'uomo delinquente*, 4th edn, Turin: Bocca.
Lombroso, C. (1890a), "Sulla diffusione della antropologia criminale," in L. M. Drago, *I criminali nati*, V–XXXIX, Turin: Bocca.
Lombroso, C. (1890b), *Sulla medicina legale del cadavere*, Pinerolo: Tipografia Chiantore-Mascarelli.
Lombroso, C. (1891a), "Illustrative Studies in Criminal Anthropology: The Physiognomy of the Anarchists," *The Monist*, 1 (3): 336–43.
Lombroso, C. (1891b), *The Man of Genius*, New York: Charles Scribner's Sons.
Lombroso, C. (1892a), "Introduction," in A. MacDonald, *Criminology*, VI–X, New York: Funk & Wagnalls.
Lombroso, C. (1892b), *Les applications de l'anthropologie criminelle*, Paris: Félix Alcan.
Lombroso, C. (1893a), "Anti-Semitism," *The Menorah*, August: 74–82.
Lombroso, C. (1893b), *Aplicaciones judiciales y médicas de la antropología criminal*, Madrid: La España Moderna.
Lombroso, C. (1893c), "Der Antisemitismus," *Neue Freie Presse*, June 11: 1–2.
Lombroso, C. (1893d), *Escritos de polémica*, Madrid: Alfredo Alonso.
Lombroso, C. (1893e), *Le più recenti scoperte e applicazioni della psichiatria ed antropologia criminale*, Turin: Bocca.
Lombroso, C. (1894a), *Der Antisemitismus und die Juden im Lichte des modernen Wissenschaft*, Leipzig: Wiegand.
Lombroso, C. (1894b), *Gli anarchici*, Turin: Bocca.
Lombroso, C. (1894c), *L'antisemitismo e le scienze moderne*, Turin: Roux.
Lombroso, C. (1894d), *L'uomo di genio*, 6th ed., Turin: Bocca.
Lombroso, C. (1894e), *Los anarquistas*, Madrid: Sucesores de Rivadeneyra.
Lombroso, C. (1895a), *Die Anarchisten*, Hamburg: Verlagsanstalt und Druckerei.
Lombroso, C. (1895b), *Gli anarchici*, 2nd ed., Turin: Bocca.
Lombroso, C. (1895c), *Los anarquistas*, Buenos Aires: Imprenta Elzeviriana.
Lombroso, C. (1895d) "Nordau's "Degeneration": Its Value and Errors," *The Century*, 50: 936–41.
Lombroso, C. (1896), *L'homme de génie*, Paris: Georges Carré.
Lombroso, C. (1897a), *Atlante*, Turin: Bocca
Lombroso, C. (1897b), *Les anarchistes*, Paris: Flammarion.
Lombroso, C. (1897c), *L'uomo delinquent*, 5th ed., Turin: Bocca.
Lombroso, C. (1897d), "Why Homicide Has Increased in the United States. I," *The North American Review*, 165 (493): 441–648.
Lombroso, C. (1898a), "Lucheni y el anarquismo en la raza latina," *La Nación*, October 28.
Lombroso, C. (1898b), "Why Homicide Has Increased in the United States. II," The *North American Review*, 166 (494): 1–11.
Lombroso, C. (1899), *L'antisémitisme*, Paris: Giard & Brière.
Lombroso, C. (1900a), "El clericalismo en Francia," *Tribuna Tibertaria*, May 27.
Lombroso, C. (1900b), "Gaetano Bresci," *La Nación*, November 2.
Lombroso, C. (1900c), *Medicina legal*, Madrid: La España Moderna.

Lombroso, C. (1900d), "Una carta de Lombroso," *La patria de México*, 7: 12.

Lombroso, C. (1902), *Delitti vecchi e delitti nuovi*, Turin: Bocca.

Lombroso, C. (1903a), *El antisemitismo*, Madrid: Viuda de Rodriguez Sierra.

Lombroso, C. (1903b), "Sul vermis ipertrofico e sulla fossetta occipitale mediana nei normali, negli alienati e nei delinquenti," *APS*, 23: 34–56.

Lombroso, C. (1906a), *Evrei i nenavist knim*, Odessa: Tribuna.

Lombroso, C. (1906b), "Il mio museo criminale," *L'Illustrazione italiana*, April 1: 302–6.

Lombroso, C. (1906c), "Mi museo criminal," *APC*, 5: 288–94.

Lombroso, C. (1907a), "Come nacque e come crebbe l'antropologia criminale," in *Ricerche di Psichiatria e Nevrologia, Antropologia e Filosofia dedicate al prof. Enrico Morselli*, 501–2, Milan: Vallardi.

Lombroso, C. (1907b), "My Museum of Criminal Psychology," NYT, February 17.

Lombroso, C. (1909a), *After Death, What?: Spiritistic Phenomena and Their Interpretation*, Boston, MA: Small. Maynard.

Lombroso, C. (1909b), *Ricerche su fenomeni ipnotici e spiritici*, Turin: UTET.

Lombroso, C. (1938), "Formas específicas de locura criminal," *Revista de la Policía Boliviana*, 1 (2): 35–40.

Lombroso, C. (2006), *Criminal Man*, M. Gibson and N. Rafter (eds.), Durham, NC: Duke University Press.

Lombroso, C. and F. Bergonzoli (1874), "La fossetta occipitale mediana e il vermis cerebellaris," *Il Morgagni*, 26 (11): 801–36.

Lombroso, C. and G. Bizzozero (1873), "Sui rapporti del cervelletto colla fossa occipitale mediana," *Archivio per l'Antropologia e la Etnologia*, 3 (1): 23–5.

Lombroso, C., and G. Ferrero (1893), *La donna delinquente, la prostituta e la donna normale*, Turin: Roux.

Lombroso, C., and G. Ferrero (1896), *La femme criminelle et la prostituée*, Paris: Félix Alcan.

Lombroso, C., and G. Ferrero (2004), *Criminal Woman, the Prostitute, and the Normal Woman*, trans. N. H. Rafter and M. Gibson, Durham, NC: Duke University Press.

Lombroso, C. and H. Kornfeld (1881), "Su Guiteau," *APS*, 2: 453–459.

Lombroso, C. and R. Laschi (1890), *Il delitto politico e le rivoluzioni in rapporto al diritto, all'antropologia criminale ed alla scienza di governo*, Turin: Bocca.

Lombroso, G. (1902), "Il lavoro della donna e le leggi protettive," *Il Socialismo*, February.

Lombroso, G. (1908), *Nell'America Meridionale (Brasile-Uruguay-Argentina)*, Milan: Fratelli Treves.

Lombroso Ferrero, G. (1921), *Cesare Lombroso. Storia della vita e delle opere*, Bologna: Zanichelli.

Lombroso, G. (1927), *La donna nella società attuale*, Bologna: Zanichelli.

Lombroso, G. (2009), *Vida de Lombroso*. México: Instituto Nacional de Ciencias Penales.

López Rey, M. (1945), *Introducción al Estudio de la Criminología*, Buenos Aires: Editorial El Ateneo.

López-Ocón, L. (2001), "La Sociedad Geográfica de Lima y la formación de una ciencia en el Perú republicano," *Terra Brasilis. Revista da Rede Brasileira de História da Geografia e Geografia Histórica*, 3: 1–23.

Lorini, A. (1980), *Ingegneria umana e scienze sociali negli USA (1890–1920)*, Florence: D'Anna.

Lorini, A. (1999). *Rituals of Race: American Public Culture and the Search for Racial Democracy*, Charlottesville: University of Virginia Press.

Lorini, A. (2013), "Il pensiero antirazzista negli Stati Uniti: W. E. B. Du Bois e Franz Boas," in P. P. Poggio (ed.), *Il capitalismo americano e i suoi critici. L'altro Novecento. Comunismo eretico e pensiero critico*, III, 211–33, Milan: Jaca Book.
Lorini, A. (2019), "'Cartoline dall'inferno': Storia e memoria pubblica dei linciaggio negli Stati Uniti," in *C'era una volta l'America. Saggi sul disincanto della modernità*, Perugia: Morlacchi.
Lorini, A. (2023), *Le statue bugiarde. Immaginari razziali e coloniali nell'America contemporanea*, Rome: Carocci.
"Love and Suicide" (1895), *The Morning Call*, 77 (76), February 24: 5.
Lozano, G. (1889), *La Escuela antropológica y sociología criminal (ante la sana filosofía)*, La Plata.
Lucchini, L. (1886), *I semplicisti (antropologi, psicologi e sociologi) del diritto penale. Saggio critico*, Turin: UTET.
Lucchini, L. (1888a), "La Escuela antropólogica en materia de criminalidad," *Revista forense chilena*, 4 (4): 637–640.
Lucchini, L. (1888b), "L'École anthropologique en matière de criminalité. Lettre de M. Luigi Lucchini, professeur de droit pénal à l'Université de Bologne, à M. Charles Lucas, membre de l'Institut de France," *Revue critique de Législation et de Jurisprudence*, 17: 637–40.
Lucchini, L. (1889), "La Escuela antropólogica en materia de criminalidad," *El Foro. Diario de Derecho, Legislación y Jurisprudencia*, 16 (32): 112.
Luconi, S. (2010), "La rappresentazione degli italiani nell'immaginario statunitense," *Diacronie. Studi di Storia Contemporanea*, 5 (4): 1–16.
Lugon, O. (2008). *Lo stile documentario in fotografia. Da August Sander a Walker Evans (1920–1945)*, Milan: Mondadori Electa.
Luschan, F. von (1892), "Die antropologische Stellung der Juden," *Correspondenz-Blatt der deutschen Gesellschaft für Anthropologie, Ethnologie und Urgeschichte*, 23: 94–100.
Lyons, M. (2012), *The Writing Culture of Ordinary People in Europe, c. 1860–1920*, Cambridge: Cambridge University Press.
M. B. S. (1887), "Beltrani Scalia, La detenzione a tempo indeterminato ed il riformatorio di Elmira (S. U. di America)," *Rivista di discipline carcerarie*, 17: 303–311.
Mac Mahon R. (2016), "Histories of interpersonal violence in Europe and North America (1700–present)," in P. Knepper and A. Johansen (eds.), *The Oxford Handbook of the History of Crime and Criminal Justice*, 111–31, Oxford: Oxford University Press.
Macedo, C. M. (1911), *Algunas variaciones anatomicás de los antiguos cráneos peruvianos*, Doctoral thesis in Natural Sciences, Lima: Tipografía Fabbri.
Mackert, N. (2014), "Danger and Progress: White Middle-Class Juvenile Delinquency and Motherly Anxiety in the Post-War US," in H. Ellis (ed.), *Juvenile Delinquency and the Limits of Western Influence, 1850–2000*, 199–223, Basingstoke: Palgrave Macmillan.
Maehle, A.H. (1993), "The Search for Objective Communication: Medical Photography in the Nineteenth Century," in R. G. Mazzolini (ed.), *Non-Verbal Communication in Science Prior to 1900*, 563–86, Florence: Olschki.
Maggie, Y. (1992), *Medo do feitiço. Relações entre magia e poder no Brasil*, Rio de Janeiro: Arquivo Nacional.
Mailhe, A. (2013), "El laberinto de la soledad del genio, o las paradojas de El hombre mediocre," *Varia Historia*, 29 (49): 197–216.
Maio, M. C., ed. (2010). *Raça como questão: história, ciência e identidades no Brasil*, Rio de Janeiro: Editora Fiocruz.

Maldonado, J. M. (1903), *Proceso Zuazo. Contestación el escrito publicado por la señora María V. de Zuazo*, La Paz: Imprenta y Litografía Artística.
Mallereal, J. (2012), "La medicina: historia, saber y poder. El higienismo como dispositivo de defensa social," in H. Palma and R. Pardo (eds.), *Epistemología de las ciencias sociales*, 249–74, Buenos Aires: Editorial Biblos.
Mamani Yanque, Y. D. (2021), "Los aymaras y el aymara en el tiempo," *Revista del Piensamento Critico Aymara*, 3 (1): 21–34.
Montaldo, S. and C. Cilli (eds.), *The Lombroso Museum: "Cesare Lombroso" Museum of Criminal Anthropology, University of Turin*, Turin: Hapax (2024).
Mantegazza, P. (1871), "Della capacità dell'orbita nel cranio umano e dell'indice cefalorbitale," *Archivio per l'Antropologia e la Etnologia*, 1 (2): 149–66.
Marteau, J. (2003), *Las Palabras del Orden. Proyecto Republicano y Cuestión Criminal en Argentina (Buenos Aires, 1880–1930)*, Buenos Aires: Editores del Puerto.
Martínez Baca, F. (1899), *Los tatuajes. Estudio psicológico y médico-legal*, Mexico City: Tipografía de la Oficina Impresora del Timbre.
Martínez Baca, F., and M. Vergara (1892), *Estudios de antropología criminal*, Puebla: Imprenta, Litografía y Encuadernación de Benjamín Lara.
Martínez Baca, F and M. Vergara (1894), *Studi di antropologia criminale:Memoria presentata all'Esposizione Internazionale di Chicago (versione dallo spagnuolo)*, Turin: Bocca.
Martinez, F. (2021), *Regenerar la raza. Política educativa en Bolivia (1898–1920)*, La Paz: Vicepresidencia del Estado Plurinacional-CIS.
Martucci, P. (2014), "Migrazioni e criminalità nella storia della criminologia. Le vicende della Lega per la restrizione dell'immigrazione negli Stati Uniti," *Rassegna Italiana di Criminologia*, 2: 112–19.
Matos, J. (1984), *Manual das doenças mentais*, Porto: Campos & Godinho Editores.
Mattos, H. (1998), *Das cores do silêncio: os significados da liberdade no. Sudeste escravista, Brasil século XX*, Rio de Janeiro: Nova Fronteira.
Matus, J. P. (2007), "El positivismo en el derecho penal chileno. Análisis sincrónico y diacrónico de una doctrina de principios del siglo XX que se mantiene vigente," *Revista de Derecho*, 20 (1): 175–203.
Matus, J. P., and R. Carnevali (2007), "Análisis descriptivo y cuantitativo de los artículos de Derecho penal y Criminología de autores chilenos en revistas publicadas en Chile (1885–2006)," *Política Criminal*, 3: 1–138.
Mazzarello, P. (2024), *Il darwinista infedele. Lombroso e l'evoluzione*, Milan: Hoepli.
McKelway, A. J. (1909), "Child Labor in the Carolinas," *Charities and the Commons: A Weekly Journal of Philanthropy and Social Advance*, 21 (18): 743–57.
McLeod, M.C. (1998), "Undesirable Aliens: Race, Ethnicity, and Nationalism in the Comparison of Haitian and British West Indian Immigrant Workers in Cuba, 1912–1939," *Journal of Social History*, 31: 599–623.
Medrano Ossio, J. (1940), *Responsabilidad penal de los indígenas*, Potosí: Tipografía P. Magne.
Mella, R. (1896), *Lombroso y los anarquistas. Refutación*, Barcelona: Ciencia Social.
Mello, J. de M. (1934), "Otto volte omicida!," *AAC*, 54: 397–412.
"Men, Women and Pain" (1892), *The Helena Indipendent*, 33 (125), June 26.

Mendoza, Q. (1907), *Juicio seguido contra doña Leonor Collazos Lara por homicidio involuntario, perpetrado en la persona del que fue doctor Abelardo Renjel*, Oruro: Imprenta de El Ferrocarril.

Menéses, A. (1892), "La Escuela Antropológica," *El Diario Judicial*, August 22–September 9.

Merlo, F. (2024), "The Water Jugs," in S. Montaldo and C. Cilli (eds.), *The Lombroso Museum*, 150–2. Turin: Hapax.

Merriman, J. (2016), *The Dynamite Club: How a Bombing in Fin-de-Siècle Paris Ignited the Age of Modern Terror*, London: Yale University Press.

Milicia, M. T. (2014), *Lombroso e il brigante. Storia di un cranio conteso*, Rome: Salerno.

Miller, J.G. (1991), *Last One Over the Wall: The Massachusetts Experiment in Closing Reform Schools*, Columbus: Ohio State University Press.

"Ministerio de Justicia e Instrucción pública" (1893), *El Comercio*, February 11: 1.

Miranda, R. (1947), "Alcoholismo, factor de desnutrición y degradación de nuestro pueblo," *Revista de los Carabineros de Chile*, 8: 79–83.

Miró Quesada, O. (1916), "El caso del asesino Montes. Ensayo de criminología práctica," *Revista Universitaria*, 11 (2), September–October: 165–299.

Miró Quesada, O. (1922), *Breves apuntes de mesologia criminal peruana*, Lima: E.R. Villarán.

Monroy, A. (1893), "Una carta de Lombroso," *Periódico Oficial del Gobierno del Estado de Puebla*, 51 (11): 142.

Montague (1908), "Editorial Comment: The American Jew E.G.," *Emanu-El*, October 30: 3.

Montaldo, S., ed. (2015), *Il Museo di Antropologia criminale Cesare Lombroso dell'Università di Torino*, Turin: Silvana.

Montaldo, S. (2018a), "Le début de la pensée raciste de Lombroso (1860–1871)," in A. Aramini and E. Bovo (eds.), *La pensée de la race en Italie. Du romantisme au fascisme*, 87–100, Besançon: Presses universitaires de Franche-Comté.

Montaldo, S. (2018b), "Lombroso: The Myth, The History," *Crime, History & Societies*, 22 (2): 31–61.

Montaldo, S. (2019), *Donne delinquenti: Il genere e la nascita della criminologia*, Rome: Carocci.

Montaldo, S. (2023), "Il giovane apprendista e il vecchio maestro: Fernando Ortiz e Cesare Lombroso," in L. Gaffuri, S. Guerra, and A. Trisciuoglio (eds.), *Italia e Cuba / Cuba e Italia: Incontri e nuove identità (Secoli XV–XXI)*, 325–48. Turin: Otto.

Monteiro, F. (2020), "O ´racialista vacilante´: Nina Rodrigues e seus estudos sobre antropologia cultural e psicologia das multidões (1880–1906)," *Topoi*, 21 (43): 193–215.

Montoro, O. (1930), "El Doctor Israel Castellanos y el Premio Lombroso," *Vida Nueva*, 25: XXVII–XXVIII.

Moore, R. (1997), *Nationalizing Blackness: Afrocubanismo and Artistic Revolution in Havana, 1920–1940*, Pittsburgh: University of Pittsburgh Press.

Morales Macedo, C. (1911), *Algunas variaciones anatómicas de los antiguos cráneos peruanos*, Ph.D. diss., Faculty of Natural Sciences, Lima: Tipografía Carlos Fabbri.

Morón Ponce, H. E. (2021), "Criminalidad y modernización punitiva en Lima. 1862–1892," Bachelor's thesis, Facultad de Ciencias Sociales, Escuela Profesional de Historia, Universidad Nacional Mayor de San Marcos, Lima.

Morton, S. G., and G. Combe (1839), *Crania americana; or, A comparative view of the skulls of various aboriginal nations of North and South America. To which is prefixed*

an essay on the varieties of the human species, Philadelphia: John Penington; James Madden & Co.
Mott, F. L. (1950), *American Journalism: A History of Newspapers in the United States through 260 Years: 1690 to 1950*, New York: MacMillan.
Moyano Gacitúa, C. (1894), *Notas de filosofía penal. Sobre el anarquismo*, Cordoba: La Patria.
Mudimbe, V. (1988), *The Invention of Africa: Gnosis, Philosophy, and the Order of Knowledge*, London: James Curray.
Muhammad, K. G. (2010), *The Condemnation of Blackness: Race, Crime, and the Making of Modern Urban America*, Cambridge, MA: Harvard University Press.
Muñiz, M. A. (1891), "Positivismo científico y Antropología criminal. (Fragmentos de un discurso)," *La Gaceta Judicial*, 1 (2/129), August 27.
Nani, M. (2009), "Lombroso e le razze," in S. Montaldo and P. Tappero (eds.), *Cesare Lombroso cento anni dopo*, 165–74, Turin: UTET.
Naranjo Orovio, C. (2016), *Fernando Ortiz. Estudio critico*, Madrid: Fundacion Larramendi.
Natale, S. (2016), *Supernatural Entertainments: Victorian Spiritualism and the Rise of Modern Media Culture*, University Park: Pennsylvania State University.
Navitski, R. (2017), *Sensational Cinema and Journalism in Early Twentieth-Century Mexico and Brazil*, Durham, NC: Duke University Press.
"New Books" (1892a), *The Sun*, 59 (229), April 16: 7.
"New Books" (1892b), *The Sun*, 60 (122), December 31: 7.
"New Books" (1895), *The Sun*, 62 (295), June 22: 7.
Nina Rodrigues, R. (1890), "Os mesticos brasileiros," *Gazeta Medica da Bahia*. April–May: 21 (9) (1890): 401–7.
Nina Rodrigues, R. (1894), *As raças humanas e a responsabilidade penal no Brasil*, Bahia: Almeida.
Nina Rodrigues, R. (1897) "Ilusoes da catechese no Brasil," *Revista Brasileira*, 9: 321–35.
Nina Rodrigues, R. (1899), "Metissage, degenerescence et crime," *Archives d'Anthropologie Criminelle. Reprinted in História, Ciências, Saúde-Manguinhos*, 15: 1151–80 (2008).
Nina Rodrigues, R. (1902), "A propos du memoire: 'La folie des foules,'" *APC*, 1: 290–3.
Nina Rodrigues, R. (1938 [1894]), *As raças humanas e a responsabilidade penal no Brasil*, Rio de Janeiro: Guanabara.
Nina Rodrigues, R. (2010 [1933]), *Os Africanos no Brasil*, esp. ch. II, "Os negros maometanos no Brasil," 44–77, Rio de Janeiro: Centro Edelstein de Pesquisas Sociais.
Nordau, M. (1895), "To Professor Caesar Lombroso, Turin," *Degeneration*, New York: D. Appleton and Company.
N[ordau], M. (1906), "Lombroso, Cesare," in *Jewish Encyclopedia: A Descriptive Record of the History, Religion, Literature and Customs of the Jewish People from the Earliest Times to the Present Day*, vol. 8, 154–5, New York: Funk and Wagnalls.
Nordau, M. (1909), "Zionismus und Antisemitismus [1899]," in Nordau, *Zionistische Schriften*, 299–306, Cologne: Jüdischer Verlag.
"Nordau and His Master" (1895), *The Morning Time*, October 7: 4.
"Nordau's Errors" (1895a), *The Ravalli Republican*, 2 (13), November 13: 1.
"Nordau's Errors" (1895b), *The Arizona Silver*, 18 (34), November 16: 1.
"Not Consoling to Geniuses" (1892), *The Evening Star*, 81 (20.362), September 10: 13.
"Nowe idee Lombrosa" (1895), *Dziennik Chicagoski*, 163, July 16: 2.
Noyes, W. (1887), "The Criminal Type," *American Journal of Social Science*, 24: 31–42.

Oda, A.M., G. Raimundo, and P. Dalgalarrondo (2000), "Juliano Moreira: um psiquiatra negro frente ao racismo científico," *Memória, Revista Brasileira de Psiquiatria*, 22 (4): 178–9.

Oficina Nacional de Inmigración, Estadística y Propaganda geográfica (1904), *Censo General de la población de la República de Bolivia (según empadronamiento de 1 de septiembre de 1900)*, vol. II, Resultados definitivos, La Paz: Talleres José M Gamarra.

Okrent, D. (2019), *The Guarded Gate. Bigotry, Eugenics, and the Law that Kept Two Generations of Jews, Italians and Other European Immigrants out of America*, New York: Scribner.

"Opinión de Zola. Acerca de la locura de Guy de Maupassant" (1892), *El Imparcial*, June 4.

Oppenheimer, F. J. (1908), "Jewish Criminality," *The Independent*, September 17: 640–2.

Orlandi, F. (2024), "Lombrosians after Lombroso: Criminal anthropology in the age of fascism, 1909–1945," Ph.D. diss., KU Leuven, Leuven, and University of Turin, Turin.

Ortiz, F. (1906), *Hampa Afro-Cubana. Los Negros Brujos (apuentes para un estudio de etnología criminal)*, Madrid: Librería de Fernando Fé.

Ortiz, F. (1916), *Los negros esclavos*, Havana: Revista Bimestre Cubana.

Ortiz, F. (1917), *Hampa Afro-Cubana. Los Negros Brujos*, 2nd ed., Madrid: Editorial América.

Ortiz, F. (1923), *Un catauro de cubanismos. Apuntes lexicograficos*, Havana: Harana.

Ortiz, F. (1926), *Proyecto de código criminal cubano*, Havana: Librería Cervantes.

Ortiz, F. (1987 [1940]), *Contrapunteo cubano del tabaco y el azúcar*, Caracas: Biblioteca Ayacucho.

Ortiz, F. (1995a), *Cuban Counterpoint Tobacco and Sugar*, Durham, NC: Duke University Press.

Ortiz, F. (1995b), *Los negros brujos*, Havana: Editorial de Ciencias Sociales.

Ortiz, F. (2012 [1915]), *La filosofía penal de los espiritistas*, San Juan, Puerto Rico: Editorial Nuevo Mundo.

Ortiz, F. (2022 [1946]), *El engaño de las razas*, Granada: Editorial Universidad de Granada.

O'Squarr, Flor (1892), *Les coulisses de l'anarchie*, Paris: Nouvelle Librairie Parisienne.

"Our Boston Literary Letter: Autorship, Crime and Travel," *Springfield Weekly Repubblican*, September 19 (1890): 3.

Paiva, T. (1926), *Catálogo da notabilíssima, escolhida e variada bibliotheca que pertenceu ao erudito homem Dr. Elysio de Carvalho*, Rio de Janeiro: Virgilio.

Palafox, A. (2021), "Construcción de una etiología de la violación en los discursos de la medicina legal y la criminología chilena (1900–1950)," *Atenea*, 524: 265–86.

Palma, C. (1897), "El porvenir de las razas en el Perú," Bachelor's thesis, University of San Marcos, Lima. Available online: https://cybertesis.unmsm.edu.pe/item/4aead725-53a6-4ec3-99a4-8e51874d0f8a, 1–24.

Palmié, S. (2002), *Wizards and Scientists: Explorations in Afro-Cuban Modernity and Tradition*, Durham, NC: Duke University Press.

Pandora, K. (2009), "Popular Science in National and Transnational Perspective: Suggestions from the American Context," *Isis*, 100 (2), June 2009: 346–58.

"Paris Letter" (1879a), *Daily Cairo Bulletin*, 38, August 9: 1

"Paris Letter" (1879b), *The Lafayette Advertiser*, 42, August 16: 2

Parmelee, M. (1911), "Introduction to the English Version," in C. Lombroso, *Crime: Its Causes and Remedies*, XI–XXXII, Boston: Little Brown.

Pavez Ojeda, J. (2009), "El retrato de los «negros brujos»: Los archivos visuales de la antropología afrocubana (1900–1920)," *Aisthesis*, 46: 83–110.

Pavez Ojeda, J. (2021), "The Fetishes of Fernando Ortiz," *H: Journal of Ethnographic Theory*, 11 (1): 122–40.

Peard, J. (2000), *Race, Place, and Medicine: The Idea of the Tropics in Nineteenth-Century Brazil*, Durham, NC: Duke University Press.

Pedersson, A. (2018), "A Science of Nature, a Science of Crime: The Reception and Embedding of Positivist Criminology in Sweden," *Crime, History & Societies*, 22 (2): 63–81.

"Pellagra" (1872), *Der Deutsche Correspondent*, 206, August 29: 2.

Pérez, D. (1915), "Antropófagos y hechiceros. La obra de Carpena," *La Esfera*, II (74): 27–9.

Pérez Firmat, G. (1989), *The Cuban Condition. Translation and identity in modern Cuban Literature*. Cambridge: Cambridge University Press.

"Personal and Pertinent" (1895), *The Daily Herald Brownsville*, May 17.

Petit, C. (2010), "Lombroso et l'Amérique," *Revue de science criminelle et de droit pénal comparé*, 1: 17–29.

"Physical Structure of Italians" (1870), *Appletons' Journal of Literature, Science and Art*, 3, March 19: 334.

"Physicians and Scientists," *River Falls Journal*, 30 (14), July 29: 1.

Piasere, L. (2020), "Quando Boas studiava gli italiani," *Voci. Annuale di Scienze Umane*: 40–70.

Piccato, P. (2001), *City of Suspects: Crime in Mexico City, 1900–1931*, Durham, NC: Duke University Press.

Pick, D. (1989), *Faces of Degeneration: A European Disorder c. 1848–c. 1918*, Cambridge: Cambridge University Press.

Pifferi, M. (2013), *L'individualizzazione della pena: Difesa sociale e crisi della legalità penale tra Otto e Novecento*. Florence: Giuffrè.

Pifferi, M (2022), "From responsability to dangerousness? The failed promise of penal positivism," in M. Pifferi (ed.), *The Limits of Criminological Positivism: The Movement for Criminal Law Reform in the West, 1870–1940*, 255–79, London: Routledge.

Pineda Iglesias, G. (1899), "¿Se justifica la pena capital en el nuevo campo del positivismo?," Bachelor's thesis, *Anales de la Universidad Mayor de San Marcos de Lima*, 26: 65–86.

Piñero, O. (1886), "El tercer congreso internacional penitenciario y el antropológico-criminal," *Revista Jurídica*, III, 1051–60.

Piñero, N. (1887a), "Derecho Criminal. Discurso del Dr. Norberto Piñero al inaugurar la cátedra correspondiente en la Facultad de Derecho," *Revista Jurídica*, 4: 163–77.

Piñero, N. (1887b), *Programa de Derecho Criminal*, Buenos Aires: Imprenta y Librería de Mayo.

Piñero, N. (1888), "Problemas de Criminalidad. Sobre las causas de las criminalidad," *Revista Jurídica*, 4: 163–77.

Polar, J. (1900), "Aptitudes políticas de nuestra raza," Bachelor's thesis, *Anales de la Universidad Mayor de San Marcos de Lima*, 27: 159–71.

Pollak, O. (1950), *The Criminality of Women*, New York: A. S. Barnes and Company.

Ponce, A. (1946 [1930]), "Un cónclave de metapsíquicos," in A. Ponce, *Obras completas*, Buenos Aires: Matera.

Portella, J. E. (1905), "Algunas observaciones sobre la escuela penal positiva," *El Comercio*, November 11.

Porto, A. (2010), "Romance sensacional e histórias de crime no Rio de Janeiro de início do século XX," *Escritos*, 4: 281–317.
Portocarrero, G. M. (2004), "El fundamento invisible: función y lugar de las ideas racistas en la República Aristocrática," in A. Panfichi H. and F. Portocarrero (eds.), *Mundos interiores: Lima 1850–1950*, 219–60, Lima: Centro de Investigación de la Universidad del Pacífico.
Posnansky, A. (1923), *Impulsos atávicos. El caso de Polonia Méndez. Consideraciones antropológicas psiquiátricas referentes a un crimen llamado pasional*, La Paz: Imprenta Velarde.
Prack, G. (1892), *El Delito ante la Nueva Ciencia Penal*, Buenos Aires: Imprenta San Martin.
Prado y Ugarteche, J. (1980 [1894]), "Estado social del Perú. (Fragmento) 1894," in L. Zea (ed.), *Pensamiento positivista latinoamericano*: 324–335. Caracas: Biblioteca Ayacucho.
Prado y Ugarteche, J. (1985 [1889]), "El metodo positivo en el Derecho Penal," *Ius et Práxiz. Revista de la Facultad de Derecho. Universidad de Lima*, 6: 108–179.
Prado y Ugarteche, M. I. (1899–1900) "El tipo criminal. Estudio de antropología jurídica," *El Ateneo*, I: 5–6; II: 7, 9, 10, 12.
"Professor Lombroso" (1891a), *The Weekly Union Times*, 27 (31), July 31: 1.
"Professor Lombroso" (1891b), *Forest Republican*, 24 (16), August 12: 1.
Pugliese, N. (2023), "Fotografia giudiziaria a Cuba tra XIX e XX secolo: I detenuti del Presidio de La Habana nell'Archivio del Museo di Antropologia Criminale Cesare Lombroso," in *Italia e Cuba / Cuba e Italia: Incontri e nuove Identità (Secoli XV–XXI)*, 393–409, Turin: Otto.
Quinta, H. (2018), "A trajetória de um libertário: Pietro Gori na América do Sul (1898–1902)," Foz do Iguaçu: EDUNILA.
Quisbert, P. (2005), "The Glory of the Race: Arturo Posnansky and Tiwanaku," in J. Farré, F. Martinez, and I. Olivares (eds.), *Hommes de science et intellectuels européens en Amérique latine (XIXe–XXe siècles)*, 283–304, Paris: Editions Le Manuscrit.
Rafter, N. (2009), "Gli Stati Uniti," in S. Montaldo and P. Tappero (eds.), *Cesare Lombroso cento anni dopo*, 277–87, Turin: UTET.
Rafter, N. and P. Y. Ystehede (2009), "Lombroso e la cultura di massa in Europa (1890–1930)," in S. Montaldo and P. Tappero (eds.), *Cesare Lombroso cento anni dopo*, 185–90, Turin: UTET.
Rafter, N. H. (1992), "Criminal Anthropology in the United States," *Criminology*, 30: 525–45.
Rafter, N. H. (1997), *Creating Born Criminals*, Urbana: University of Illinois Press.
Rafter, N. H. (2006), "Criminal Anthropology: Its Reception in the United States and the Nature of Its Appeal," in P. Becker and R. F. Wetzell (eds.), *Criminals and Their Scientists: The History of Criminology in International Perspective*, 159–81. New York: Cambridge University Press.
Ramos Mejía, F. (1888), "Antropología Jurídica. Principios Fundamentales de la Escuela Positiva de Derecho Penal," *Revista General de Administración*, 4: 31–7, 112–26.
Ramos Mejía, J. M. (1878–82), *Las neurosis de los hombres célebres en la historia argentina*, 2 vols., Buenos Aires: Martín Biedma.
Rauty, R. (2010), "Il sogno americano. Rappresentazione dell'emigrazione italiana nei classici della sociologia statunitense," *Italies*, 14: 33–50.
Rebelo, F., and S. Caponi (2007), "O gabinete do doutor Edelvito Campelo D'Araújo: a Penitenciária Pedra Grande como espaço de construção de um saber (1933-1945)," *História, Ciências, Saúde-Manguinhos*, 14 (4): 1217–38.

Reiss, R. A. (1913), *Polícia Technica. Resumo das conferências realizadas no Rio*, Rio de Janeiro: Biblioteca do Boletim Policial.

Relatório da Secretaria de Justiça de São Paulo (RSJSP) (1893).

"Remarkable skulls found in Peru" (1834), *Scientific intelligence: The Dublin Journal of Medical and Chemical Science*, 5: 475–80.

Renneville, M. (1994), "La reception de Lombroso en France (1880–1900)," in L. Mucchieli (ed.), *Histoire de la Criminologie Française*, 107–35, Paris: L'Harmattan.

"Results of Observation of Criminals" (1875), *The Daily Clarion*, 2, January 6: 3.

"Retaliation" (1892), *St. Paul Daily Globe*, 14 (329), November 24: 6.

Ribak, G. (2014), "'The Jews Usually Left Those Crimes to Esau'. The Jewish Responses to Accusations about Jewish Criminality in New York 1908–1913," *AJS Review*, 38 (1): 1–28.

Riis, J. A. (1890), *How the Other Half Lives: Studies Among the Tenements of New York*, New York: Charles Scribner's Sons.

Rios, A. (1898), "El positivismo penal," Ph.D. diss., *Anales de la Universidad Mayor de San Marcos de Lima*, 25: 75–116.

Ripley, W. Z. (1899), *The Races of Europe: A Sociological Study*, New York: Appleton.

Rivacoba y Rivacoba, M. (1991), *Evolución histórica del derecho penal chileno*, Valparaíso: EDEVAL.

Riviale, P. (2002), "Alcide d'Orbigny, 'l'homme péruvien' et les débuts de l'anthropologie," in M. Bertrand and L. Vidal (eds.), *À la redécouverte des Amériques*, 37–52, Toulouse: Presses universitaires du Midi.

Rodríguez, A. M. (1898), "Reflexiones antropológicas relativas al hombre universal, al americano y al peruano," Ph.D. diss., University of Lima, Faculty of Science, *Anales de la Universidad Mayor de San Marcos de Lima*, 25: 339–432.

Rodríguez, A. M. (1899), "Estudios Criminológicos. Primera Parte. Los caracteres del hombre criminal," Bachelor's thesis, University of Lima, Faculty of Medicine.

Rodriguez, J. (2006), *Civilizing Argentina. Science, Medicine and the Modern State*, Chapel Hill: University of North Carolina Press.

Roosevelt, T. (1891), "Letter from Theodore Roosevelt to Ann Roosevelt," March 21, Harvard College Library, Theodore Roosevelt Center. Available online: theodorerooseveltcenter.org/Research/Digital-Library/.

Roosevelt, T. (1908), "Letter from Theodore Roosevelt to Guglielmo Ferrero," November 14. Collection: Library of Congress Manuscript Division.

Ross, E. A. (1901a), "The Causes of Race Superiority," *Annals of the American Academy of Political and Social Science*, 1: 67–89.

Ross, E. A. (1901b), *Social Control. Survey on the Foundation of Order*, New York: Macmillan.

Ross, E. A. (1914), *The Old World in the New: The Significance of Past and Present Immigration to the American People*, Project Gutenberg.

Rotondo, F. (2014), *Itinerari alla periferia di Lombroso. Pietro Gori e la "Criminologia moderna" in Argentina*, Naples: Editoriale Scientifica.

Rouma, G. (1913), *Les indiens quitchouas et aymaras des hauts-plateaux de la Bolivie*, Brussels: Misch & Thron.

Ruggiero, K. (2004), *Modernity in the Flesh. Medicine, Law and Society in Turn of the Century Argentina*, Stanford, CA: Stanford University Press.

Russell, F. (1900), "Studies in Cranial Variations," *The American Naturalist*, 34 (405): 737–45.

Rutsch, M. (2007), *Entre el campo y el gabinete. Nacionales y extranjeros en la profesionalización de la antropología mexicana (1877–1929)*, Mexico City: Instituto Nacional de Antropología e Historia/Universidad Nacional Autónoma de México.

Saavedra B. (1900), *Estadística judicial 1897–1898*, La Paz: Oficina Nacional de Inmigración, Estadística y Propaganda Geográfica, Taller Tipo-litográfico Ayacucho.

Saavedra, B. (1903), "La criminalidad aymara," in *El Ayllu*, La Paz: Imprenta Artística Velarde, Aldazosa y Ca.

Sabadell, A. L., and D. Dimoulis (2022), "Limits and displacements in the adoption of criminological positivism in Brazil (1890–1940)" in M. Pifferi, *The Limits of Criminological Positivism: The Movement for Criminal Law Reform in the West, 1870–1940*, 231–54, New York: Routledge.

Saco, José A. (1932), *Historia de la esclavitud de los indios del Nuevo Mundo*, vol. I, Havana: Cultural.

Salazar, J. M. (1903), "La represión de la delincuencia infantil. Debe ser organizada conforme a las conclusiones de la Criminología moderna," Bachelor's thesis, *Anales de la Universidad Mayor de San Marcos de Lima*, 30: 37–73.

Sale, S. (1900), "Can We redeem the Criminal?," *The Jewish Voice*, November 2: 5.

Salessi, J. (1995), *Médicos maleantes y maricas. Higiene, criminología y homosexualidad en la construcción de la nación argentina (Buenos Aires: 1871–1914)*, Rosario: Beatriz Viterbo.

Salla, F. (1999), *As Prisões em São Paulo (1822–1940)*, São Paulo: Annablume-Fapesp.

Salvatore, R. (1996), "Penitentiaries, Visions of Class and Export Economies: Brazil and Argentina Compared," in R. Salvatore and C. Aguirre (eds.), *The Birth of the Penitentiary in Latin America*, 194–223, Austin: University of Texas Press.

Salvatore, R. (2006), "Positivist Criminology and State formation in modern Argentina (1890–1940)," in P. Becker and R. Wetzell (eds.), *Criminals and their scientists*, 253–79, Cambridge: Cambridge University Press.

Salvatore, R. (2016), "Evidencia empírica y explicación teórica en *Los Hombres de Presa* de Luis M. Drago," Jornadas Crimen y Sociedad. 10 años de estudio sobre delito, policía y justicia en perspectiva histórica, UDESA-UNRN-Agencia Nacional Científica y Tecnológica-CONICET.

Salvatore, R. and C. Aguirre (1996), "The Birth of the Penitentiary in Latin America: Toward an Interpretative Social History of Prisons," in R. Salvatore and C. Aguirre (eds.), *The Birth of the Penitentiary in Latin America*, 1–43, Austin: University of Texas Press.

Salvatore, R., C. Aguirre, and G. Joseph, eds. (2001), *Crime and Punishment in Latin America. Law and Society Since Colonial Times*, Durham, NC: Duke University Press.

Sánchez, F. (1956), "Influencia del factor económico en la criminalidad," *Revista de los Carabineros de Chile*, 56: 9–10.

Sansone, L. (2022), *La Galassia Lombroso*, Bari: Laterza.

Sansone, L. (2023), *Field Station Bahia: Brazil in the Work of Lorenzo Dow Turner, E. Franklin Frazier and Frances and Melville Herskovits, 1935–1967*, Leiden: Brill.

São Paulo (1924), *Decreto n. 3.706, de 29 de abril de 1924.*

Scarzanella, E. (1999), *Italiani Malagente. Immigrazione, Criminalità, Razzismo in Argentina, 1890–1940*, Milan: Franco Angeli.

Schaack, M. J. (1889). *Anarchy and Anarchists. A History of the Red Terror and the Social Revolution in America and Europe. Communism, Socialism, and Nihilism in Doctrine and in Deed. The Chicago Haymarket Conspiracy, and the Detection and Trial of the Conspirators*, Chicago: F.J. Schulte & Company.

Schorn, J., and D. Williams (2017), "The Theft of Authorship: Crime Narrative in Post-Revolutionary Early American Literature," in C. Raczkowski (ed.), *A History of American Crime Fiction*, 27–40, Cambridge: Cambridge University Press.

Schwab, M. (1891), "A Convicted Anarchist's Reply to Professor Lombroso," *The Monist*, 1 (4): 520–4.

Schwarcz, L. M. (2005), *O espetáculo das raças: cientistas, instituições e questão racial no Brasil, 1870–1930*, 6th edn. São Paulo: Companhia das Letras.

Schwartz, S. (2022), "On Social Photography," in *Documentary Genealogies: Photography 1848-1917 Exhibition, Madrid, Museo Nacional Centre de Arte Reina Sofia, from November 16, 2022 to February 27, 2023*, 243–9, Madrid: Museo nacional centre de arte Reina Sofia.

Schwartz, S. R. (1991), *The Emergence of Jewish Scholarship in America: The Publication of the Jewish Encyclopedia*, Cincinnati: Hebrew Union.

"Science and Crime: What Savants Know of the Natural History of Criminals" (1890), *The Sunday Herald and Weekly National Intelligencer*, 25 (13), June 15: 13.

"Science and the Spirits: Schiaparelli and Lombroso on mediumistic phenomena" (1893), *The Sun*, 60 (172), February 19: 6.

"Scientific Notes" (1913), *The Hebrew Standard*, September 5: 13.

Secord, J. A. (2004), "Knowledge in Transit," *Isis*, 95: 654–72.

Sekula, A. (1986), "The Body and the Archive," *October*, 39: 3–64.

Serafini, S. (2025), "Atavism, Recidivism, and Prison System: Cesare Lombroso in the British Popular Press, 1887–1896," *Journal of Modern Italian Studies*.

Sheldon, W. H. (1949), *Varieties of Delinquent Youth: An Introduction to Constitutional Psychiatry*, New York: Harper & Brothers Publishers.

Sheldon, W. H. (1957), "Mesomorphs in Mischief," *Contemporary Psychology*, 2 (5): 125–6.

Shepherd, J. (2024), "A History of Future Crime: Prediction, Youth, and the Organisation of Suspicion in Criminology and American Society, 1900–1960," Ph.D. thesis, Durham University, Durham.

Sherman, A. F., and P. Mesenhöller (2005), *Augustus F. Sherman: Ellis Island Portraits, 1905–1920*, New York: Aperture.

Sicherman, B. and C. Hurd Green. 1980a. "Dreier Mary Elisabeth," in *Notable American Women: The Modern Period. A Biographical Dictionary*, 204–6, Cambridge, MA: Belknap Press.

Sicherman, B. and C. Hurd Green. 1980b. "Kellor Frances," in *Notable American Women: The Modern Period. A Biographical Dictionary*, 393–5. Cambridge, MA: Belknap Press.

Siegel, L. J. (1983), *Criminology*, St. Paul: West Publishing Co.

Sighele, S. (1891), *La folla delinquente*, Turin: Bocca.

Sighele, S. (1892), *La muchedumbre delincuente*, Madrid: La España Moderna.

Sighele, S. (1906), *Letteratura tragica*, Milano: Fratelli Treves.

Sighele, S. (1908), "A litteratura dos processos," *Boletim Policial*, 7: 284–93.

Sighele, S. (1910), *Literatura trágica*, Madrid: Imprenta de Enrique Teodoro y Alonso.

Simon, J. (2001), "Sanctioning Government: Explaining America's Severity Revolution," *University of Miami Law Review*, 56: 217–53.

Simon, J. (2006), "Positively Punitive: How the Inventor of Scientific Criminology Who Died at the Beginning of the Twentieth Century Continues to Haunt American Crime Control at the Beginning of the Twenty-first," *Texas Law Review*, 84: 2134–72.

Smart, C. (1976), *Women, Crime and Criminology: A Feminist Critique*, Boston: Routledge and Kegan Paul.

Smith, M. (2023), *The First Resort: The History of Social Psychiatry in the United States*, New York: Columbia University Press.

"Socialism and Insanity" (1886a), *The Universalist*, 39, September 25: 2.

"Socialism and Insanity" (1886b), *Thomas County Cat*, 39, October 7: 2.

"Socialism and Insanity" (1886c), *Savannah Courier*, 40, October 7: 1.

"Sociedad Agustín Aspiazu," *El Diario*, December 14, 1909, p. 2.

Solano, S. (1937), *El Estado peligroso. Algunas de sus formas clínicas no delictivas*, Lima: Universidad de San Marcos.

"Some New Books" (1890), *The Sun*, 57 (273), May 31: 7.

Soria Galvarro, R. (1907), *Proceso célebre: Leonor Collazos Lara. Acusada por asesinato del doctor Abelardo Renjel*, Oruro: Imprenta de 'El Industrial'.

Sozzo, M. (2006), "Traduttore Traditore. Importación Cultural, Traducción e Historia del Presente de la Criminología en América Latina," in M. Sozzo (ed.), *Reconstruyendo las Criminologías Críticas*, 353–431, Buenos Aires: Ad-Hoc.

Sozzo, M. (2007), "Florencio Varela y el Nacimiento del Liberalismo Penal en la Argentina," *Nueva Doctrina Penal*, B: 635–48.

Sozzo, M. (2015), *Locura y Crimen. Nacimiento de la Intersección entre Dispositivo Penal y Dispositivo Psiquiátrico*, Buenos Aires: Didot.

Sozzo, M. (2017), "Los usos de Lombroso. Tres variantes en el nacimiento de la criminología positivista en Argentina," in M. Sozzo and L. Caimari (eds.), *Historia de la cuestión criminal en América Latina*, 27–69, Rosario: Prohistoria.

Speckman, E. (1992), *Crimen y castigo. Legislación penal, interpretaciones de la criminalidad y administración de justicia (Ciudad de México, 1872–1910)*, Mexico City: El Colegio de México/Universidad Nacional Autónoma de México.

Spiro, J. P. (2009), *Defending the Master Race: Conservation, Eugenics, and the Legacy of Madison Grant*, Lebanon: University of Vermont Press.

Spitzka, E. C. (1883), "A Contribution to the Question of the Mental Status of Guiteau and the History of His Trial," *The Alienist and Neurologist*, 4: 201–20.

Stanislawski, M. (2001), *Zionism and the Fin-de-Siècle: Cosmopolitanism and Nationalism from Nordau to Jabotinsky*, Berkeley: University of California Press.

Staples, B. (2019), "How Italians Became 'White'," NYT, October 12.

Starr, F. (1897), "Study of the Criminal in Mexico," *American Journal of Sociology*, 3 (1): 13–14.

Stocking, George W. Jr. (1974), *A Franz Boas Reader. The Shaping of American Anthropology, 1883–1911*, Chicago: University of Chicago Press.

Stone, D. (2008), " 'Not a Race but only a People after all': the Racial Origins of the Jews in Fin-de-Siècle Anthropology," *Patterns of Prejudice*, 42 (2): 133–49.

Suriano, J. (1990), "El estado argentino frente a los trabajadores urbanos: política social y represión, 1880–1916," Anuario 14, Escuela de Historia: 109–37.

Sutherland, E. H. (1951),"Critique of Sheldon's Varieties of Delinquent Youth," *American Sociological Review*, 16 (1): 10–13.

Tamassia, A. (1874), "Craniometria degli alienati e dei delinquenti in rapporto all'Antropologia e alla medicina legale," *Archivio per l'Antropologia e la Etnologia*, 4 (1): 164–89.

Tejera, V. (1929), "Castellanos, La delincuencia femenina en Cuba," *Revista de Medicina legal de Cuba*, 8: 302–4.

"Tendencias devastadoras," *La Industria*, May 16, 1899: 1.

Teti, V. (2011), *La razza maledetta: origini del pregiudizio antimeridionale*, Rome: Manifestolibri.

"The Criminal Type" (1887a), *The Wichita Daily Eagle*, 9 (112), September 26: 8.
"The Criminal Type" (1887b), *The Smirna Times*, 33 (19), October 26: 1.
"The Criminal Type" (1887c), *The Sauk Centre Herald*, 21 (23), October 27: 4.
"The Criminal Type" (1887d), *The Columbus Journal*, 18 (28), November 2: 1.
"The Criminal Type" (1887e), *The Dillon Tribune*, 8 (48), November 25: 2.
"The Death of Cesare Lombroso" (1909), *The Hebrew Standard*, October 22: 4.
"The Evil" (1908), *The Hebrew Standard*, October 16: 8.
"The Holmes Horror" (1895a), *Mower County Transcript*, 28 (22), August 7: 7.
"The Holmes Horror" (1895b), *Pine Bluff Daily Graphic*, 2 (298), September 6: 3.
"The Revolutionists" (1886), *The Fairfield News and Herald*, 51, July 21: 1.
"The Sensibility of Women" (1892), *The Morning Call*, 72 (103), September 11: 10.
"The Spiritualists" (1892), *Medical Record: A Weekly Journal of Medicine and Surgery*, July 30: 132.
Thomas, W. I. (1907), *Sex and Society: Studies in the Social Psychology of Sex.* Chicago: University of Chicago Press.
Thomas, W. I. (1923), *The Unadjusted Girl*, Boston: Little, Brown.
Torrelio, B. (1903), *Proceso criminal. Escrito presentado ante el señor Juez de Acusación, en el sumario instruido para la averiguación de el agente ocasional de la muerte del doctor Manuel Zuazo*, La Paz: Imprenta y Litografía Artística.
Triplett, R. A., ed. (2018), *The Handbook of the History and Philosophy of Criminology*, Hoboken: Wiley.
Ugarte, E. (1947), "Generalidades sobre el alcoholismo," *Revista de los Carabineros de Chile*, 7: 80.
Ulloa, J. C. (1890a), "La locura impulsiva ante los tribunales del Peru,'" *El Diario Judicial*, 1 (nos. 136–42, 144, 146–8, 150–2, 157–8, 161–2, 165–6, 168, 170–1, 174–9, 182, 189, 196–8), September 9–November 22.
Ulloa, J. C. (1890b), "Demostraciòn positiva", *El Diario Judicial* 1 (200), November 25.
Ulloa, J. C., M. Macedo, and M. C. Barrios (1890), "Informe de una comisión de la Academia Libre de Medicina," in J. C. Ulloa, "La locura impulsiva ante los tribunales del Perú," *El Diario Judicial*, 1 (nos. 137–142, 144, 146–148), September 9–22.
Urías, Beatriz (2000), *Indígena y criminal. Interpretaciones del derecho y la antropología en México, 1871–1921*, Mexico City: Universidad Iberoamericana.
Valdizán, H. (1910), "La delincuencia en el Perú. Ensayo de Criminología Nacional," Bachelor thesis, *La Crónica Médica*, 27 (nos. 512, 513, 514, 518, 520, 521), April 4–September 15.
Valdizán, H. (1918), "Peritaje. Un imbecil criminal," *Revista de Psiquiatría y disciplinas conexas*, 1: 166–76.
Valentin, P. (1906), "Fantasmas y espíritus materializados," *APC*, 5: 40–9.
Valentino, S. (2011), "L'Archivio "Cesare Lombroso," in S. Montaldo and P. Novaria (eds.), *Gli Archivi della Scienza. L'Università di Torino e altri casi italiani*, 75–88. Milan: Franco Angeli.
Valette, P. (1903), *De l'érostratisme ou vanité criminelle*, Lyon: A. Storck.
"Various Manifestations" (1891), *The Sun*, October 25: 24.
Venda Fortuna, S. (2013), *Revisitando Nina Rodrigues: um estudo sobre as religiões afrobrasileiras e o conhecimento científico no século XIX*, Maringá: Eduem
"Verbrechen" (1878), *Freie Press für Texas*, 706, March 14: 4.
Verga, A. (1872), "Della fossetta occipitale media dell'osso occipitale," *Archivio per l'Antropologia e la Etnologia*, 2 (1): 273–6.

Verga, A. (1876), "Sulla fossetta media dell'osso occipitale del cranio umano. Nuove ricerche," *Rendiconti*, 9 (1): 11–15.
Vergara Lope, D. (1890), *Refutación teórica y experimental de la teoría de la Anoxihemia del Doctor Jourdanet*, Mexico City: Secretaría de Fomento.
Vezzetti, H. (1985), *La locura en Argentina*, Buenos Aires: Paidós.
Vicuña, J. (1910), *Coa. Jerga de los delincuentes chilenos. Estudio y vocabulario*, Santiago: Imprenta Universitaria.
Viderique, I. (1903), *Proceso Zuazo. Contestación al escrito publicado por la señora María V. de Zuazo*, La Paz: Imprenta y Litografía Artística.
Vieira, C. (1915), "Polícia e publicidade," in *A lucta technica contra o crime: conferências jurídico-policiais*, Rio de Janeiro: Biblioteca do Boletim Policial.
Villa, R. (1985), *Il deviante e i suoi segni. Lombroso e la nascita dell'Antropologia criminale*, Milan: FrancoAngeli.
Villavicencio, V. M. (1930), *Algunos aspectos de nuestra sociología criminal*, Lima: Talls Grafs. de la Penitenciaria.
Villavicencio, V. M. (1933), *Defensas criminales*, Lima: Librería y Editorial Peruana.
Villegas Díaz, M. (2021), "La responsabilidad penal de los indígenas en el pensamiento de José Medrano Ossio," *Criminalia*, 88 (1): 149–67.
Vivado, A., C. Larson and V. Arroyo (1939), "La asistencia psiquiátrica en Chile," *Revista de psiquiatría y disciplinas conexas*, 3: 155–74.
Vucetich, J. (1902), "Delirio sistematizado religioso," *APC*, 1: 164–71.
Walby, K. and N. Carrier (2010), "The Rise of Biocriminology: Capturing Observable Bodily economies of 'Criminal Man'," *Criminology and Criminal Justice*, 10 (3): 261–85.
Wald, L. D. and A. Kellor (1910), "The Construction Camps of the People," in *The Survey: Social, Charitable, Civic: A Journal of Constructive Philanthropy*, 23: 449–65.
Ward, P. (2018), *Lamarck's Revenge*, New York: Bloomsbury.
Weber, M. (1949), *On the Methodology of Social Sciences*, New York: The Free Press.
Webster, W. (1895), "Lombroso on Love and Suicide," *The Alienist and Neurologist*, 16: 86–9.
Weissmann, P. (1999), "Francisco de Veyga. Prolegómenos de la clínica criminológica en la Argentina," *Temas de Historia de la Psiquiatría Argentina*, 7.
Wetzell, R. F. (2000), *Inventing the Criminal: A History of German Criminology, 1880–1945*, Chapel Hill: University of North Carolina Press.
"Why are the Jews Long Living?" (1900), *The Hebrew Standard*, August 24: 1.
Wigmore, J. H. (1911), "Memorial to Lombroso," *Journal of the American Institute of Criminal Law and Criminology*, 2 (4): 491–2.
Winlow, H. (2006), "Mapping Moral Geographies: W. Z. Ripley's Races of Europe and the United States," *Annals of the Association of American Geographers*, 96 (1): 119–41.
Wit, C. W. V. P. de. (2021), "Entre o cárcere e o lar: trabalho e ressocialização feminina na Penitenciária de Florianópolis (1930–1963)," MA diss., Universidade do Estado de Santa Catarina, Florianópolis.
"Woman's Power to Endure Pain" (1892), *Port Gibson Reveille*, 17 (2), April 6: 1.
"Woman's Sensibility" (1892a), *Semi-Weekly Interior Journal*, 20 (68), October 21: 3.
"Woman's Sensibility" (1892b), *Bridgeton Pioneer*, 46 (2322), November 3: 2.
"Women as Prevaricators" (1892), *St. Paul Daily Globe*, 14 (319), November 14: 3.
"Women Endure Pain" (1892), *The Pittsburgh Dispatch*, 47, July 31: 16.
"Women's Criminal Instincts" (1895), *The Indianapolis Journal*, July 10: 2. 50: 936–941.

Wood J. C. (2016), "Crime, News and the Press," in P. Knepper and A. Johansen (eds.), *The Oxford Handbook of the History of Crime and Criminal Justice*, 301–19, Oxford: Oxford University Press.

Zamorano, G. (2011), "Fisonomía del traidor. Fotografía y la racialización de los indígenas bolivianos por la Expedición Créqui-Montfort (1903)," *Anuario del ABNB*, 17: 635–74.

Zedner, L. (1991), "Women, Crime, and Penal Responses: A Historical Account," in M. Tonry (ed.), *Crime and Justice: A Review of Research*, 337–42, Chicago: University of Chicago Press.

Zimmerman, E. (1994), *Los liberales reformistas. La cuestión social en la Argentina, 1890–1916*, Buenos Aires: Sudamericana.

Zimmern, H. (1893a), "Criminal Woman," *Popular Science Monthly*, 44: 218–23.

Zimmern, H. (1893b), "One of the Great Men. Cesare Lombroso. The Great Italian Philosopher of Crime, Insanity, and Genius," *The Sun*, June 11.

Zimmern, H. (1893c), "Reformatory Prisons and Lombroso's Theories," *Popular Science Monthly*, 43: 598–609.

Zuñiga Rodriguez, L. (1991), "El nuevo Código Penal peruano," *Anuario de Derecho Penal y ciencias penales*, 44 (2): 515–24.

Contributors

Martín Albornoz is a researcher at CONICET and professor at the University of San Martín, Argentina. He earned his Ph.D. in History from the University of Buenos Aires. His research focuses on the global impact of anarchism in Buenos Aires, viewed through the social and cultural history of the press and police surveillance. He is the author of *Cuando el anarquismo causaba sensación* (2021).

Viviane Borges is a professor at the State University of Santa Catarina (UDESC), Brazil, and a researcher affiliated with the Institute for the History of Present Time (IHTP), France. Her research focuses on the history of prisons, prisoners' writings and minors in conflict with the law, (auto)biographies of marginalized subjects, archives, public history, difficult heritage, and prison heritage.

Laura Cházaro García is a researcher and professor at the Center for Research and Advanced Studies of the National Polytechnic Institute (IPN), Mexico. She specializes in the history of science and medicine in the nineteenth and twentieth centuries. In recent years, she has focused on the material culture of science, particularly on the uses, practices, and circulation of scientific and medical instruments in Mexico and Europe.

Gabriella Chiaramonti is a former Associate Professor of Latin American History at the University of Padua, Italy. She has studied the political, institutional, and constitutional history of Peru in the twentieth century, focusing on the processes of citizenship and representation. She is the author of the books *Perú, Ecuador e Bolivia: Le repubbliche impervie* (1992) and *Ciudadanía y representación en el Perú* (2005 and 2021).

Emanuele D'Antonio is a postdoctoral fellow in history at the University of Turin, Italy. His primary research interests include Cesare Lombroso and the history of the Jews and anti-Semitism in nineteenth-century Italy. His works include the monograph *Il sangue di Giuditta: Antisemitismo e voci ebraiche nell'Italia di metà Ottocento* (2020).

Diego Galeano is an Associate Professor of Contemporary History at the Pontifical Catholic University of Rio de Janeiro, Brazil. He is a member of the Brazilian National Council for Scientific and Technological Development. His research focuses on the history of urban policing and transnational crime in Latin America. He is the author of *Escritores, detectives y archivistas* (2009) and *Delincuentes viajeros* (2018), also published in Brazil (2016), where he received the National Research Award.

Gerardo García Rojas is a Ph.D. student at the Center for Research and Advanced Studies of the National Polytechnic Institute (IPN), Mexico. Among his publications is the book *Educar para Regenerar* (2024). His research focuses on racialization processes based on scientific and educational technologies from a historiographical perspective.

Mary Gibson is a Professor Emerita of History at John Jay College and the Graduate Center, City University of New York, United States. Her most recent book, *Italian Prisons in the Age of Positivism, 1861–1914* (2019), was translated into Italian in 2022. She has translated, with Nicole Hahn Rafter, the two classic works of Lombroso: *Criminal Man* (2006) and *Criminal Woman, the Prostitute and the Normal Woman* (2004).

Marco Antonio León León is a Full Professor at the University of the Bío-Bío, Chile. He is a FONDECYT-ANID researcher and evaluator for the Advanced Human Capital Program of ANID (Agencia Nacional de Investigación y Desarrollo). His research specializes in the sociocultural history of criminality and abnormality in Chile and Latin America in the nineteenth and twentieth centuries.

Alessandra Lorini is a former Associate Professor of North American History at the University of Florence, Italy, and has been a visiting professor at several American universities. Her publications include *Rituals of Race* (1999), *L'impero della libertà e l'isola strategica: Gli Stati Uniti e Cuba tra Otto e Novecento* (2008), and *Le statue bugiarde* (2023).

Alejandra Mailhe is a researcher at CONICET and Professor of History of Social Ideas in Latin America at the National University of La Plata, Argentina. She has published numerous articles in specialized journals in Argentina, Brazil, Mexico, Spain, and Canada. Her works include *En busca de la alteridad perdida* (2023), *Archivos de psiquiatría y criminología* (2016), and *Brasil: Márgenes imaginarios* (2011).

Françoise Martinez is a Full Professor of Latin American History at Sorbonne University, France, and a researcher at the Centre for Interdisciplinary Research on the Contemporary Iberian World (CRIMIC). Her research focuses on contemporary political history in Bolivia and Mexico. She has led and participated in several research programs on these themes and has published articles, thematic issues, and books, including *"Régénérer la race": Politique éducative en Bolivie (1898–1920)* (2010) and *Fêter la nation: Mexique et Bolivie pendant leur premier siècle de vie indépendante (1810–1925)* (2017), both also translated and published in Spanish.

Maria Teresa Milicia is an Associate Professor of Cultural Anthropology at the University of Padua, Italy. Since 2011, she has been involved in a multisited ethnographic study related to the repatriation request for the remains of Giuseppe Villella from the Cesare Lombroso Museum of Criminal Anthropology in Turin. Her research focuses on political anthropology, postcolonial legacies of scientific racism, museum collections of human remains and repatriation movements, symbolic constructions of locality, and the politics of identity, particularly in southern Italy.

Silvano Montaldo is a Full Professor of Modern and Contemporary and Academic Director of the Cesare Lombroso Museum of Criminal Anthropology at the University of Turin, Italy, whose cataloguing, rearrangement, and public opening he oversaw. He has published several works on the history of this museum and its collections, including the catalogue, available in Italian and English (2024). He is also the scientific director of the Lombroso Project.

Franco Orlandi is a cultural historian and former doctoral fellow of the Research Foundation Flanders (FWO). He holds a Ph.D. from KU Leuven, Belgium, and the University of Turin, Italy. His research interests center on the history of criminology, deviance, and the human sciences.

Nadia Pugliese is a Ph.D. student in Cultural Heritage and Historical-Artistic, Audiovisual, and Multimedia Production at the University of Turin, Italy. Her project investigates the photographic heritage held at the Cesare Lombroso Museum of Criminal Anthropology. Her research interests lie at the intersection of the history of photography, historical-scientific archives, and media studies.

Pablo Quisbert is a historian and Ph.D. student in History at the University of Tarapacá, Chile, specializing in Bolivian history and historical anthropology. He has authored numerous articles on the colonial period and the Imperial Villa of Potosí in the sixteenth and seventeenth centuries. His interests also include political myths and imaginaries in contemporary Bolivian history, and he coauthored *Pachakuti: El retorno de la nación: Estudio comparativo del imaginario de nación de la Revolución Nacional y del Estado Plurinacional* (with Vincent Nicolas, 2014).

Fernando Salla is a researcher at the Center for the Study of Violence (NEV-USP) of the University of São Paulo, Brazil. He holds a master's degree and a Ph.D. in sociology from the same university. He is the author of several articles and books on prisons in Brazil. His research work focuses on public safety policies, juvenile justice, and studies about prisons.

Livio Sansone is a Full Professor of Anthropology at the Federal University of Bahia (UFBA), Brazil. His best-known English publication is *Blackness Without Ethnicity: Creating Race in Brazil* (2003). His most recent works are *La Galassia Lombroso: L'Africa e l'America Latina* (2022) and *Field Station Bahia* (2023).

John Shepherd holds a Ph.D. in philosophy from Durham University, UK. His research interests include the history of criminology, surveillance, and the human sciences. His Ph.D. thesis traces the history of psychiatric and statistical efforts to predict and pre-empt criminal behavior in the twentieth-century United States.

Maximo Sozzo is Professor of Sociology of Law and Criminology at the National University of Litoral (Argentina) and Ramon y Cajal Researcher at the University of A Coruña (Spain). His research focuses on the past and present of criminology and punishment in Latin America. His last books are *Punishment in Latin America* (edited with L. dal Santo, 2025) and *Los viajes de las ideas sobre la cuestión criminal desde y hacia Argentina (1880–1955)* (edited with J. Nuñez, 2024).

Mario Valero is an Associate Professor at the Fashion Institute of Technology of New York City, United States. His interdisciplinary scholarship bridges economics, art history, and cultural studies to examine the construction of racial categories in modern Latin America, particularly in the human sciences and visual media. His forthcoming book analyzes the intersection of racial theories and visual documentation on the work of Euclides da Cunha and Fernando Ortiz, seminal thinkers in modern Latin American social thought.

Index

www.ingramcontent.com/pod-product-compliance
Ingram Content Group UK Ltd.
Pitfield, Milton Keynes, MK11 3LW, UK
UKHW020238290926
15470UKWH00002B/611

9 781350 571211